BEYOND RESISTANCE!

Youth Activism and Community Change

Critical Youth Studies

Series Editor: Greg Dimitriadis

Beyond Resistance! Youth Activism and Community Change:
New Democratic Possibilities for Practice and Policy for
America's Youth
Shawn Ginwright, Pedro Noguera, and Julio Cammarota

BEYOND RESISTANCE!

Youth Activism and Community Change

New Democratic Possibilities for
Practice and Policy for America's Youth

Edited by
Shawn Ginwright • Pedro Noguera • Julio Cammarota

Routledge
Taylor & Francis Group
New York London

Published in 2006 by
Routledge
Taylor & Francis Group
270 Madison Avenue
New York, NY 10016

Published in Great Britain by
Routledge
Taylor & Francis Group
2 Park Square
Milton Park, Abingdon
Oxon OX14 4RN

© 2006 by Taylor & Francis Group, LLC
Routledge is an imprint of Taylor & Francis Group

10 9 8 7 6 5 4 3 2 1

International Standard Book Number-10: 0-415-95251-4 (Softcover)
International Standard Book Number-13: 978-0-415-95251-4 (Softcover)
Library of Congress Card Number 2005027676

Library of Congress Cataloging-in-Publication Data

Beyond Resistance! : youth activism and community change : new democratic possibilities for practice
    and policy for America's youth / edited by Shawn Ginwright, Pedro Noguera and Julio
    Cammarota.
        p. cm. -- (Critical youth studies)
    Includes bibliographical references and index.
    ISBN 0-415-95250-6 (hb : alk. paper) -- ISBN 0-415-95251-4 (pb : alk. paper)
    1. Social work with youth--United States. 2. Community-based social services--United States. 3.
Youth--United States--Political activity. 4. Community development--United States. I. Ginwright,
Shawn A. II. Noguera, Pedro. III. Cammarota, Julio. IV. Series.

HV1431.A638 2006
362.7083'0973--dc22   2005027676

Taylor & Francis Group
is the Academic Division of Informa plc.

Visit the Taylor & Francis Web site at
http://www.taylorandfrancis.com

and the Routledge Web site at
http://www.routledge-ny.com

Contents

Series Editor Foreword

The publication of *Beyond Resistance! Youth Activism and Community Change: New Democratic Possibilities for Practice and Policy for America's Youth* is good news indeed for academics, activists, and others concerned with the plight of contemporary youth as well as the future of civic life and the civic sphere more broadly. Drawing together exemplars from around the U.S., editors Shawn Ginwright, Pedro Noguera, and Julio Cammarota help document the ongoing struggles of youth to become agents in their futures and the futures of their communities.

The gesture is critical. Young people today face an unprecedented set of risks and challenges, including vastly diminishing economic and social possibilities. Moreover, social policy initiatives aimed at youth have been almost wholly punitive. From the imposition of the No Child Left Behind legislation and its barrage of (extremely) high stakes tests, to the shameful expansion of the prison system, young people are assumed a problem to be controlled, maintained, and policed. That the U.S. was the only nation in the world, with Somalia, to refuse to sign on to the United Nations' "Convention of the Rights of the Child" only underscores this seismic moral shift.

Challenging this zeitgeist, the authors in this collection address the wide range of sites and forums where young people are engaging in critical activism. From New York City to Los Angeles, university classrooms to after-school centers, high schools to cultural centers, the editors and authors offer a sweeping, panoramic view of the range of organizations and peoples struggling to think and act "otherwise" at this critical social and historic juncture.

Turning our gaze towards youth in this fashion helps opens up key sets of questions to be addressed as well as concepts to be rethought. For example, much traditional work in psychology has treated "youth" at a pre-social stage, implicitly assuming that young people are "not yet ready" to act on their own social environs. As the editors and authors show, such a position does injustice to the lived realities of (often marginalized) young people, precluding a discussion about their own roles in shaping their own futures. Young people can—indeed, must—be charged with this vital task.

This more expansive notion of "youth" also asks us to look beyond the ways schools are organized today. In particular, schools often infantilize young people, treating them as "empty vessels" to be filled in by the more powerful and all-knowing adult teacher. High stakes testing regimes have only further constricted what can happen in such settings today. Schools are increasingly focused on narrow sets of skills, linked to testable outcomes. In the end, such tests create a culture of suspicion and remediation—a disposition challenged on every single page of this collection.

Finally, these editors and authors ask us to re-think the very terms of democracy itself. As they so powerfully demonstrate, the terrain of negotiation here is often limited to electoral politics and a fairly circumscribed and pre-figured set of issues. Many young people are turning away from this system—but they are not giving up on democracy itself. The young people here are struggling with issues and concerns linked to their own set of circumstances and conditions. In doing so, they give us an emergent vision of political activism today, where it happens and around what issues.

In addition to the wide-ranging exemplars, the editors and authors provide an overarching language to understand youth, framing the next round of discussion on young people and the civic sphere. Indeed, the editors and authors give us all cause to contest what Freire so famously called "reality sickness." Now endemic to much U.S. life, "reality sickness" is the often overwhelming sense that the future has already been written, that our job is to struggle within its prefigured parameters. Such a disposition can radically shrink the potentials and possibilities for dialogue with youth, making it seem useless and superfluous. The authors and editors, rather, evidence the kind of trust, love, and commitment necessary to enter into such emergent dialogue with young people. The outcomes here are not the formal, predictable outcomes of high stakes tests. But they are democratic to their very core.

I am reminded here of James Baldwin's (1985/1963) prophetic words about education, written at the dawn of the Civil Rights movement:

> The crucial paradox which confronts us [today] is that the whole process of education occurs within a social framework and is designed to perpetuate the aims of society. Thus, for example, the boys and girls who were born during the era of the Third Reich, when educated to the purposes of the Third Reich, became barbarians. The paradox of education is precisely this—that as one begins to be conscious one begins to examine the society in which he is being educated .... But no society is really anxious to have that kind of person around. What societies really, ideally, want is a citizenry which will simply obey the rules of society. If a society succeeds in this, that society is about to perish. (p. 326)

If nothing else, *Beyond Resistance! Youth Activism and Community Change: New Democratic Possibilities for Practice and Policy for America's Youth* underscores Baldwin's powerful sentiment—that both our schools and society will ultimately crumble if young people simply "obey" their predetermined rules and work within their parameters. The future, again, cannot be written beforehand.

In closing, I'm humbled that this volume inaugurates my new series with Routledge, "Critical Youth Studies." Volumes in this series look to renegotiate the terms on which and through which "education" is discussed, practiced, and researched today. Drawing together the work of both well-known and emerging scholars, this series will focus on "youth studies" as a self-constituting, trans-disciplinary area of inquiry, highlighting the wide span of cultural forms that young people are using to navigate their everyday lives today, including popular music, fashion, dance, and art; the unofficial educative sites and settings young people are turning to as schools become increasingly standardized and homogenized; new articulations of the local and the global, with a particular emphasis on new ways of understanding "the urban"; the importance of multi-methodological and inter-disciplinary work for grappling with the emergent and unpredictable nature of youth culture today. Drawing on a range of methods and approaches, volumes treat the span of issues most relevant to youth today.

I again thank the editors and chapter authors of *Beyond Resistance! Youth Activism and Community Change: New Democratic Possibilities for Practice and Policy for America's Youth.* We are all indebted to you!

Greg Dimitriadis
Buffalo, New York
February, 2006

Reference

Baldwin, J. (1985). A talk to teachers. In *The price of the ticket* (pp. 325–332). New York: St. Martin's Press. (Originally published 1963).

Introduction

SHAWN GINWRIGHT AND JULIO CAMMAROTA

As hundreds of young people descended on Oakland's City Hall in August 2002, they chanted in unison, "You can't stop the power of the youth, 'cause the power of the youth won't stop." Confronting Mayor Jerry Brown's decision to spend nearly $70 million to hire 100 police officers to patrol Oakland's underfunded schools, young people collectively forced the city to allocate $7 million to youth programs throughout the city. Youth activism has always played a central role in the democratic process and continues to forge new ground for social change. Young people's participation in movements in South Africa to end apartheid, in China's infamous Tiananmen Square, and in the hills of Chiapas, Mexico to bring greater sovereignty to indigenous people all remind us how young people struggle for justice against all odds. One lesson we draw from these movements is that young people are agents of social change. It is precisely this notion of agency that gives rise to important democratic movements throughout our history.

What happens, however, when young people are silenced and restricted from participating in important civic affairs? In what ways do young people push, shove, and elbow their way into the democratic process? What stands in young people's way in their relentless pursuit of social change? This book addresses these questions head on; it is the product of a series of conversations about how policy and research may shape new opportunities for youth. While having lunch at the American Educational Research Association meeting in Chicago in 2003, the editors of this volume debated whether or not educational researchers effectively advocated for issues they studied. We asked ourselves, Do researchers effectively shape policies that make a difference in young people's lives? Shawn Ginwright raised an intriguing question to Julio Cammarota and Pedro Noguera: What if we could organize a group of researchers who share a common vision of youth, in order to impact policy and practices in schools and communities? Both Julio and Pedro agreed that such an effort would be worthwhile and could yield promising results. In October 2004, with support from the Ford Foundation, we convened an inter-disciplinary group of researchers who have written about youth and various forms of activism. The group was given the formidable task to write about how youth participate in school and community activities for change, and to make explicit how knowledge about these activities might contribute to more effective policy for youth.

The authors herein took on this challenge, and have provided us with remarkable insight into communities where young people are resisting unfair laws, changing policies to better meet their needs and in some cases trans-forming schools. This book offers a comprehensive discussion of how young people respond to major patterns of institutional failure in their schools and communities. Unfortunately, the broader social context where change is occurring is inhospitable to youth, particularly youth of color. For example, during the past 7 years, 43 states have instituted legislation that facilitated the transfer of children accused of crimes from juvenile to adult courts. The result of these laws was the dismantling of a long-standing belief on the part of juvenile courts that special measures were necessary to protect children and youth from the effects of the adult justice system, and to ensure rehabilitation (Poe-Yamagata & Jones, 2000; Polakow, 2000; and Polakow-Suransky, 2000).

These policies are a reflection of a larger shared national consciousness about young people and their rights. For example, one of the most significant steps toward an equitable youth policy occurred in 1990, when 191 nations around the world adopted the Convention on the Rights of the Child, which outlines a vision for children and youth around the world, promotes national strategies, and protects the rights and dignity of children in developed and developing nations. The convention is a legal instrument to protect children from a variety of issues ranging from participation in armed conflict to prohibiting the use of child labor. As of 2005, the United States is the only developed nation in the world that has not adopted the Convention on the Rights of the Child. Unfortunately, the inability of the U.S. to adopt the con-vention raises serious questions about its commitment to American children and youth.

The passage of the No Child Left Behind (NCLB) Act is yet another example of imposing punitive strategies in an attempt to improve schools and educa-tional outcomes. By imposing tougher accountability standards on America's public schools without addressing the underlying weaknesses in these schools, the new law has had the opposite effect of its stated goal—leaving no child behind. NCLB has contributed to rising dropout and failure rates by holding children and youth accountable for meeting higher educational standards, while little has been done to expand and improve their educational opportunities.

Yet, there is a strange silence among both progressives and conservatives about the status of America's youth. Despite our collective agreement that "youth are our future," policy makers, researchers, and teachers have voiced little concern about how these policies severely cripple America's democratic vision and destroy opportunities for young people on the margins. The editors of this volume have been deeply concerned about the role that young people in America play in the democratic process. For nearly 20 years, we have worked in communities as practitioners, teachers, youth workers, organizers, and researchers and have witnessed firsthand institutional failure to support young people in poor communities. Our combined experiences have given us a powerful lens through which to conceptualize the promise of youth activism and the challenges young people inevitably must confront.

We share Alexis de Tocqueville's concern about American democratic participation—namely, how can we reconcile entrenched social inequality with the promise of democracy, and to whom do we grant full participation (Tocqueville 1969)? In many ways, youth particularly from working poor communities occupy second-class citizenry. Similar to the ways that Jim Crow laws limited democratic participation for African Americans, youth today are subjected to hostile laws and unfair policies but have no rights or power to change them.

Despite broad institutional failure on the part of public schools, health care, and employment for young people, youth in America's urban communities are not passive victims. Rather, they find remarkable ways to work collectively to improve the quality of their lives. The authors in this collection argue for a more nuanced understanding of youth agency in urban communities and avoid the pitfalls, common among social scientists, of focusing only on the most egregious activities among urban youth. These chapters brilliantly illustrate how youth respond to community and school conditions through forms of civic engagement vaguely understood by social science researchers.

It is our intent that these chapters serve as a launching pad for new conversations about young people that ultimately will carve out new territory for youth policy. The pages that follow at times are rough and gritty. They illustrate without apology how young people struggle for justice in their communities. Whether it is Puerto Rican young people's struggle to preserve their barrio from encroaching gentrification, or how African Americans and Mexican Americans create a community high school amid the tensions of ethnic conflict, these chapters push researchers, policy makers, and practitioners to "keep it real" when representing young folks' lives.

It is not by accident that these authors share a common vision for youth. In fact, we toiled for quite some time about how we might frame these chapters in ways that departed from more traditional treatments of youth behavior. We asked how we could highlight the struggles, victories, and defeats in young people's lives without romance while at the same time avoiding nihilism. We want you to travel with us—to community meetings in church basements, to street corners where young people connect, into classrooms where they are inspired, to the small, underfunded storefront nonprofit organizations that change lives on shoestring budgets.

We hope to illuminate how youth agency contributes to more vibrant and inclusive democracy and informed public policy. Our lessons come from youth on the margins of society (those of racial, sexual, and/or language minorities) as they struggle for inclusion and equality. In order to align our conceptual framing of youth, we asked the contributors of this volume to consider four guiding principles that together shape our collective understanding of youth. These principles guide our journey as we discover new forms of youth participation and inform a more democratic vision for young people.

Principle 1: Young People Should Be Conceptualized in Relationship to Specific Economic, Political, and Social Conditions

The ways in which we theorize about young people have not sufficiently addressed questions regarding the influences of economic, political, and social conditions on the developmental process. We argue that in order to understand more fully the developmental process, we must bring sociopolitical issues to the foreground. This means understanding how, for example, demographic changes and neoliberal policies create significant differences among groups of young people. Now, more than at any other time in history, the older generations in American society are whiter and wealthier while the younger generations are browner and poorer (see Males, chapter 17, this volume). This racial and class divide between generations fosters political tensions that prompt conservative constituencies to roll back the gains of people of color and preserve white privileges.

For example, over the past decade, we have seen the evanescence of affirmative action, removal of multicultural and bilingual education in numerous schools, assault on public education, and the political scapegoat of immigrants (Giroux, 2003). Meanwhile, the number of prisons, and the degree of police and security on school campuses, have dramatically increased (Noguera, 2003). These policies, in combination with structural economic changes that severely limit job opportunities for youth, have a devastating impact on the developmental process toward adulthood. In fact, some have argued that these same factors not only shift our conceptualization of youth, but also force us to reconsider static notions of adulthood as well (Ginwright, 2005). For example, researchers have highlighted how welfare reform has required black and Latino youth from low-income communities to assume greater adultlike responsibilities (Brooks, Hair, & Zaslow, 2001). Researchers concluded that, increasingly, youth from welfare-dependent families are expected to assume responsibilities held by their parents. Such responsibilities included paying bills, caring for younger siblings, purchasing clothes, and/or finding housing for the family because their parents are required by new welfare regulations to work more hours and therefore have less time to complete household responsibilities (Brooks et al., 2001). By considering how youth are shaped by specific social, political, and economic conditions, we have a more complete picture of the youth development process.

Principle 2: The Youth Development Process Should Be Conceptualized as a Collective Response to the Social Marginalization of Young People

Conceptualizing youth development in relationship to specific social, political, and economic conditions also allows us to reframe the ways in which youth respond to limited economic and social opportunities. Given these constraints and opportunities, we highlight the collective dimensions of the developmental process, particularly among youth of color in working-poor neighborhoods. Wyn and White (1997) have noted that marginalization yields a number of collectively shared experiences for youth, such as lack of money, being under constant state surveillance, and feelings of powerlessness. The youth development process therefore cannot be separated from the collective dimensions of community life. However, community life is not without collective resistance, and it is through the collective dimensions of community life that notions of social justice and acting on behalf of the common good are made evident.

This view of the youth development process acknowledges structural constraints in communities and views youth as active participants facilitating neighborhood change through strong social networks. Much of the contemporary study of youth, particularly in urban communities, focuses almost entirely on the most egregious aspects of youth behaviors without sufficient analysis of the structural determinates of their social positioning. By shifting the focus from "problem"-driven assumptions of youth behavior to "collective" dimensions of youth development, we develop a more nuanced understanding of how young people navigate their environments.

Recent formulations of social capital provide a useful framework for conceptualizing the collective dimensions of youth behaviors (Sampson, Morenoff, & Earls, 1999). Sampson and colleagues (1999) have noted that discussions of social capital usually treat social networks as perfunctory, task-specific relationships that translate to individual opportunities (see also Portes, 1998; Putnam, 1993). As a result, we don't understand the collective dimensions of social capital—the willingness, trust, and motivations that encourage or prohibit groups to act on behalf of the common good. Borrowing from Sampson (2001) we argue that youth development for youth of color in working poor neighborhoods comprises not simply individual relationships but is shaped by collective efficacy, "the linkage of mutual trust and the shared willingness to intervene for the common good ..." (p. 95).

For Sampson (2001), youth engagement occurs through intergenerational ties, exchanging information and advice with young people, and establishing clear pathways for civic participation for young people in a community-change context. Thus, central to our understanding of the youth development process is precisely the collective dimensions of community life, such as xviii • Introduction

understanding how a group of young people develop crews on the basis of racial and ethnic identities, how young people participate at hip-hop concerts, or why young people engage in collective action to improve safety at their neighborhood park.

One way to understand collective dimensions of youth collective action is through the lens of social movement theory. Unlike theorists who view youth collective action as irrational, violent, emotional, and deviant (Smelser, 1968; Useem, 1985), we contend that youth collective action is a rational response to the state intervention and repression in their lives. Researchers have documented the various ways that people act collectively to respond to state repression (Fantasia, 1988; Gamson, 1990; Muller & Opp, 1986; Olson, 1971).

Other researchers have argued that when institutional means of social change are not available to groups who have grievances, they employ the only means of transformation available to them (Piven & Cloward, 1979). Youth, who grossly lack political and economic power, use school walkouts, marches, and other forms of civil disobedience, which revive the dormant dynamic qualities of state institutions and render them responsive to change (Carmichael & Hamilton, 1969; Carson, 1981; Martínez, 1998; Newton, 1973; Piven & Cloward, 1979). For example, HoSang, James, and Chow-Wang (2004) have found that youth groups frequently address issues related to unfair suspension and expulsion policies, armed police officers on campus, unsanitary bathrooms, and inadequate public transportation to and from school. The authors also highlight the fact that young people frame these issues through a broader political analysis of power and operate within networks of intergenerational allies, collaborations with other youth groups, and partnerships with larger political organizations. These forms of capital—social, political, and human—are important elements for effective community mobilization for young people (Sampson et al., 1999).

Principle 3: Young People Are Agents of Change, Not Simple Subjects to Change

Youth collective action tends to be absent from the perspectives on young people held by many policy makers, education researchers, and youth development practitioners. The dominant paradigm of psychological approaches to development allows only for a view of young people as empty and inert vessels that competent and qualified adults must fill with the apposite kinds of knowledge, attitudes, and norms. When they finally reach adulthood and move beyond the rights of passage set out in adolescence, young people supposedly evolve into social actors and thus independent contributors to society.

This paradigm of adolescent development and dependency is not only inaccurate—young people have been agents who have changed practices and social relations in families since childhood—but also detrimental to their capacity to participate in democratic society. When educators apply this paradigm, which they so often do, young people learn to be passive subjects who wait for others—particularly adults—to tell them what to do, how to think, and what to say. The learning of passive subjectivities contradicts the main objective of democracy—allowing the independent, freethinking voices of citizens to be heard on some level.

We suggest a Freirian perspective of young people, one that posits their capacity to produce knowledge to transform their world. In this regard, youth should be recognized as *subjects* of a knowledge production that underpins their agency for personal and social transformation. If democracy still seems to be a noble ideal, then supporting youth agency should be considered a high priority. The only chance for democracy to expand in the next generation is for young people to be perceived of and treated as vital agents of social transformation. Limiting their agency by undermining their efforts to improve community conditions will render them *objects* of knowledge—vessels to be filled. The advancement of an active and engaged citizenry requires the edifying practice of acknowledging and supporting youth agency, and young people's capacity to become subjects of knowledge and social transformation.

We are mindful however, not to overromanticize youth agency. In fact, we acknowledge that youth are often constrained by economic and political forces rather than controlled by them. That is, we wish to convey the idea that the personal choices that young people make are often subject to the constraints and opportunities available to them. Wyn and White remind us that "where one lives and grows up has a major influence on how one literally sees the world" (1997, p. 124) and the choices available. Taking the bus to school through congested city traffic is quite different from walking to school on a quiet path through the woods. Often the banal choices young people make are profoundly influenced by their social position.

Principle 4: Young People Have Basic Rights

The category of *youth* as a socially distinct group of people fundamentally imposes a second-class status upon young people. Wyn and White (1997) argue that our concept of youth "in transition," "becoming" or "adults to be" all positions our focus on the future of what young people may become, ignoring the present day reality of young people's lives (p. 115). By focusing entirely on the future, there is little need for young people to have decision making responsibilities about issues that impact their lives in the present.

Young people's engagement with the democratic processes of civil society has largely been through compulsory education and the labor market. In fact, the success of democratic societies often hinges upon a social contract that implies that by participation in civic society—voting, volunteering, or serving as jurors—citizens are afforded rights to ensure the sustenance of healthy democratic life through protections offered through the state systems of schools, government, and law enforcement.

However, the state has nearly abandoned its role of facilitating basic social welfare and has increasingly adopted the role of what Wacquant (2001) refers to as the penal state—the omnipresent influence of institutions such as police, schools, and prisons who in concert encroach upon young people's lives through surveillance, zero-tolerance policies, or imprisonment in the name of public safety. Rather than building mutual trust, democratic participation, and community building, Wacquant argues, the penal state threatens the vitality of democratic engagement among youth.

While the state enacts policies that affect the lives of young people, youth rarely have a voice in policy making. Vital to healthy democratic life is exercising one's right to change, challenge, or disrupt policies, laws, and regulations that unfairly create inequality. For youth, the lack of opportunity to enjoy such democratic activities as voting, creating policies, and having a voice in local government represents a forfeiture of basic citizenship rights. Furthermore, the focus on the category of youth as "future" citizens further obscures the fact that youth already participate in civic life by navigating the laws and policies made by adults (Wyn & White, 1997). Furthermore, young people, more than anyone else, have the best vantage point for understanding what they need for securing a healthy, safe, and productive existence.

This conceptual shift from youth as "future citizens" to "present civic actors" forces us to think more boldly about the nature of rights for youth and how to ensure these rights. Therefore, we suggest that one basic right applicable to all youth is the *right to civic representation and decision making*, where young people are represented as much as possible in law- and policy-making arenas; this will ensure that state institutions meet their needs and interests. Youth can realize their right to fair representation by becoming members of school boards and city councils or establishing youth caucuses in legislative bodies. The right to real political power is essential for young people to shape their social contexts to facilitate a healthy transition into adulthood.

An Overview of the Chapters

The chapters in this volume brilliantly illustrate how these principles provide us with new insights into various forms of youth agency. The book is organized in four sections. The first section, "Reframing Youth Resistance: Building Theories of Youth Activism," articulates what we consider the building blocks for conceptualizing youth activism and democratic engagement. From case studies that illustrate key concepts from social theory, the authors in this section weave together—from seemingly divergent perspectives—a cogent argument about how youth resistance, community change, and civic engagement contribute to more effective and democratic policy making in local communities. In the second section, "Learning for Justice: Innovative Pedagogies for Justice in Schools," the authors demonstrate—through research carried out with young people both inside and outside of schools—how engaging young people in learning need not be an onerous chore if educators take time to understand the interests, hopes, and dreams of urban youth. These authors remind us that the learning process becomes richer when it is made relevant to young people's lives and sensibilities. The central element to this task is a recognition that many young people can and must be actively engaged in schools and communities if they are to succeed academically.

The third section, "Street-Corner Democracy: Youth, Civil Society, and Community Change," considers the role of youth agency in community change activities. Considering conditions engendered by larger political economic forces such as failing schools, environmental degradation, and gentrification, this section explores how young people struggle against diminishing living standards for communities and their families. This section pays particular attention to sites where notions of social justice among youth are fostered, developed, and sustained. These chapters focus on how young people create space—in conditions where there aren't any established spaces—in which to engage their communities and promote social justice. Two chapters (see Strobel, Osberg, & McLaughlin, chapter 11; and O'Donoghue, chapter 13) examine the extent that community-based organizations represent that space in which young people can express their political needs, while others point to organizing campaigns (see Kwon, chapter 12, & Aguilar-San Juan, chapter 14) or arts-based cultural centers (see Flores-González, Rodríguez, & Rodríguez-Muñiz, chapter 10).

The fourth section, "Perspectives on Youth Civic Engagement and Youth Policies," unapologetically raises the questions public policy advocates, researchers, and practitioners have simply avoided. What role do youth play in sustaining a healthy democracy? How has public discourse about youth shaped opportunities for civic participation among America's most vulnerable youth populations? The chapters in this section challenge both views toward young people—protective and punitive—and illustrate how democratic engagement fosters not only healthy youth but also stronger communities.

References

Brooks, J. L., Hair, E. C., & Zaslow, M. J. (2001, July). Welfare reform's impact on adolescents: Early warning signs. *Child Trends Research Brief.* Washington, DC: Child Trends.

Carmichael, S., & Hamilton, C. (1969). Black power: Its need and substance. In J. McEvoy & A. Miller (eds.), *Black power and student rebellion* (pp. 237–253). Belmont, CA: Wadsworth.

Carson, C. (1981). *In struggle: SNCC and the black awakening of the 1960s.* Cambridge, MA: Harvard University Press.

Fantasia, R. (1988). *Cultures of solidarity: Consciousness, action, and contemporary American workers.* Berkeley and Los Angeles: University of California Press.

Fuchs, E. R., Shapiro, R. Y., & Minnite, L. C. (2001). Social capital, political participation, and the urban community. In S. Seagert, P. Thompson, & M. Warren (Eds.), *Social capital in poor communities* (pp. 290–324). New York: Russell Sage Foundation.

Gamson, W. (1990). *The strategy of social protest.* Belmont, CA: Wadsworth.

Ginwright, S. (2005). On urban ground: Understanding African American intergenerational partnerships in urban communities. *Journal of Community Psychology, 33*(1), 101–110.

HoSang, D., James, T., & Chow-Wang, M. (2004). Youth Organizing for Public Education Reform: A Preliminary Scan and Assessment. Report to the Edward Hazen and Surdna Foundation, Mosaic and Movement Strategy Center.

Martínez, E. S. (1998). *De colores means all of us: Latina views for a multi-colored century.* Cambridge, MA: South End.

Muller, E. N., & Opp, K.-D. (1986). Rational choice and rebellious collective action. *American Political Science Review, 80,* 471–487.

Newton, H. P. (1973). *Revolutionary suicide.* New York: Writers and Readers.

Noguera, P. (2003). *City schools and the American dream.* New York: Teachers College Press.

Olson, M. (1971). *The logic of collective action: Public goods and the theory of groups.* Cambridge, MA: Harvard University Press.

Piven, F., & Cloward, R. (1979). *Poor people's movements: Why they succeed, how they fail.* New York: Vintage.

Poe-Yamagata, E., & Jones, M. (2000). And Justice for Some. Washington, DC: National Council on Crime and Delinquency, p. 30.

Polakow, V., (Ed.) (2000). *The public assault on America's children. Teaching for social justice.* New York: Teachers College Press.

Polakow-Suransky, S. (2000). America's least wanted: Zero tolerance policies and the fate of expelled students. *The Public Assault on America's Children.* V. Polakow, (Ed.) New York: Teachers College Press.

Portes, A. (1998). Social capital: Its origins and application to modern sociology. *American Sociological Review, 24,* 1–24.

Putnam, R. D. (1993, Spring). The prosperous community: Social capital and community life. *American Prospect,* pp. 35–42.

Sampson, R. (2001). Crime and public safety: Insights from community-level perspectives on social capital. *Social capital in poor communities.* S. Seagert, P. Thompson, & M. Warren, Eds., New York: Russell Sage.

Sampson, R. J., Morenoff, J. D., & Earls, F. (1999). Beyond social capitol: spacial dynamics of collective efficacy for children. *American Sociological Review, 64,* 633–660.

Smelser, N. (1968). Social and psychological dimensions of collective behavior. In *Essays in sociological explanation* (pp. 92–121). Englewood Cliffs, NJ: Prentice-Hall.

Tocqueville, A. de. (1969). *Democracy in America.* New York: Doubleday.

Useem, B. (1985). Disorganization and the New Mexico prison riot of 1980. *American Sociological Review, 50,* 677–688.

Wacquant, L. (2001). The advent of the penal state is not destiny. *Social Justice, 28*(3), 81–87.

Wyn, J., & White, R. (1997). *Rethinking youth.* London: Sage.

Section I
Reframing Youth Resistance: Building Theories of Youth Activism

Deeply embedded in our understanding of America's urban youth is the notion that young people are disinterested or disengaged from civic affairs. The idea particularly applies to poor youth of color who, many have argued, "need to be fixed" before they enter the fray of civic life. The chapters in this unit reframe this perspective and view youth as important civic actors in the democratic process. By introducing new theoretical discourse about youth and social justice, these chapters address the following questions:

1. In what ways does identity facilitate political consciousness among ethnic youth?
2. How do we describe the process of youth participation in community and social change efforts?
3. What role do community-based organizations play in developing political identities among youth of color?
4. How should we theorize about youth activism?

In chapter 1, Daniel HoSang argues that perceptions of young people are key in shaping local policy. When young people can reframe the perceptions and issues that they organize around, there is a greater likelihood of success. HoSang argues for an alternative space where youth organizing challenges the discourse about youth as neighborhood problems. Using two case studies (Los Angeles and New York), Hosang demonstrates how youth-led activist groups contest the ways in which the public in general and policy makers in particular define community issues. Youth, however, do not work in isolation; rather, they work closely with experienced adult organizers who can serve as critical social capital for young community activists.

Reporting on a 1-year study of 11 youth activist organizations, Heather Lewis-Charp, Hanh Cao Yu, and Sengsouvanh Soukamneuth illustrate in chapter 2 how youth civic participation shapes the youth-development process. Through what they have termed *civic activism*—a process through which youth are engaged in addressing issues related to identity, community, and activities toward social change—the authors describe how the personal becomes political for youth activists.

In chapter 3, Ben Kirshner unpacks the complex interchange between adults and youth in efforts toward community change and argues for a more nuanced understanding of youth-led social change. Theorizing about the intergenerational community change efforts, Kirshner argues for an understanding of youth-center apprenticeships where adults model behavior, coach youth regarding skills, and then fade into the background so that youth can genuinely lead efforts toward community change. In doing so, these young people tap dimensions of social capital that are not on the radar of most social scientists. In chapter 5, A. A. Akom illustrates that social science researchers have been largely restricted to Putnam's formulations of social capital and unable to interrogate how race shape the production and sustenance of social capital for youth.

These activities for community change among youth are a reflection of the deeper sociopolitical awareness. But how is sociopolitical awareness developed? What are the psychological determinates for civic and community involvement for youth? In chapter 4, Roderick Watts and Omar Guessous argue that youth-development theory is incomplete without a deeper understanding of the broader political, economic, and cultural forces at work in young people's lives, and explain the complex relationships among oppression, social justice, and the youth-development process.

CHAPTER 1

Beyond Policy: Ideology, Race and the Reimagining of Youth

DANIEL HOSANG

The 50th anniversary of the U.S. Supreme Court's *Brown v. Board of Education* ruling in 2004 connected two contrasting moments of ideological conflict and struggle over the meaning of race. In 1951, 16-year-old Barbara Johns and her classmates at Robert Russa Moton High School decided they could no longer tolerate conditions in their segregated rural Virginia school, where overcrowding had grown so bad that classes were held on school buses and in tarpaper shacks set up in the schoolyard. Johns hatched a plan to distract the principal while the students assembled in the auditorium; they soon voted to go on strike and walk off the campus. Their actions won the support of their parents and the National Association for the Advancement of Colored People, resulting in a desegregation lawsuit that became of one of the five cases reviewed by the U.S. Supreme Court under the *Brown* decision. Twelve years before the March on Washington brought the civil rights crisis fully onto the national agenda, Johns and her fellow students put the experiences and struggles of young people of color at the center of a national effort to restructure long-standing policies and social norms. They confronted the prevailing framework, which justified and naturalized the idea that state and society had few obligations to educate and support black youth. Though the local district fought desegregation efforts relentlessly during the next two decades, John's activism was to be repeated in countless communities as young people joined social movements for democracy and justice (Wormser, 2003).

Fifty-three years later, at a black-tie gala in Washington, D.C., to commemorate the *Brown* anniversary, entertainer and philanthropist Bill Cosby offered his own account of the crisis in public education that has endured in spite of the desegregation imperative. Against Johns's account of an institution and society failing its young people, Cosby insisted it was "lower economic people" who were "not holding up their end in this deal." Rehearsing the profile of black pathology in its most venomous dimensions, Cosby railed against young people "...with names like Shaniqua, Taliqua and Mohammed and all of that crap, and all of them are in jail" and those "standing on the corner [who] can't speak English." Despite holding a doctorate in education, Cosby remained silent on the conditions in many high schools that have improved little in the post-*Brown* era: armed police officers patroling high schools plagued by over-crowding, crumbling classrooms, and a shortage of basic learning materials. Instead, Cosby proposed that hypersexed black women, violent black men, and a vapid youth culture conspire to extinguish the possibilities opened by *Brown*. Of today's black youth, Cosby explains "50 percent drop out, the rest of them are in prison" (Black Commentator, 2004).[1]

If we take seriously the role that language and discourse play in constituting and constructing political conflicts, rather than just expressing or representing them, then Cosby has offered an exemplary recital of the most commanding discourse on the failures and defects of black youth in particular and the racial-ization of large groups of youth in general. That is, while it has been through specific regressive shifts in policy and legislation—such as the expansion of "zero tolerance" law enforcement and cuts in public-education funding—that the possibilities for racial justice in the post–Civil Rights period have been undermined, those shifts have been naturalized and secured through signifi-cant ideological struggles and symbolic conflicts.

Here, we must think of political discourse as more than just "language games" or the "marketing" of political issues through clever framing strategies developed by communications specialists (e.g., rechristening estate or inherit-ance tax as "the death tax"). To be sure, in any immediate political conflict, language, messaging, and issue framing are critical; as the linguist George Lakoff and other media strategists have demonstrated, people comprehend political issues through a repertoire of narrative frameworks, and organizers and advocates must frame their campaign demands and policy proposals to resonate within these existing schemes. But as Gilmore (2004b) notes, an emphasis on short-term issue frames alone risks reifying those narrative cate-gories as "a-historic durables" rather than historically contingent and con-tested ideological concepts.

A more expansive interpretation of political discourse—and its broader ideological dimensions—involves not simply which words or slogans are used to advance political issues, but a recognition that to exercise long-term politi-cal power requires interventions into the way people formulate, imagine, and identify themselves within the social world. As mediators of experience, dis-courses establish the terrain on which people understand their identities, experiences, and interests, constituting the "common sense" they draw upon in their negotiations and calculations of day-to-day life. Political discourses are central to the engagement and contestation of all power relations because they provide coherent frameworks through which people view the world, understand their identities in relation to others, and make meaning from their experience (Purvis & Hunt, 1993). As the contrasting accounts of the crisis in public education provided by Johns and Cosby affirm, the ability of a discourse to structure a particular field of meaning—to regulate what constitutes its specific "truths," common sense, and logics—matters a great deal in understanding, interpreting, and responding to social problems.[2]

Fortunately, for the millions of youth of color whose prospects for happiness and life remain tenuous, the legacy of Barbara Johns rather than the punditry of Bill Cosby still holds promise. This chapter discusses the contributions of contemporary youth-led organizing in refashioning the ideological landscape through which particular racialized representations of "youth" are constructed and naturalized. Focusing on what theorist Stuart Hall (1988b) describes as the "political-ideological" dimensions of social change and transformation, I pay particular attention to the role youth organizing can play in challenging the dominant or hegemonic political discourse that has explained the abandonment of large portions of the youth population as not only justifiable but both natural and inevitable. I suggest that community organizing, which is rooted in directly challenging relations of power, exposing contradictions within existing social relations, and collectivizing the experiences of exploited and oppressed groups so that they can organize on their own behalf is uniquely situated for this type of ideological struggle because of its potential to transform the day-to-day experiences and practices that shape and validate competing ideological frameworks.

Using case studies of organizations in Los Angeles and New York City in particular, I examine how these youth-led activist groups use community organizing campaigns to contest the discourses used to define and explain social problems and crises and to reimagine the world through alternative logics, ideas, and frameworks. I begin with a brief review of the shifting ideological terrain that has governed the racialization of many groups of youth during the last 30 years and describe the emergence of youth-led social justice organizations as a response.

Historicizing Youth Activism

The 1950 walkout led by Barbara Johns unfolded amid a rich postwar legacy of young people leading direct-action social change movements. Four years before Martin Luther King Jr.'s 1963 March on Washington, civil rights leader Baynard Rustin (himself a product of the Young Communist League) led a youth march for integrated schools in the nation's capitol. Soon after, teenage college students initiated the first successful challenges to lunch-counter segregation. And in 1963, a thousand children as young as six years old emptied the Sixteenth Street Baptist Church in Birmingham, Alabama, singing freedom songs as they were blasted with fire hoses and attacked by police dogs. Hundreds spent the night in police commisioner Bull Connor's jail (Blumberg, 1991).

The faces of the leading antiracist formations of the era such as the Student Non-Violent Coordinating Committee, the Black Panthers, the Young Lords, the American Indian Movement, and the Brown Berets were the faces of youth. All of the notable U.S. social movements of the 1960s and 1970s—antiwar, feminist, gay rights, and free speech—drew their leadership and base in part from politically committed youth activists. Together with earlier generations of political strategists, organizers and leaders, they proved critical in provoking the crisis in political authority in full view by 1968. This groundswell of youth protest led Congress to extend the franchise to 18- to 20-year-olds in 1971, implicitly acknowledging that youth old enough to be drafted should not be barred from the voting booth. In short, young people played a central role in securing the (downward) redistribution of material resources and social status and recognition achieved by the early 1970s. These shifts benefited social groups within every generation, from first-generation college students, to blue collar workers and their families, to senior citizens living on fixed incomes (Duggan, 2003).

Not coincidentally then, the conservative counterattack epitomized and escalated by Ronald Reagan's capture of the presidency in 1980 turned in many ways on profiling and constructing young people of color as threats toward, rather than allies of, national hopes for peace and prosperity. The narratives mobilized by conservative opinion leaders to arrest the growth of the welfare state and the leveling of economic and civic hierarchies—the breakdown of the family, the primacy of individual responsibility over government intervention, the intergenerational "culture of poverty"—almost required an antagonistic stance toward youth raised outside the sanctity of white middle- and upper-class life. For example, California's dramatic turn from setting the global standard for a public education system in the 1970s toward its dismal record on teaching, learning, and access today, secured in large part through conservative antitax initiatives, became politically acceptable only by profiling the growing numbers of young black and brown Californians as both menacing and undeserving (Schrag, 1998). From this perspective, "youth" itself became a pejorative identity, emblematic of the failure of family, values, and nation.

Predictably, while recreation centers and youth jobs programs shut their doors, racially charged profiles of "wilding" youth offenders and remorseless teen moms increasingly found their way into political speeches and evening news sound bites. By the 1990s, any winning political script seemed to require some heavy-handed gesture toward young people—and black and brown youth in particular. Suggesting the offspring of the "failed family" had come home to roost, conservative academics warned that an upswing in the teenage population would spawn a wave of violent youth crime. Curfew laws and antigang taskforces proliferated. President Bill Clinton's 1994 crime bill allowed more juveniles to be tried as adults, and 41 states followed suit with their own versions of this policy. A 1996 *Newsweek* headline story titled "Superpredators Arrive" posed the policy question of the day: "Should we cage the new breed of vicious kids?" (Annin, 1996). From 1984 to 1997 the arrests of juveniles nationally jumped 30 percent. By 1998, polls showed that two-thirds of Americans believed youth under the age of 13 accused of murder should be tried as adults (Ginwright, 2001; HoSang, 2003; Males, 1996).

Meanwhile, nearly every state's reformed welfare laws placed draconian restrictions on benefits to teen parents while mandating that schools adopt an "abstinence-only" approach to sex education, drawing upon racialized pronouncements of irresponsible and immoral young mothers draining taxpayers of their hard-earned dollars. Parental consent laws limiting abortion access for young women proliferated. The effort to ban undocumented immigrants from public schools in California and to eliminate bilingual education programs in many states raised the specter of hoards of immigrant children running public schools into the ground.[3] Higher education costs soared while earnings for workers with no college degree declined. Liberal and conservative policymakers alike eagerly stripped the affirmative action and antidiscrimination protections that afforded young people of color limited opportunities in education and the marketplace.

That the apocalyptic prophecies proved wrong ultimately mattered little to opinion leaders. Demography was not destiny for teen crime, pregnancy, or any other of the imagined youth-fueled crisis: 60,000 fewer young people were arrested for homicide, rape, robbery, and assault in 2001 than in 1994, despite a large increase in the teen population. According to the FBI, young people in 2001 accounted for just 5 percent of the nation's homicides and 12 percent of violent crimes—both historic lows (Males, 1996). But the 20-year project of racializing youth of color through a profile emphasizing depleted morality, indolence, and violence had taken its toll (Ginwright, 2001). From 1980 to 2000, California built 21 new prisons but did not open a single new University of California campus; nationally the population of the nation's prisons, jails, juvenile facilities, and detention centers has quadrupled to more than two million people during this time (Krisberg, Wolf, & Marchionna, 2005).

As sociologist Amy Ansell (1997) explains, these racializing "political spectacles" or conflicts crafted by the conservatives in the United States in the last decade around affirmative action, immigration policy, crime and other issues have sought to not only amend particular laws but also "to rearticulate and contest the 'truths' dominant in … society for strategic and partisan advantage." That is, the discourses they mobilize through these conflicts seek to naturalize a particular vision of the social world—one in which inequality is normal, inevitable, and beyond the ambit of state intervention. By regulating the frameworks through which people understand issues in public life and the identity positions they claim for themselves and ascribe to others, a hegemonic discourse stakes out in advance the limits of legitimate debate (Giroux, 1997; Howarth, 1995). It is through the work of this dominant discourse, for example, that in California during the last two decades it has become commonsensical to build a prison complex unmatched in human history for its reach and cost but is regarded as absurd to devote similar efforts toward constructing the hundreds of new schools the current generation of California youth require. Similarly, California's once vaulted 1960 Master Plan for Higher Education guaranteeing a tuition-free college education for all in-state high school graduates sounds absurd within the prevalent political discourse, yet the practice of literally caging (on occasion, in four-square-foot holding pens) thousands of youth in California Youth Authority "warehouses'" seems both necessary and inexorable.[4] Producing this "truth"—that prisons for brown, black, and poor bodies are a "required" expenditure but schools for those same bodies "throw money at the problem"—is not just the work of powerful lobbyists or the sensational coverage of big money media. It results from the active public contests over the discourses society will use to establish such truths in the first place.

In the case studies that follow, I explore the ways in which the issue-based organizing campaigns of two youth groups *might* play a role in disrupting and reorganizing the larger ideological terrain that we currently confront. To be sure, no individual organization or advocacy project can transform the broad contours of this terrain single-handedly or over a short period of time; such renovations are better measured in decades than years, and by their nature grow well beyond the impact and influence of social justice organizations alone. But as I suggest below, the efforts of groups such as InnerCity Struggle in Los Angeles and FIERCE! in New York City might gesture toward the role that organized groups of young activists can play in facilitating or contributing toward such a transformation, and stand in sharp contrast to policy advocacy or litigation efforts that actually endorse, rather than disrupt, dominant ideological frameworks.

The "Disappeared Students": Re-Imagining Public Education in East Los Angeles

In the East Los Angeles offices of the 11-year-old community group InnerCity Struggle (ICS), a large chart titled "The Disappeared Students" hangs above a modest meeting room packed with student organizers from several nearby high schools.[5] The chart tells us that every year at neighboring Roosevelt High School, an average of 68 percent of the students "disappear," leaving school before graduation. Though Roosevelt's official enrollment of more than 5,100 students makes it one of the largest high schools in the nation, only a fraction of entering 9th graders earn their diplomas; only 1 in 15 members of a student body that is 99 percent Latino goes on to a four-year college (Brenes, 2003; Vasquez, 2004).

In the prevalent education policy discourse and mainstream news accounts, the annual decline in student population at Roosevelt and many hundreds of other schools is attributed to "dropouts," implicitly explaining the problem through the volition and decisions of individual students. In this discourse, the students reject the opportunity afforded them because they lack some combination of motivation, self-discipline, or intellectual ability (Giroux, 1997). Both heavy-handed zero-tolerance policies that expel students permanently for technical violations of school code and more sympathetic interventions such as mentoring programs still take the individual student to be the object of change. Though budget-starved Roosevelt crams as many as 65 students in classrooms built for 30, and provides one college guidance counselor for the entire student body and only a handful of college preparatory courses, the students are understood as the primary authors of the school's failure (Brenes, 2003). Drawing on long-standing narratives of people of color as unable or uninterested in learning and intellectual development, the crises of student dropouts, failure on standardized tests, and school violence are produced and rationalized through thinly veiled references to the students' myriad deficiencies.

The "disappeared students" information sheets, signs, and chants that student leaders from ICS carry to their meetings with their school principals, to press conferences before the school board, and to statewide mobilizations at the capitol in Sacramento represents more than a clever campaign slogan. Coined by an allied group of student organizers affiliated with the South Los Angeles–based Community Coalition for Substance Abuse Prevention and Treatment, the "disappeared students" framework emphasizes the burdens and loss borne by the youth and suggests that the failures of their schools and the decision makers who regulate them is not accidental. The shift away from student "dropouts" embodies the oppositional discourse both organizations use to analyze and explain the conditions facing students and to craft alternative explanations and courses of action.[6]

ICS, which organizes students and parents in three East Los Angeles high schools and several middle schools, demonstrates the ways in which issue-based organizing campaigns can seek short-term policy reform while contesting the broader ideological terrain. Organizing by ICS to win additional guidance counselors, college preparation classes, and a new high school to serve the neighborhood understands that progressive social change is realized in part through specific policy reforms, increased political power, and expanded relations of accountability. But for poor Latino students from East Los Angeles, profiled as intellectually apathetic and unworthy of significant public investment, modest policy ameliorations alone will not transform their security in a racially structured polity. Following scholar-activist Ruth Wilson Gilmore's (2004a) formulation, this profile "extinguishes" their innocence; that is, because of their ascribed status as dangerous, undeserving, and thus "guilty," they relinquish their standing to demand social equity and make claims for public resources. Moreover, within the logics of the broad culture of neoliberalism, in which competition, social hierarchy, and insecurity are valorized, the students' "failure" to graduate from high school and attend college represents a naturalization and rationalization of these inevitable inequalities rather than a consequence of them. Only by contesting and disrupting the racialized discourses and the commonly understood "truths" that constitute them as guilty (and other groups, by contrast, as innocent) can they secure more enduring transformations.

The organization's leadership understands clearly the contours of this struggle over ideology and representation—it chooses organizing issues and campaigns that will allow it to challenge and destabilize prevailing narratives about students of color. ICS director Luis Sanchez explains these dominant assumptions:

> First [there is] the assumption that only some kids can learn. The idea that only some kids should go to college is rooted in both ideas about a *learned* versus a *laboring* class, and racist ideas about people of color not being capable of learning; second, the assumption that because people of color are criminals, schools have to be run like prisons.... In all of our campaigns, we ask, "What kind of world views do we want to change?" (Sanchez, personal communication, 2005)

ICS meets this imperative at multiple scales. Through United Students (US), its campus-based organizing component, an activist core of 75 to 100 students at Roosevelt and two other neighborhood high schools conducts weekly lunchtime meetings to discuss the issues students confront in their everyday lives. But US student organizers address these issues through alternative frameworks and language that challenges rather than naturalizes existing inequalities and norms. For example, their analysis of the pervasive presence of military recruiters at their school (a US survey reported that three of every four Roosevelt students had heard a military recruitment presentation in their classroom by their senior year) contested the popular rhetoric about the singular opportunities for personal and career fulfillment awaiting those who enlisted. Instead, through their Students Not Soldiers educational campaign, the group focused on the ways recruiters target students in failing schools who may feel they have few other opportunities; the campaign promotes non-military options in support of a vision of nonviolence (Brenes, 2003). All of the organizing campaigns and discussions implicitly ask students to conjure up their own positive visions for their schools and communities. Thus, in these local and immediate settings, among students, teachers, and even some school administrators, the organization mobilizes a discourse based on the students' own aspirations and their power to "organize against their abandonment" by state and society (Gilmore, 2002).

It is also important to note that this campus-based organizing seeks to counter the hierarchies and divisions often at work among students themselves. If the organization's work exclusively focused on increasing college access opportunities, it would risk implicitly marginalizing and excluding those students not placed in the existing "high achievement" tracks—simply repositioning the "extinguished innocence" status onto another portion of the student body. But ICS presses for college access opportunities while simultaneously addressing such issues as suspension and truancy policy, school construction, and military recruitment, all within the broader "disappeared students" framework. This approach intentionally confronts divisions around language, immigration status, and experience, and the academic labels imposed on all students (e.g., "college-bound" versus "troublemaker").

Because many of the most important policy debates and the related discourses shaping the conditions at individual high schools are produced at higher levels of decision making, ICS also focuses its attention beyond the local campuses. In addressing Los Angeles Unified School District decisions over school funding, curriculum, and school construction in particular, it deploys the same student-centered discourse before this broader public, often through mobilizations targeting the school board and meetings with district officials. In one of its most successful efforts to date, ICS joined with the Community Coalition and other local parent and student activist groups to compel the school board to make a rigorous college preparatory curriculum the standard for all high school students. If implemented by 2008 (as the board has pledged it will be), the policy will open up the "college track" to many students customarily denied access to such rigorous courses because of overcrowding, traditional tracking, or mistakes in course programming. Notably, the campaign has shifted the local debate over student achievement to questions of educational adequacy, resources, opportunity and student self-determination; when more than five hundred students and parents rallied in support of the policy at a May 2005 board meeting, they wore shirts emblazoned with the declaration Let Me Choose My Future—an assertion retold in dozens of subsequent media accounts (Hayasaki, 2005).

Indeed, in the last two years, four *Los Angeles Times* feature stories have profiled the group's activities and analysis, and dozens of local radio, television, community, and Spanish-language press accounts have done the same. Staff organizers and student leaders run regular media advocacy trainings and workshops to better frame and project their account of "disappeared students" and to contest the frameworks typically employed to deliberate problems within public education (Sanchez, personal communication, 2005).

Likewise, parents and residents in the surrounding East Los Angeles neighborhoods are challenged to rethink their assumptions about the students, their capacity to learn, and their right to participate in defining the needs of the neighborhood. In their two-year quest to win funding for a new high school and elementary school, student leaders talked with hundreds of residents in their homes, in schools, and in churches to redefine the problem and build support for the school construction project. In spite of the vocal resistance of a small group of local homeowners, the students successfully realigned a significant number of residents to support the project, and initiated a parents' organizing group to build on this collaborative approach (Sanchez, personal communication, 2005). The community organizing strategies utilized by ICS, which emphasize collective participation, confrontation, and the exposure of contradictions in relations of power, give participants (including the student organizers as well as the residents, policy makers, and journalists they engage) new experiences and frameworks with which to understand and interpret existing social problems.

Finally, ICS actively joins and organizes regional and statewide coalitions with organizations and advocates that share its ambitions and analysis. In 2000, its Schools Not Jails network mobilized to raise public awareness against a successful statewide ballot initiative that would try more juvenile offenders as adults and increase sentencing penalties. More recently, the groups have focused on federal legislation to expand police powers and prosecutions in the name of fighting "gang violence." Campaigns for statewide legislation to increase access to public universities for undocumented high school graduates and to standardize college preparation curriculums in all high schools capture the proactive racial justice visions of these same groups. Though exercising significant influence on statewide policy can be limited because of California's size and political geography, legislative victories are not the only objectives. By refusing to cede the debate exclusively to the norms, logics, and frameworks of their opposition, the group and its allies can gain some ground through the strategic use of the media, even in moments of short-term defeat.

Again, while it is premature to suggest that ICS and its Los Angeles allies alone stand poised to reverse the decades-long exclusion and subordination of large sectors of the youth population, their efforts are aligned with a growing number of similar projects around the country which similarly emphasize the politicoideological dimensions of their advocacy efforts around public education. In Denver, youth organizers with the groups Padres Unidos/ Jovenes Unidos (Parents United/Youth United) and Students 4 Justice issued reports on several high schools documenting dramatic racial disparities in the uses of discipline and the availability of college-track classes and other resources for students. As in Los Angeles, the student-researched and -written reports have received significant media attention and have begun influencing the terms of the local debate. In Mississippi, affiliates of the Jackson-based organizing network Southern Echo are challenging the Schoolhouse 2 Jailhouse pipeline that confines growing numbers of black youth. Led by groups such as Citizens for Quality Education in Lexington, the coalition focuses the attention of elected officials, the media, and the public on the relationships among resource-starved schools, austere classroom disciplinary policies (which still include corporal punishment in many schools), and the state's Orwellian juvenile "training schools" that institutionalize and detain students expelled from public schools. Generation Y, a multiracial group of student activists, has successfully organized against zero-tolerance policies in the

Chicago school system, replacing them with "peer courts" as an alternative dispute resolution system. Again, the organizing group both secured important policy reforms to benefit youth of color in particular while contesting the logics that discourses of punishment and reprisal offered the only framework to respond to conflicts between youth. Youth groups in Philadelphia, New York, and the San Francisco Bay Area, among other communities, have developed equally generative and compelling interventions into the discourses and ideologies that construct and racialize particular groups of youth.[7]

Whose Quality of Life? Living FIERCE! in Greenwich Village

While ICS and its allies have used the crisis in public education to challenge one form of exclusion faced by youth whose innocence has been "extinguished," along the Hudson River on the western edge of Manhattan's Greenwich Village, another group of youth activists contest a different set of racialized narratives in their struggle for recognition in public discourse and public space.[8] The Christopher Street Pier has traditionally provided one of the few safe spaces of kinship and community for lesbian, gay, bisexual, and transgender (LGBT) youth of color and homeless youth from across New York City. By one estimate, LGBT youth constitute one-third to one-half of the City's estimated 22,000 homeless youth, though transitional housing and service programs specifically serving queer youth provide less than 100 beds (Karp, 2002). The pier has historically provided an important, if tenuous, respite to the harassment and violence such youth face in most other public spaces and a place where youth could find one another and create their own networks of support and sustenance. Service providers conducting outreach on the pier connected youth to important medical, mental health, housing, and employment services.

But as the area became the focus of a $330 million community redevelopment plan to develop the pier into a "green and blue oasis for all New Yorkers to enjoy," powerful interests sought to ensure that "all New Yorkers" did not include the pier's most steadfast users. Though police statistics showed major crime decreasing in the area, high-profile sweeps resulted in the arrests of hundreds of youth of color for violating myriad "quality of life" statutes. Residents and merchants in the surrounding neighborhoods, city politicians, elite developers, and police spokespersons agreed that the principle "threat" to the peace and security of the community was the violence and turmoil young people inevitably brought to "their" neighborhood. A *New York Times* article titled "Tolerance in Village Wears Thin" portrayed a place besieged by "noisy visitors" turning the area into a "sinkhole of vice" (Worth, 2002). An ad hoc group calling themselves Residents in Distress (RID) sponsored a Take Back Our Streets rally while the local precinct brought in 23 rookie officers to carry out its zero-tolerance initiative, which included a 1:00 A.M. curfew near the river and new "security" cameras on public streets. Absent from nearly all these discussions were any studied references to the stories, challenges, and interests of the youth themselves (Goldstein, 2002; Lee, 2002).[9]

In 2000 a group of youth activists founded Fabulous Independent Educated Radicals for Community Empowerment! (FIERCE!) to organize, educate, and support LGBT youth of color and homeless youth in the area struggling against both growing police harassment and their general abandonment by the polity.[10] FIERCE! launched a Save Our Space organizing campaign to deliberately shift the terms of the "quality of life" debate to focus on the experiences, needs, and struggles of the young people drawn to the West Village, and their "quality of life" concerns. Conducting outreach near the pier and to nonprofit organizations serving LGBT youth of color, FIERCE! has mobilized hundreds of youth to attend various community meetings on police and safety issues to confront those who view surveillance and arrest as the only viable solution to the conflict. Youth in the group produced *Fenced OUT*, a documentary about the issue that connects the struggle to "past generations of queer peoples' fight for use of public spaces at Christopher Street and the piers." Community awareness activities such as the daylong public celebration Reclaim Our Space: A Festival of Resistance highlight the race- and gender-based profiling stemming from neighborhood gentrification efforts (Amateau, 2002). FIERCE! leaders have met with police representatives, leaders of the neighborhood community board, and local politicians in an unswerving effort to counter the prevailing discourse on "youth deviance" marking the early debates.

Through these activities and others, the oppositional discourse FIERCE! draws upon and mobilizes includes three critical dimensions. First, the organization has used the public outcry on youth congregating in the West Village to focus attention on the myriad forms of prohibition and exploitation LGBT youth of color face in their own efforts to survive in a climate of shrinking economic opportunities and public services. FIERCE! situates the concerns over prostitution in residential neighborhoods within a larger analysis of the overwhelming discrimination and exclusion queer youth of color face in realizing any economic security—sex work is often the only viable alternative. The group has also joined other progressive formations in linking the city's "quality of life" campaigns to the tremendous growth in the numbers of young people of color brought under the supervision of the criminal justice system: young gay black men who come to the Village to socialize face arrest for the mildest transgression while rowdy middle-class whites spilling out of neighborhood bars will rarely know the enduring pain of spending hours in handcuffs. Extending the important work to advance public awareness of racial profiling, it exposes the contradictions and duplicity behind the "quality of life" discourse. Quite notably, FIERCE! calls attention to the specific ways in which such profiling is experienced and enforced with regard to gender and sexuality (Block, 2003; Goldstein, 2002).

In addition, the group has fashioned proactive alternative solutions to discredit the claims that police sweeps, "resident patrols," curfews, and surveillance cameras represent the only possible response to conflicts between residents and the LGBT youth in the neighborhood (Martinez, 2002). In particular, FIERCE! has called for the city and state to fund a late-night, drop-in center for LGBT youth in the area, demanding the reallocation of funds intended for an expanded juvenile detention center. At neighborhood meetings, they constantly address the lack of services and support available to homeless youth and LGBT youth of color, and insist that such resources be included in any comprehensive "quality of life" campaigns.

Finally, the youth leadership of the organization, struggling with issues of harassment, abuse, and profiling in their own lives, invests substantial time in understanding and identifying the root social, political, and economic dimensions of the issue. The organization conducts a wide range of workshops and training sessions devoted to understanding the historical dimensions of struggle and control over public space in the West Village and how developer-fueled gentrification has intensified those conflicts. Before neighborhood meetings, press conferences, meetings with city officials and their own peers, they have become authoritative commentators on the rapid transformations besetting the area (J. Ehrensaft-Hawley, personal communication, 2005). Their nuanced analysis implicitly discredits the regressive efforts to profile the youth who gather near the pier as infantile, rebellious, and self-absorbed.

Thus, FIERCE! organizes both to secure concrete policy reforms that will benefit its constituents and to transform the broader public discourses in which such policies are understood and debated. FIERCE! demonstrates the particular ways that racialized discourses are inflected and expressed through the modalities of gender, class, and sexuality because their members experience these hierarchies all together. While the city continues to prioritize law enforcement solutions for conflicts in the West Village, FIERCE! has won the support of many local residents, preventing relatively small groups such as RID from speaking for the neighborhood as a whole. It is important to note that FIERCE! has ensured that local debates now at least consider the needs, interests, and lives of the LGBT youth who gather in the neighborhood, thwarting those groups who treat queer youth as loathsome and disposable. Like ICS and other youth organizing groups, FIERCE!'s emphasis on collective action, confrontation, and disruption provides the groundwork for new frameworks and experiences. The organization's long-term political strategy seeks to restructure the ideological terrain that constructs LGBT youth of color as "problems" by demanding their consideration as important, vital subjects. Again, while enormous work remains to be done to transform this terrain more significantly, FIERCE!'s organizing demonstrates how issue campaigns focused on policy reform can contribute to long-term renovations.

Youth organizing groups in other parts of the country echo FIERCE!'s groundbreaking work at the interstices of race, class, gender, and sexuality.

In Portland, Oregon, the youth-led community group Sisters in Action for Power waged an impressive organizing campaign to force the school district to address sexual harassment in the public schools. The group has now turned its attention to an analysis of the racial and gender justice dimensions of the gentrification and public housing crisis besetting the city. In Albuquerque, New Mexico, Young Women United has launched a student-led campaign to challenge restrictive "abstinence-only" sex education programs in local high schools, responding in part to the ways traditional discourses of "teen pregnancy" construct and represent young women of color. In Long Beach, California, Khmer Girls in Action organizes young working-class Cambodian American women, and also secured a new school district policy regarding sexual harassment.[11]

Conclusion

To be sure, groups like ICS, FIERCE! and their contemporaries face a long haul to substantively transform the ideological terrain on which key youth policy debates unfold: limited access to funding; frequent turnover in leadership, membership, and staff; and the complexity and endurance of the dominant discourses linking youth and race render their short-term impact uneven and incomplete. But at a time when approaches to youth development focus almost entirely on pragmatic and piecemeal legislative reforms, policy triage, and "innovative practices," the struggles waged by the youth organizing groups discussed here are all the more important.[12] They remind us of the centrality of ideological conflict and struggle in transformative social justice movements. Moreover, if we conceptualize these formations as contemporary (albeit underdeveloped) forms of political parties for large numbers of young people of color not represented in the formal party system, then we can consider Antonio Gramsci's prescient explanation of the roles such groups must play in modern politics. Gramsci asserts the imperative of such formations lies "in the elaboration and diffusion of conceptions of the world" because "what they do is to work out the ethics and the politics corresponding to these conceptions and act, as it were, as their historical 'laboratory'" (cited in Hall, 1988a, p. 188), that is, groups such as ICS and FIERCE! provide structured, strategic spaces and experiences through which young people and their allies can make sense of the vexing and contradictory forces that shape their lives, and allow them to test new avenues of struggle and resistance.

If we take the political ideological dimensions of youth organizing work seriously, three opportunities for youth-led organizing groups, intermediaries, funders, scholars, and public policy strategies seem promising.

First, funders and intermediaries in particular should consider giving youth organizing groups more resources and opportunities to further develop their already rich work in this area. Resources for documentation of existing approaches and convenings to discuss this dimension of their organizing could be particularly important.

Second, scholars, training intermediaries, and funders could devote resources and attention toward understanding how to better expand and strengthen this work, how it might be documented and evaluated, and how promising practices and approaches might be proliferated.

Third, while a renewed interest among progressive activists in general has emerged over the centrality of issue framing and strategic communications in a divisive political moment (the well-known "How do we talk to the red states?" conundrum), this attention has generally turned on narrower questions of crafting persuasive "messages" and sound bites. Such pragmatic concerns are clearly important to winning short-term policy debates, but they risk leaving the broader frameworks and ideological underpinnings that define those debates undisturbed.[13]

This danger looms particularly large over debates surrounding the "problems" posed by young people of color. Too often, liberal policy advocates rehearse the dominant logics of these debates in support of modest policy reforms—"Yes, our youth are troubled and dysfunctional, but that's why we need more job training programs"—rather than challenging and contextualizing their underlying assumptions. The experiences of FIERCE! and ICS challenge us to remain vigilant about the imperative to contest, rather than reproduce, such narratives.

Notes

1. For a more extended discussion of the Cosby controversy, see Dyson, 2005.
2. For more of the rich theoretical literature on this point, see, especially, Edelman, 1998; Hall, 1988b; Laclau & Mouffe, 1985.
3. See Gibbs & Bankhead, 2001.
4. For an excellent account of the ongoing organizing against the California Youth Authority's warehousing of youth offenders see the work of Books Not Bars (http://ellabakercenter.org/bnb.html).
5. This case study is built in part on a set of organizational publications in the author's possession. See also Hayasaki, 2003 and the group's website (http://www.innercitystruggle.org).
6. For more on the Community Coalition for Substance Abuse Prevention and Treatment and its youth organization South Central Youth Empowered Thru Action (SC-YEA), see its website (http://www.ccsapt.org).
7. See, as examples of this work, Browne, 2003; Mitchell, 2004.
8. This section is based in part on several organizational publications in the author's possession.
9. See Goldstein, 2002; Lee, 2002. RID tended to articulate the most reactionary and sensationalist accounts of the dispute, and attracted much of the initial media attention. RID had much less influence on the negotiations and debates that followed, which involved local politicians, resident councils, the police, and FIERCE! and its allies (J. Ehrensaft-Hawley, personal communication, 2005).
10. See the organization's website (http://www.fierceny.org). FIERCE! specifically describes itself as "a community organizing project for Transgender, Lesbian, Gay, Bisexual, Two Spirit, Queer, and Questioning (TLGBTSQQ) youth of color in New York City." The more familiar abbreviation LGBT is used here, though the organization's careful attention to expansive language in its description is instructive.

11. See the Funders' Collaborative on Youth Organizing website (http://www.fcyo.org) for information on these organizations.
12. As one among many examples of this type of approach, see Kelotra, 2004.
13. See, for example, the work of the Frameworks Institute (http://www.frame-worksinstitute.org) and the Rockridge Institute (http://www.rockridgeinsti-tute.org), and the work of linguist George Lakoff (especially Lakoff, 2004).

References

Amateau, A. (2002, October). Queer youth protest, celebrate. *Gay City News* (New York), *1*(20). Retrieved May 11, 2004 from http://www.gaycitynews.com/GCN20/protest.html.

Annin, P. (1996, January 19). Superpredators arrive. *Newsweek*, p. 57.

Ansell, A. E. (1997). *New Right, new racism: Race and reaction in the United States and Britain.* New York: New York University Press.

Black Commentator. (2004, June 3). Bill Cosby's Confused Notions of "Responsibility." *Black Commentator.* (Editorial) Retrieved May 6, 2004 from http://www.blackcommentator.com/93/93_cover_cosby.html.

Block, J. (2003, November 19–25). Street sweeping: Bloomberg plan sends prostitutes cycling from city jails to local corners. *Village Voice.* Retrieved May 4, 2004 from http://www.villagevoice.com/news/0347,block,48779,5.html.

Blumberg, R. L. (1991). *Civil rights: The 1960s freedom struggle* (Rev. ed.). Boston: G. K. Hall.

Brenes, M. (2003, Summer). High school students in East L.A. win changes for quality education. *The Struggle* (newsletter published by InnerCity Struggle of East Los Angeles), pp. 1–2.

Browne, J. A. (2003). *Derailed! The schoolhouse to jailhouse track.* Washington, DC: Advancement Project.

Duggan, L. (2003). *The twighlight of Equality? Neoliberalism, cultural politics, and the attack on democracy.* Boston: Beacon.

Dyson, M. E. (2005). *Is Bill Cosby right? Or has the black middle class lost its mind?* New York: Basic Civitas.

Edelman, M. (1998). *Constructing the political spectacle.* Chicago: University of Chicago Press.

Gibbs, J. T., & Bankhead, T. (2001). *Preserving privilege: California politics, propositions, and people of color.* Westport, CT: Praeger.

Gilmore, R. W. (2002). Fatal couplings of power and difference: Notes on racism and geography. *Professional Geographer, 54*(1), 15–24.

Gilmore, R. W. (2004a). Profiling alienated labor: racialization, externalities, and re-partitioned geographies. (Unpublished paper in author's possession.)

Gilmore, R. W. (2004b). *Scholar-activists in the mix.* Paper presented at the Presidential Plenary, Association of American Geographers, Philadelphia.

Ginwright, S. (2001). Critical resistance: African American youth and US racism. *Youth Development Journal, 3*, 15–24.

Giroux, H. A. (1997). Ideology and agency in the process of schooling. In H. A. Giroux (Ed.), *Pedagogy and the politics of hope: Theory, culture, and schooling* (pp. 71–94. Boulder, CO: Westview.

Goldstein, R. (2002, April 24). Street hassle. *Village Voice,* Retrieved May 4, 2004 from http://www.village voice.com/news/0217.goldstein,34171,1.html.

Hall, S. (1988a). Gramsci and us. In *The hard road to renewal: Thatcherism and the crisis of the Left* (p. 171). London: Verso.

Hall, S. (1988b). *The hard road to renewal: Thatcherism and the crisis of the Left.* London: Verso.

Hayasaki, E. (2003, May 21). Schools see "an awakening" of student activism. *Los Angeles Times*, p. B2.

Hayasaki, E. (2005, June 15). College prep idea approved in L.A. *Los Angeles Times,* p. B1.

HoSang, D. (2003). *Youth and community organizing today.* New York: Funders' Collaborative on Youth Organizing.

Howarth, D. (1995). Discourse theory. In D. Marsh (Ed.), *Theory and methods in political science.* London: Macmillan.

Karp, D. (2002). Fierce gay youth confront distressed West Village residents. Retrieved May 25, 2004, from http://www.jrn.columbia.edu/studentwork/children/2002/karpgay.asp

Kelotra, R. (2004, March/April). FAIRNESS: The Civil Rights Act of 2004. *Poverty and Race, 13,* 5–7.

Krisberg, B., Wolf, A., & Marchionna, S. (2005). *California corrections at the crossroads (FOCUS).* Oakland, CA: National Council on Crime and Delinquency.

Laclau, E., & Mouffe, C. (1985). *Hegemony and socialist strategy* (2nd ed.). London: Verso.

Lakoff, G. (2004). *Don't think of an elephant! Know your values and frame the debate.* White River Junction, VT: Chelsea Green.

Lee, D. (2002, March 31). Street fight. *New York Times,* p. 1.

Males, M. (1996). *The scapegoat generation: America's war on adolescents.* Monroe, ME: Common Courage.

Martinez, G. (2002). A FIERCE fight against gay harassment. Retrieved May 25, 2004, from http://www.gothamgazette.com/commentary/145.martinez.shtml.

Mitchell, N. (2004, March 17). North High students issue call for reforms. *Rocky Mountain News.*

Purvis, T., & Hunt, A. (1993). Discourse, ideology, discourse, ideology, discourse, ideology.... *British Journal of Sociology, 44*(3), 473–499.

Schrag, P. (1998). *Paradise lost: California's experience, America's future.* New York: New Press.

Vasquez, R. (2004, February 5). Schools needed now. *Eastside Sun* (Los Angeles), p. 1.

Wormser, R. (2003). Profile of Barbara Johns. Retrieved May 5, 2004, from http://www.pbs.org/wnet/jimcrow/index.html.

Worth, R. (2002, January 19). Tolerance in village wears thin. *New York Times,* Sect. B, p. 1.

CHAPTER 2

Civic Activist Approaches for Engaging Youth in Social Justice

HEATHER LEWIS-CHARP, HANH CAO YU,
AND SENGSOUVANH SOUKAMNEUTH

In the last decade, the youth development field had successfully shifted the public dialogue and research base of youth work from one that was deficit oriented to one that articulated the kinds of supports and opportunities young people need to become healthy and functioning adults (Connell & Gambone, 2000; Gambone & Arbreton, 1997; Pittman & Irby, 1996). While youth development research and policies had created a more holistic public dialogue about the developmental process, it did so without due attention to the environments and sociopolitical context in which development occurs (Ginwright & James, 2002; Mohamed & Wheeler, 2001). Neighborhood and community factors such as poverty, unemployment, violence, and underresourced schools impede civic participation and are serious barriers to the developmental process (Bronfenbrenner, 1979; Brooks-Gunn, Duncan, & Aber, 1997; Chalk & Phillips, 1996; Garbarino, 1995). Examining such factors is an important step to addressing the systematic barriers that impede the positive development of young people.

In order to address this gap in the research, many youth development scholars began to take a harder look at context in efforts to address the needs of vulnerable adolescents (Granger, 2003; Lerner, Taylor, & von Eye, 2002). More specifically, there is growing consensus that effective youth programs need to address the cultural, social, and political contexts that support or impede young people's healthy development (Phelan, Davidson, & Yu, 1998). Scholars in Community Youth Development (CYD) have addressed context by advocating for an approach that channels the power of youth to take action in their communities, while simultaneously challenging communities to embrace their role in the development of youth (Cahill, 1997; Gambone, Klem, & Connell, 2002; Hughes & Curnan, 2002; Irby, Ferber, Pittman, Tolman, & Yohalem, 2001).

Despite the emerging interest in youth action and political engagement, few empirical studies exist in this area—particularly studies of youth in low-income urban communities. Most research has focused on the benefits of traditional forms of political engagement and/or community service (see Walker, 2002; Youniss & Yates, 1997; Youniss & Yates, 1999). Few empirical studies have explicitly explored the relationship between youth development and youth activism. Emerging scholarly works on the development of an activist orientation and sociopolitical capacity, however, have begun to lay the groundwork for a study in this area. Watts, Williams, and Jagers (2003), for example, explore concepts relevant to sociopolitical development among African American youth. Building on concepts from community psychology, such as oppression, liberation, critical consciousness, and culture, Watts et al. claim that sociopolitical development is a key process by which individuals acquire the knowledge, analytical skills, and emotional faculties necessary for participation in democratic processes and social change efforts.

The study of civic activism we conducted and discuss in this chapter is one step toward addressing this void in the research literature, as we focus explicitly on the engagement of marginalized youth in social justice efforts. The study focuses on the work of civic activism groups because of their applied strategy for engaging youth as actors and "experts" on issues of public policy and community concern. By supporting political skills and knowledge, civic activism efforts support young people's capacity to engage directly with power brokers, decision makers, and institutions in their communities. Such efforts have the potential to transform the capacity of families and communities to provide for young people (Forum for Youth Investment, 2001). It is through the politicized analysis of the inequitable contexts and policies that shape young people's day-to-day lives (schools, healthcare, public services, etc.) that civic activism groups seek to promote the conditions for healthy youth development.

Framing Youth Activism and Identity

Our research approach assumes that social justice is not confined to the public sphere. It has an explicitly personal dimension, one classically illustrated by the feminist anthem, "The personal is political." That is, social justice is embedded in the choices of individuals to resist dominant discourses and prejudices in the course of their day-to-day lives, just as it is embedded in overt action to transform the policies and institutions around them. The concept that social change involves ongoing "self-work" resonates with the theories of Jürgen Habermas, who argued that "*insights gained through critical self-awareness are emancipatory in the sense that at least one can recognize the correct reasons for his or her problems.*" (*Habermas*, 1970, p. 371). We would argue that critical self-awareness not only helps an individual identify the seeds of her own problems, but also sheds light on dominant discourses that contribute to her marginalization and oppression of others. Education about the "self" and identity is key to social transformation because it helps individuals identify and articulate what it is that needs to be changed.

The importance of this aspect of social justice work is best captured in identity-based social movements. Bernstein argues that identity is an end goal of collective action in that "activists may challenge stigmatized identities, seek recognition for new identities, or deconstruct restrictive social categories." (Bernstein, 1997, p. 538) In line with this argument is research that illustrates that identity support includes both the opportunity to form a positive identity through relationships with adults and peers who once struggled through similar identity issues, and the opportunity to critique mainstream institutions and values (Ginwright & James, 2002; Lewis-Charp, Yu, Soukamneuth, & Lacoe, 2003; Tatum, 1997). Moreover, research on young people's participation in identity-based movements can contribute to our understanding of young people's social and political development (Inglehart, 1990; Johnston, Laraña, & Gusfield, 1994). As youth make the connection to broad social movements, their understanding of how civil rights apply to their context and their notions of social justice are likely to be affected.

Our examination of civic activism looks explicitly at the role that identity plays in creating an orientation toward social justice in marginalized young people and sowing the seeds for their social and political development. While researchers have well documented identity-based movements among young adults in the civil rights era (e.g., McAdam, 1988), we know very little about the complex dimension of identity-based collective action in the post–civil rights era. As will be discussed further in our presentation of findings, we argue that civic activism groups facilitate collective action among marginalized youth in two key ways. First, they nurture collective forms of identity by helping young people come to understand their connections to others who share their race, gender, sexual orientation, social class, and so on. Second, they make social change tangible through systematic work on issues that youth find meaningful and relevant to their lives.

The research questions guiding our analysis and reporting of the study include:

1. How do civic activism groups provide a forum for youth to actively address social justice issues?
2. How do civic activism groups promote a social justice orientation among marginalized youth?
3. What implications do our findings have for youth development practice and policy?

Methods

Our data was gathered during two visits to 11 youth civic activist organizations, approximately one year apart (2001–2002). These visits lasted 2 or 3 days and included in-depth interviews with youth participants, program staff, and community members. We also observed program activities such as meetings, rallies, trainings, retreats, or cultural activities to provide a context for our evaluation and better understand the programs offered by the organizations. Thorough training for our researchers ensured a high level of consistency and reliability of data collected from the 11 organizations. Prior to each round of site visits, we conducted document reviews for each organization, including reviews of their annual reports, newsletters, and organizational planning documents.

Study Sample of Youth

The youth in our sample come from unique backgrounds that may affect their engagement in youth development programs. Table 2.1 highlights the key challenges faced by young people across civic activism groups studied. When compared to statistics on the general U.S. youth population, youth in civic activism organizations face a high percentage of barriers and risk factors. For instance, a high percentage of the youth within these organizations come from single-parent households (50%), come from families that receive public assistance (43%), and have limited proficiency in English (12%). Histories of drug and alcohol use (29% and 32%, respectively) are also high relative to the

Table 2.1 Risk Factors Faced by Youth in Study Sample and National Statistics
(N = Participants from 9 organizations)

	Civic Activism Groups	National Average
Single-parent household	50%	31%
On public assistance	43%	9%
Alcohol abuse	32%	5%
Drugs	29%	5%
Physical abuse	28%	1%
Language other than English is spoken at home	26%	17%
Incarceration	20%	18%
Attempted suicide	19%	9%
Sexual abuse	19%	1%
Limited English proficiency	12%	5%
Pregnancy	11%	27%

Source (for national data): Yu & Lewis-Charp, 2003.

general youth population, as are histories of sexual abuse (19%) and attempts at suicide (19%).

Further, given the very focused recruitment strategies of some organizations, these risk factors look more serious when examined by individual organization. For example, in one organization, 85% of youth come from single-parent households. Meanwhile, 100% of youth at two of the organizations come from homes where a language other than English is spoken. In another organization, 70% come from families that are on public assistance. Similarly, 72% of youth at one organization face problems with drug use, compared to a cross-site average of 29%. Thus, some of the civic activism organizations recruit and serve youth with risk factors that are above and beyond the cross-site and national average.

Summary of Findings

This chapter represents a summary of findings from qualitative research of these 11 diverse civic activism organizations.[1] We begin our summary with a brief discussion of the characteristics of civic activism organizations. Subsequently, we present civic activism practices that inform our understanding of how civic activism organizations engage marginalized youth by (1) nurturing collective forms of identity, (2) making social change tangible, and (3) coaching strategies to foster lifelong activism. After the reporting of findings, we articulate the implications of these research findings for youth policy and practice.

Characteristics of Civic Activism Organizations

We really focus on developing people. A lot of times, organizers are focused on quantitative measures of membership.... We develop qualitative goals around analysis, around leadership development, around personal growth .... We look at people's minds and people's beliefs as centrally important.

—Staffer at C-Beyond, in Concord, California

As illustrated by the above quote, the priority that civic activism groups place on young people's personal growth distinguishes their work from that of more adult-led traditional community organizing. Civic activism groups provide diverse young people, largely from resource poor communities, opportunities to explore and act on social issues. They use varied activities from the fields of multicultural counseling and community organizing, such as critical education on prejudice and discrimination, support groups, political education, issue identification, advocacy for the rights of marginalized populations, and direct action.

The civic activism groups we studied valued youth leadership, and most had youth on staff or in core leadership positions, youth members on their board, youth steering committees, and so on. The tendency for high levels of youth involvement in decision making within civic activism is partially an outcropping of the philosophical value for grassroots leadership that characterizes most organizing efforts (Alinsky, 1971). Within civic activism organizations, there is a sense that young people are the only ones who know their own experience and therefore are the only ones who can mobilize their peers to take action on issues that are relevant to youth.

Nurturing Collective Forms of Identity

> *We believe that before you go out into the community and make change, you have to really understand where you're coming from and understand yourself. This is about identity development, the history of your people, where your people stand in the bigger picture.*

—Staffer at CAPAY (Coalition for Asian Pacific American Youth), in
Boston, Massachusetts

As evidenced by this quote, civic activism organizations focus on raising awareness and strengthening individuals' ability to navigate and negotiate the challenges they face. In doing so, they seek to "make the personal political" among youth from marginalized social groups in the United States. Civic activism organizations recruit youth from marginalized ethnic, racial, or cultural groups; within our study, there were organizations focused explicitly on African American, Native American, Asian American, and gay, lesbian, bisexual, transgendered, and questioning (GLBTQ) identity. There were other organizations that coalesced around larger identity categories, such as youth of color.

We found that there was a clearly defined need for identity support among the young people within these organizations. Youth we interviewed described that before joining these groups they had a poor view of themselves, had been ignorant about their history, and/or had been involved in self-destructive behaviors. For instance, as one youth explained, "When I first realized I was queer I felt really powerless and really scared of myself. And that was really scary; to be scared of who you are is totally diminishing." Other youth said that they "didn't know there were so many different kinds of Asians," "didn't know about self-hatred," or didn't "understand what really happened in the civil rights movement; schools didn't really give you more than the basics." The need for identity affirmation, therefore, within these youth populations was particularly strong. It is important, however, to point out that civic activism organizations moved beyond mere identity affirmation, gearing their work in such a way as it set the groundwork for a broader social justice orientation.

Most organizations offered "critical education" on prejudice and discrimination as an entry point for social justice issues in order to help youth understand the legacy of oppression and identify present-day challenges facing their identity group. One organization, for example, believed that the barriers faced by African American youth are best addressed once youth have considered the legacy and impact of their own history, including the painful scars left by slavery and segregation. They encouraged youth to reflect on and "heal" these scars so that they could transcend internalized racism and learn to effectively function in society. This approach is consistent with Watts et al.'s argument that African Americans benefit from an understanding of the social structure of power and privilege. In their struggle against oppression, African Americans can "benefit from a strong sense of self that incorporates both the cultural and sociopolitical aspects of their African American heritage" (2003, p. 188).

Civic activism organizations move beyond the exploration of the history of particular identity groups, seeking to emancipate youth through a process of deep critical analysis and reflection. Some organizations are intentional about pushing youth out of their "comfort zone" by asking that they interrogate their assumptions about themselves, each other, and about the society around them. One youth captured this aspect of this approach when he said,

> I don't think it's about being comfortable all the time. It's about learning different circumstances that make you uncomfortable, where you have to stand up for what you say, even if it's not the majority opinion. It's about getting over the discomfort you feel.

Thus, youth within these organizations are pushed to extend their thinking, to confront their own biases, and to ask hard questions of the leaders within their communities. Further, they analyze issues of oppression and consider how their own personal experiences relate to the struggles of others within and outside of their own community. This kind of identity support, in turn, creates a sense of purpose in young people to take a civic activist stance and to work with others in their communities to end various forms of oppression.

Making Social Change Tangible

> *Social change happens at the personal level, at the gut level, and has to come out of self-interest. People mobilize because their daughter has asthma and they need to do something about it.*
>
> —Staffer at 21st Century Youth Leadership Movement, in Selma, Alabama

As captured by this quote, the desire for social change is often rooted in personal needs and experiences, and as such, connection to collective forms of identity can be a precursor to social action. Civic activism, however, also depends on the identification of tangible goals for social change, an articulation of a coherent strategy for reaching those goals, and a belief in the power and efficacy of groups of people to effect change.

Further, we have found that the social change goals or "wins" that civic activism groups use to measure their own progress are, by design, incremental so that youth can remain engaged in the process. These include press coverage of their issues, the number of people they recruit to attend rallies or events, and the number of meetings they hold with people in power. Over the course of the study, civic activism groups achieved some relatively large-scale community wins. These include one organization's success in closing down a cement plant in their community, another's successful defeat of a city council measure to create a daytime curfew for teens, and a third organization's successful effort to have a sexual harrassment policy created for their school district. These types of victories fueled young people's sense of purpose and their belief that they could make a difference. The following quote from one youth is illustrative of the sense of enthusiasm and competence that young people within these groups radiated.

> We have a big voice. There aren't a lot of other youth who are as involved as we are.... But, we're at the point now where we are taken seriously. We earned their respect by the actions we take. When we were opposing the cement plant, the owner challenged us at a city council meeting. He told us to be more "productive." So, we went out and got 1,000 signatures opposing his plant and that shut him up and impressed the city council people.

Civic activism groups use a variety of strategies to build the capacity of youth leaders to effect change. One of most universal and potent strategies used by organizing groups is political education. This approach enables youth to learn about social movements (e.g., the civil rights movement), political processes (the electoral process) and current events (e.g., racial profiling and the effects of 9/11 on immigrant communities). Through political education, youth organizing groups hope to support critical-thinking skills and develop values and attitudes that move youth to act against injustice. Political education sessions often seek to make connections between larger social issues and young people's day-to-day lives, and center on such issues as policing, school quality, environmental justice, and immigrants' rights. On one level, youth are seen as experts on these issues, and they are encouraged to share their experiences as well as compose and defend their own opinions. On another level, youth are pressed by program leaders to think about these issues abstractly, on a scale beyond their individual experience, including a consideration of the international or global characteristics of power and oppression.

From a base of political education, civic activism groups have progressed toward the development of a clear and manageable community-change agenda. They have sought, at the most basic level, to empower youth to take leadership on issues in their lives, emphasizing their role as grassroots leaders within their communities. The first step in that process is to identify the issues most salient to the youth who participate in the organization. The second step is to ask youth to actively seek out the perspectives and concerns of other community members, in an effort to find issues of broad concern that can serve as the basis for sizable coalitions and collective action. Thus, the issues that civic activist groups address are reflective of issues that community members face. The process of listening to and raising awareness about such issues is seen as a high priority in and of itself. Issues identified as most relevant to youth and their communities include the lack of recreational spaces, lack of green spaces, environmental pollution, sexual harrassment in schools, policing and the increased incarceration of youth offenders, and unfair working conditions.

Coaching Strategies for Fostering Lifelong Activism

Without grounding youth in the larger sociohistorical context of social movements and introducing them to concrete strategies for social change, impassioned youth would be at a loss to translate their ideas and beliefs into action. Civic activism groups use a variety of mechanisms or levers ("direct actions") for change, including education, letter-writing campaigns, petitions, public presentations, meetings with people in power, protests, and boycotts. In taking such approaches to civic engagement, youth activism groups dispel some of the stereotypes that characterize their work as "oppositional." They emphasize the need to work within the system to the extent possible (i.e., through participation in decision-making bodies), while always being prepared to apply pressure from outside the system (i.e., through protests and boycotts). In the words of one program director, "We're clear that being in the system or out isn't important. It's a strategy that's rooted in systems change that is important." Further, civic activism groups embrace a philosophy of nonviolent and peaceful activism; they are concerned that youth develop a social justice orientation that is positive and affirming, because they believe that this is necessary to sustain social action in the long run. The following quote, by a staff member at one organization, speaks to this issue:

> We don't organize out of hate, but out of love—our love for people. Because hate is very defeating, and can motivate and charge you to do something about injustices. But [we ask youth], how long is your hate going to sustain your commitment to social justice?

Hence, these organizations promote spiritual and/or human rights arguments for social justice. In doing so, they seek to strike a delicate balance, supporting young people's ability and opportunity to actively question authority while at the same time enabling youth to resist cynicism that could potentially lead to social distrust and/or alienation.

Reflections on the Role of Identity in Youth Activism

Our findings indicate that civic activism organizations provide crucial forms of identity support and build practical social justice skills. Indeed, identity can play a powerful role in shaping youth involvement in social activism, serving as an important "hook" to engaging youth in the issues that are most pressing to them. At the same time, however, the identity-based issues that define youth work today are complex and multifaceted. Participants in identity-based social movements during the civil rights era fought against very concrete discriminatory laws and practices, such as Jim Crow laws. In contrast, young people today find themselves fighting against discriminatory institutional policies and practices that pretend to be "color-blind" and to offer "fairness" and "equal opportunity." The increasingly covert nature of discrimination means that youth activism organizations often find themselves spending increasing amounts of time educating about the insidious nature of power and oppression. Groups are discovering that it is not as easy to galvanize large groups around identity issues, because the reasons behind disparities in outcomes for different groups are often very complex and diverse. Further, the "target" is often more difficult to identify and to communicate to others.

In our study, it became clear that the identity support offered to youth provides strength and resilience in their activist roles. We also learned that although identity drives a lot of youth activism, the identities that drive an individual's work may be fluid, changing as the issue changes. The composition of the membership of some of the youth activism organizations we studied would vary depending on the current campaign. For instance, a campaign to end a youth curfew would draw in a very racially diverse constituency, while a campaign to fight against an antibilingual education policy might draw a primarily Latino constituency. Because some groups need to maximize membership and leverage, many gravitate toward large identity categories, such as "youth identity" and "youth of color," to attract a large number of youth. This strategy enables youth to form a strong collective identity, further bridging differences across identities that might otherwise separate them because of the issues they care about. Moreover, some organizations, particularly those that attract immigrant groups, need to form ethnic alliances based on common "American" racial schemas and categories in an effort to find common ground among diverse youth. In these cases, the organizations must dedicate time to building a sense of group or collective identity (i.e., as a person of color) so that commonalities in the experiences of different groups can be drawn out.

Many social-change theorists argue that identity-based movements can be insular and that emphasizing the uniqueness of a given group's experience can inhibit an individual's ability to identify common ground and to work across difference to effect change (Stryker, 2000; Wood, 2002). Our findings also suggest that emphasizing identity-based activism can be a challenge for some organizations. For instances, youth within many of the organizations we studied are struggling with the boundaries of identity; some members struggle with what it means to be Asian and American; some with whether there is room in the GLBTQ movement for heterosexuals; some with how skin color affects racial identification, and so on. Some groups examine prejudice within identity groups, such as prejudice against transsexuals within the GLBTQ community, gender discrimination and homophobia within the African American community, class discrimination, and so on. The preoccupation with defining an identity group and its agenda does have a potential to detract from a shared or common social change agenda, and may not bode well for external solidarity. Those groups that are most effective at achieving broad social change goals tend to be diverse and inclusive in orientation. The strategies that these organizations use to bridge differences include not only creating a shared identity—such as "youth of color"—but also galvanizing around pressing social problems that affect youth of varied identities, such as youth rights and liberties in the schools and communities.

In summary, support for healthy and efficacious identities is crucial for marginalized youth, especially given the harmful messages they so often receive from societal institutions, such as schools and the media. Yet identity politics in the 21st century is increasingly complex and contested, in ways that it may not have been during the civil rights era. Identity-based strategies that nurture identity, while forming coalitions across difference, can help young people understand the connections between their personal experience and the pressing social justice issues facing their communities.

Implications for Policy

Our findings and recommendations extend two important conclusions presented in the National Research Council's review of the current science of adolescent health and development. In this report, Eccles and Gootman (2002) conclude that a persistent segment of the youth population remains at risk because they often live in poor, high-risk neighborhoods and repeatedly experience racial and ethnic discrimination. As well, effective, high-quality youth programs must be flexible enough to adapt to the existing diversity among young people and the communities in which they operate. We believe that civic activism addresses these issues by providing promising models for extending and deepening the youth development approach, so that it can be (1) more inclusive of older marginalized youth and (2) more successful at engaging youth as actors in their communities. As such, we make a series of recommendations.

Recommendation 1: Public and Private Funders Should Be Mindful of the Organizational Support Needed for Civic Activism Work

The infrastructure of support for civic activism groups remains weak. As small grassroots organizations, civic activism groups often lack strong infrastructures and a coherent and stable funding base to sustain their work. Their fund-raising efforts, both for foundation and government grants, are complicated by the ongoing perception that civic activism is "radical" or "contentious." As shown in this research study and others, civic activism approaches can have a host of benefits, such as enabling traditionally marginalized youth to actively engage in community action. Thus, there is a definite need for policy and funding streams that legitimize youth-led social action and make investments that help stabilize civic activism within the fields of youth development and community organizing. Beyond issuing grants to civic activism organizations to support direct programming, we recommend that funders and policy makers take note of the capacity building needs of civic activism groups. We have found that these groups critically need support for staff training, better staff compensation, staff retention, and development of organizational systems that institutionalize their innovative approaches, particularly in times of leadership transitions.

Recommendation 2: Youth Policy Should Consider Specific Ways in Which to Engage Adolescents of Color and Marginalized Populations

Youth policy does not thrive in a climate that sees young people's generic "assets" without recognizing the overwhelming challenges facing so many families, communities, and young people today. We need youth policy that is unapologetic about tailoring programs to the racial history, culture, and community of marginalized groups in this country. Findings from our studies suggest that civic activism programs hold promise in reaching out to youth in a manner that sustains their interests and builds their leadership skills while also celebrating their racial and cultural backgrounds (Lewis-Charp et al., 2003). Without programs that recognize the uniqueness of different groups, general youth programs may miss attracting and retaining diverse youth who can benefit most from unique and meaningful experiences for positive development.

Recommendation 3: Youth Policy Should Recognize the Value of Social Action as a Means Toward Broad Civic Engagement Among Traditionally Marginalized Youth

If we expect our adolescents to develop into social actors and engaged citizens, then we need to support youth programs that raise their consciousness about issues in their lives and in the lives of others. In the tradition of popular education, it is crucial that such strategies draw from young people's experience rather than being imposed from the outside (i.e., indoctrination). Strategies such as systematic issue identification, political education, historical analysis, and power analysis increase young people's awareness of the social and political issues that are most relevant to their communities and the larger societal and historical context. These strategies have potential for broader application in youth and civic education programs, as they enable young people to reflect on how their experiences can be applied in the public sphere.

Recommendation 4: Youth Policy Should Emphasize the Importance
of Hands-On and Real-World Learning Opportunities for Young
People—Particularly Those from Marginalized Groups

If the youth development field hopes to be more effective at engaging adolescents and young adults, then we need to provide youth with authentic roles in their community. When young people have opportunities to engage in real-world learning and apply their cognitive and critical thinking skills on problems and policies that matter to them, civic engagement and leadership development take on new meaning. We cannot continue to express dismay about disconnected and alienated youth populations while at the same time keeping adolescents and young adults outside meaningful decision-making opportunities.

In conclusion, our research shows that civic activism has the potential to stimulate youth participation in their communities to contribute to the larger social good. Civic activist organizations have raised the bar for what youth can do. Their youth participants are seriously engaged in critical reflection about themselves and their society, uniting with their peers in positive collective action against social injustices, and engaging community leaders to see uncommon and innovative solutions to chronic problems in our society. Policy makers can support young people by being open to creating, learning, replicating, and supporting models and programs of youth empowerment so that youth determine for themselves how to solve problems and make our society a better and more just place to live.

Note

1. This article summarizes qualitative findings that are reported in more detailed elsewhere; see Lewis-Charp, Yu, Soukamneuth, & Lacoe, 2004.

References

Alinsky, S. (1971). *Rules for radicals.* New York: Random House.
Alinsky, S. (2003). "Protest Tactics." In J. Goodwin & J. M. Jasper, Eds., *The social movements reader: Cases and concepts* (pp. 225–228). Oxford: Blackwell.
Bernstein, M. (1997). Celebration and suppression: The strategic uses of identity by the lesbian and gay movement. *American Journal of Sociology, 103*(3), 531–565.
Bronfenbrenner, U. (1979). *The ecology of human development.* Cambridge, MA: Harvard University Press.
Brooks-Gunn, J., Duncan, G. J., & Aber, J. L. (1997) *Neighborhood poverty: Context and consequences for children* (Vol. 1). New York: Russell Sage Foundation.
Cahill, M. (1997) *Youth development and community development: Promises and challenges of convergence.* Takoma Park, MD: Forum for Youth Investment.
Chalk, R., & Phillips, D. A. (1996). *Youth development and neighborhood influences.* Washington, DC: National Academy Press.
Connell, J. P., Gambone, M. A., & Smith, T. J. (2000). Youth development in community settings: Challenges to our field and our approach. In Youth development: Issues, challenges and directions (pp. 281–300). Public Private Ventures, Report prepared for the Community Action for Youth Project.

Eccles, J., & Gootman, J. A. (2002). *Community programs to promote youth development.* Washington, D.C.: National Academy Press.

Forum for Youth Investment. (2001). *Youth development and community change: A guide to documents and tools developed through the Forum's Ford Foundation funded projects 1997–2001.* Community and Youth Development Series. Tacoma Park, MD: Forum for Youth Investment/International Youth Foundation.

Gambone, M., Yu, H. C., Lewis-Charp, H., Sipe, C., & Lacoe, J. (2004). A comparative analysis of community youth development strategies. Paper presented at the Society of Research on Adolescence, Baltimore, 2004.

Gambone, M. A., Klem, A. M., & Connell, J. P. (2002). *Finding out what matters for youth: Testing key links in a community action frame-work for youth development.* Philadelphia: Youth Development Strategies/Institute for Research and Reform in Education.

Gambone, M. A., & Arbreton, A. J. A. (1997). Safe havens: The contributions of youth organizations to healthy adolescent development. Retrieved January 30, 2001, from http://www.ppv.org/content/youthdev.html.

Garbarino, J. (1995). *Raising children in a socially toxic environment.* San Francisco: Jossey-Bass.

Ginwright, S., & James, T. (2002). From assets to agents of change: Social justice, organizing, and youth development. *New Directions for Youth Development: Theory, Practice, and Research, 96,* 27–46.

Granger, R. (2002). Creating the conditions linked to positive youth development. *New Directions for Youth Development: Theory, Practice, and Research, 95,* 149–164.

Habermas, J. (1970). Toward a theory of communicative competence. *Inquiry, 13,* 371.

Hughes, D., & Curnan, S. (2002). Towards shared prosperity: Change-making in the CYD movement, *CYD Anthology 2002,* retreived September 15, 2003 from http://www.cydjournal.org/2002Winter/Framework.pdf.

Inglehart, R. (1990). Values, ideology, and cognitive mobilization in new social movements. In R. J. Dalton & M. Kuechler (Eds.), *Challenging the political order: New social and political movements in western democracies* (pp. 43–66). New York: Oxford University Press.

Irby, M., Ferber, T., Pittman, K., with Tolman, J., & Yohalem, N. (2001). *Youth action: Youth contributing to communities, communities supporting youth.* Community and Youth Development Series (Vol. 6). Takoma Park, MD: Forum for Youth Investment/International Youth Foundation.

Johnston, H., Laraña, E., & Gusfield, J. R. (1994). Identities, grievances, and new social movements. In E. Laraña, H. Johnston, & J. R. Gusfield (Eds.), *New social movements: From ideology to identity.* Philadelphia: Temple University Press.

Lerner, R. M., Taylor, C. S., & von Eye, A. (Eds.). (2002). Pathways to Positive Development among Diverse Youth [Special issue]. *New Directions for Youth Development: Theory, Practice, and Research, 95.*

Lewis-Charp, H., Yu, H. C., Soukamneuth, S., & Lacoe, J. (2003). *Extending the reach of youth development through civic activism: Outcomes of the youth leadership development initiative.* Oakland, CA: Social Policy Research Associates.

Mohamed, I. A., & Wheeler, W. (2001). *Broadening the bounds of youth development: Youth as engaged citizens.* Chevy Chase, MD: Innovation Center/Ford Foundation.

McAdam, D. (1988). *Freedom summer.* New York: Oxford University Press.

Phelan, P., Davidson, A. L., & Yu, H. C. (1998). *Adolescents' worlds: Navigating family, peers and school.* New York: Teachers College Press.

Pittman, K. J., & Irby, M. (1996). Preventing problems or promoting development: Competing priorities or inseparable goals? Retrieved August 1, 2002 from http://www.iyfnet.org/document.cfm/22/general/51.

Stryker, S. (2000). Identity competition: Key to differential social movement participation? In S. Stryker Sheldon, T. J. Owens, and R. White (Eds.), *Self, identity, and social movements* (pp. 21–41). Minneapolis: University of Minnesota Press.

Tatum, B. D. (1997). *Why are all the black kids sitting together in the cafeteria? And other conversations about race.* New York: Basic.

Walker, T. (2002). Service as a pathway to political participation: What research tells us. *Applied Developmental Science, 6*(4), 183–188.

Watts, R. J., Williams, N. C., & Jagers, R. J. (2003) Sociopolitical development. *American Journal of Community Psychology, 31*(1–2), 185–194.

Wood, R. (2002). *Faith in action: Religion, race, and democratic organizing in America.* Chicago: University of Chicago Press.

Youniss, J., & Yates, M. (1997). *Community service and social responsibility in youth.* Chicago: University of Chicago Press.

Youniss, J., & Yates, M. (1999). *Roots of civic identity: International perspectives on community service and activism in youth.* Cambridge: Cambridge University Press.

Yu, H. C., & H. Lewis-Charp. (2003). *Collaborating to meet the organizational challenges of promoting youth civic activism.* Social Policy Research Associates.

CHAPTER 3

Apprenticeship Learning in Youth Activism

BEN KIRSHNER

As other chapters in this volume illustrate, youth activism groups have fought successfully in recent years to improve conditions for young people in their communities and schools (e.g., HoSang, 2005; Kwon, 2005; O'Donoghue, 2005). Such efforts defy pervasive deficit-based misconceptions about youth and enable them to challenge punitive social policies (Ginwright, Cammarota, & Noguera, 2005).

These grassroots social action campaigns, which require sophisticated planning, organizing, and advocacy skills, are noteworthy not just for their political impact, but also because of the insights into teaching and learning that they provide. For example, consider the cognitive and social tasks that student activists mastered in their efforts to address funding inequities and school overcrowding in Chicago public schools: youth organizers learned how to think analytically, develop and maintain long-term plans, work collaboratively, speak in public, and respond flexibly to unexpected contingencies (Larson & Hanson, 2005). Campaigns such as this exemplify a democratic ideal in progressive education in that they help young people address meaningful problems through project-based, collaborative work (Dewey, 1902; Perlstein, 2002).

Although recent scholarship has begun to highlight developmental outcomes of youth activism (Larson & Hanson, 2005; Lewis-Charp, Cao Yu, & Soukamneuth, 2005; Watts & Guessous, 2005), few researchers have focused on pedagogical strategies in community-based youth activist groups. How do high school students, especially those who go to schools that by many measures are failing academically, learn how to perform complex demands of campaigns effectively? If "teaching," with its corresponding image of an authority figure who transmits knowledge, is not the right term to describe adult guidance, then what is? These questions are relevant not only to adults in the youth activism field, but also to the broader community of educators and policy makers interested in supporting youth participation in public policy.

In this chapter I draw on ethnographic research to describe teaching practices in a multiracial organizing group called Youth Rising. Adults provided a "youth-centered apprenticeship" in skills such as community organizing, persuasive speech, and problem framing. Before discussing research findings I will briefly review research about civic engagement among urban youth and explain the theoretical framework for this study.

Youth Organizing

The emergence of youth organizing and activism as a youth development strategy should be understood against the backdrop of deindustrialization and disinvestment from American cities in the 1980s and 1990s. Despite the creation of new wealth associated with the burgeoning "information economy" of the 1990s, the "dot com" boom only accentuated the stratified character of many cities, where affluent enclaves thrive next door to areas of concentrated poverty (Noguera, 2003). Young people in urban neighborhoods confront low-performing schools, limited job opportunities, declining social services, and few opportunities to participate in civic life (Akom, this volume; Ginwright, 2005; Hart & Atkins, 2002; Rubin, Billingsley, & Caldwell, 1994). Moreover, social constructions of urban youth of color as dangerous and disengaged, reflected in policies such as Proposition 21 in California,[1] further contribute to youth's marginalization (Mahiri & Cooper, 2003; McLaughlin & Heath, 1993).

Although after-school programs and youth organizations can provide a sanctuary from toxic social conditions, many argue that this is not enough, that youth must also have the opportunity to speak up and transform institutions shaping their lives (Ashley, Samaniego, & Cheun, 1997; Ginwright & James, 2002). Organizing groups, for example, help young people come together around problems that they care about and find ways to address them through community organizing and political advocacy (Akom, chapter 5, this volume; Sherman, 2002). Across the country, young people have led or participated in grassroots efforts to make an impact on local problems in a meaningful and lasting way (Tolman & Pittman, 2001). As Ginwright and James (2002) write, such groups treat youth "as agents capable of transforming their toxic environments, not simply developing resiliency and resistance to them" (p. 40).

One challenge that such groups face, however, pertains to the development of egalitarian, respectful, and culturally responsive partnerships between adults and youth (Ginwright, 2005; Zeldin, Camino, & Larson, 2005). Youth activism groups are often made up of youth leaders and adult allies who seek to reorganize hierarchical adult-youth relations and place youth in charge of significant decisions (Kirshner, 2005). But it is not uncommon for young people to be novices when it comes to planning effective campaigns or engaging in policy discussions. Moreover, youth's past experiences with adults may lead them to hold preconceptions of adults as condescending, authoritarian, or dismissive (Jarrett, Sullivan, & Watkins, 2005). Adult staff members, therefore, experience dilemmas about how to provide assistance to youth while still supporting their freedom and voice (O'Donoghue & Strobel, 2003; Larson, Walker, & Pearce, 2005).

Dilemmas Facing Adult Staff Members

Some dilemmas arise when the task demands of a campaign appear to conflict with principles of youth leadership. For example, an adult leader might have personal contacts with members of the city council that could be of strategic use, but is concerned that too much involvement would undermine youth leadership. Or a veteran activist might be aware that a particular rally is unlikely to succeed without greater organization, but prefers to let youth learn from their mistakes. Conversely, in cases when the political stakes are high, adult advisors may choose to complete necessary tasks, such as arranging for buses to get people to an event or completing a survey analysis on a tight deadline (Larson & Hanson, 2005).

Dilemmas may also arise when it comes to discussing young people's political beliefs. On one hand, a principled commitment to youth voice could lead adults to adopt a neutral stance, where they withhold their beliefs and encourage youth to develop their own ideas about the origins of problems they face in their schools and neighborhoods. Such a view would be consistent with constructivist teaching approaches that have been common among some progressive educators in the United States (Perlstein, 2002), as well as developmental theories that stress the value of peer interaction (Piaget, 1965; Rogoff, 1990). On the other hand, educators in the tradition of Paolo Freire or Myles Horton question the notion that teachers should put aside their values or defer to students' experience as the sole guide for learning (see Freire, 2002; Kilgore, 1999). Because cultural scripts promoting the myth of individualism and the "level playing field" are powerful throughout the United States (Crocker, Major, & Steele, 1998; Markus, Mullally, & Kitayama, 1997), many suggest that youth empowerment requires attention to broader structures of inequality and racism in the United States (Ginwright & James, 2002; Perlstein, 2002).

Dilemmas such as these exist in part because of widespread pressure for youth leadership programs to be "youth led" (programs in which youth exercise greater control over decision making, and adults are primarily facilitators and mentors [Larson, Walker, & Pearce, 2005]). Although the "youth led" notion is politically appealing because it affirms the capacity of young people to be capable democratic actors, it leaves unexamined the critical roles that adults can, and often do, play. Such omissions are problematic, not just from an empirical standpoint, but also because adults are left with few strategies for helping youth become effective activists. Ironically, empowerment approaches that privilege youth voice at the expense of adult input may reinforce the widespread problem of age segregation in the United States, in which youth have few opportunities to work collaboratively or collegially with adults (Heath, 1999). In this paper I argue that theories of apprenticeship learning offer a useful way of avoiding the youth-led versus adult-led trap.

Theoretical Lens: Youth-Centered Apprenticeships

Apprenticeship is a term that has been employed in recent years to describe how people learn through participation in meaningful, goal-oriented activity, such as selling Girl Scout cookies (Rogoff, 1995), carrying out projects in youth organizations (Heath, 1999), or becoming a master tailor (Lave, 1990). Interactions between experts and novices in apprenticeships are less likely to resemble those that are familiar from school, in which a teacher instructs students about fixed facts or procedures, and more likely to resemble collaborative activity, in which novices receive just enough guidance from experts to pursue a shared goal (Halpern, 2005; Rogoff, 2003). According to this theory, interaction with experienced members of a cultural group can be as essential for development as interaction with peers (Vygotsky, 1978). In optimal cases, the expert engages in modeling, coaching, and fading: experts begin a task or project by modeling best practices and coaching learners, but over time they fade back to let the learner perform tasks without support (Brown, Collins, & Duguid, 1989; Heath, 1999).

In addition to specific assistance strategies, apprenticeship also signals entry into a community of people who are linked by a shared set of goals and norms (Lave & Wenger, 1991). Participants not only learn the cognitive dimensions of a discrete task, but also take up identities as members of a social practice (Holland & Lave, 2001). Newcomers, through interacting with "old hands," begin to envision a trajectory of participation; in this sense apprenticeship involves both cognitive learning and changes in identity (Nasir & Saxe, 2003; Packer & Goicochea, 2000).

Sometimes apprenticeships are organized in a hierarchical, potentially exploitative manner, such as when a boss holds more power than his employee (Lave & Wenger, 1991), or when an adult supervisor overrules the decisions of youth volunteers (Hogan, 2002). Apprenticeship learning, however, can also be organized in a democratic and youth-centered manner. Here *youth-centered* refers to learning environments that are responsive to young people's skill levels and interests, honor their everyday experiences, and foster feelings of community and safety (McLaughlin, 2000). When approached in a youth-centered manner, apprenticeship learning can help youth develop the skills required for meaningful and effective political action. In the remainder of this chapter I discuss an empirical example of a youth-centered apprenticeship taken from my fieldwork with an organizing group called Youth Rising.

Youth Rising Background

Youth Rising is a multiracial youth organizing group housed in a larger youth advocacy nonprofit agency in a midsized city in the western United States (here called Marshall).[2] At the time of my fieldwork, the group met two afternoons per week during the school year. Participants, called "youth organizers," received bimonthly stipends for their work, which included organizing student clubs at their schools, planning and carrying out a campaign for student power, and leading monthly membership meetings to attract additional students to the campaign. Two young adult staff members, Alonzo and Elsa, coordinated the group's activities part time. Both coordinators had been active in local organizing groups as teenagers. They were in turn supported by Vanessa, the nonprofit organization's executive director.

Participants. Rather than only seek out the officially recognized student leaders, Youth Rising also reached out to young people who might have had trouble with the juvenile justice system or who struggled in school. This is consistent with the research finding that youth organizing groups engage urban youth who are less likely to show up at more traditional youth development programs (Lewis-Charp, Yu, Soukamneuth, & Lacoe, 2003). Several male youth were recruited through their interest in music—Alonzo and a handful of youth worked together to write and record hip-hop songs that were eventually released on a self-produced compact disk. Throughout the year there were roughly 8 to 12 youth organizers, with some leaving and some joining. Of the 12 youth organizers who were involved for at least two months, there were 10 African Americans (7 males and 3 females) and 2 Asian Americans (1 male and 1 female). They ranged from 9th graders to 12th graders. The adult staff members who worked directly with youth organizers included 1 African American male, 1 Latina female, and 1 Asian American female.[3]

Community and School Context. The Youth Rising offices were located in downtown Marshall on the second story of a nondescript office building situated in a business district scattered with inexpensive restaurants, niche retail stores, and nonprofit organizations. Inside the office was a large meeting room with two couches, a handful of rolling chairs, and more than enough folding chairs to accommodate the membership meetings, where as many as 30 students were sometimes in attendance. Posters of Malcolm X and Bob Marley adorned the walls. A handwritten poster outlining group agreements, such as "respect others" and "step back so that others can step up" hung next to the entranceway.

Youth organizers attended three public high schools in Marshall: Central, Northside, and Franklin.[4] Student achievement at these schools was low relative to state and national standards: across the schools, between 20% and 37% performed at or above national averages in reading and between 15% and 27% completed coursework required for admission to state colleges. The economic profile of students across these three schools helps to put in context the low achievement scores. Pooling data from across the schools, between 53% and 60% were supported by the state's free and/or reduced-price lunch program.

The majority of youth participants lived in an ethnically diverse residential district that was characterized by a mixture of modest family homes and public housing. In 1999 Elmwood was comprised of 50% African Americans, 38% Latinos, 6% Asian and Pacific Islanders, and 4% European Americans (2% reported two or more races). Designated a "concentrated poverty neighborhood," 48% of residents reported an income of less than $30,000 per year. One-third of residents participated in public assistance programs, either through welfare or subsidized medical care. Of residents above the age of 25, 6% had completed college or held a graduate degree; 39% did not have a high school degree.

Community strengths included a strong sense of political activism and working-class alliances. Residents organized projects such as midnight basketball games, public health safety patrols, and employment initiatives. Also, spurred by the organizing efforts of local churches and community groups, several larger schools were in the process of transitioning to small schools at the time of my research. In 2003, local technology centers received grants to expand services with the intention of bridging the "digital divide." Developments such as these suggest that, despite challenges posed by deep poverty and struggling schools, local groups and organizations were working alongside Youth Rising to address public problems and create opportunities for young people.

Campaign Overview. At a retreat in September 2002, youth organizers came to the conclusion that the dropout rate was the most pressing problem facing youth in Marshall. After a period of reflection, discussion, and pilot research, the group decided that greater student voice in high school governance would lead to strong academic performance and a reduction in the dropout problem. To gather support for their goals, youth organizers asked their peers to fill out school "report cards" that evaluated teachers, counselors, security guards, administration, school atmosphere, and facilities. They also enlisted fellow students in the campaign by inviting them to monthly membership meetings. Youth organizers collected over 950 report cards and entered the data into spreadsheets.

After some introductory statistics instruction from adults, youth identified and analyzed frequencies in the survey results that caught their attention. For example, they found that 26% of students felt that they could talk to school counselors about personal issues and that 66% of students said that the presence of security guards and police officers did not make them feel safer at school. Most relevant to their campaign, surveys showed that more than two-thirds of students wanted greater involvement and voice in their schools. Youth presented these results and others at a rally and press conference in front of school district headquarters in the spring of 2003. Two weeks later, Youth Rising used evidence from the report cards to lobby the school board to endorse a resolution to change the governance structures of district high schools by strengthening student councils and creating more leadership opportunities for regular students. Although changes in school district leadership stymied implementation of the resolution, Youth Rising received support from the majority of school board members and vowed to continue its efforts during the subsequent year.

Research Methods

Data Collection. My fieldwork, which included participant observation, interviews, and collection of program artifacts, spanned eight months. I recorded field notes for more than 60 hours of observation, including 21 program meetings, 5 meetings with staff members, and 5 public rallies, performances, and hearings. In return for receiving access to the program, I helped the staff with program evaluation needs and wrote a narrative about the campaign for public distribution. During meetings I participated in group team-building exercises and periodically assisted with small group tasks, such as analyzing survey results. Often I sat quietly and recorded notes as youth went about their work. In addition to regular informal conversations, I conducted semistructured interviews with eight core youth organizers and one adult coordinator, Alonzo. My analysis also drew from written artifacts, such as newsletters written by youth and documents that described Youth Rising approaches to community organizing.

Data Analysis. Data analysis was an iterative process that began while I conducted fieldwork (Miles & Huberman, 1984). Because this study was part of a broader dissertation study of three youth leadership groups, I compared youth-adult interactions across them (see Kirshner [2005] for comparison of assistance strategies in these groups). After I completed my fieldwork I worked with three colleagues, who were engaged in qualitative research in other youth programs, to develop a set of descriptive codes and decision-rules. We coded transcripts together and developed low-inference codes that could be used in our different sites. I entered codes in N6, a software application for data analysis. After coding field note and interview transcripts I looked more closely at specific occasions when adults lent assistance to youth, as well as occasions where youth performed tasks independently. For the purposes of this chapter I focused my analysis on assistance strategies that appeared to foster young people's engagement and skill development. Later, after I had written up some of my analysis, I shared a draft with program staff and made some adjustments to ensure that it was a fair and accurate representation.

Apprenticeship Practices in Youth Rising

Relationships between adults and youth in Youth Rising resembled qualities of an apprenticeship, in which expert members of a community provide assistance to novices as they pursue a meaningful, goal-oriented project. Alonzo, Elsa, and Vanessa engaged in cycles of modeling, coaching, and fading that exposed novice youth to the practices of mature activists and prepared youth to perform complex tasks independently. They did not adopt a neutral or facilitative role, as is often the case in constructivist, student-led approaches to learning. Instead, they sought to develop a shared community of activists comprised of both adults and youth. Adults often participated as colleagues with youth in discussions about social issues or preparations for upcoming events. Sometimes youth learned indirectly —through observation of adult actions or through participation in collegial interactions with adults.

To illustrate these interrelated apprenticeship practices, I discuss processes by which youth organizers learned two campaign-related tasks: *persuasive speech* and *problem framing* (see Table 3.1 for summaries). I chose these two tasks because they were both critical to the campaign. *Persuasive speech* refers to situations where youth needed to persuade others, whether peers or school board members, of the merits of their cause. In addition to public speaking skills it also involved more sophisticated rhetorical strategies for staying "on message" and providing compelling evidence for an argument. *Problem framing* refers to the ways that youth and adults framed the problem of the dropout rate, in terms of root causes and potential solutions (Hunt, Benford, & Snow, 1999).

Table 3.1 Examples of Apprenticeship Learning During the Campaign

	Persuasive Speech	Problem Framing
Modeling	Adults share examples of effective speeches in instructional situation.	Adults share political views with youth in collegial interactions.
Coaching	Youth practice speeches and adults provide feedback.	Adults provide prompts and ask critical questions to stimulate youth's thinking.
Fading	Adults retreat to the side during presentations to political decision-making bodies.	Youth shape the goals of the campaign based on their concerns and experiences.

Persuasive Speech

Several campaign tasks required youth to practice persuasive speech. Youth recruited students to fill out report cards and attend rallies. They sought permission from teachers to make announcements. And at the end of the year they proposed a school board resolution in support of greater student voice in school governance. Overall, youth organizers spoke or performed at five different political events: a rally against the exit exam, a youth organizing conference, the school board hearing, a press conference, and a transportation board hearing.

In order to help youth organizers learn how to speak persuasively, adult staff members engaged in modeling, coaching, and fading. Such a cycle can take place over an extended period of time or in a brief activity, depending on the complexity and scope of the task. One example of modeling took place in an afternoon activity toward the end of the year, when youth organizers met to prepare speeches for the public transportation hearing. In order to model an effective speech Alonzo recited a story about the positive impact of subsidized transportation on his life. When he was finished, Vanessa asked the youth organizers to talk about what he did well. They observed that Alonzo had given specific examples of how the bus pass helped him get to his job and to an after-school program; they also noticed that he thanked the board members several times for listening to him. Vanessa reiterated this last point, "Over and over, he was thanking them. Started by thanking them and ended by thanking them."

Modeling was typically followed by practice and coaching. In a coaching situation, experts provide supported opportunities for novices to carry out the task, through "hints, scaffolding, feedback, modeling, reminders, and new tasks aimed at bringing their performance closer to expert performance" (Collins, Brown, & Newman, 1989, p. 481). For example, after Alonzo's demonstration above, participants practiced their own speeches to the transportation board. Role-playing exercises such as this, in which youth practiced their speeches and received feedback, were common in Youth Rising.

The following field note excerpt describes a role-playing exercise that took place just prior to a meeting with school board members. The students hoped to persuade the school board to adopt their new student power resolution to give greater voice to student councils. Lisa and Denise, two youth organizers, practiced making their pitch to Vanessa, an adult staff member, who played the role of a school board member:

Field note observation: Role play prior to meeting with school board members.

Drawing on the report card results, Lisa says, "One out of four students surveyed said they didn't know what classes they needed to graduate and get into college." Lisa goes on to state Youth Rising's recommendations:

counselors should meet with students once per semester to help students develop a plan to fulfill high school graduation requirements. Lisa concludes by saying, "If we have more student voice in the schools then we could ask our student councils to meet with counselors and let them know our concerns."

Vanessa, posing as a school board member, says, "So that's what you want us to vote on?"

Lisa says, "Yeah."

Vanessa says, "Counselors?"

[Here it appears that Vanessa is trying to trick Lisa, because the school board is only supposed to vote on the student council resolution.]

Monique, who is sitting next to Lisa, whispers "no" in her ear.

Lisa says, "I mean, no."

Vanessa says, "Oh, so you want the student council resolution and then once you get that they can work on improving the situation with the counselors. I see…"

In this example Vanessa played the part of a naive school board member who misinterpreted what Lisa was trying to say. After the exchange, Vanessa returned to a point she had communicated earlier: it was important that the students stay "on message," a key skill for advocates and activists who need to control their communications in the public arena and not get sidetracked by members of the media or skeptical politicians.

After Lisa's turn, Denise, another youth organizer, made her pitch. In this example Vanessa tried a different strategy to distract her:

Field note observation: Role play (continued).

Denise starts her speech next, saying, "Seventy-seven percent of students surveyed want to evaluate their teachers to help them improve…."

Vanessa interrupts her: "I'm sorry, what is your name?"

Denise, who hadn't introduced herself at the beginning of her speech, says her name and tells Vanessa that she goes to Central High School.

Vanessa says, "I want to ask you about Central, you know, because that's the school in the neighborhood that I represent, and there have been some problems with the plants behind the school…"

[*Similar to the prior interaction with Lisa, Vanessa appears to be trying to divert Denise from the message about student councils.*]

Denise says, in her attempt to stay on message, "We'll get to that."

By this time both Vanessa and Denise are smiling; they appear to be having a good time playing these roles. Others are laughing because they see that Vanessa was trying to trick Denise into getting off message, but Denise has successfully parried Vanessa's diversion.

Like her interaction with Lisa, in this example Vanessa tried to get Denise to digress. But Denise had mastered the principle that Vanessa hoped to teach; she discerned Vanessa's efforts at manipulation and stayed focused on the student voice resolution.

These examples suggest that Vanessa sought to prepare youth to be seasoned advocates, rather than just hope that the adult policy makers would go easy on them because they were young. The youth organizers appeared to enjoy the activity, perhaps because Vanessa's impersonation appealed to their experience of what adults sometimes do to youth—alter their words, trip them up, catch them off guard.

Coaching episodes like these prepared youth for direct, real-world interactions with adult policy makers. During such interactions adults faded from their coaching role, and youth organizers—including the shyest ones—shared speaking responsibilities. For example, at the school board hearing, the adults' fading was physically embodied by their location in the auditorium. Whereas youth organizers and their peers sat in the center front rows, Alonzo sat several rows back near the aisle and Vanessa stood in the aisle to the side of the auditorium. Each youth was responsible for his or her statements, presented directly to the board. Some students wrote down what they wanted to say, and others improvised on the spot.

Later I asked one of the speakers, Denise, how she felt about the school board presentation:

I think we did good! We had a lot of people … and then [the school board president] … was like … "I agree." And he was looking around like, "Who else is going to [agree] … ?" So I think we did good. I liked that one.

So you felt like they were listening to you guys when you were talking up there?

Yeah. Finally. And that's why a lot of people were … noticing and saying, "Oh my God, I'm being listened to!" And some of them were like, "If they listen to me I'm about to really bring it!" So, like me, personally, I was like, "Oh, are they listening to me? I'm about to ... I'm not even going to shut up." You know? That's how I was. I was like, "I'm finally being listened to. I might as well say everything I've got to say and not hide no words."

Denise's description conveys her personal investment, and that of her peers, in the school board presentation; she sought to make the most of a rare opportunity. Such encounters with adult policy makers embodied a form of authentic assessment, in which new skills were "tested" in real-world, practical contexts, in contrast to school contexts where skill assessments are often several steps removed from their practical use (Shepard, 1999).

Adults also faded during the monthly membership meetings. The young people facilitated most of the agenda items, such as team-building exercises, discussions, and workshops about political issues. Adult participation was more peripheral; they observed from the side or joined the activities as participants. One youth in particular, Ahmad, was described by his peers as the most effective leader because he had a sense of humor, was not afraid to speak in front of groups, and conveyed passion for the cause. Vanessa seconded this assessment, telling me, "When Ahmad talks, people listen." On multiple occasions Ahmad offered inspirational speeches to his peers about the importance of succeeding in their campaign and the merits of getting involved with the student clubs.

Although descriptions of fading reflected the young people's sense of ownership for the campaign, adults did not fade so far as to appear indifferent or detached. At times adults participated as equal members, by helping out with campaign tasks that needed to get done. For example, in February 2003, Elsa took the criteria that youth developed for the report cards and crafted it into a formatted survey that resembled a "report card," which she then brought back to the group for feedback and comment. Also, Alonzo took responsibility for distributing report cards at Franklin at a time when there was only one youth organizer who attended that school. Such participation was justified according to a principle articulated in Youth Rising materials: "It's about the *work*, not the worker." In other words, the group's social change objectives meant that everyone had to pitch in.

Alonzo fostered a sense of shared purpose with youth organizers by sharing his advice about tactics, and using language that underlined his own membership in the group. I observed an example of Alonzo's emphasis on community during a meeting when the young participants prepared "talking points" for their upcoming student clubs at their schools. The activity began with them working in pairs to write down what they should say. Later Alonzo brought people together so that they could practice in front of the whole group. Here is another excerpt from my field notes:

Field note observation: Practice for student club meetings.

Erik, a new member of Youth Rising, expresses reluctance to speak before the group. Alonzo reassures him by letting him know he isn't expected to know all of the details about the campaign. Alonzo says, "You're new, we ain't trippin'.... You're around family."

After everyone practices their talking points Alonzo asks one of the veteran organizers to facilitate a check-in about how people feel about the upcoming student club meetings .... After others speak, Alonzo concludes the check-in by offering some words of support and guidance: "I got faith in ya'll ... you guys are ready. At Franklin, I'll be right there with you, so anything you forget I can say. Also, I don't want you to think that having hella [a lot of] people is the goal. We just wanted to be sharing our energy, wanting to resist. Even two people will be successful if they keep coming back."

In this example, Alonzo supported the youth in a variety of ways. He reiterated the priority of the meetings—recruiting two students who cared about the campaign goals would be better than recruiting a large group of youth who attended for other reasons. Moreover, by using collective language—"You're around family"—Alonzo signaled his own membership in the campaign, rather than adopting a neutral or detached pose. And later, in his effort to support the students at Franklin, he said that he would be right there with them to help if necessary.

By conveying his membership in the group, Alonzo signaled his personal commitment to the campaign and its various tasks. One could imagine that if he adopted a more detached view, attributing ownership strictly to youth, it could send a message that perhaps the project was not important to him, that the stakes were less real, or that he was more like a traditional teacher. Alonzo's identification with the campaign was common among adults in Youth Rising, which contributed to the sense that it was a community of youth and adults working toward a shared goal.

Sociopolitical Problem Framing

Problem framing refers to interpretive practices in social movements. How a group frames the root causes and political solutions of a problem is central to its identity (Hilliard, 1996; Hunt, Benford, & Snow; 1999). Adults in Youth Rising framed the problem of high dropout rates in Marshall in terms of broader social conditions and district policies. This focus on systemic factors departed from individualistic interpretations that attribute the causes of social problems primarily to personal responsibility (MacLeod, 1987).

The process by which youth learned to interpret problems in terms of systemic influences looked different from the persuasive speech example. Distinctions between novices and experts in public speaking are fairly straightforward, but such distinctions are more complex when it comes to political beliefs, which tend to vary based on a young person's family upbringing or her emerging identity. Perhaps for these reasons, adults encouraged youth to construct their understanding of political issues based on their own experiences in their schools and neighborhoods. At times the young people voiced diverging ideas about the causes of school failure, attributing responsibility to school policies, to fellow students, or to combinations of both.

The process of modeling, coaching, and fading, therefore, took on a different character with regard to problem framing. Modeling, for example, was not limited to instructional situations where adults showed youth how to complete a particular task. Modeling also took place in informal conversations where experts or "old hands" articulated their thinking strategies and beliefs.

One example of this kind of indirect modeling took place during a "check-in" conversation on the day of the U.S. invasion of Iraq, March 20, 2003. Check-ins were typical in Youth Rising: they were a way to start the meeting in an informal and egalitarian way, with everyone responding to the question at hand, which was often generated by a youth organizer. On this day Raymond asked, "Do you agree or disagree with the war? And, how does it affect you, directly?" Raymond said he agreed with the war, but other youth were against it. Two youth said the war did not affect them directly; several others focused on their personal fear of a terrorist attack. The responses from the adult staff members were markedly different because they emphasized the ways in which the war was linked to broader concerns about social justice. For example, Elsa framed her answer in terms of the war's consequences for the working class, by talking about her relative in the military and saying that the war is "affecting us the most and benefiting us the least." Vanessa mentioned that the money used to purchase one warplane, $17 million, could be of immense use to the Marshall school district.

This interaction was unlike a class or training, but it still had educational qualities, because older members of the group modeled their own meaning-making strategies for younger members of the group through conversation and sharing of personal experiences. Informal activities like this provided valuable opportunities for youth to learn through observation and interaction—in short, by participation in group conversations rather than activities designed for didactic instruction.

Adults coached students in their problem-framing skills in a variety of ways. At times adult staff members encouraged youth to remember to reframe the problem from one that focused on individuals to one that focused on a broader system. For example, after a discussion in which youth talked about the report cards as a way to highlight some of the bad teachers at their school, one of the coordinators, Elsa, reminded them that there was a bigger goal at stake, saying that their goal was not just to blame teachers, but to focus the campaign on problems in Marshall's schools generally—"budget cuts, no money for schools, the bigger issues."

Adults also exposed youth to problem-framing strategies through workshops and activities that were intended to help them think about the broader social context for the dropout rate. Adults encouraged youth to question the status quo and recognize that social phenomena are not inevitable. From the perspective of adult staff members, "youth voice" would have been an empty promise if not accompanied by critical perspectives on social issues. Activities included interactive skits, board games, discussions, and, on one occasion, a mini-lecture about school funding laws. One thinking strategy that adults stressed was the importance of understanding the root cause of a problem. This was communicated in a "hint" that was part of a board game created by Youth Rising:

> If you were coughing because you had cancer, and the doctor gave you a prescription for cough medicine, that wouldn't be the right analysis of the problem; therefore you need the right analysis of the problem in order to make effective change.

This hint did not dictate a specific answer to the task, but at the same time it used a metaphor to challenge youth organizers to think critically about the issue at hand, as well as to appreciate the ways in which the diagnosis of the problem was necessary for its prevention.

In interviews, youth organizers described Youth Rising as a place where they began to view their neighborhoods and schools in new ways. For example, when I asked Coretta if she had changed in any way since joining Youth Rising, she said, "I feel that I'm actually viewing the community as it is. I mean, I'm not going to lie … this community does need a lot of changing." When I asked Raymond to compare Youth Rising to school, he said the two were different: "The school is going to teach you the good side of everything, but up in here, they going to show you the good side, the bad side. They going to show you all four corners of everything." I asked Ellie if she thought students at school wanted to have a voice and cared about student power. She said that "the ones that don't get involved just go through life not noticing anything." These statements suggest that Youth Rising was a place where members le arned to see the world differently, to "view the community as it is" and "notice" the problems that exist.

Adults "faded" by leaving room for young people to come to their own conclusions about issues pertinent to the campaign. For example, the campaign itself was generated by youth organizers, who attended a retreat at the beginning of the year where they reflected on problems facing Marshall's young people and chose to focus on student voice issues. Also, after the "report cards" had been entered into a database, the youth took responsibility for identifying trends in student responses; youth organizers highlighted those findings that were most important to them and used them to shape the student voice resolution. Finally, the Youth Rising quarterly newsletter offered a youth-authored space for organizers to express their opinions about social issues. In his interview with me, Raymond described Youth Rising as a place where

> You just get to ... speak your opinion. You get to say how you feel about everything. Instead of just having everybody else tell you what they going to do and how they going to do it. You get to put your way, how you want something to be done.

Raymond's description of Youth Rising as a place where you "get to speak your opinion" corresponded to my own observation that youth appeared to feel safe to express their views. On occasions when youth, including Raymond, raised alternative or dissenting views, these were discussed and explored by the whole group.

Summary of Apprenticeship Practices

This paper has examined apprenticeship practices in Youth Rising by analyzing two tasks that were critical to the effectiveness of their campaign—persuasive speech and sociopolitical problem framing. In the case of persuasive speech, novices received necessary supports in early stages of learning, but over time developed enough mastery to be able to speak before policy makers and other audiences without adult guidance. Modeling, coaching, and fading looked different in the sociopolitical domain, because adults adopted a variety of strategies, which ranged from activities designed to examine the systemic and historical origins of social problems to informal interactions with young people where they shared political viewpoints.

These assistance strategies should be understood in the broader context of adult and youth relationships in Youth Rising. Unlike the teacher-student relationship in typical classrooms, adults saw themselves as partners with youth in the broader effort to make schools better for youth in Marshall. When I asked them if Youth Rising was a youth-run group, an adult-run group, or a group of youth and adults working together, all eight of the youth I interviewed described it as some form of collaboration. For example, Sitha responded by saying,

> I think it is youth and adults working together. We get to put in our input and adults get their input in there too. They are also helping us with our campaign and stuff, but they don't really take it over. But they want us to do most of the stuff.

Monique described how her feelings about Youth Rising changed over time:

> I thought this was going to be a job, like, just say "Hi" and "Bye," you know? And I didn't think I was really going to be attached to all these

people and it is like my family now and it is just crazy. I never thought I would have been here this long. I thought I was going to be fired, I was going to quit or something, but now it is like the only thing in my head.

Implications

Developing Young Leaders

Sometimes adults seek to foster ownership and intrinsic motivation among youth by limiting adult input and facilitating a youth-led process. The rationale is that, if given authentic opportunities to determine lines of action independently of adults, youth will be more committed and engaged. But feelings of engagement and ownership can also be fostered when adults participate and share their expertise.

Youth Rising followed the second strategy, relying on what I call *youth-centered apprenticeship*. Adults modeled expert practices, such as how to make a persuasive speech or how to mobilize community members. They coached youth by organizing role-playing exercises, testing their ability to stay on message, and helping them think about the social and political origins of the dropout rate. And, at key moments, adults faded in order for youth to advance their goals and participate fully on the public stage. Adults also interacted in a collegial manner with youth, such as during check-ins at the beginnings of meetings. During these times they candidly shared their own interpretations of political issues and contributed to a shared community. In this sense they shared their activist identities with young people.

One potential criticism of the apprenticeship approach stems from Piaget's theory that children develop new social and moral perspectives through peer interaction rather than "asymmetrical" discussions with adults (Piaget, 1965; see also Rogoff, 1990). According to Piaget, interactions with adults do not necessarily lead to qualitative shifts in reasoning, but instead to temporary adaptations to adult authority. From this viewpoint, for example, the systemic political framework espoused by adults may not have stimulated true shifts in thinking among youth participants.

The data from my study does not provide a definitive answer to this criticism. One limitation of this Piagetian critique, however, is that it does not take into account the proposition that people's sociopolitical attitudes are mediated by broader cultural narratives about individualism and meritocracy in the United States (Gee, 1996; Varenne & McDermott, 1999; Wertsch, 1998). By asking critical questions and exploring the origins of social problems, adults can help youth examine their assumptions about the sociopolitical world. According to adults in Youth Rising, such efforts were necessary to combat internalized racism and sexism common among urban youth.

Apprenticeship strategies had other related benefits. First, youth designed and implemented—with adult assistance—a campaign that was taken seriously based on its merits, rather than just out of a sense of noblesse oblige toward youth. Second, youth learned essential skills for civic participation, which ranged from speaking in public to analyzing complex sociopolitical problems. Third, perhaps because of the authenticity of the campaign, youth were invested in its outcome. In this case adult involvement did not undermine youth ownership, but instead helped to foster it.

Reconceptualizing Youth Voice

Calls for youth voice sometimes convey essentialist assumptions about youth and reinforce age segregation between youth and adults. Age segregation is evident in the finding that youth in the United States have few opportunities to engage in sustained cycles of planning and executing tasks with adults (Heath, 1999; Jarrett, 2005; Schlegel & Barry, 1991). At precisely the time when adolescents should be transitioning into mature roles in the lives of their communities, their interactions with adults are often restricted to the school building, which itself is divided by fairly rigid role distinctions between teachers and students. Youth-led initiatives that limit adult involvement may unwittingly reproduce their own forms of age segregation.

This chapter has proposed an alternative, more fluid conception of youth and adult roles, which puts static definitions of *youth* and *adult* aside in favor of broader concerns about social justice and effective policy making. Such an approach builds on the expertise and social capital of adult activists to facilitate meaningful and competent participation by young people.

Notes

1. Proposition 21 increased the penalties for juvenile offenses and the range of cases that could be tried in adult courts. For information about the details of the law, see the website of the state legislative analyst at www.lao.ca.gov/initiatives/2000/21_03_2000.html.
2. All names are pseudonyms to protect the anonymity of participants.
3. There were two additional adult staff members whose work focused on other aspects of the nonprofit agency mission, but who were not directly involved with Youth Rising.
4. The data sources for school and community context are kept confidential to protect the identity of participants. Please contact the author at ben.kirshner@colorado.edu if you would like further information about these or other data.

References

Ashley, J., Samaniego, D., & Cheun, L. (1997). How Oakland turns its back on teens: A youth perspective. *Social Justice, 24*, 170–177.

Brown, J. S., Collins, A., & Duguid, P. (1989). Situated learning and the culture of learning. *Education Researcher, 18*(1), 32–42.

Collins, A., Brown, J. S., & Newman, S. E. (1989). Cognitive apprenticeship: teaching the crafts of reading, writing, and mathematics. In L. B. Resnick (Ed.), *Knowing, learning, and instruction: Essays in honor of Robert Glaser* (pp. 453–494). Hillsdale, NJ: Lawrence Erlbaum Associates.

Crocker, J., Major, B., & Steele, C. M. (1998). Social stigma. In D. Gilbert, S. T. Fiske, & G. Lindzey (Eds.), *The handbook of social psychology* (Vol. 2; pp. 504–553). Boston: McGraw-Hill.

Delpit, L. D. (1988). The silenced dialogue: Power and pedagogy in educating other people's children. *Harvard Educational Review, 58,* 280–298.

Dewey, J. (1902/1990). *The child and the curriculum.* Chicago: University of Chicago Press.

Flanagan, C., & Faison, N. (2001). *Youth civic development: Implications of research for social policy and programs.* Ann Arbor, MI: Society for Research in Child Development.

Freire, P. (2002). *Pedagogy of the oppressed.* New York: Continuum. (Original work published 1970).

Gee, J. (1996). *Social linguistics and literacies.* London: Taylor & Francis.

Ginwright, S. (2005). On urban ground: Understanding African-American intergenerational partnerships in urban communities. *Journal of Community Psychology, 33*(1), 101–111.

Ginwright, S., & James, T. (2002). From assets to agents of change: Social justice, organizing, and youth development. *New Directions for Youth Development, 96,* 27–46.

Halpern, R. (2005). Instrumental relationships: A potential relational model for inner-city youth programs. *Journal of Community Psychology, 33*(1), 11–20.

Hart, D., & Atkins, R. (2002). Civic competence in urban youth. *Applied Developmental Science, 6*(4), 227–236.

Heath, S. B. (1999). Dimensions of language development: Lessons from older children. In A. S. Masten (Ed.), *Cultural processes in child development* (Vol. 29; pp. 59–75). Mahwah, NJ: Lawrence Erlbaum Associates.

Hilliard, D. (1993). *This side of glory: The autobiography of David Hilliard and the story of the Black Panther Party.* Boston: Little, Brown.

Hogan, K. (2002). Pitfalls of community-based learning: How power dynamics limit adolescents' trajectories of growth and participation. *Teachers College Record 104*(3), 586–624.

Holland, D., & Lave, J. (2001). *History in person: Enduring struggles, contentious practice, intimate identities.* Santa Fe, NM: School of American Research Press.

Hunt, S. A., Benford, R. D., & Snow, D. A. Identity fields: Framing processes and the social construction of movement identities. In E. Laraña, H. Johnston, & J. R. Gusfield (Eds.), *New social movements: From ideology to identity* (pp. 185–207). Philadelphia: Temple University Press.

Jarrett, R. L., Sullivan, P. J., & Watkins, N. D. (2005). Developing social capital through participation in organized youth programs: Qualitative insights from three programs. *Journal of Community Psychology, 33*(1), 41–55.

Kilgore, D. W. (1999). Understanding learning in social movements: a theory of collective learning. *International Journal of Lifelong Education, 18*(3), 191–202.

Kirshner, B. (2005). *Assistance strategies in three youth activism groups: Facilitation, apprenticeship, and joint work.* Manuscript submitted for publication.

Larson, R. W., & Hansen, D. (2005). The development of strategic thinking: Learning to impact human systems in a youth activism program. *Human Development, 48* (6), 327–349.

Larson, R., Walker, K., & Pierce, N. (2005). A comparison of youth-driven and adult-driven youth programs: Balancing inputs from youth and adults. *Journal of Community Psychology, 33*(1), 57–74.

Lave, J. (1990). The culture of acquisition and the practice of understanding. In J. W. Stigler, R. A. Shweder, & G. Herdt (Eds.), *Cultural psychology: Essays on comparative human development* (pp. 309–328). Cambridge: Cambridge University Press.

Lave, J., & Wenger, E. (1991). *Situated learning: Legitimate peripheral participation.* New York: Cambridge University Press.

Mahiri, J., & Cooper, E. (2003). Black youth violence has a bad rap. *Journal of Social Issues: Youth Perspectives on Violence and Injustice, 59*(1), 121–140.

Markus, H. R., Mullally, P. & Kitayama, S. (1997). Selfways: Diversity in modes of cultural participation. In U. Neisser & D. Jopling (Eds.), *The conceptual self in context: Culture, experience, self-understanding.* Cambridge: Cambridge University Press.

McLaughlin, M. W. (2000). *Community counts: How youth organizations matter for youth development.* Washington, DC: Public Education Network.

McLaughlin, M. W., & Heath, S. B. (1993). Casting the self: Frames for identity and dilemmas for policy. In S. B. Heath & M. W. McLaughlin (Eds.), *Identity and inner-city youth: Beyond ethnicity and gender* (pp. 210–239). New York: Teachers College Press.

Nasir, N., & Saxe, G. (2003). Ethnic and academic identities: A cultural practice perspective on emerging tensions and their management in the lives of minority students. *Educational Researcher 32*(5): 14–18.

Noguera, P. (2003). *City schools and the American dream: Reclaiming the promise of public education.* New York: Teachers College Press.

O'Donoghue, J. L., & Strobel, K. R. (2003). Directivity and Freedom: the Role of Adults in Youth Civic Empowerment. Paper presented at the International Conference on Civic Education, New Orleans, November 16–18, 2003.

Packer, M., & Goicoechea, J. (2000). Sociocultural and constructivist theories of learning: Ontology, not just epistemology. *Educational Psychologist 35*(4): 227–241.

Perlstein, D. (2002). Minds stayed on freedom: Politics and pedagogy in the African-American freedom struggle. *American Educational Research Journal, 39*(2), 249–277.

Piaget, J. (1965). *The moral judgment of the child.* New York: Free Press.

Rogoff, B. (1990). *Apprenticeship in thinking: Cognitive development in social context.* New York: Oxford University Press.

Rogoff, B. (1995). Observing sociocultural activity on three planes: Participatory appropriation, guided participation, and apprenticeship. In J. Wertsch, P. Del Rio, & A. Alvarez (Eds.), *Sociocultural studies of mind.* New York: Cambridge University Press.

Rogoff, B. (2003). *The cultural nature of human development.* New York: Oxford University Press.

Rubin, R. H., Billingsley, A., & Caldwell, C. (1994). The role of the black church in working with black adolescents. *Adolescence, 29*(114), 251–266.

Schlegel, A., & Barry, H. (1991). *Adolescence: An anthropological inquiry.* New York: Free Press.

Sherman, R. (2002). Building young people's lives: One foundation's strategy. *New Direction for Youth Development, 96,* 65–82.

Shepard, L. A. (2000). The role of assessment in a learning culture. *Educational Researcher 29*(7), 4–14.

Tolman, J., & Pittman, K., with Cervone, B., Cushman, K., Rowley, L., Kinkade, S., Phillips, J., & Duque, S. (2001). *Youth acts, community impacts: Stories of youth engagement with real results.* Community and Youth Development Series (Vol. 7). Takoma Park, MD: Forum for Youth Investment.

Varenne, H., & McDermott, R. P. (1999). *Successful failure: The school America builds.* Boulder, CO: Westview.

Vygotsky, L. S. (1978). *Mind in society: The development of higher psychological processes.* Cambridge, MA: Harvard University Press.

We Interrupt This Message. (2002). *Speaking for ourselves: A youth assessment of local news coverage.* San Francisco: Youth Media Council.

Wertsch, J. V. (1998). *Mind as action.* New York: Oxford University Press.

Wilson, W. J. (1996). *When work disappears: The world of the new urban poor.* New York: Alfred A. Knopf.

Zeldin, S., Larson, R., Camino, L., & O'Connor, C. (2005). Intergenerational relationships and partnerships in community programs: Purpose, practice, and directions for research. *Journal of Community Psychology, 33*(1), 1–10.

CHAPTER 4

Sociopolitical Development: The Missing Link in Research and Policy on Adolescents

RODERICK J. WATTS AND OMAR GUESSOUS

Sociopolitical Development Is Neglected in Scholarship and Policy on Youth Development

We are writing this chapter with three objectives. The first is to make a case for including sociopolitical development (SPD) and social-justice activism in scholarly work on civic development and youth development—with particular emphasis on psychology. The second is to present a theory of SPD and some related research findings. In the conclusion we will explore the implications of this work for enhancing youth-related policy.

In their paper on social justice and youth policy, Ginwright, Cammarota, and Noguera (unpublished manuscript), have identified three impediments to scholarship on youth development and building the connection between it and youth-led social justice work. They note that much of the conventional literature on youth development sees youth "as objects of policy rather than as actors who possess the rights and abilities to shape policy." Thus, the adults-only approach to intervening in social problems can disempower youth, and fail to mobilize their "capacity to resist and challenge unjust institutional practices." Ginwright et al. have also lamented the

> lack of social theory [that] has contributed to a set of anecdotal propositions about the youth development process, which tend to emphasize individual behavior rather than collective responses to marginalization. The myriad of lists, models, and principles commonly found in youth

development literature has ties to important psychological concepts, but are grossly disconnected from social theory and an analysis of social context .

One alternative to conventional theories of youth psychological and social development is liberation psychology, which is distinguished by its emphasis on human rights and social equity. Exposing social injustice, creating just societies, promoting self-determination and solidarity with others, and ending oppression (and healing its effects) are its core tenets. A central aim is to articulate the relationship between the collective battle against social ills and the advancement of personal well-being. Liberation psychology is better known outside of the United States, but that is beginning to change.

This chapter focuses on SPD as an aspect of liberation psychology. It is an effort to remedy the shortcomings in conventional theorizing described by Ginwright et al. by retaining "ties to important psychological concepts" while forging much stronger connections to social theory and context.

We define *sociopolitical development* as a product of both liberation and developmental psychology. It is the evolving, critical understanding of the political, economic, cultural, and other systemic forces that shape society and one's status within it, and the associated process of growth in relevant knowledge, analytical skills, and emotional faculties (see Watts, Williams, & Jagers, 2003). It broadens or replaces a narrow focus on adjustment, coping, resilience, and similar concepts that connote accommodation with the more empowering notions of a collective sense of agency, commitment to action, and activism. Although our work on SPD includes many elements of conventional thinking about human behavior, it explicitly acknowledges oppression and the influence of social forces outside the individual. Sociopolitical development theory aims to social justice activism, with an eye toward cultivating it more effectively and accelerating its inclusion in mainstream psychological theory. Because SPD is a developmental process, it is consistent with developmental psychology, which in recent years has come to appreciate that grappling with civic issues is part of identity consolidation in adolescence (Youniss & Yates, 1997). Flanagan (2004), a leading scholar in the field, believes that civic—if not political—development has established itself, even if theory and research have not yet caught up. For example, Westheimer and Kahne (2003) argue that the "good citizen" can be framed in three ways, through (1) citizenship manifested in individual acts such as volunteering; (2) citizenship in local community affairs, staying informed on local and national issues; and (3) the justice-oriented citizen who, like the participatory citizen, emphasizes collective work toward community betterment while maintaining a more critical stance on social, political, and economic issues. Their third point suggests a window of opportunity for establishing sociopolitical development and social justice activism as a core area of research and a legitimate target for youth development policy and intervention—once there is evidence to support the theory. Of course, for many of us, the true test of its value is its utility on the front line.

Theorizing on Sociopolitical Development

How an activist identity develops remains one of the basic questions in social psychology and social movement research today.

—Corning and Myers, 2002 (p. 703)

Five questions have shaped our research on sociopolitical development:

1. What are the most important psychological determinants of "societal involvement" (i.e., community service, civic engagement, and social justice activism)?
2. In general, does the data support the model of SPD proposed in this paper?
3. What is the relationship between youth societal involvement and conventional indicators of healthy youth development?
4. How can what we learn be useful in encouraging future scholarly research on SPD?
5. What implications do the findings have for social policy on youth development?

Our model of SPD, which is informed by the work of activists, and scholars of activism, is based on four propositions—each with links to researchable concepts (see Figure 4.1):

Proposition 1: An Analysis of Authority and Power is Central. In their study, Lewis-Charp, Yu, and Soukamneuth (this volume, chapter 2) contend, "It is through the *politicized* analysis of the inequitable contexts and policies that shape young people's day-to-day lives" that youth organizing groups promote healthy youth development. This critical analysis or "critical consciousness" (Freire, 1990) is central to our theory of SPD. For young people, social power operates through adult and parental authority and then through formative institutions such as schools. Sociopolitical development requires young people to contend with that power in each of these settings. These formative venues offer them an early taste of institutional power. Psychology is a resource for youth development because analysis is a learned mental process that produces emotional effects. Critical consciousness is therefore psychology's subject matter.

Ginwright (2002) has detailed the importance of social analysis to youth organizing for social justice, especially in helping young people make connections between life in their communities and larger social forces. Although many other activist scholars stress the importance of critical consciousness or,

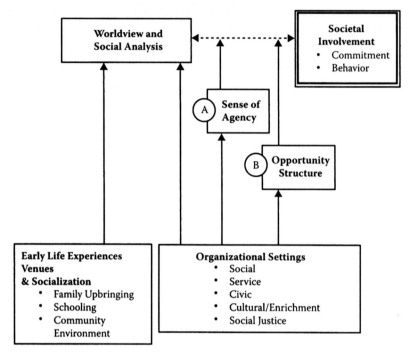

Fig. 4.1 A Theory of Sociopolitical Devlopment.

more narrowly, *social analysis,* the field of psychology has yet to devise a means of researching it. Figure 4.1 depicts our working theory of SPD. At the left is social analysis, where at one end of the continuum there is the individualist view. Here people are the architects of their own destiny and they get what they deserve. According to this view society is fair and personal circumstances reflect personal capabilities, fate, or unseen forces beyond one's control.

At the other end of the continuum is a systems view that sees failed or oppressive social institutions as the cause of personal circumstances. From this perspective sociopolitical systems, rather than persons, are the problem. These contrasting ideas of social causation are reflected in the just world belief construct in social psychology (Rubin & Peplau, 1975). According to the theory, individuals who see the world as unjust believe that people do not necessarily get what they deserve because there are social forces beyond their control. Consequently, they are more likely than their counterparts to offer contextual rather than individual explanations for social problems. This theory has been supported repeatedly in empirical research: adult activists tend to endorse an unjust world and they are motivated by perceptions of injustice and outrage (O'Neill, Duffy, Enman, Blackmer, & Goodwin, 1988). This latter study found evidence of systems-level thinking, awareness of injustice, and belief in an unjust world to be especially prevalent among people of color. At the macrolevel, those who believe that the world is just tend to blame the poor for their fate (Furnham & Gunter, 1984), while those who reject just world beliefs tend to blame world economic systems for poverty, exploitation, and war (Harper & Manasse, 1992). We used the Global Belief in a Just World Scale created by Lipkus (1991) to assess social analysis in this study.

Because most of our research participants are of African descent, we also examined race as a component of social analysis in the form of racialized cultural identity. This is a politicized conception of social identity (related to black nationalism) that has long been a feature of black liberation movements (e.g., Fredrickon, 1995; Karenga, 1993). We used two measures to assess this: Sellers, Shelton, Rowley, and Chavous's (1998) multidimensional scale of racial identity, and the Cultural Pride Reinforcement Subscale of Stevenson's (1994) Racial Socialization Scale. Lewis-Charp et al. (chapter 2, this volume), among others, have argued that identity support—especially stigmatized identities—is an important theme in youth development, and one that is emphasized by youth organizers.

Proposition 2: A Sense of Agency Is Essential: People Take Action When They Believe They Can Make an Impact. There are several different ways to think about sense of agency. Collective efficacy looks at it as a shared experience. Sense of agency implies a belief in the capacity of the group to pull together and realize shared aspirations or address shared problems (Bandura, 2001; Sampson, Raudenbush, & Earls, 1997). According to experimental studies, when individuals identify with a group they are more willing to forgo individual gain in order to enhance the collective good (Brewer & Gardner, 1996). Empowerment has been described in both personal and collective ways, and defined by Zimmerman and Rappaport (1988) as "a combination of self-acceptance and self-confidence, social and political understanding, and the ability to play an assertive role in controlling resources and decisions in one's community." Empowerment can be viewed as a special case of self-efficacy that is specific to community and political action. Two versions of this concept are especially relevant to the proposed research. The concept of perceived control, developed by Schulz, Israel, Zimmerman, and Checkoway (1995) measures self-efficacy in community action activities with others. Zimmerman and Zahniser's (1991) measure of sociopolitical control queries self-confidence, the desire to lead others, and attitudes about political involvement. They found that young African American men who scored high on this scale also reported fewer symptoms of psychological distress, despite their exposure to a variety of stressors. Although sense of agency and leadership skills are not synonymous, they are related to one another. Lewis-Charp et al. (chapter 2, this volume) talk about the importance of both in their emphasis on documenting "wins" in youth-led campaigns, which contribute to a sense of agency in young people.

Proposition 3: Action Requires Opportunity. Theories in sociology and political science that explain societal involvement stress the importance of opportunity structures (Keeter, Zukin, Andolina, & Jenkins, 2002). National studies indicate that 29% of early adolescents are not reached by community youth programs at all (U.S. Department of Education, 1990). Opportunities afforded by faith-based groups to practice organizational and leadership skills and to be recruited into civic action are one of the few ways that people of lower socio economic status overcome these class disparities (Verba, Schlozman, & Brady, 1995). We are exploring ways to make an objective determination of opportunity structure, but in the meantime we use a subjective measure that captures the options respondents see as accessible or desirable. Developmental psychology has established the influences of peers during adolescence, so this information is important to collect.

Proposition 4: Commitment and Action Are Sociopolitical Development Outcomes. In the model proposed here, the sociopolitical development outcome of interest is action, which is thought to occur once the factors of social analysis, opportunity, and agency make effective action possible. Emotional and intellectual commitment is seen as a proxy for action when the opportunity structure provides few options for action. Although it is simplest to depict the elements of Figure 4.1 in a linear way, the reality is likely to be more complex; there are probably reciprocal effects between societal involvement, social analysis, and sense of agency. Leading scholar activists such as Freire (1970) and Martín-Baró (1994) argue that the action-reflection cycle is central to political development. Of particular interest is the transition from "armchair activist" to true activist. Although the armchair activist possesses an analysis of social problems, she does not report activist behavior.

Measuring societal involvement is fairly straightforward. It can be done through an inventory of possible societal involvement behavior: community service (learning), civic activity (conventional involvement in social and political institutions), and sociopolitical action. Pancer, Pratt, and Hunsberger (2000) developed two measures of societal involvement especially for young people. The Youth Responsibility Scale assesses attitudes, and it corresponds to the "commitment" component of societal involvement (see Figure 4.1). The other is called the Youth Inventory of Involvement, and it focuses on behavior. It is necessary to measure commitment because there is often a limited opportunity structure for societal involvement that is appropriate for teenagers. A measure of commitment, intent, or interest may provide a more sensitive measure and one less influenced by the opportunity structure.

It is useful to do more than count instances or frequency of involvement (though they are important). A number of researchers have found that the role that young people have in a project influences its impact on their lives. Research by Morgan and Streb (2001) indicates that "student voice" in a project is essential. They describe four items for assessing this—to which students should answer "yes": "I had real responsibilities, I had challenging tasks, I helped plan the project, I made important decisions."(p. 160) Findings from this research further support the contention that a sense of agency—both as an antecedent to and as an outcome of societal involvement—is essential to consider. Yates and Youniss (1996) have found that within the existing range of community service activities, those that provide opportunities for intense experiences and social interactions are the most strongly associated with our variables of interest—sense of agency and political awareness (as well as social relatedness). Flanagan's (2003) review of the literature on youth civic programming further highlights the importance of agency: she found that successful programs provide participants with a range of possible roles and with a balance between freedom and structure. Thus, "voice"—demanding opportunities that confer real power—appears to be a potentiating feature of societal involvement behavior. All of these findings play to the strengths of youth organizing where the aim is to partnering with youth and cocreating program roles and objectives.

Societal Involvement and Positive Youth Development

Our third research question asks about the role of sociopolitical development in positive youth development overall. Along with understanding and enhancing SPD there is a need to move this area of research and action closer to the mainstream of youth development theory. The lack of an empirically tested psychological theory of SPD is accompanied by a dearth of information on how it is related to conventional psychological outcomes such as social competence, mental health indicators, and intellectual development. Figure 4.2

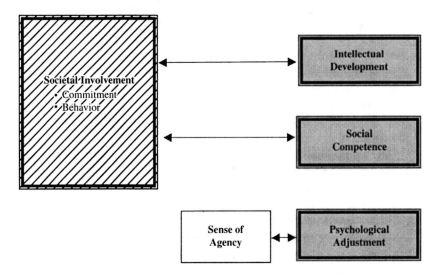

Fig. 4.2 Relationships among indicators of societal involvement and positive youth development.

makes a case for how these variables may be related to societal involvement behavior and sense of agency. With a few notable exceptions, the research literature on these question is sparse and equivocal (Sherrod, Flanagan, & Youniss, 2002). A well-respected Brandeis University study found no effect of service learning at the high school level on communication skills, work orientation, or risky behavior (Center for Human Resources, 1999). Nonetheless, Morgan and Streb (2001) have argued that civic engagement activity can enhance self-concept and political self-efficacy. They contend that civic engagement experiences ought to enhance academic performance, and their prediction appears to have been borne out by the Brandeis study. The Brandeis group found improvements in academic performance among students who participated in community service learning. They also found a significantly stronger affect among students of color as compared to white students.

Rather than adopting a narrow focus on academic achievement, we decided to examine intellectualism. Young people can be intellectually curious and active and still receive low grades due to rebellious behavior and alienation from schools (McLaren, 1991). Efforts to foster critical consciousness and social analysis may potentiate critical thinking and academic performance, which seem to draw on related competencies (Freire, 1970; Martín-Baró, 1994; Watts, Abdul-Adil, & Pratt, 2002). The connection shown in Figure 4.2 between societal involvement behavior and intellectual development reflects our desire to find empirical evidence of an association between the two.

We also suspect that the sustained collective effort associated with activism both builds and benefits from social competence. It is logical to predict that cooperation, effective communication, self-control, and similar behaviors are all part of teamwork. The longitudinal component of this study will allow for a better understanding of how societal involvement contributes to social competence. Although it is not shown as an outcome variable in the model, it is reasonable to predict that successful societal-involvement projects also lead to a greater sense of agency, and perhaps a positive feedback loop. Thus, if societal involvement behavior strengthens sense of agency over time, it is useful to view agency as an ancillary output of SPD and also an input for positive youth development.

The limited findings that link SPD and psychological adjustment are encouraging. Sociopolitical control was found to predict general health and depressive symptoms in a randomized, Midwestern African American community sample (Parker, Lichtenstein, Schulz, Israel, Steinman, & James, 2001). It also predicted self-rated health in a European adult sample (Ruetten, von Lengerke, et al., 2000). Also, research by Zimmerman, Ramirez-Valles, and Matton (1999) has suggested that sociopolitical control made male African American adolescents less vulnerable to the effects of helplessness on their mental health.

The Research

Participants and Procedures

Participants lived inside the highway that circles the city of Atlanta or frequented a school, program, or organization within this perimeter. Given this study's focus on societal involvement behavior, youth who were involved in some type of civic, community, or political activity were oversampled. This was done by actively identifying and recruiting from settings that encouraged community engagement. African American youth make up the majority in the city, and so this is reflected in the sample. The measures reflected our desire to explore links among SPD and racial identity, culture, and a social analysis based on race.

Settings were contacted if there was reason to suspect that they might work with or serve a youth population—regardless of whether youth were their primary focus. As a result, the settings that participants were recruited from vary with respect to their size and budget, philosophy and values, mission, approach to youth work, standards of success, and so on. For example, whereas some organizations focused on artistic development, others focused on academic, social, and/or political development.

The paper-and-pencil surveys used in this study were administered in a group format by trained undergraduate and graduate research assistants. More often than not, data was collected on-site at the school or organization where youth were recruited, once parental consent forms had been signed and returned.

Of the 131 youth who have so far participated in the study, over half (58%, N = 76) were female and 79% self-identified as black or African American (N=103). The remaining 21% were white (N = 20), multiracial (N = 5), Asian American (N = 1), or Native American (N = 1). The mean age was 15.8 and the median age 15. Over half of the sampled youth (54%, N = 71) were in their first two years of high school (grades 9 and 10). Most of the black participants attended a public school, whereas most of the white youth attended a private school—a reflection of Atlanta area schools' racial makeup.

Measures

Each variable of interest was assessed using 1–3 survey-type instruments that were answered on a numerical scale. All of the following measures achieved a minimum coefficient of reliability (alpha) of .70.

The Global Belief in a Just World Scale. The Global Belief in a Just World Scale (GBJWS; see Lipkus, 1991) is a 7-item scale that assesses the extent to which a person believes that the world is a just place and that people get what they deserve and deserve what they get. This was used to assess social analysis.

The Communalism Scale. The Communalism Scale (CS; see Boykin, Jagers, Ellison, & Albury, 1997) is a 31-item measure that assesses the degree to which a person is oriented toward social obligation and interdependence; this orientation is seen as a feature of African (American) culture. This scale was used to assess one aspect of worldview and to explore how culture can be an asset in building political solidarity.

The Multidimensional Inventory of Black Identity—Short Form. From the Multidimensional Inventory of Black Identity—Short Form (MIBI—short form; see Sellers et al., 1998) we present two subscales in this analysis: Racial Centrality and Private Regard. The 4-item Racial Centrality Subscale examines the degree to which race is a self-defining characteristic, and the 3-item Private Regard Subscale assesses one's affective evaluation of being black. The MIBI was used to assess racial identity and one aspect of cultural worldview.

Scale of Racial Socialization for African American Adolescents. The Scale of Racial Socialization for African American Adolescents (SORS-A; see Stevenson, 1994) was designed to assess adolescents' opinion about the appropriateness of racial socialization processes in educational, family, and societal venues. One subscale from this instrument was administered to all African American participants: Cultural Pride and Reinforcement. The SORS-A was used to assess a second aspect of cultural worldview.

The Sociopolitical Control Scale. The Sociopolitical Control Scale (SPCS; see Zimmerman & Zahniser, 1991) is a 17-item scale that assesses thinking, motivation, and personality as they relate to a person's belief that their actions in the social and political system can lead to desired outcomes. This instrument was used to assess one aspect of sense of agency: sociopolitical control.

Experience of Agency. Experience of Agency (EOA; see Morgan & Streb, 2001) is a 4-item scale that was created to assess the level of student "voice" in the design and implementation of service-learning projects. These items were adapted for the current study to assess the extent to which participants had been involved in community or political projects that allowed them to exert and further develop their individual sense of agency.

The Youth Social Responsibility Scale. The Youth Social Responsibility Scale (YSRS; see Pancer et al., 2000) was developed to assess teenagers' commitment to societal involvement, using such items as "More young people should become active in political parties and organizations" and "Young people have an important role to play in making the world a better place." It was used to measure commitment to societal involvement.

The You and Your Neighborhood Scale. The You and Your Neighborhood Scale (YYN; see Watts, unpublished) is a 10-item instrument that was developed to assess young neighborhood residents' beliefs about the worth and effectiveness of community-level individual and collective action, as well as their commitment to community involvement. It was used to assess commitment to societal involvement.

The Youth Inventory of Involvement. The Youth Inventory of Involvement (YII; see Pancer et al., 2000) is a 30-item scale that was devised to assess subtype and extent of youth societal involvement behavior. Respondents indicate how much, in the past year, they have participated in each of the activities using a 5-point scale. The YII was used to assess societal involvement behavior.

Data Analysis

The survey data was entered into the SPSS and checked for data-entry errors and for violations of the assumptions associated with the statistical analyses described below. Next, basic correlational analyses were conducted in order to examine bivariate associations among the study variables as well as between the study variables and demographic characteristics. A set of hierarchical linear regressions were then conducted to test for main effects of variables of interest. The outcome variable of interest was entered as the dependent variable, and the predictor variable of interest was entered as an independent variable at step 3. One demographic variable—gender—was associated with the main outcomes of interest and was therefore entered at step 1 of each regression model. These 2-step hierarchical regression models allowed us to partial out the effect of demographics variables in order to determine the unique effect of the predictor variables of interest. Finally, a moderation analysis was conducted to test the hypothesis that sense of agency moderates the relationship between social analysis and societal involvement.

Research Findings

Three sets of findings are presented. First, we describe some of the main effects findings that we identified for societal involvement commitment and behavior. Second, we examine in more detail two direct-effects models in predicting commitment to societal involvement. Third, we present support for the moderator role of sense of agency in the relationship between social analysis and societal involvement behavior.

Main Effects Findings for Societal Involvement

Societal Involvement Commitment—As Distinct from Behavior. Consistent with most research on civic and political development, girls tended to express higher levels of commitment. As predicted, social involvement (SI) commitment was related to social analysis and cultural worldview, as well as to sense of agency. In the case of social analysis, those who believed the world is *unjust* tended to indicate a stronger commitment to societal involvement. Cultural worldview was positively related to commitment as well: those who endorsed a more communal orientation also expressed a higher level of commitment. Similarly, among the black participants, those who held their race in a higher regard and those who expressed greater pride in their culture demonstrated higher levels of commitment. Finally, respondents with a stronger sense of agency tended to have higher commitment levels.

We conducted some preliminary tests of our theoretical models. In the first model, the social analysis and sense of agency variables (leadership competence, policy control, and experience of agency) were entered together in the second step of a hierarchical multivariate model. The model altogether accounted for 46% of variance in commitment ($R^2 = .458$) and all four predictors—just world belief ($B = -.185$, $p < .01$), leadership competence ($B = .251$, $p < .001$), policy control ($B = .327$, $p < .001$), and experience of agency ($B = .199$, $p < .01$)— significantly and uniquely contributed to levels of commitment.

We also examined the relationship of commitment to the cultural and racial identity variables. This model accounted for 33% of the variance in commitment ($R^2 = .330$), although only communalism ($B = .462$, $p < .001$) significantly contributed to SI commitment. When all the data are in we intend to explore ways of combining the racial and cultural variables as an index of racialized cultural identity, as described earlier.

Notably, even when all three variables—social analysis, sense of agency, and cultural worldview—were simultaneously entered into a regression model, each of them remained significant. This additive model, which accounted for 60% of variance in commitment ($R^2 = .601$), suggests that each variable *uniquely* and *independently* plays an important part in the development of commitment to societal involvement.

Societal Involvement Behavior: Political Activity. Although our predictor variables, as indicated in Table 4.1, had a number of significant and medium- to large-sized direct effects on *commitment* to societal involvement, these same predictors largely failed to directly predict *behavior.* However, as predicted, *experience* of agency—as measured by four questions more closely related to behavior and project roles than the questions we initially intended to use—moderated the relationship between just world belief and societal involvement in community and political activities. Indeed, the interaction term between just world belief and experience of agency was significantly related to the behavioral outcome variable, even after controlling for demographic variables and the predictor variables' main effects (see Table 4.2). As illustrated in Table 4.2, a post-hoc analysis indicated that at higher levels of experience of agency, belief in an unjust world was positively related to societal involvement behavior. At lower levels of experience of agency, the relationship was reversed; viewing the world as unjust was negatively related to behavior.

Table 4.1 Predicting Societal Involvement Commitment

Predictor Variables	SI Commitment (R^2)
Demographic Variables	
Gender	.05
Social Analysis	
Just world belief (GBJWS)	.08 (−)
Sense of Agency	
Leadership competence (SPCS)	.23 (+)
Policy control (SPCS)	.25 (+)
Experience of agency (EOA)	.10 (+)
Cultural Worldview	
Communalism (CS)	.29 (+)
Cultural pride reinforcement (SORS)	.16 (+)
Racial Identity	
Centrality (MIBI)	.05 (+)
Private regard (MIBI)	.11 (+)

Note: The table shows R^2 change values at step 2, after entering the predictor variable. The value is a percentage indicating how much predictive power the predictor adds, above and beyond that of the demographic variables that were entered at step 1.

Table 4.2 Moderation Analysis of the Social Analysis–Societal Involvement Behavior Link

Post-hoc Analysis

Experience of Agency		Beta	Sig.
Below average:	Constant		.777
	JWB	.239	.021
Above average:	Constant		.000
	JWB	−.330	.046

Note: Outcome variable = community and political activities.

Discussion of the Research Findings

Psychological determinants of societal involvement

As expected, we were able to identify predictors for both the behavioral and the attitudinal aspects of SI, although commitment was more consistently and strongly related to the hypothesized predictors (see Figure 4.1).

Youth who, based on their social analysis, did not believe that people are treated fairly in society were more committed to societal involvement. Those who endorsed a communal worldview (that is, social duty and interdependence) were also more committed to societal involvement. This was also true for youth who felt a greater sense of agency. Finally, black respondents with a strong and positive connection to their racial and cultural heritage as determined by measures or racial identity and cultural pride reinforcement tended to be more committed to societal involvement. Often items on both race and culture were on the same surveys, indicating a connection between the politics of race and elements of an African (American) cultural worldview. At a later point we intend to consider an index of racialized cultural identity that combines some of these measures.

Overall, the preliminary findings lend some early support to our theoretical model of sociopolitical development. We currently lack the statistical power to test for the moderating effects of opportunity structure and sense of agency depicted in Figure 4.1.

How Can Findings from This Study Inform Future Scholarly Research?

Increasingly, leaders in research and education have lamented the weakness associated with the way universities separate disciplines into discreet areas. In the case of youth development, the separation of political science, sociology, psychology, and kindred disciplines has impeded the development of a multileveled view of the human condition, one that incorporates sociopolitical as well as psychological processes. The findings described in this paper show a link between what is good for the individual and what is good for society. Yet social science lacks an interdisciplinary model of youth development that addresses growth in both these domains. To date, U.S. psychology has provided us with information about personal development, but it has neglected conceptions of social (in)justice, and the social processes that lead to a collective striving for liberation. We also know little about how individual well-being and striving for social liberation are related. So then, the argument to explore and advance in academe is that *the qualities young people need to develop and improve themselves are related to the qualities they need to develop and improve their society; these two domains of development are synergistic.*

Liberation psychology, and particularly mesolevel constructs like sociopolitical development (see Table 4.3) offer ways of linking the two together. However, traditional psychological thinking is not equipped to move in this

Table 4.3 Examples of Conceptual Integration Across Levels of Analysis

Microlevel (Personal Focus)	Mesolevel (Intermediate Focus)	Macrolevel (Societal Focus)
Psychology	Political Science, Anthropology, Sociology	
Sense of agency*	Collective efficacy/empowerment*	Social power
Personal identity	Social/ethnoracial identity*	Political solidarity and nationalism
Moral development	Sociopolitical development*	Ideological development*
Self-actualization and* well-being	Civic engagement/community building	Social movements/liberation
Coping and adjustment	Strategic resistance and action	Social policy change/ revolution
Interpersonal capacity	Community capacity	Sociopolitical capacity

Note: Examples marked * were included in this study.

direction alone; collaboration with other social science disciplines is essential. Table 4.3 provides examples of how conceptual integration might occur, and how this study makes a contribution. By reading across the rows some of the conceptual similarities among disciplines become evident. The last row shows the three levels of capacity that Ginwright (2002) describes as "youth development outcomes." They help to connect the columns in the table to practical ways of thinking about youth development. Note that until psychology expands its level of analysis, sociopolitical considerations remain difficult to consider. Similarly, until the other social sciences noted apply their ideas to work on the front line with individuals and small groups, their concepts are of limited value in youth work.

What Implications Do the Findings Have for Social Policy on Youth Development?

Opportunities in Civic Education: Federal Youth Policy and Foundation Funding. The existing windows of opportunity are not wide open, but there are opportunities nonetheless. The most obvious opportunities come under the headings of youth civic engagement and service learning. As a whole, U.S. citizens tend to be apolitical, distrustful, and disengaged from politics, and the new generation of young voters, by all accounts, need engagement. Only about 50% of the electorate bothers to cast ballots, even in significant national elections (State Stats, 1996; Putnam, 2000). Furthermore, over one-third of eligible voters were not registered to vote in the 2000 presidential election. Statistics such as these make the United States second to last in voting behavior among major democracies (Putnam, 2000). It is not surprising, then, that participation in activities that are more demanding than voting, such as working on a political campaign, was even lower—16% in 1998. The political socialization literature has consistently found that young people follow the path of their parents when it comes to political behavior, and our data in this study supports this: we found that youth activism was associated with parental activism. In contrast to decreases in political behavior, the statistics on volunteering are more positive: young people see service work as more likely to produce tangible results and personal outcomes. Fifty-three percent of surveyed 18- to 25-year-olds said they volunteered on a regular basis (National Association of Secretaries of State, 2000).

Foundations are another sector to target for policy change; some of the major ones have put substantial resources behind conventional forms of political participation such as voting. In 2003, the Pew Charitable Trust (PCT) funded 97 grants on "supporting civic life" worth a total of over $38 million. This window of opportunity requires a broad definition of civics, but as the PCT notes, "Engagement takes a wide variety of satisfying and useful forms." The term *civic engagement* also has the advantage of name recognition among traditional youth-serving institutions. Watts and Flanagan (in press) have called for "pushing the envelope on youth civic engagement: so that it includes youth organizing and other social justice work with youth." More specifically, the PCT notes the following:

> Art inspires, informs and often challenges us to see our world in new ways.... The health and welfare of Americans is the concern of all, because protection of and support for society's most vulnerable individuals and families is the acid test of responsible civic stewardship. Voting is the life-blood of a thriving democracy.... When citizens can actually visit and see for themselves the documents that established our nation's principles and the icons that have come to symbolize these ideals, they may be inspired to become more active in contemporary policy and political debates. (Pew Charitable Trusts, 2005)

Similarly, the White House Task Force on Disadvantaged Youth, in a report commissioned in 1992 and released in 2003 (National Clearinghouse on Families and Youth, 2003), opened the civics window as part of its "Aspirations for Disadvantaged Youth." According to the executive summary of the report (pp. 1–2; emphasis added):

> Our comprehensive Federal response begins with our Vision for Youth in the form of a national youth policy framework. This is an outcome-focused approach designed to express what we as a country want for disadvantaged youth and for all children. Namely, we want them to grow up:

• Healthy and Safe

• Ready for Work, College, and Military Service

• Ready for Marriage, Family, and Parenting

• Ready for Civic Engagement and Service

That civics is mentioned, irrespective of the surrounding political rhetoric, is an indication that policy makers want the idea on the table. Of course, the question is who defines it, and how. One obvious challenge in the current federal climate is to shift the language from a deficit perspective to a strengths perspective. For example, the press release for the Task Force's creation spoke of the "failure" of youth to develop the skills they need for success. More surprising and disturbing was that the Forum on Youth Investment (in conjunction with the Kellogg Foundation and the W. T. Grant Foundation) adopted this language as it described "efforts to address the problems of failure among disadvantaged youth." (Forum for Youth Investment, 2003, p. 1). Because these foundations are major funders of youth initiatives, it is essential that their analysis expand to include the failures of society and the resources youth bring to solving larger social problems.

Opportunities in Educational Policy. One of the key elements of sociopolitical development is social analysis; our findings indicate that it was associated with commitment to societal involvement and, to a lesser extent, with a sense of agency. *Social analysis,* as we defined it for research purposes, is akin to critical consciousness, and critical consciousness is a politicized version of critical thinking (CT). Because critical thinking is seen as central to a quality education among many scholars and educational policy makers, supporting advocates of critical thinking is a way of promoting SPD. Facione, Sánchez, Facione, and Gainen (1995; P. A. Facione also authored a commercialized scale of critical thinking) tell us,

Hardly a college or university in the nation would fail to identify the development of CT as a vital outcome of its core curriculum. Regional and professional accrediting associations have begun to require student assessment measures of CT as a curricular outcome (National League for Nursing, 1990; Western Association of Schools and Colleges, 1990; North Central Association of Colleges and Schools, 1992). In 1990 President [George H. W.] Bush, in concert with the Governors of the 50 States, preeminent among them being Governor Clinton, articulated five national educational goals. Goal 5 states that adult *Americans will possess the knowledge and skills necessary to compete in a global economy and exercise the rights and responsibilities of citizenship.* (p. 2; emphasis added)

Speaking of secondary education in British Columbia, Wright (2003) declares, "The centrality of critical thinking has been impressed upon us in the social studies literature and in curriculum guides for so long that it has taken on motherhood status" (p. 1). There is little doubt that critical thinking, a cousin to critical consciousness and social analysis, provides an opportunity to infuse a progressive version of civic education into schools. For example, the senior author of the present chapter successfully marketed a program to the Chicago public school system, based on the critical thinking (and critical consciousness) skills that were part of his SPD development program for young African American men, called Young Warriors (Watts, Griffith, & Abdul-Adil, 1999; Watts, Abdul-Adil, & Pratt, 2002).

A second opportunity in the field of education is in service learning. According to the National Service Learning Clearinghouse (NSLC), two studies—one regional (Maloy & Wohlleb, 1997) and one national (U.S. Department of Education, 1997)—indicate that 96% of school districts offered service learning opportunities and 84% offered academic credit for this work. About 17% have a service learning requirement and over 12 million young people in grades 6–12 participate. Yearly, about 26% participate "regular[ly]." But to go beyond traditional service work, the definition of *service learning* must be stretched. According to the NSLC, examples of service learning projects include: preserving native plants, designing neighborhood playgrounds, teaching younger children to read, testing the local water quality, creating wheelchair ramps, preparing food for the homeless, developing urban community gardens, starting school recycling programs, and the like. Although the work itself may not have a justice focus, the *analysis* of the work's social context can still contribute to SPD by broadening students' perspective on the work. Service learning in combination with youth leadership development internships in organizations that stress youth organizing can make an even greater impact. For example, the present chapter's junior author successfully codesigned and institutionalized an advanced undergraduate honors course based on service learning. The course primarily consists of undergraduate students of color attending a large, primarily white state university, and promotes systems-level critical analysis and personal reflection. The service component consists of mentoring youth of color from the local black and Latino communities, which are communities from which the college students largely feel disconnected.

The range of associations we found between cultural worldview and SPD suggests that the emergence of multicultural and cultural socialization programs is an opportunity to advance a SPD agenda. Indeed, the Seven Principles of Blackness (*Nguzu Saba*) that are part of the African American celebration of Kwanzaa stress communalism, nationalism, and cultural pride, all of which are related to our construct of "commitment" to societal involvement. Evidence of the benefits of culturally conscious, emancipatory education is emerging in the scholarly research literature (see Potts, 2003).

Finally, the association we have observed between parental and youth activism, which is consistent with the political socialization literature, suggests a window of opportunity with parenting-skills training that is totally unexplored as far as we can determine. Many parents are concerned about the emotional, cognitive, social, moral, spiritual, and physical development of their children, but what of their sociopolitical development? Given the influence parents have on this as well nearly every other aspect of their children's development, it is important that parent training and support programs include sociopolitical and cultural development themes in their curricula.

One challenge in formulating a policy strategy in mainstream institutions is determining how much of the "political" must be retained as we negotiate with these institutions if we are to remain true to the spirit of social justice activism. Social values, youth empowerment, and social justice are at the center of liberation psychology and the whole of the community youth organizing field. At what point do campaigns that have more to do with cleaning up vacant lots or feeding the hungry fall unacceptably short? Is it enough to bring a systems analysis to the work, or must the work itself contribute to social change? The less radical and more pragmatic among us would argue that traditional community service and civic engagement activities can contribute to social change if crafted properly. Theory and research can help us determine which activities move young people toward a commitment to social justice. In any case, it is clear that the youth resources devoted to youth social justice work are miniscule compared to the resources available to community service and civic projects.

We believe the research process itself must move closer to the work of practitioners. Too often the two diverge and fail to inform one another. The study described here is both theoretical and quantitative, but we also have an applied action component involving a partnership with youth. We hope they will help us craft and understand our findings so that their voices are more clearly heard by us, and by the adult policy makers we intend to inform.

References

Bandura, A. (2001). Social cognitive theory: An agentic perspective. *Annual Review of Psychology, 52,* 1–26.

Boykin, A. W., Jagers, R. J., Ellison, C., & Albury, A. (1997). The Communalism Scale: Conceptualization and measurement of an Afrocultural social ethos. *Journal of Black Studies, 27,* 409–418.

Brewer, M. B., & Gardner, W. (1996). Who is this "we"? Levels of collective identity and self representations. *Journal of Personality and Social Psychology, 71,* 83–93.

Corning, A. F., & Myers, D. J. (2002). Individual orientation toward engagement in social action. *Political Psychology, 23*(4), 703–729.

Facione, P. A., Sánchez, C. A., Facione, N. C., & Gainen, J. (1995). The disposition toward critical thinking. *Journal of General Education, 44(1),* 1–25.

Flanagan, C. A. (2004). Volunteerism, leadership, political socialization, and civic engagement. In R. M. Lerner & L. Steinberg (Eds.), *Handbook of adolescent psychology.* New York: Wiley.

Flanagan, C. A. (2003) Developmental roots of political engagement. Political Science and Politics, *36*(2), 257–261.

Forum for Youth Investment. (2003). *All youth, one set of goals: Thoughts on a comprehensive federal response to reduce youth failure and increase youth opportunities recommendations for the White House Task Force on Disadvantaged Youth.* Washington, DC: Forum for Youth Investment.

Freire, P. (1990). *Education for a critical consciousness.* New York: Continuum.

Furnham, A., & Gunter, B. (1984). Just world beliefs and attitudes to the poor. *British Journal of Social Psychology, 23,* 265–269.

Ginwright, S. (2002). Youth Organizing: Expanding possibilities for youth development. *Occasional papers on youth organizing series,* no. 3. Retrieved from www.fcyo.org

Ginwright, S. A., Cammarota, J., & Noguera, P. (in press). Youth, social justice, and communities: Toward a theory of urban youth policy.

Harper, D. J., & Manasse, P. R. (1992). The just world and the Third World: British explanations for poverty abroad. *Journal of Social Psychology, 132*(6), 783–785.

Karenga, M. (1993). *Introduction to black studies* (2nd ed.). Los Angeles: University of Sankore Press.

Keeter, S., Zukin, C., Andolina, M., & Jenkins, K. (2002). *The civic and political health of the nation: A generational portrait.* College Park, MD: University of Maryland Center for Information and Research on Civic Learning and Engagement.

Laird. (2003) p. 19.

Lipkus, I. (1991). The construction and preliminary validation of a global belief in a just world scale and the exploratory analysis of the multidimensional belief in a just world scale. *Personality and Individual Differences, 12*(11), 1171–1178.

Maloy, R., & Wohlleb, B. (1997). Implementing community service in K–12 schools: A report on policies and practices in the eastern region. Amherst, MA: University of Massachusetts School of Education, Eastern Regional Information Center.

Martín-Baró, I. (1994). *Writings for a liberation psychology.* Cambridge, MA: Harvard University Press.

McLaren, P. (2002). *Life in schools: An introduction to critical pedagogy in the foundations of education* (4th ed.). Needham Heights, MA: Allyn & Bacon.

Morgan, W., & Streb, M. (2001). Building citizenship: How student voice in service-learning develops civic values. *Social Science Quarterly, 82*(1), 154–169.

National Association of Secretaries of State. (2000). *New millennium project, part 1: American youth attitudes on politics, citizenship, government, and voting.*

National Clearinghouse on Families and Youth. (2003). *White House Task Force for Disadvantaged Youth.* Silver Spring, MD: National Clearinghouse on Families and Youth.

O'Neill, P., Duffy, C., Enman, M., Blackmer, E., & Goodwin, J. (1988). Cognition and citizen participation in social action. *Journal of Applied Social Psychology, 18*(12), 1067–1083.

Ortega, V. (2000). *Psicología social y liberación en América Latina* [Social psychology and liberation in Latin America]. Mexico City: Universidad Autonoma de Mexico, Unidad de Iztapalapa.

Pancer, M., Pratt, M., & Hunsberger, B. (2000, July). The roots of community and political involvement in Canadian youth. Paper presented at the sixteenth biennial meetings of the International Society for the Study of Behavioral Development, Beijing.

Parker, E. A., Lichtenstein, R. L., Schulz, A. J., Israel, B. A., Steinman, K. J., & James, S. A. (2001). Disentangling measures of individual perceptions of community social dynamics: Results of a community survey. *Health Education & Behavior, 28*(4), 462–486.

Pew Charitable Trusts. (2005). Supporting civic life; Retrieved from http://www. pewtrusts.com/ideas/area_index.cfm?area=3.

Potts, R. (2003). Emancipatory education vs. school-based prevention in African American communities. *American Journal of Community Psychology, 31,* 173–184.

Putnam, R. D. (2000). Bowling alone: The collapse and revival of American community. New York: Touchstone.

Rubin, Z., & Peplau, L. A. (1975). Who believes in a just world? *Journal of Social Issues, 31,* 65–90.

Ruetten, A., von Lengerke, T., Abel, T., Kannas, L., Lueschen, G., Diaz, J. A. R., et al. (2000). Policy, competence and participation: Empirical evidence for a multilevel health promotion model. *Health Promotion International, 15*(1), 35–47.

Sampson, R., Raudenbush, S., & Earls, F. (1997). Neighborhoods and violent crime: A multilevel study of collective efficacy. *Science, 277,* 918–924.

Schulz, A. J., Israel, B. A., Zimmerman, M. A., & Checkoway, B. N. (1995). Empowerment as a multi-level construct: Perceived control at the individual, organizational and community levels. *Health Education Research, 10*(3), 309–327.

Sellers, R. M., Shelton, J. N., Rowley, S., & Chavous, T. M. (1998). Multidimensional model of racial identity: A reconceptualization of African American racial identity. *Personality and Social Psychology, 2*(1), 18–39.

Sherrod, L., Flanagan, C., & Youniss, J. (2002). Dimensions of citizenship and opportunities for youth development: The *what, why, when, where* and *who* of citizenship development. *Applied Developmental Science, 6*(4), 264–272.

Stevenson, H. C. (1994). Validation of the scale of racial socialization for African American adolescents. *Journal of Black Psychology, 20*(4).

Stolle, D., & Hooghe, M. (2002, August). The roots of social capital: The effect of youth experiences on participation and value patterns in adult life. Paper presented at the Annual Meeting of the American Political Science Association, Boston.

U.S. Department of Education, Office of Educational Research and Improvement, National Center for Education Statistics. (1990). *National education longitudinal study of 1988: A profile of the American eighth.*

Verba, S., Schlozman, K. L., & Brady, H. E. (1995). *Voice and equality: Civic voluntarism in American politics.* Cambridge, MA: Harvard University Press.

Watts, R. Unpublished manuscript.

Watts, R., Flanagan, C. (in press). Pushing the envelope on youth civic engagement: a developmental and liberation psychology perspective. *Journal of Community Psychology.*

Watts, R., Griffith, D., & Abdul-Adil, J. (1999). Sociopolitical development as an antidote for oppression: Theory and action. *American Journal of Community Psychology, 27,* 255–272.

Watts, R., Williams, N., & Jagers, R. (2003). Sociopolitical development. *American Journal of Community Psychology, 31*(1–2), 185–194.

Watts, R. J., Abdul-Adil, J. K., & Pratt, M. (2002). Enhancing critical consciousness in young African American men: A psycho-educational approach. *Psychology of Men and Masculinity, 3*(1), 41–50.

Westheimer, J., & Kahne, J. (2003). *Teaching democracy: What schools need to do.* Phi Delta Kappan, 85(1), 34–40, 57–66.

Wright, I. (2003). The Centrality of Critical Thinking in Citizenship Education. *Canadian Social Studies, 38.*

Yates, M., & Youniss, J. (1996). A developmental perspective on community service in adolescence. *Social Development, 5*(1), 85–111.

Youniss, J., & Yates, M. (1997). *Community service and social responsibility in youth.* Chicago: University of Chicago Press.

Zimmerman, M. A., Ramirez-Valles, J., & Maton, K. L. (1999). Resilience among urban African American male adolescents: A study of the protective effects of sociopolitical control on their mental health. *American Journal of Community Psychology, 27*(6).

Zimmerman, M. A., & Rappaport, J. (1988). Citizen participation, perceived control, and psychological empowerment. *American Journal of Community Psychology, 16*(5), 725–750.

Zimmerman, M. A., & Zahniser, J. H. (1991). Refinements of sphere-specific measures of perceived control: Development of a sociopolitical control scale. *Journal of Community Psychology, 19*(2), 189–204.

CHAPTER 5

The Racial Dimensions of Social Capital: Toward a New Understanding of Youth Empowerment and Community Organizing in America's Urban Core

A. A. AKOM

Introduction

I'm standing on a corner in West Oakland. One of my students is telling me the story of a 16-year-old boy who was shot and murdered one block from her house. The week before another young black man was killed in the house behind her backyard. Raymond glides over on his bicycle. Raymond is a thirty something-year-old African-American male. Long and sturdy, he stands six-foot-two with dreadlocks covered in cowrie shells. Raymond is also what Elijah Anderson (1990, p. 69) refers to as an old head—a person who believes it is his job to "teach, support, encourage, and in effect, socialize young men to meet their responsibilities with regard to the work ethic, family life, the law, and decency."[1]

In *Streetwise* (1990, p. 70) Anderson argues, "As economic and social circumstances of the urban ghetto have changed, the traditional old head has been losing prestige and credibility as a role model." This is due to an intergenerational gap between "old heads" and "new old heads." Old heads, as the name implies, are from the civil rights generation. They are people who embody the values of the civil rights movement: "decency," "willingness to sacrifice for their children," and a fundamental belief that "hard work pays off," learned from their experiences during the manufacturing era.

However, "as meaningful employment has become increasingly scarce, drugs more accessible, and crime a way of life for many young black men"

(1990, p. 69), new old heads have begun to emerge. The new old head, according to Anderson, is "younger and may be the product of a street gang making money fast and scorning the law and traditional values" (1990, p. 69). According to Duneier, Anderson's view of urban social change as a movement from the "old head of the formal economy to the new head of the underground economy," while powerful, overlooks the question of what other kinds of mentoring relationships are happening in urban communities in the midst of racial and spatial transformation (Duneier, 1999, p. 40).

Raymond is not a gang banger or a drug dealer. Yet his occupation as a hustler—a person who defies traditional social norms by sometimes working outside of the formal economy, often without the privilege of possessing mainstream educational credentials—places him squarely on the bottom of the new urban economy.[2] Without health care and with little education his presence reminds us that the new old head, more than anything else, is the product of a racialized and highly segregated urban housing and educational system designed to increase low wage labor and feed the growing prison industrial complex.

Yet Raymond cares about young black men. The lessons he imparts—at Raider games, on fishing expeditions, on camping trips—are of local legend. Raymond's influence is rooted in caring not intimidation. Raymond cares enough about black children and youth to give respect and demand that he be respected. Raymond cares enough to avoid senseless violence and instill a sense of discipline and self-worth in young black men because "it's the right thing to do." By working outside the formal economy and providing a level of social support and personal encouragement not found in many urban educational institutions, it is possible that Raymond affects the lives of young black men more than he might if he took a job as a local school teacher in an apartheid-like educational system designed to reproduce social inequality and racial hierarchy.

Raymond's "hood habitus" (use of black English and slang, Hip Hop style of dress, knowledge of local history, "streetwiseness," and commitment to mentor some of the most downtrodden segments of a heterogeneous black community) contributes to his ability to mentor "at risk youth" marginalized by mainstream American institutions.[3] Raymond's commitment to teach black youth how to critically resist and navigate a highly visible racial hierarchy suggests that there are alternative models to the old head–new head, decent-street binary presented by Anderson; and that perhaps there is a dynamic, multidirectional, contradictory social praxis happening on the ground level that heretofore had been undertheorized–because the truth of the matter is that most of the action takes place somewhere in-between.

With this in mind, this essay seeks to illuminate the racial dimensions of social capital. More specifically, I examine how racially explicit experiences and practices are not explicitly conceptualized as racial by the leading theorist of social capital (Pierre, 2006). Instead, racially explicit practices are coded as cultural or social with little or no attention to structural inequalities (Pierre, 2004). By using cultural rather than structure as an explanation of the subordinate position of blacks, social capital theory tends to reduce the African American experience to a set of stereotypes reminiscent of the culture of poverty thesis (Gomez, 2004).

This chapter offers a framework for understanding this form of cultural racism by asking two central questions. First, how do seemingly non-racial theories like social capital simultaneously mark youth of color as "highly visible" (in terms of race and class) while at the same time rendering our unique forms of social and cultural capital as pathological at best and invisible at worst? Second, how do social scientists like Anderson and Putnam divorce processes of social and cultural capital from processes of racialization and institutionalized racism?

Social capital theory, in its current academic deployment, recodes structural notions of racial inequality as primarily cultural, social, and human capital processes and interactions. Such a "post-racial" reformulation, where issues of racism and racial discrimination operate just beneath the surface, are problematic for at least two reasons. First, recoding allows racialized social practices and public policy to remain unmarked, invisible, and unnamed, effectively placing the burden of social change on communities of color, while masking social capital theory as race neutral, which continues to perpetuate white privilege. Second, recoding fails to illuminate the ways in which race, space, place, gender, and sexual orientation influence both the accumulation of social capital and its efficacy as a mobility resource.

These questions are central to the emerging field of youth development because they reflect tensions between how we theorize social capital and urban youth and what young people are actually experiencing on the ground level. While time and space considerations do not permit a thorough review of the enormous literature on social capital, I begin by briefly reviewing its origins and applications. In particular, I pay careful attention to how the term's uses and meanings have changed over time in relation to community youth development theory and practice. Surprisingly, the concept of social capital is used widely in this emerging field (especially in the form of civic engagement); however, the field as a whole lacks definitional clarity with respect to the racial dimensions of social capital, how social capital is measured, and when social capital began to theoretically develop.

The Theoretical Origins of Social Capital

"How are social capital and social justice related?" (Seagert, Thompson, & Warren, 2001, XV). Ironically, western scholarship traces the introduction of social capital, as a theoretical concept, to the work of L. Judson Hanifan, a young progressive educator and social reformer who worked on overcoming poverty in rural Appalachia nearly a century ago (Seagert, Thompson, & Warren, 2001). According to Hanifan, "the individual is helpless socially, if left to himself" (1916, p. 130). Hanifan continues, "If he comes into contact with his neighbor, and they with other neighbors, there will be an accumulation of social capital, which may immediately satisfy his social needs and which may bear a social potentiality sufficient to the substantial improvement of living conditions in the whole community."

In the years since Hanifan introduce the concept of social capital, a deluge of scholarship has emerged seeking to operationalize the term and contextualize its meaning. Surprisingly, however, much of this scholarship does not examine the ways in which race is implicated in structuring everyday life and the politics of identity in low-income communities. For example, the notion of social capital developed in France, by Pierre Bourdieu, offers no specific articulated notion of racial justice, and does not name the racial hierarchy that informs local realities (i.e., in 2006 there was only one black senator and there has never been a black president; thus, even for upwardly mobile blacks there is a glass ceiling, let alone for the black poor who are more structurally vulnerable). Instead, Bourdieu's understanding of social capital is part of a broader theory of capital that characterizes class positionality, as absent from, and unconnected to, racial privilege. According to Bourdieu, social capital is "the aggregate of the actual or potential resources which are linked to possession of a durable network of more or less institutionalized relationships of mutual acquaintance or recognition" (Bourdieu, 1985, p. 248).

Bourdieu's definition is important because it highlights two key processes that are overlooked in contemporary discussions of social capital and youth development. First, he makes explicit the importance of institutionalized power in relation to helping individuals or groups achieve social mobility. Second, he emphasized social capital's connection with processes of social inclusion and exclusion.[4]

For Bourdieu, microprocesses of inclusion and exclusion are some of the most invisible, pervasive, and effective forms of marking social and cultural distance, leveraging privilege, and creating and maintaining unequal access to institutional resources (especially when combined with other forms of capital). By themselves, inclusive social networks can lead directly to economic resources (well-paying jobs, subsidized loans, and cheaper goods and services). Conversely, social exclusion (or lack of social capital in the form of social networks) can lead to social isolation, decreased opportunities, and more expensive goods and services (Bourdieu, 1985).

Over the years, Bourdieu's conception of social capital has been criticized for failing to incorporate an explicit understanding of the dialectics of race into his theory of power, and for largely concentrating on white middle-class cultural competencies, norms, networks, and styles while underemphasizing the cultural competencies, norms, networks, and styles of individuals and groups form different racial and socioeconomic locations.[5] In its totality, Bourdieu's framework is far more complex than what can be stated here, yet his conceptualization of power (i.e., norms, networks, and the negotiation of public and private space) as non-racial ignores a complicated set of historical realities that serve to reify and reinforce the existing racial hierarchy.

In an effort to understand how racial practice, racial praxis, and racial privilege occur within the broader dimensions of historical and contemporary white supremacy, economist Loury was the first to develop, extend, and racialize the notion of social capital in the United States. Loury's work emerged in the context of his larger critique of neoclassical theories of race and income inequality (DeFilippis, 2001; Portes, 1998). Loury argued that traditional economic theories relied too heavily on Adam Smith's (1993) conceptualization of individualism, whereby an individual's chance to succeed or fail depended solely on his innate ability. Loury's work invoked both the literature on the intergenerational transmission of income inequality as well as an analysis of private wealth to illustrate the role of race in social mobility. According to Loury,

> The merit notion that, in a free society, each individual will rise to the level justified by his or her competence conflicts with the observation that no one travels that road entirely alone ... social origin has an obvious and important effect on the amount of resources that is ultimately invested ... It may thus be useful to employ a concept of "social capital" to represent the consequences of social position in facilitating acquisition of the standard human capital characteristics. (1977, p. 176)

Loury's work is important when analyzing the ways in which urban youth, like Raymond, resist and respond to urban decay and economic deprivation, for at least two reasons. First, Loury takes seriously the racial dimensions of social capital by arguing that racial subordination is one the most important sociological and economic variables to explain African Americans' current and past social standing. Second, Loury situates the actions of individuals in the context of their local conditions. In other words, he conceptualizes the behaviors of urban adults and youth within the political economy of urban communities while taking into consideration the historic racialization of federal, state, and local policies aimed at limiting the democratic participation of people of color (Ginwright & Cammarota, Introduction, this volume; Oliver & Shapiro, 1995).[6] For Loury, "no one goes to school in isolation from the context in which that school is located, administered, or funded" (DeFilippis 2001, p. 783).[7] Loury's racially based critique provides an important alternative to the narrowly individualistic and myopic understanding of the culture of poverty discourse that has managed to reinvent itself and dominate much of today's social commentary on urban communities (Gomez, 2004).

Race, Poverty, and Social Capital in Urban Communities

All social discourses, particularly those about black people and poverty, are engaged, according to Pierre (2006), in the "ideological struggle to define identity and construct community" (4). In asking how mentorship in urban communities is related to the development of social capital in the "hood," it is important to reflect on the poor black men and women who live in West Oakland struggling to define and construct community.

With this in mind, on Tuesday Narobi and I are standing in front of an abandoned house used for illegal dumping when Narobi, a fifty-six-year-old black parent, begins to read the neighborhood for me. According to Goffman (1959) reading involves paying close attention to a variety of symbols that people display, then using those symbols to interpret and define a social situation. In reading the neighborhood Narobi begins to construct a community identity for me: a *we* who fought to get diesel emissions out of the air, a *we* who mortgaged and lost our homes to buy this church…a *we* who sees illegal dumping not just as another eyesore, but as a threat to the built environment. He says:

> You see that vacant lot over there … it used to be a church…a place of worship for Godsakes … and now look at it … (the narrow lot is littered with trash … a toilet boil … beer cans … needles … and rusted out auto parts …) "Now look at it … it's a Goddamn dump … with a toilet boil in the middle … isn't that fitting … Have you ever been to Africa or a third-world country?

> AA: Yea …

> N: And when you were there didn't it make you sick to see all the trash in the streets … kids playin' in filth … that's what it's like livin' in this neighborhood … It's filthy … you know what I'm sayin'… I mean here in West Oakland we don't live by the NIMBY principle … Nawh … we're forced to live by the PIBBY principle …

> AA: What's the PIBBY principle?

> N: (He laughs) The PIBBY principle stands for Put in Blacks Back Yard … Get it … white people say NIMBY out of one side of their mouth … but out of the other they say PIBBY … So whenever you hear of NIMBY think of PIBBY too … cause there's two sides to every coin …

Narobi's PIBBY principle doesn't just name a local problem. The potency of garbage as a symbol of disorder and a threat to black communities is nothing new. In fact, there is growing empirical evidence that indicates that toxic-waste dumps, municipal landfills, garbage incinerators, and similar toxic facilities are not randomly scattered across the American landscape—rather there is a strong association between race and the location of hazardous-waste facilities (Bullard, 1990). According to a 1995 study by the National Law Journal:

> There is a racial divide in the way the U.S. government cleans up toxic waste sites and punishes polluters. White communities see faster action, better results, and stiffer penalties than communities where blacks, Latinos, and other minorities live. This unequal protection often occurs whether the community is wealthy or poor.

Narobi doesn't need government statistics to illuminate his lived experience. He has two asthmatic children from the airborne toxins circulating in his neighborhood. In his own words, "there's not a day that goes by that I don't think about the toxic waste in this community."

For over a year I followed Narobi and other members of the Citizens for West Oakland (CWO), a neighborhood organization dedicated to improving living conditions for Oakland's poorest community. During this time I have witnessed this volunteer organization grow into one the strongest community-based organizations in West Oakland.

Closer examination of CWO activities demonstrates that in addition to serving as a community watchdog and information agency, they organized a number of public service activities to increase the social capital supplied to the community:

- Rehabilitating and cleaning up dysfunctional or abandoned housing stock;
- Having bi-annual Clean Air festivals and monthly neighborhood cleanups;
- Monitoring and tracking diesel emissions in West Oakland.

The presence of the CWO as a form of informal social control to protect segments of the black community illustrates the ways in which black communities are not solely pathological or dysfunctional and how spatial context, racial justice, and poverty levels are important factors when measuring levels of social capital (as civic engagement) in low-income communities. According to Portney and Berry (1997), "the participation rates of low socioeconomic status (SES) residents in predominantly African American neighborhoods is almost twice that of low SES residents of low minority population neighborhoods" (p. 637). Similarly, Assensoh (2002), focusing on race, poverty, and neighborhood composition, finds that civic engagement (in the form of community meeting attendance) is higher in high-poverty, low-income areas. These findings indicate that "residence in concentrated poverty neighborhoods can facilitate social capital and civic engagement by spurring citizens to seek political redress for existent inequalities" (Assensoh, 2002, p. 887), even though those living in black urban communities must negotiate a set of local relationships "dominated by white capital and white lending institutions ... (and) by the cultural products of the white West" (Mills, 1998, p. 102).

These racialized relationships work to underdeveloped social capital in black urban communities both in theory and in practice. In theory, research on race and urban poverty overwhelmingly focuses on those areas of black urban life that are pathological, dysfunctional, and differ from the mainstream. Terms such as "poverty pimp" and "welfare queen" are bantered about while the majority of poor black community members are "creating new political and social formations that are invisible to social scientists looking for social capital in all the old places (national data sets) and in all the traditional forms" (Cohen, 2001, p. 270; Sullivan, 1997).

In other words my findings point toward the development of a new model of social capital that takes into account social practices that, due to processes of racialization and stigmatization, are usually ignored or discounted by the mainstream. Such a framework will analyze the lives of Raymond and Narobi through a broader lens that will include a variety of context-dependent variables missing from most current models of social capital, such as racial and economic inequality, poverty rates, homeownership, unemployment, underemployment, types of employment, segregation indices, youth participation, number of community-based organizations, and some measure of community history, to name a few (Bedolla & Scola, 2004, p. 14). By developing more racially and cultural nuanced measures of social capital, we deepen our understanding of the various forms of social capital at work in low-income communities, while at the same time ensure that we do not dilute the concept to such an extent that it is rendered meaningless (Portes, 1998).

Race, Youth, and Civil Society

One way to more precisely conceptualize social capital and civic engagement in urban communities is through community activism among youth. Cohen (2001) argues that Putnam and others overlooked community-based struggles largely because they focused their analysis on national databases of political participation and did not spend any time, in the "hood," with urban youth. For those of us who do spend time with urban youth, we know that young people in urban communities rarely have the power to make decisions about policies that shape their lives, yet activism remains an important form of social capital in the urban milieu.

Saegert, Thompson, and Warren (2001) acknowledge the challenges associated with conceptualizing social capital in the context of poor communities. Their edited volume is important because it discusses how urban youth, constrained and restrained by racial subordination and white privilege in most social spaces, come to understand different articulations of social capital, in different community settings, how social capital evolves over time, and how it is connected to different racial projects—of labor, education, the media, the police, etc. Yet, even though Saegert, Thompson, and Warren (2001) do not declare, as Putnam does, that social capital is declining in urban communities, they do avoid an analysis of how race itself shapes organizing strategies, group solidarity, collective action, and grassroots mobilization in poor communities. The ethnographic vignettes of Raymond and Narobi, as well as "thick descriptions" such as Gregory's ethnography of the Lefrak community in Queens New York, serve as important counternarratives that remind us of the continuing significance of race in relation to social capital, precisely because they hightlight how disputes over racial meanings can foster political networks, engage residents in civic affairs, and spark activism in communities among youth and adults.

As it stands now many of the leading theories of social capital are silent on the issue of race, ignoring the fact that young people in poor communities contribute to rich social networks (i.e., membership in voluntary associations, trust in political authorities, cooperation for mutual benefit). These networks often exist as a way for youth to learn how to resist and cope with persistent racial marginalization. These are significant omissions, and limiting factors in the potential uses of social capital frameworks in community youth development theory and practice because Americans in general, and youth in particular, "define their core political identities in terms of their race, gender, religion, ethnicity, and culture" (Smith, 1997, p. 4; DeFilippis, 2001, p. 791).

Thus, the important question is not, Has social capital in the form of civic engagement declined for urban youth? but rather, What conditions promote or inhibit different articulations of social capital and why?" And what role do race, age, gender, and sexual orientation play in the development or underdevelopment of social capital in poor black communities and other communities of color (Ginwright, 2006)?

Works by Aguilar–San Juan; Duncan-Andrade; Flores-González, Rodríguez, and Rodríguez-Muñiz; Kwon; HoSang; and others (all in this volume) demonstrate that urban communities are rich sites of social capital and civic engagement, particularly among youth of color. This body of work highlights a disjuncture between the experiences of urban youth who are mobilizing in inner-city neighborhoods, and the prescriptions for urban youth development coming from "fragmented models of community action and youth agency" (Ginwright & Cammarota, this volume). This disjuncture has led funders and practitioners to begin questioning the utility of social capital frameworks that do not bring issues of identity (race, class, gender, sexual orientation), and political organizing to the forefront of community youth development theory and practice (Mohamed & Wheeler, 2001).

Conclusion

My characterization of social capital theory and practice, as a process thoroughly structured by constructions of race, racial privilege, racial hierarchy, intersectionalities of class, and the politics of identity, is itself a radical claim. In the current environment of "postracial," "colorblind," "cultureblind," and "meritocratic" theories of identity and politics, where notions of racism (structural or cultural) are immediately dismissed as remnants of the past, it is more important than ever to understand the racial dimensions of social capital. Given the dearth of research and analysis on race and social capital it is important to remind those who study urban communities (as well as suburban and rural communities) to include race and racism in their analysis of human capital, cultural and social capital, and political economy. Contemporary scholarship on social capital is explicitly implicated in the process of "conceptual and epistemological de-racialization" of social capital theory (Pierre, 2006, p. 13).

A new model needs to be developed that directly addresses "global white supremacy as a political system ... a particular kind of polity, so structured, as to advantage whites" (Mills, 1998, pp. 99–100). This model should incorporate a broader understanding of social capital that pays careful attention to: (1) race, racism, and processes of racialization; (2) identity-based frameworks; (3) context dependency; and (4) issues of power within and outside the ghetto. We have to move to the point where the very act of naming and mapping processes of racial subordination is not particularly radical or activist, but rather, part of a collective, normalized goal of worldwide black emancipation. I am hopeful.

Notes

I wish to thank Shawn Ginwright for his belief and patience in this project and the invaluable research of my students Ashely Moore and Jeannine Villasenor.

1. Anderson also notes that there are female oldheads whose responsibility it is to socialize young men and women.
2. At times Raymond vacillates between working odd jobs, working as a handyman, and selling stolen goods that he "does not steal himself" for a living. At the same time Raymond does not believe that "the youth should steal," and "values an education that teaches about black history and culture."
3. The concept of "Hood Habitus" evolved from my work in low-income communities with the Nation of Islam, as well as through conversations with one of my graduate students, Rashawn Ray, at the University of Indiana, Bloomington.
4. According to Bourdieu, "the volume of the social capital possessed by a given agent ... depends on the size of the network of connections he can effectively mobilize and on the volume of the capital (economic, cultural, or symbolic) possessed in his own right by each of those to whom he is connected" (1986, p. 249).
5. Even though Bourdieu developed his theory of forms of capital in Algeria and France, the framework still lacks a dynamic understanding of race and culture.
6. Ginwright & Cammarota (this volume) refer to the "hostile laws and unfair policies" that African Americans (of all ages) endure as a part of a "second-class citizenry."
7. This seems to be stating the obvious, but apparently this is still not self-evident to human capitalist theorists who continue to dominant labor theories in American

economics. As a point of fact, the idea of meritocracy has become even more widely accepted in the popular imagination since Loury first presented his piece.

References

Anderson, E. (1990). Streetwise: Race, class, change in an urban community. Chicago: University of Chicago Press.

Anderson, E. (1999). *Code of the street: Decency, violence and the moral life of the inner city.* New York: W. W. Norton.

Assensoh, Y. (2002). Inner city contexts, church attendance, and African-American political participation. Journal of Politics, *63*, 886–901.

Bedolla, L. G., & Scola, B. (2004). Race, social relations, and the study of social capital. Paper presented at the 2004 meeting of the American Political Science Association, Chicago.

Bonilla-Silva, E. (2001). *White supremacy and racism in the post–civil rights era.* Boulder, CO: Lynne Rienner.

Bourdieu, P. (1980). *The logic of practice.* Stanford, CA: Stanford University Press.

Bourdieu, P. (1985). The forms of capital. In J. Richardson (Ed.), *Handbook of theory and research for the sociology of education* (pp. 241–258). New York: Greenwood.

Bullard. R. (1990). Dumping in Dixie: Race, class, and environmental quality. Boulder, CO: West View Press.

Carpini, M.X.D. (2000). Gen. com. Youth, civic engagement, and the new information environment. Political Communication, 17, 341–349.

Cohen, C. (2001). Social capital intervening institutions and political power. In Social capital in poor communities. S. Seagert, P. Thompson, & M. Warren (Eds.). New York: Russell Sage.

DeFilippis, J. (2001). The myth of social capital in community development. *Fannie Mae Foundation, Housing Policy Debate, 12*(4), 781–806.

Duneier, M. (1999). Sidewalk. New York: Farrar, Straus, and Giroux.

Edwards, B., & Foley, M. (1998). Is it time to disinvest in social capital? Unpublished manuscript.

Gambone, M. A., Yu, H. C., Lewis-Charp, H., Sipe, C. Y., & Lacoe, J. (2004). *A comparative analysis of community youth development strategies.* Oakland, CA: Social Policy Research Associates.

Ginwright, S. (2003). Youth organizing: Expanding possibilities for youth development. *Funders Collaborative on Youth Organizing, 3*, 4–17.

Ginwright, S. (2006). *Toward a politics of relevance: race, resistance and african american youth activism.* http://www.ya.ssrc.org

Goffman, E. (1959). *The Presentation of self in everyday life.* Garden City, NY: Doubleday.

Gomez, M. (2004). *The nine lives of the culture of poverty.* Unpublished manuscript.

Hanifan, L.J. (1916). The rural school community center. *Annals of the American Academy of Political and Social Science, 67*, 130–138.

Lavelle, M., & Coyle, M. (1992). Unequal protection: The racial divide in environmental law. *National Law Journal*, September *21*, 1–2.

Lopez, M. L., & Stack, C. (2001). Social capital and the culture of power: lessons from the field. In *Social capital in poor communities*. S. Seagert, J.P. Thompson, & M. Warren (Eds.). New York: Russell Sage.

Loury, G. (1977). *A dynamic theory of racial and income differences.* In P. Wallace & A. LaMond (Eds.), *Women, minorities, and employment discrimination* (pp. 153–188). Lexington, MA: Heath.

McLain, P. (2003). Social capital and diversity: An introduction. *Perspectives on Politics, 1*, 101–102.

Mills. C. (1998). Blackness visible: Essay on philosophy and race. Ithaca: Cornell University Press.

Mohamed, I., & Wheeler, W. (2001). *Broadening the bounds of youth development.* Chevy Chase, MD: Innovation Center for Community and Youth Development/ Ford Foundation.

Oliver, M., & Shapiro, T. (1995). *Black wealth white wealth: A new perspective on racial inequality.* New York: Routledge.

Patillo, M. (1999). Black picket fences: Privilege and peril among the black middle class. Chicago: University of Chicago Press.

Pierre, J. (2004). Black immigrants in the United States and the "cultural narratives" of ethnicity. In Identities: global studies in culture and power (pp. 141–170). New York: Routledge.

Pierre, J. (2006). Activist groundings or grounding for activism?: The study of racialization as a site of political engagement. Unpublished manuscript.

Pittman, K. (2000). Balancing the equation: Communities supporting youth, youth supporting communities. *Community Youth Development Journal, 1,* 19–24.

Portes, A. (1998). Social capital: Its origins and applications in modern sociology. *Annual Review of Sociology, 24,* 1–24.

Portney, K., & Berry, J. (1997). Mobilizing minority communities: Social capital and participation in urban neighborhoods. *American Behavioral Scientists, 40,* 632–644.

Putnam, R. (1993a). *Making democracy work: Civic traditions in modern Italy.* Princeton, NJ: Princeton University Press.

Putnam, R. (1993b). The prosperous community: Social capital and public life. American Prospect, Spring, 35–42.

Putnam, R. (1995). Bowling alone: America's declining social capital. *Journal of Democracy, 6,* 65–78.

Putnam, R. (1998). Foreword. Housing Policy Debate 9(1), v–viii.

Putnam, R. (2000). *Bowling alone: The collapse and revival of American community.* New York: Simon and Schuster.

Rodney, W. (1972). *How Europe underdeveloped Africa.* Washington DC: Howard University Press.

Seagert, S., Thompson, J. P., & Warren, M. (Eds.) (2001). Social capital and poor communities. Ford Foundation Series on Asset Building. New York: Russell Sage.

Skocpol, T. (1996, March–April). Unraveling from above. *American Prospect,* pp. 20–25.

Skocpol. T., & Fiorina, M. (Eds.). (1999). *Civic engagement in American democracy.* Washington, DC: Brookings Institution.

Smith, A. (1993). *The wealth of nations.* New York: Oxford University Press. Original work published 1776.

Smith. R. (1997). *Civic ideals: Competing visions of citizenship in U.S. history.* New Haven, CT: Yale University Press.

Smith, R. M. (2003). *Stories of peoplehood: The politics and morals of group membership.* Cambridge: Cambridge University Press.

Stack, C. (1974). *All our kin.* New York: Harper & Row.

Sullivan, L. (1997). Hip-hop nation: The undeveloped social capital of black urban America. *National Civic Review, 86*(3), 235–243.

Wacquant, L. J. D. (1996). Negative social capital: State breakdown and social destitution in America's urban core. *Netherlands Journal of the Built Environment,* Special issue on Ghettos in Europe and America, Burgers, J., & van Kempen, R. (Eds.).

Yates, M., & Youniss, J. (1998). Community service and political identity development in adolescence. *Journal of Social Issues, 54*(3), 493–512.

Section II
Learning for Justice: Innovative Pedagogies for Justice in Schools

Why should students seek to achieve higher grades and test scores and pursue the rewards that are ostensibly available to those who are academically "successful"? With public officials and educational leaders working with considerable intensity to raise student achievement and improve academic outcomes for students across the United States, it is amazing that very little thought has gone into this question. There appears to be an unstated assumption that all youth want to achieve and readily accept the educational goals that have been laid out before them as the end products of academic success: access to college, a good job, a middle-class life.

Yet is this assumption accurate? Can young people be motivated to achieve in school and perform well on standardized tests by hanging the threat of failure over their heads with high-stakes exams? Some might argue that even if young people do not embrace the goals that have been adopted by policy makers, particularly since the advent of the No Child Left Behind Act, then such policies can be used to coerce young people into following its mandates. If pursuit of the rewards—access to college and financial security in adulthood—is not sufficient as a motivator, then perhaps fear of failure, in the form of unemployment, a life of poverty, social ostracism, and permanent membership in the underclass will do the trick.

Does it work? Are the assumptions about student motivation that appear to guide educational policy at the state and federal levels accurate? Are young people merely passive participants in an educational process controlled by adults—governors, legislators, administrators, and teachers—or do they have agency, the capacity to make choices and take actions that influence the character of the education they receive?

If the answer to the latter question is yes, and most adults who have worked with young people or who have a vague recollection of their own youth may be inclined to venture that it is, then perhaps we are approaching the task of improving education in the United States through a strategy that is fundamentally flawed. If the strategy assumes that it is the work of adults that will lead to higher levels of achievement among youth but that young people have no role other than to show up at school and do what they are told, then perhaps this strategy needs to be reexamined, if not entirely revised.

It may well be the case that for middle-class and affluent youth, assumptions about student motivations to achieve are accurate. Children from families headed by professional, college-educated parents may indeed be more likely to accept the notion that pursuit of high levels of achievement is a worthwhile goal, and therefore the sacrifices necessary—long hours of study, putting up with boring and difficult classes, weekends spent in SAT preparation classes, and the like—are a necessary means to a desirable end. The fact that many, though clearly not all, middle-class and affluent youth go along with the educational strategy that currently guides educational policy suggests that perhaps for these students the underlying assumptions are accurate.

Yet what about the remainder of America's youth—those who are poor, nonwhite, and who have no guarantee that hard work in school will lead to a middle-class life? Do these assumptions work for them? Does the fear of failure serve as an effective means to motivate? Are they likely to be moved by the possibility that education will serve as their ticket to a better life?

Undoubtedly for some low-income youth of color, the assumptions underlying current education policy do hold true. There are many examples of young people who defy the odds and demonstrate tremendous resilience and perseverance in the pursuit of opportunity through education. This is particularly true for many immigrant youth who are often more likely to demonstrate a strong work ethic and are more willing to comply with school rules and show deference to adult authority figures (Ogbu, 1988; Suarez-Orozco, 2002). However, there are also many other young people who clearly do not. These are the students who drop out or are pushed out of school. They are also the ones who show up at school regularly but who do little more than passively go through the motions of "doing" school. More often than not they are bored—not with learning, necessarily, but with the schooling they have been subjected to.

The authors in this section demonstrate through research carried out with young people both inside and outside of school that engaging young people in learning need not be an onerous chore if educators take time to understand the interests, hopes, and dreams of urban youth. These authors remind us that when learning is made relevant to young people's lives, the educational process is more meaningful and constitutes a richer context for active student engagement. The central element of this task is a recognition that many young people can and must be actively engaged in their education if they are to succeed academically.

In chapter 6, David Stovall's ethnography of a Chicago community's struggle to create a community school painstakingly chronicles the vitality of youth engagement in democratic decision making. Partnering with adult community members, Stovall illustrates how young people can rupture seemingly unyielding barriers to educational change. While Stovall focuses on what occurs outside of the boundaries of schools, Ernest Morrell examines in chapter 7, how young people in urban communities can be trained as "critical researchers" who examine the conditions in their communities. Morrell argues, through a well-documented case study of youth who participated in a summer seminar with college students, that the process of engaging in student-centered, community-based research taps into students' funds of knowledge, increases students' sense of efficacy, and helps students to develop literacies of power. Similarly, in chapter 8, Jeffrey M. R. Duncan-Andrade focuses primarily on pedagogical strategies that highlight and facilitate critical literacy among urban youth. Duncan-Andrade argues that this pedagogical approach presents powerful pathways to develop student agency as they confront conditions of urban social inequality.

In chapter 9, Korina M. Jocson offers us insight into how poetry can influence how urban youth make sense of their social world and shape their identities. Through a case study of young people who participated in a poetry writing program, Jocson demonstrates how poetry serves as a "form of cultural politics and reveals the power of words as youth make sense of their lives and their agentive roles in communities."

CHAPTER 6

From Hunger Strike to High School: Youth Development, Social Justice, and School Formation

DAVID STOVALL

This chapter seeks to identify the attempt of two communities (one Mexican American, one African American, both low-income) to authentically involve young people in the development and planning process of a community high school. Recognizing the adverse conditions faced by African American and Latinoa high school students (constant marginalization at the hands of school teachers and administrators, criminalization through school policy, high suspension rates, low graduation rates, etc.), this chapter documents the necessity of youth empowerment in creating a neighborhood high school. Having operated as an active participant in the process, the author utilizes the tenets of participatory action research to discuss the challenge and struggle to authentically include young people in the process of neighborhood school development. Throughout the progression of the initiative, participants realized that one of the most viable means through which to foster sustainable community collaboration is a practice that includes young people in the decision-making process. For the duration of the initiative (from the initial hunger strike to the submission of the proposal for the high school to central office), young people were central to dialogue and coalition building, highlighting commonalities between two cultures with distinct histories and realities.

A Brief Note on Participatory Action Research and Method

Throughout the process of developing this chapter, I have operated on two specific fronts: as participant researcher and as concerned community member. In these spaces I have consciously chosen political spaces that may make the chapter appear "unsettling." However, for the purpose of this document, such disquiet is important in completing the required inquiry. Throughout the process I continually challenge myself to study my praxis (theory plus practice) in the hope of working in concert with community members, community organizations, teachers, students, and administrators to develop a community high school. Echoing the sentiment of Michael Apple (1994), I understand my work as raising "intensely personal questions about ourselves (myself)—as raced, gendered, and classed actors—and where we fit into the relations of power, of domination and subordination, in our societies" (Apple, quoted in Gitlin, 1994, p. x).

As an African American teacher/professor with a background in community organizing, I am intimately acquainted with the relations of power among municipal bodies (in this case an urban public school system), community organizations, and community residents. Such research is "grounded" in my experience as a community organizer and the transition to high school social studies teacher and college professor. In so doing, the attempt is to document my experiences as a member of a design team for one of the high schools as our proposal for the school awaits approval from central office.

Situating myself in the position of researcher and concerned community member can complicate matters in terms of research. Participatory action research locates me as insider and outsider, depending on the situation. Wearing my "prejudice on my sleeve" in this case would seem a dangerous exercise, as qualitative researchers are often chided for incorporating data often deemed "too interpretive" to quantify. Nevertheless, in the attempt to present a representative account of my participation and observations, the attempt is to "test out the principles of reflection and action upon the world in order to transform it" (Crotty, quoted in Tickle , 2001, p. 346). As a concerned community member, I made numerous visits to the hunger strike site and also was one of the first persons outside of the hunger strikers to be consulted on issues of curriculum. Consequently, it is my belief that research can be "reconceptualized so that it can more powerfully act of some of the most persistent and important problems of our schools, namely those surrounding issues of race, class and gender" (Gitlin, 1994, p. ix). The following account, in documenting the inclusion of young people in the planning of a school, is an explicit attempt to discuss the intersection of race, class, and power.

Documenting such events as a participant required significant dependence on field notes and tape-recordings. Along with field notes taken from meetings, interviews with community members have been transcribed to provide context to the events leading to the inclusion of young people in the initiative. Coupled with the gathering of primary and secondary documents (community flyers, requests for proposals, historical accounts, newspaper clippings, the addresses of related websites, memoranda between community organizations, etc.), the following sections attempt to provide synthesis between oral and printed qualitative data. From the organizing that led to the hunger strike, to the approval of the high school, the process is multifaceted and requires analysis of the factors that impact youth inclusion.

Beginnings: The Need for Drastic Action

The Mexican American community examined here, on Chicago's southwest side, has been steeped in community action and resistance. From the struggle to develop bilingual education programs in the public schools to assisting in the election of Chicago's first African American mayor, the community of South Lawndale (more commonly known as Little Village hereafter) has a history of community activism. The events leading to the onset of the hunger strike on May 13, 2001 should be understood as part of the continuum of community efforts. Through these efforts we can locate the struggles of a community to gain access to equitable education for its students.

Beginning as early as 1995, members of the Little Village community, through political and grassroots organizing, began to place pressure on the central office of the Chicago Public Schools (CPS) system to create a high school for their neighborhood. Currently, the community is one of the youngest in the city, with 4,000 children of high school age and with only one public high school, which has a capacity for 1,800 students (Nambo et al., 2004, p. 5). Twenty-five percent of the adult residents have incomes below $15,000. Only 17% of Little Village residents have a high school diploma, while 5.5% have college degrees. Adding to these concerns is the fact that the neighborhood high school currently servicing the community has a dropout rate of 17% and a graduation rate of 55%.

Recognizing these issues to be of immediate concern, Little Village community members organized to lobby for a new high school in their neighborhood. After consistent pressure on the school board from the community, $30 million was allocated to build a high school. While the request from residents of Little Village was that a neighborhood school with open enrollment be built, the city of Chicago had set plans to create four selective-enrollment high schools across the city. Selective-enrollment schools, unlike neighborhood schools, require applicants to have a particular composite test score upon entry. In addition, applicants to a selective-enrollment school are not allowed to take the entrance exam if they do not have the required composite score. As the selective enrollment high schools were given first priority, plans for new neighborhood schools were overlooked by the school board's central office. In Little Village, despite the $30 million dollar allocation, no construction took place. Community members, after numerous exchanges with elected officials in the neighborhood, sought to address the problem through the protocols of CPS. Outraged at the decision to build the selective enrollment schools, Little Village residents approached CPS. They were told that the funds originally allocated to build their high school had been spent. Because the funds were nonrenewable, high school construction was postponed indefinitely. After the indefinite postponement, Little Village community members were subsequently told that CPS had come to a final decision not to build a high school.

In response to the CPS decision, members of the Little Village community decided to stage a hunger strike, beginning on May 13, 2001. Protest in the form of a hunger strike was chosen because it demonstrated the seriousness of the community. It was not a decision couched in desperation. Instead, it was an intensely planned strategy to alert CPS of the community's staying power. The hunger strike took place on the site originally planned for the school, which was now named Camp Cesar Chavez after the one-time leader of the United Farm Workers. Because some of them were senior citizens, careful attention was given to the hunger strikers as the days progressed; medical staff remained on-site in case of emergency. Although there were only 14 hunger strikers, community support surpassed the participants' expectations. During the 19 days the community staged related theater events, community rallies, and prayer vigils. All were key in keeping the hunger strikers in good spirits.

Of the 14 strikers, 2 were under the age of 20. One was still in high school at the time, while the other was a college student at a downstate university. Recognizing the importance of young people to the development of the community-led initiative, it was agreed on the part of the hunger strikers that all events following the hunger strike in the planning of the school would include young people. Within this time period the strikers forced CPS to the negotiating table, resulting in the approval of the high school complex originally set for construction in 1998. Within the structure, four schools—one for the visual and performing arts; one for math, science, and technology, one for world languages; and one for social justice—were be housed in the complex, which opened September 6, 2005. Remembering the spirit of the hunger strikers and the participation of young people in the initiative, the original planning committee vowed that the new high school complex would be a space that reflected the core values of democracy, community ownership, self-discipline, flexibility, collaboration, lifelong learning, innovation, accountability, leadership development, cross-cultural respect, efficacy, teamwork, and empowerment. As discussed in later sections, key to the core values was the inclusion of the African American community, as students from two distinct ethnicities and cultural backgrounds converged to create effective schooling.

Organizational Structure: Inclusion and Community Context

Indicative to many community planning/organizing initiatives, groups choose an organizational structure through which to operate. In this case, in addition to the hunger strikers, members of the neighborhood block clubs (along with community residents at large) who supported the hunger strike came together to organize themselves as the school planning committee. With the help of the

Little Village Community Development Organization (LVCDC), the planning committee organized itself into three main committees: one for curriculum, one for community services, and one for school design.

Originally part of the curriculum committee, the youth council came into existence as a separate entity as the planning committee transitioned to an advisory board (later known as the Transition Advisory Committee, or TAC). The multifaceted nature of the process is important in that members of the various committees remained committed to ensuring youth representation in the development of the school. By remaining accountable to the core values of the initiative, the shifts and transitions in community organizing were critical in the documentation of the project's development. As committees phased out, dissolved into existing committees, or became new committees altogether, the chronology became important in order to provide a sense of the work that took place to maintain continuity throughout the process.

The authentic inclusion of young people became the responsibility of the TAC. In order to secure permanent spaces for young people in the planning process of the school, the TAC created a position for youth advocates. Responsibilities of the youth advocates included holding youth council meetings and representing youth concerns on the advisory board. Remaining accountable to both communities, the youth advocate positions were shared by two youth workers from North Lawndale and a youth worker from Little Village (the two from North Lawndale shared the position, as they alternated in attendance at TAC meetings).

Upon first glance, the process may appear contradictory to "authentic" youth participation. Often youth initiatives claiming to include the opinions of young people use youth participants symbolically. Rarely are youth trained to make leadership decisions that determine the direction of the organization. In the attempt to break from such practices, the youth advocates were active in providing youth the necessary leadership development to make informed decisions on policies that would govern the four high schools. The representative youth advocate positions came about for logistical reasons. In the transition from the planning committee to the TAC, many of the meetings were held at night (due to the work schedules of TAC members). Because many of the members of the youth council were aged 11 to 14, many parents were worried about their safety in traveling the neighborhood at night. To accommodate parental concerns, youth council meetings were held in the afternoon. The youth advocates of the TAC, in organizing the youth council meetings, became responsible for reporting back to the advisory board and the youth council. Stressing the authentic participation of young people, it became crucially important for the youth advocates to operate as liaison between the TAC and youth council. Any conflicts between the two groups in terms of ideology would have to be negotiated by the youth advocates.

The Infusion of Community Organizations and African American Residents in North Lawndale

As African American residents of the neighboring community of North Lawndale were included in the school formation process through a consent decree to desegregate, the infusion of community organizations in North Lawndale became of ultimate importance. Operating under a desegregation mandate since 1982, CPS has been required by the federal government to engage in a concerted effort to desegregate its schools. Critical to the decree, however, is the fact that there aren't enough white students in Chicago public schools to "desegregate" the student populace. In the attempt to operate in compliance with the desegregation mandate, CPS interpreted it as integrating the four high schools in South Lawndale with the neighboring African American community of North Lawndale. Under the consent decree, each high school would be required to maintain a population that was at least 30% African American and no more that 70% Latinoa. As a loose interpretation of the desegregation mandate, CPS could now argue to the federal government that its attempts at new school development remain in agreement with the legal statute.

In comparison to the statistics cited earlier for Little Village, 42% of residents in North Lawndale live below the poverty line. Median income for the area hovers around $18,000. Fifty-two percent of the families with children under the age of 18 live below the poverty line. Reflective of trends in many urban, low-income African American communities, 58% of families with one or more children under the age of 18 indicated a grandparent as primary caregiver. In terms of school, 18.6% of North Lawndale high school students perform at or above the state standard. The high school graduation rate is 26.2%, with only 3% of its residents going on to earning a college bachelor's degree (Nambo et al., 2004 , p. 6).

In order to bring residents of North Lawndale to the table, members of the TAC contacted community organizations in the neighborhood. The organization known as the Crib Collective (CC) became central to the inclusion process. Recommended by a community organizer working at LVCDC on a project separate from the hunger strike, his experience with a member of the CC in a national community support organization provided members of the advisory board a space to meet with residents of North Lawndale. The meeting space was a house CC members converted into a community space. The name Crib Collective came from the popular nickname for a house in communities of color (a "crib") and the collective of artists and organizers who occupied the residence. Currently, the building houses five members. Two are art students employed in a local arts program, one is a community organizer, another is a student who is also employed as a parks and recreation worker, and one is a direct-service worker ("direct service" can refer to social work, drug rehabilitation, ex-offender employment programs, etc.). In addition to the collective's own fund raising, it has secured various grants and fellowships to keep the operation afloat.

Currently two members of the CC serve as youth advocates for the TAC. Developed as a community organization with a focus on youth, the CC began with a group of community members who desired a safe space in which young people could express their issues and concerns. A central focus of the group was social entrepreneurship. Different from economic entrepreneurship, with a monetary goal in mind, the goal of the social entrepreneur is to create positive systemic change. The focus came about from interviewing numerous young people throughout the neighborhood. Upon surveying young people in the North Lawndale community, they inquired as to what they felt the community lacked.

Responding to the concerns of young people, the first project of the CC was a dinner and "open mike" night at which artists could sign in and give impromptu performances. Many members of the collective with experience in community organizing began to meet among themselves to develop other strategies through which to engage the community. Following the concept of meeting people where they are, they wanted a practical approach that would not turn community members away. To draw community residents into the work of the CC, the open mike nights were accompanied by a Sunday dinner for the residents on the block where the collective is located. Each CC member went door to door and alerted community members about the dinner and open mike performances. At first, the community was cool to the concept, as a group of artists and organizers who were not from the community appeared suspect. However, with consistency and support from connections through informal networks (mainly word of mouth from young people in North Lawndale), community residents began to frequent the community dinners and open mikes. The dinners provided young people the space to discuss their concerns about the neighborhood. Discussions included concerns with neighborhood safety, drug sales and proliferation, antagonistic relationships with local police, and the lack of a community center for young people.

Whereas the first dinners and open mikes were not well attended, the following events developed momentum, simultaneously creating the desired forum for expression. As young people who attended the open mikes desired to engage in other substantive work, the work of the collective expanded the concept of social entrepreneurship to the arts, violence prevention, and employment (all areas of concern for youth in the community).

For the purposes of the high school complex, the two adult youth advocates assembled the youth council, which would be responsible for fielding the concerns of young people as the opening day of high school neared. The youth council would meet biweekly, facilitated by a youth advocate from the TAC. Once the school was up and running, the youth council members (currently in sixth, seventh, and eighth grades) would transition to the youth councils of each of the four high schools in the complex. At the time, organizers from the CC and the LVCDC took the lead in securing the position of young people in the remaining months of the initiative. Both youth advocates from the CC were college students, responsible for facilitating youth meetings and providing reports to the TAC. Upon the opening of the school complex, the TAC would then shift its leadership responsibility to the four schools, and the task of the youth advocate and the youth committee would now be to ensure permanent student input and participation in governance throughout the life of the school complex. Currently, the four high schools are required by the TAC and the partners in the CPS system to demonstrate how young people will be included in the daily decision making of each school.

Struggle and Process

It would be incorrect to state that there are fuming tensions between the communities of Little Village and North Lawndale. However, due to the segregation of many of Chicago's neighborhoods, the dynamic deserves some discussion in that there is potential for tensions to escalate as Mexican Americans and African Americans are scheduled to convene in the same place. Currently the local high school serving both communities is riddled with problems (e.g., low graduation rates, high truancy, fights, low student morale, etc.). Tensions often escalate as rival gangs convene in the same place. Students, with little knowledge of one another's culture, are often skeptical of engaging each other inside classroom space and school grounds. Because residents in both neighborhoods know little about the other's community and culture, a concerted effort by the TAC and community members is needed to maintain school support. In fact, when the idea surfaced that African American and Mexican Americans would be going to the same school, some members of the youth council felt the concept would never work. However, with the involvement of the youth advocate, many members of the community realized the importance of interracial, cross-cultural collaboration to make the project work.

For the first couple of youth council meetings, it was difficult to get young people from Little Village and North Lawndale to engage in conversation. First, the initial tensions of language and unfamiliarity became clear as young people from both groups sat on separate sides of the room while the youth advocates explained the purpose of the council. In order to get the youth on the same page in understanding why having a peaceful and constructive coexistence was critical to the development of the process, the youth advocates had to communicate the history of the two communities. From this discussion, young people began to understand the ability of their neighborhoods to work collaboratively.

One of those sessions included a discussion of prominent community and political figures in Chicago. Because the city remains segregated, students are often unaware of a time when African Americans and Latinoas worked collectively to end corruption in the political sphere. For a brief moment in the mid-1980s, there was great political collaboration between both communities in the election of Harold Washington, Chicago's first African American mayor.

Labor organizers from the 22nd Ward, under the leadership of Rudy Lozano, helped secure a victory for Washington by mobilizing Latinoa voters throughout Chicago. In other areas of the city, Washington was adamant about the inclusion of Latinoas in government, employment, and education. While serving as a state representative, Washington was one of the first African American legislators to sign the Illinois State Board of Education's Bilingual Education provision. Upon Lozano's assassination in the summer of 1983 and the death of Washington four years later, many of those connections were lost. In both organizers was the hope of making the necessary connections in the quest for racial, social, and economic justice. Relying on the same spirit that Washington and Lozano took to communities to identify common goals, the youth advocates had the responsibility of creating and sustaining the same energy to ensure racial understanding among the future students of the high school complex.

Successful Youth Inclusion in High School Development

Because the four high schools had yet to open, the majority of my work was on the level of the design team. The school of social justice design team (of which I was a member) had taken the responsibility of studying the attempts by schools across the country to incorporate young people in areas of school governance, discipline, and curriculum. Through their struggles we learned of the importance of young people in guiding the process of authentic inclusion. The process took us to schools in New York City; Oakland, California; and Providence, Rhode Island. Through various examples we discovered a set of common themes. First, none of these establishments exists without conflict. To say that people are able to get students from different cultures and backgrounds together in the same place to operate harmoniously through osmosis is false. Instead, teachers and administrators must be prepared to have upfront, often confrontational discussions with regard to race, class, gender, and sexuality. When these conversations are placed out in the open before a crisis event, students are able to develop a sense of trust with adults in the school. Second, the mission and vision of the schools should reflect a commitment to young people. Third, all of the institutions have an operating youth council with power that goes beyond mere recommendations. Often in these schools students build curriculum collaboratively with teachers, and disciplinary decisions are shared with members of the youth council. Fourth, each of the institutions incorporates leadership development in curricular practice. Finally, community inclusion is central to the process. Many schools have partnered with local community organizations to assist them in the inclusion of community members in the day-to-day functions of the school. Some schools have developed their own community organizations, comprised of parents and students, to address community concerns.

Our process of youth inclusion was difficult on the social justice design team. While we have experienced relative success in the participation of parents, young people were slow to participate in the process. Because many of our meetings included dealing with operational budgets and staffing concerns we relied heavily on the youth council to provide curricular ideas and concerns. A summer institute was held by the LVCDC to provide young people from the Little Village and North Lawndale communities with leadership training centered on the importance of community inclusion in school development. The process is Freirian in the sense that it is centered on empowering those most disposed with the skills and abilities to act as change agents. Training young people in community mapping, political economy, and community assessment has been beneficial as they provide recommendations to the TAC. During the transition to fully functional high school, the responsibility remains for the adult leadership to remain accountable to the principle of community (youth) inclusion as an original principle of the hunger strike.

Based on What We Know, What Do We Do Now?

As stated at the outset of this chapter, participatory research should not be viewed as a finite field of research that will provide a blanket solution to the issues of urban education. Instead, from instances like the hunger strike to the development of the youth council, we can begin to understand the nuances that impact issues of youth and school development. With this take we are forced to transition from the broad-based educational policy solutions suggested by our current government to ones centered in the site-specific needs of communities. Broad-based (e.g., city, county, state, national) policy should be used to monitor and support the progression of young people instead of developing punitive systems grounded in deficit. As discussed in this chapter, one of the most sensible means by which to do so is to consult with the persons who will be affected by said policies the most.

Presently, the work at the Little Village Multiplex is incomplete. Because it is a school in formation, we are unable to provide a comprehensive account of the relationships among young people, community organizations, and schools. However, the story of the hunger strike demonstrates the severe means communities often have to take to guarantee educational access. Working with both communities, the need for neighborhood cooperation is at a premium in that the high school represents an experiment in race and class, as two distinct ethnic communities are being served. Although they share the realities of class, it is yet to be seen if the work of the community and youth council will prevent expected clashes among young people in both neighborhoods. Still, in fact, the attempt must be made. As a participant in the process I have been able to observe and carry on dialogue about the concerns for the high school nearing its opening day. Working on the design team for the school of social justice has enabled me to understand the nuances involved in preserving the integrity of the initial hunger strike. From the drafting of the initial proposals, we remained critically concerned about the suggestions the CPS central office would make concerning our approach. Before the school's opening, we were in negotiations with CPS on the proposed class schedule and budget of our school. Coupled with hiring teachers and securing an operating community center for the school, the process was sometimes uneven and difficult. However, the community has continued to support us throughout the process. Despite our own infighting and inability to come to consensus on some issues, we moved forward with the idea of making the school a reality.

From working in this community, four specific policy recommendations have come to fruition. They are not new to those who have engaged in community organizing, but they are critical in ensuring community representation and input.

Community Accountability

Any community initiative must remain accountable to its constituents. Accountability can take the form of community reports on new policy, community forums to collect issues and concerns, or checking in with residents on whether or not the information disseminated is accurate.

Youth Inclusion

The authentic inclusion of young people in community initiatives should involve a process by which young people's perspectives are respected and incorporated into any existing work. The process should also be one that is able to adjust to new issues and concerns held by young people. This can include (but is not limited to) youth councils, policy implementation of youth concerns, and the like.

Autonomy

In order for community processes to incorporate the issues and concerns of residents, autonomy must be given to the creators of the policy to engage new and innovative approaches.

Evaluation

Throughout any community process, evaluation will be key in revisiting any initiative to make suggested improvements for any new developments.

Although basic from the outset, these processes were developed independently from the influence of "official" sources (i.e., local government, school boards, etc.). Developed naturally from the initiative of the hunger strike, the aforementioned points remain critical to the school's formation. While these may operate as points of contention, members of the youth council, the TAC, and members of the design teams still struggle to keep these points at the center of our work.

Unfortunately, many adults are still overcome with a distrust of young people. On the contrary, it would behoove us to return to a very practical understanding: young people do not have all the answers (no one does), but given the chance, we will discover their expertise in their lives. As youth development has become in vogue and youth organizing is receiving significant funding from major philanthropic organizations, we must remain keenly aware of how the paradigm is defined. It cannot be a situation where youth development becomes equated to "giving those poor people of color what they so desperately need." Again, the rhetoric of deficit inhibits our ability to understand the importance of youth inclusion. Youth development requires a balanced approach. The contributions of young people and adults are critical if our projects, organizations, and schools are to succeed. We must look to the examples of work that draw on young people and adults, such as the summer program of the Institute for Democracy, Education, and Access at the University of California–Los Angeles. If we are advocating for youth inclusion in policy decisions, studies and reports can benefit from participatory action research by placing the work of young people at the center. The process can sometimes appear daunting, because one places one's theories out to be tested or rejected. Instead of viewing this negatively, participatory action research allows us to welcome such success and failure, with the hope of moving the project of social justice forward.

References

Ayers, W., Hunt, J. A., & Quinn, T. (Eds.). (1998). *Teaching for social justice.* New York: Teachers College Press.

Ayers, W., Klonsky, M., & Lyon, G. (Eds.). (2000). *A simple justice: The challenge of small schools.* New York: Teachers College Press.

Benson, P. (1997). *All kids are our kids: What communities must do to raise caring and responsible children and adolescents.* San Francisco: Jossey-Bass.

Calhoun, E. (2002). Action research for school improvement. *Educational Leadership 59*(6), 1–8.

Evans, M., Lomax, P., & Morgan, H. (2000). Closing the circle: Action research partnerships towards better learning and teaching in schools. *Cambridge Journal of Education, 30*(3), 1–12.

Ginwright, S. (2004). *Black in school: Afrocentric reform, urban youth, and the promise of hip-hop culture.* New York: Teachers College Press.

Gitlin, T. (Ed.). (1994). *Power and method: Political activism and educational research.* New York: Routledge.

Heath, S. B., & McLaughlin, M. (Eds.). (1993). *Identity and inner-city youth: Beyond ethnicity and gender.* New York: Teachers College Press.

Levine, E. (2002). *One kid at a time: Big lessons from a small school.* New York: Teachers College Press.

Lipman, P. (1998). *Race, class, and power in school restructuring.* Albany: State University of New York Press.

Lipman, P. (2004). *High stakes education: Inequality, globalization, and urban school reform.* New York: Routledge/Falmer.

McLaughlin, M. (2000). *Community counts.* Washington, D.C.: Public Education Network.

McLaughlin, M., Irby, M., & Langman, J. (1994). *Urban sanctuaries.* San Francisco: Jossey-Bass.

Nambo, C., Childress, T., DeLeon, S. J., Meier, D., & Merriwether, S. (2004). Overview of Little Village and North Lawndale Communities. (Unpublished draft document.)

Noguera, P. (2003). *City schools and the American dream: Reclaiming the promise of public education.* New York: Teachers College Press.

Price, J. (2001). Action research, pedagogy and change: The transformative potential of action research in pre-service teacher education. *Journal of Curriculum Studies, 33*(1), 43–74.

Schepers, E. (2003, June 14). Rudy Lozano, 20 Years Later. Retrieved Feb. 20, 2005 from www.pww.org/article/view/3595/1/167/.

Skrla , L., & Scheurich, J. (Eds.). (2004). *Educational equity and accountability: Paradigms, policies and politics.* New York: Routledge/Falmer.

Stoer, S., & Cortesao, L. (2001). Action research and the production of knowledge in a teacher education based on inter/multicultural education. *Intercultural education, 12*(1), 65–78.

Tickle, L. (2001). Opening windows, closing doors: Ethical dilemmas in educational action research. *Journal of Philosophy of Education, 35*(3), 345–359.

Villarruel, F., & Lerner, R. (1994). *Promoting community-based programs for socialization and learning.* San Francisco: Jossey-Bass.

Zygouris-Coe, V. I., Page, B. G., & Weade, R. (2001). Action research: A situated perspective. *International Journal of Qualitative Studies in Education, 14*(3), 390–412.

CHAPTER 7

Youth-Initiated Research as a Tool for Advocacy and Change in Urban Schools

ERNEST MORRELL

Overview

Though some important gains have been made, most scholars and policy makers revisit the 1954 *Brown v. Board of Education* ruling with an acute sense of the distance yet to be traveled toward equitable schools that grant meaningful access to all students. Research conducted in the 50 years following *Brown* reveal that problematic trends persist in spite of the rhetoric of reconciliation and progress. America's classrooms and schools remain, for the large part, racially and socioeconomically segregated spaces (Orfield and Eaton, 1997). There are also huge spending discrepancies between the wealthiest and poorest districts (Kozol, 1991) and large gaps in academic achievement (Ladson-Billings, 1994; Noguera, 2002).

We know from this research that students in poor urban areas continue to have differential access to learning resources such as rigorous coursework, credentialed teachers, textbooks, lab equipment, and digital technology (Fine, 1991; Oakes and Lipton, 2004; Valenzuela, 1999). These students also frequently attend schools that fail to offer the basic necessities such as heat, water, healthy food, or toilet facilities. Most important, however, these schools fail to offer students the access they need to a quality education—an education that will largely determine their access to a well-paying stable job and the skills needed for critical citizenship in a multicultural democracy.

Sociologists of education are working diligently to confront these problems. Research on the inequitable conditions and achievement gaps have been important in promoting honest and candid dialogue about the state of America's urban schools. There have been many of us, however, who have not been satisfied only with promoting these sorts of conversations. We have become more interested in impacting the conditions of urban schools than we are in studying them at present. In this project of critical sociology, we have attempted to work with parents, students, teachers, and community members to transform the inequitable conditions of urban schools. One important aspect of this work has been the engagement of urban teens as collaborators in the critical research project. For the past six summers I, along with a team of colleagues at the University of California–Los Angeles Institute for Democracy, Education, and Access (IDEA), have convened a seminar in which local teens are apprenticed as critical researchers who develop and carry out research projects in urban schools and communities. This chapter will examine the production associated with two consecutive summer research seminars that apprenticed Los Angeles area youth as critical researchers of the conditions of Los Angeles area schools. Particularly, this chapter will explore youth research related to an Educational Bill of Rights and a School Accountability Report Card to understand more about how youth research can be used as a tool for advocacy and social change.

I begin by explaining the conceptual framework of the seminar; that is, I describe our notions of critical research and critical learning through apprenticeship in communities of practice. I then briefly describe the structure of the summer seminars and the research foci during the summers of 2001 and 2002. I devote a section each to describing and presenting the research activities and products associated with each of these seminars. The penultimate section describes the dissemination and advocacy associated with the student research. I talk about how the work was disseminated and some important structural changes that occurred largely as a result of the student research. I conclude with some commentary on the impact of the seminar on the students and the university researchers who participated, along with recommendations for policy makers at the school, city, state, and national levels.

Conceptual Framework: Critical Research in Communities of Practice

Critical research can be defined by the *who,* the *what,* and the *why* that have come to be associated with the term. By *who,* I mean to challenge the assumption of what persons have the right to participate in socially sanctioned research. Foucault (1972) suggests that discourses internally regulate themselves by limiting the numbers of people who have the will to truth or the right to make truth statements. Critical research challenges the exclusions within the discourse of social science research that normally exclude nonacademics from participating in conversations about educational reform. Instead, it draws upon Gramsci's (1971) notion of the organic intellectual to argue that students and parents should legitimately work as collaborators in community-based critical research.

The *how* of critical research also differs markedly from its traditional counterpart; where traditional research is individualistic, critical research is collaborative; where traditional research is often defined by objectivity or distance from research subjects, critical research is defined by proximity, even intimacy between researchers and populations researched. Kincheloe and McLaren (1998) argue that trustworthiness is a better criterion than objectivity in evaluating the merit of critical research projects. Critical research is messy and near, but no less "worthy" than more traditional forms of research. Philosophers dating back to Frankfurt School theorists like Max Horkheimer (2002) have reminded us that all scholarship is ideological or susceptible to ideology—even work that imagines itself as objective or neutral. Indeed, the most current iteration of critical thought has been as a reflexive discourse used to unpack the relationship between the unwitting work of dominant discourses and the maintenance of existing, often inequitable power relations. Critical research, then, is not a derivative or inferior form of traditional scholarship; rather, it offers a compelling counterargument for an entirely different approach to knowledge production (Merriam, 1998).

Perhaps the most significant difference in critical research concerns its "*why.*" That is itself part of a process of transforming the world . Kincheloe and McLaren (1998), for example, define a *criticalist* as a researcher or theorist who attempts to use her work as a form of social or cultural criticism and who accepts certain basic assumptions that all thought is fundamentally mediated by power relations that are social and historically constituted; that facts can never be isolated from the domain of values or removed from some form of ideological inscription; that the relationship between concept and object and between signifier and signified is never stable or fixed and is often mediated by the social relations of capitalist production and consumption; and that the oppression that characterizes contemporary societies is most forcefully reproduced when subordinates accept their social status as natural, necessary, or inevitable (p. 263). In the process of articulating the politics, purposes, and practices of critical research, they offer the following:

> To engage in critical postmodern research is to take part in a process of critical world making guided by the shadowed outline of a dream of a world less conditioned by misery, suffering, and the politics of deceit. It is, in short, a pragmatics of hope in an age of cynical reason. (p. 294)

Within this criticalist tradition, Denzin (1997) advocates a public, civic, or everyday life ethnography that draws on the legacies of the new journalists, that evidences a desire to connect with people and their concerns, and writes ethnographies that move people to action and "answers to a new readership—the biographically situated reader who is a co participant in a public project that advocates democratic solutions to personal and public problems" (Denzin, 1997).

Cultural psychologists believe that people learn as they participate in everyday sociocultural activity (Bruner, 1996; Cole, 1996; Lave and Wenger, 1991,

Rogoff, 1990; Vygotsky, 1978). They critique transmission models of learning often promoted in schools that assume that teachers are sole disseminators of knowledge and that students are empty vessels.

Within this school of thought, Lave and Wenger (1991) offer a social practice theory in which they contend that learning occurs when new participants are afforded legitimate peripheral participation in communities of practice. As the beginner or newcomer moves from the periphery of this community to its core, he becomes more active and engaged within the culture and hence assumes the role of expert or "old-timer." These ideas are what Lave and Wenger (1991) call "the process of legitimate peripheral participation." A community of practice is a site of learning and action where participants coalesce around a joint enterprise as they develop a whole repertoire of activities, common stories, and ways of speaking and acting. Communities of practice constitute reality in a particular manner and encourage specialized ways of acting and thinking (Wenger, 1998).

Communities of practice are social sites where people participate in activities as they become certain "kinds of persons." These activities embody distinctive ways that participants relate to each other and the broader world. Learning occurs constantly in these communities as people participate in activities that are increasingly central to the core practice. This changing participation leads participants to take on new identities that are necessarily bound up with new knowledge and skills (Lave, 1996).

Building upon these concepts of critical research and communities of practices I, along with several colleagues at UCLA, designed a seminar in which city teens would have the opportunity to learn about critical research as they collaborated with local teachers and university professors on research projects conducted in local schools and communities. In the following section I describe the structure of summer seminars in more detail and outline the themes of the two seminars around which this analysis is framed.

The Summer Seminar

Beginning in 1999, several colleagues at IDEA began convening a summer seminar at UCLA. The seminar brought together students, teachers, and parents from urban schools and communities to design and carry out critical research projects on issues of immediate concern to these schools and communities. Students were chosen from the most underperforming schools and communities in the city. They were selected only for their interest in the program, giving us students with a wide range of life and educational experiences.

The students worked in groups of four or five on research teams led by teachers from the local elementary and secondary schools. Throughout the five weeks of the seminar the students read seminal works on the sociology of education and critical methods of educational research; they developed research questions, read relevant literature, collected and analyzed data, and created research reports; and they presented these reports to university faculty, policy makers, and, on occasion, to regional and national conferences of educational researchers and practitioners. Students also wrote individual papers where they contemplated the practical applications of their research to the issues in their own schools and communities.

There were multiple goals of the seminar, but two emerged as primary. We desired to use the seminar space to help students acquire the language and tools they need to function within the academy, what we have called *academic literacy* (Morrell, 2004). Customarily, the student populations that we worked with had not been well represented within colleges and universities throughout the state. We wanted to demonstrate to the schools and universities that had dismissed these students that the students were indeed capable of college-level work. At the same time, we wanted to use the context of critical, community-based research to help the students gain the literacy tools they would need in order to be successful at these universities.

A second goal of the seminar relates to the research itself. We held the sincere belief that teachers, students, and parents were the most legitimate collaborators for the kind of community-based, praxis-oriented research that we ourselves were interested in. In other words, the research studies were not merely a context for literacy learning; the products themselves were important to the struggle for educational justice within the teacher education program, with the local districts, the greater metropolitan area, and even statewide. The student-participants and their work would influence policy and practice across all of these settings.

During the summer of 2001, students convened to articulate an Educational Bill of Rights that outlined the basic entitlements of all students in California. Student-initiated research projects sought to investigate the existence of these rights in the context of urban schools across Los Angeles. This research sought to answer the following questions:

What does every student in California deserve?
What inequalities arise in the experiences of California's students?
Why do these inequalities arise? What is our explanation for the inequalities?
What can youth do? How can they use research to play a part in legal advocacy?

Toward these ends, student groups collected data in and around Los Angeles's urban schools. Students visited classrooms, interviewed and surveyed their peers, and evaluated curricula, textbooks, and technological capabilities in order to understand the state of schools in their communities. Research from the seminar featured prominently in the ongoing work of the American Civil Liberties Union (ACLU) in its litigation against the State of California. Language from the Educational Bill of Rights was incorporated in legislation that was argued in the state assembly. Teachers, students, and administrators from the target schools were also impacted by the work of these student researchers.

In July 2002, a different group of students convened for the summer seminar. Course readings introduced students to the field of sociology of education and to critical research methods. These academic tools were used to develop research projects that would test out the possibilities of a bottom-up accountability system that enabled students and parents to monitor student opportunity to learn. The central purpose of the seminar was to understand how students could contribute information about school conditions to the state-mandated School Accountability Report Cards (SARCs).[1] This question embodied three subquestions:

What are the conditions of learning in urban schools across Los Angeles?
How can students access and contribute information about these conditions?
How can students, working in conjunction with parents and community advocates, pressure their schools and districts to include student-generated data in the official SARCs?

The seminar was divided into four student research teams, each focused on one core condition of schooling—quality teachers, a rigorous curriculum, adequate learning materials, and a positive physical and social school environment. Under the guidance of teachers, the research teams conducted field research in several Los Angeles area schools. The students explored various research and pedagogic tools (Geographic Information Systems mapping, audiotape recording, video and still digital photography, and the theater of the oppressed) for gathering and representing this data. Throughout the five-week seminar, the students also interviewed and met with educational researchers, community organizers, parent advocates, school administrators, civil rights attorneys, and elected officials to investigate how student research might become a standard part of the SARC process. On the final day of the seminar, the research teams presented their findings, methods, and analysis of the politics of implementation to a public audience of UCLA faculty, civil rights attorneys, educators, community advocates, and parents. Instruments developed during the seminar were refined and used by other students and parents to make sense of the conditions in schools across the city. The research products and tools were also featured on a website developed for teachers in the Greater Los Angeles area. Finally, a team of students presented their research to the annual meeting of the American Educational Research Association.

This chapter draws upon field notes, student interviews, digital video footage of seminar sessions and student research, student-generated products, and conversations with lawyers, community advocates, administrators, and policy makers to consider the relationship between the summer project, students' identities as agents of change, and local and state conversations about transforming urban schools. The work about which this chapter reports has major implications for who has the right to conduct research of import to urban educational reform. It also has implications for curriculum development in urban schools. I argue that it is important to consider students as partners in urban educational research. I further argue that the process of engaging in student-centered, community-based research taps into students' funds of knowledge, increases students' sense of efficacy, and helps students to develop literacies of power (i.e., academic literacies, critical literacies, civic literacies, and new media literacies). The next sections discuss in more detail the work of the seminar during the summers of 2001 and 2002.

Students' Bill of Rights: Summer Seminar 2001

In the spring of 2001, researchers in IDEA met with leaders and activists in the community over a series of lawsuits being filed by the ACLU over grievances about inequitable educational conditions in California's urban schools. Out of these conversations emerged an Educational Bill of Rights, listing what these legal activists, community leaders, educators, and educational researchers believed that every student in California deserved. The rights included:

Clear standards
Appropriate materials
Adequate facilities
Quality teachers
College preparation
Safe schools
Fair tests
Home language
Rights information
Public forums

It was against this backdrop that we began planning for the 2001 summer seminar. Our aim was to use our work with the students to learn more about what we meant by each of these rights. Particularly, we wanted to gain an understanding of what these rights might look like in practice and we also wanted to develop tools that students, parents, and community members might be able to use to determine whether these rights were being met. It is one thing to say that students have a right to a quality teacher, for instance. It is quite entirely another enterprise to agree upon a definition of a quality teacher and to assess whether the 10th-grade English teacher fits that definition.

The five research groups each took one of the 10 rights as a starting point. Groups examined access to quality teachers, a safe school environment, learning and technology resources, fair and authentic assessments, and rights to primary language. As part of their research process, these students consulted educational scholarship, used Internet research to obtain demographic data, visited schools, and interviewed and surveyed students, teachers, and administrators. Students were able to amass impressive data sets combining the most recent educational scholarship, achievement data, and their own data sets to contribute to their analysis of educational equity and access in urban schools. Consider this excerpt from the final report of the Fair and Authentic Assessment Group report:

> Standardized testing is defined by "Any set of predetermined questions given to large numbers of students under the same conditions (such as time limit) and scored in the same way" (Failing Our Kids: Why the Testing Craze Won't Fix Our Schools, 2000). This means schools around the nation, rich and poor are taking the exact same test even though some schools lack resources, funds, and even credentialed teachers. Many of these schools are schools in low-income urban cities and many of these students are students of color.
>
> Our research shows that many students are drastically being affected by these standardized tests and some are not even aware of the consequences. We found a great number of English Language Learner (a.k.a. ELL, ELD, ESL) students that take standardized tests such as the Stanford Nine (STAN-9, SAT-9, STAR) and the High School Exit Exam (HSEE) achieve low scores because of their inability to understand English fluently. It is stated that "Beginning in 1999, Spanish-speaking English Language Learners who have been in California public schools fewer than 12 months must be administered the SABE/2" (Spanish Assessment of Basic Education Second Edition).

The Fair and Authentic Assessment Group produced a well-written, well-researched report that explained many of the dangers of the current climate of high-stakes, standardized tests. For example, the group used existing research, policy documents, demographic data, and their own interviews with high school students to demonstrate that many students were poorly prepared to take the tests and others were unfairly assessed in negative ways due to language differences. The issue of language was an important one for Los Angeles students considering that the majority of students in the city come from homes where English is not the primary language. Additionally, a large number of students in Los Angeles schools are recent immigrants to the United States. The student research group was rightly concerned that students attending underperforming schools and students speaking a first language other than English were disproportionably negatively affected by the state standardized tests and the High School Exit Exam (HSEE), which has subsequently been suspended, largely due to efforts similar to the work of the students in the seminar.

It is also important to note that the research process itself was a form of advocacy. As students engaged in research on students' rights, they were also teaching other students about their rights and educating themselves. Engaging youth as critical researchers built efficacy on the part of the research practitioners, who gained confidence and tools needed to advocate for educational justice.

The following excerpt from the Language Rights Group report provides a great example of how the students began to see themselves not only as advocates, but as educators as well:

> We had many opportunities at "Shadow Side High" to get in group discussions about fair and authentic assessments. Our group felt that not only the interviews were great and powerful, but also [that] the focus groups were a way to educate the students about the injustices in the school system. The first time that we went to "Shadow Side High" we were able to have a discussion with four ELL students and an ELL teacher's aid. These students were honest and their input was incredible. We got to observe their facial expressions and there was a lot of anger, disappointment, sadness, and confusion. Many of the students that we interviewed couldn't believe that they were attending a school with such a bad reputation. These students said many times that they felt that they were cheated in many different ways. But there were some of them who also were very critical. They were conscience about the corruption in the school system. Not only did we learn from these students but we also educated them in many different ways. Our research group was a group who encouraged these students to feel proud of themselves because, believe it or not, many of these students were "ashamed" of themselves because of their low-test scores. The ELL students and our research group empowered each other with knowledge.

School Accountability Report Cards: Summer 2002

The theme for the summer of 2002 emerged in work initiated during the previous summer relating to the Educational Bill of Rights. Students, parents, and teachers throughout the state felt it unfair that all students were assessed under conditions that assumed equality of educational experience when the lived experiences of students bore out an entirely different reality. Without paying attention to context, state officials were insensitive to the plight of underperforming urban districts, essentially blaming them for their own failure. What would happen, in essence, is that the states would blame districts, who would then blame principals, who would then blame teachers, who would in turn blame students and their families. We called this process a top-down accountability system; that is, starting from the top, each unit beneath was considered responsible for failure until it came to students and their parents, the real losers in the equation, who were unable to hold anyone else accountable.

This situation created two serious problems that needed attention. First, the standardized tests existed as the only real assessment of school performance. The State of California had created an achievement index to rank schools on a scale of 1 to 10, but the only criterion for assessment remained the scores on state standardized tests. Second, parents and students had no collective mechanisms for holding schools accountable. From our conversations with local participants, we decided to create a seminar that would focus on creating a bottom-up accountability system in which local actors would have the tools to assess the degree to which their schools were adequately preparing their children. We wanted to continue with the themes

We are high school seniors researching inequality in public schools in order to make positive changes. With your help we can make a difference. Your opinion counts!!!

Demographic Info
School:
City:
Grade Level:
Gender:
Ethnicity (optional):
Age:

Rigorous, Quality, and Relevant Curriculum

My classes are preparing me for a successful future

Hell No				Hell Yeah
1	2	3	4	5

I feel like I'm being challenged in my classes

Hell No				Hell Yeah
1	2	3	4	5

I know what courses I need to graduate and go to a four-year college

Hell No				Hell Yeah
1	2	3	4	5

I often choose my own class schedule

Hell No				Hell Yeah
1	2	3	4	5

Social and Physical Environment

The bathrooms at my school are in good shape and I am able to use them

Hell no	Barely	Somewhat	Mostly	Hell Yeah
1	2	3	4	5

I am proud of the way my school looks

Hell no	Barely	Somewhat	Mostly	Hell Yeah
1	2	3	4	5

I notice segregation at my school during lunch

Hell no	Barely	Somewhat	Mostly	Hell Yeah
1	2	3	4	5

I notice segregation at my school during classes

Hell no	Barely	Somewhat	Mostly	Hell Yeah
1	2	3	4	5

When I express my opinions to the administrators they take action upon my concern

Hell no	Barely	Somewhat	Mostly	Hell Yeah
1	2	3	4	5

My school does a good job of informing parents about what goes on in my school

Hell no	Barely	Somewhat	Mostly	Hell Yeah
1	2	3	4	5

Fig. 7.1 Los Angeles Area High School Student Survey.

Quality Teaching

I consider my teachers highly qualified
Hell No				Hell Yeah
1	2	3	4	5

My teachers are often available during their free time to provide students extra help
Hell No				Hell Yeah
1	2	3	4	5

My relationship with my teachers is based on respect
Hell No				Hell Yeah
1	2	3	4	5

My teachers value other students' beliefs and ideas
Hell No				Hell Yeah

My teachers use creative methods to help me understand the lessons and materials
Hell No				Hell Yeah
1	2	3	4	5

Learning Resources

Do you have a home and class set of textbooks in all of your classes?
NO			YES	

How important is this to you?
Not very				Very important
1	2	3	4	5

Are there working computers in all of your classes with available printers?
NO			YES	

How important is this to you?
Not very				Very important
1	2	3	4	5

Are there a variety of languages and cultures represented in the books at your school library?
NO			YES	

How important is this to you?
Not very				Very important
1	2	3	4	5

Are there dictionaries and thesauruses in good condition in your English and history classes?
NO			YES	

How important is this to you?
Not very				Very important
1	2	3	4	5

Fig. 7.1 *(Continued)*

articulated in the Educational Bill of Rights, yet we wanted the research groups to develop tools that would allow students and parents to assess the schools' performance in respecting the inalienable rights of students to a fair and equitable education.

With these goals in mind, the seminar of 2002 involved four groups; one each to examine learning resources; the quality of teachers; access to a rigorous, college-going curriculum; and the social and physical ecology of schools. The students read literature relevant to the sociology of education, qualitative and quantitative research methods, and the conditions of local schools. They learned how to access Internet databases to learn about school and community demographics and academic achievement. Student groups also developed tools that they could use in their visits to neighborhood schools where they would conduct their research, and that could be used by their peers and by parents or community advocates interested in conducting research in or on neighborhood schools. For example, the groups each contributed to a Los Angeles Schools survey that was later used by a parent research group in the city (see Figure 7.1).

Unsurprisingly, the groups found that, by and large, students did not have access to these inalienable educational rights. This was significant for the students, considering the fact that they were researching their own neighborhoods and schools. The sense of frustration and resolve in the research groups is well represented in this conclusion to the Learning Resources Group's final report. For this reason, I quote it at length:

> Based on our critical research, we are able to see the obvious discrepancies that exist in our educational system. We could see that students do care about their education and that they want the same opportunity that the upper class has. They want equal access to quality resources. They want textbooks that tell their history. They do not want the Eurocentric lectures they are accustomed to hearing. Furthermore, they want the knowledge to keep pace with the Information Age. People nowadays are relying heavily on technology and Internet access. If they are not able to keep up with society, then they will be at a heavy disadvantage. The working-class students also want the simple things. They want staplers and basic materials needed for presentations. They do not have the luxury of being able to afford excess materials to enhance their presentations. They must rely on the little they have but they want the materials provided by the state educational code.

> We were able to see that what the students want and what they deserve differ greatly from what they receive. Students in urban schools are not being given the same opportunity as students in the more affluent schools. The textbooks they use are Eurocentric and unrepresentative of other cultures. They progress in the educational system not knowing the history of their own cultural background, which is also in violation of an educational code. Many students do not have access to computers. If computers are in the classroom they are not allowed to touch them. This is not an example of preparing students to engage in the new Information Age. Finally, teachers are grading some projects based on presentation and superficial qualities. The students with the most money are at a higher advantage. The students who are not able to afford the basic necessities that should be provided are looked upon as incapable and incompetent.

The differences are exposed. The demands are voiced. Like the Chicano, Black, and Women's civil rights movements before us, we are engulfed in social and educational reform. We demand equity and the preservation of our civil rights. We demand that all our schools in urban and suburban communities be taught equally and be provided with the same quality educational resources. Otherwise, how are working-class people supposed to become an active part of society? Cesar Chavez once said, "Once social change begins, it cannot be reversed. You cannot uneducate the person who has learned to read. You cannot humiliate the person who feels pride. And you cannot oppress the people who are not afraid anymore." We are educated, full of pride, and united by a common goal for social change. We cannot be uneducated nor can we be humiliated. We are no longer afraid.

The students in this group, strangers to the topic and the research process only five weeks earlier, had become powerful researchers and advocates for social change. Even though their research revealed gross inequities in access to learning resources, the group left the process with a sense of urgency to work for social change. This attitude speaks directly to the *why* of critical research that I alluded to earlier. It is so important to have youth involved in research for educational justice just because they bring so much urgency to the conversation. I'll discuss further exactly *what* these young people bring in the concluding remarks.

Report Dissemination and Advocacy for Social Change

The first and immediate form of research dissemination consisted of the final presentations. Students presented orally with their accompanying PowerPoint slides to an audience of academic faculty members, community members, parents, and elected officials. Each of the presentations during the 2001 and 2002 summers was well received. Marco Firebaugh, assembly member for the 50th District in California, sent key staff members to the 2001 presentations. They were so impressed that a series of conversations led to Assembly Member Firebaugh sponsoring state legislation based on the work of the seminar students. Assembly Bill 226 remained remarkably similar to the Educational Bill of Rights as created by local students and parents. Assembly members fervently argued the bill in committee, and several parents and researchers involved in the seminar testified on its behalf. Ultimately, the bill was defeated. The governor at the time threatened to veto the bill if it passed, anyway. Nonetheless, the bill remained an important rallying call: it significantly mobilized students, teachers, and parents across the state, and it increased momentum for two legal briefs that the ACLU filed against the state, *Williams v. State of California*, which ultimately settled in 2004 giving an additional billion dollars to California schools.

Following the seminar, student projects were uploaded into an online journal under a series of special issues. The website is accessed by thousands of teachers in the southern California area, as well as by researchers throughout the country. For the academic years 2001–2002 and 2002–2003, each month featured a different issue related to the Educational Bill of Rights and the School Accountability Report Card. The issues featured seminar work and allowed spaces for teachers and students from Los Angeles area schools to submit their own narratives and their own research. As the seminar research instruments were made available, several classrooms across the city disseminated the Los Angeles Schools survey and reported the results.

Additionally, two of the teachers from the summer seminar brought the concept back to their high school and started an after-school program focusing on critical research. Several of the student participants from the seminar played major roles in helping to establish and promote the club. These students continued with the research of the summer and even attended a march for educational equality. Two students attending this school ran for student office and were elected as president and vice president of the associated student body. Under their tenure they lobbied the district and were successful in creating a diversity liaison to ensure that the needs of the students of color were being met.

Following the summer seminar of 2002, several students traveled to Chicago to present their research to the annual meeting of the American Educational Research Association. The symposium, which featured the summer research projects, was well attended by scholars throughout the country, several of whom are now instituting similar projects with urban youth in their cities.

One of the more significant outcomes pertains to the changes in the youth themselves. Students leave the seminar not only having participated in worthwhile projects for educational change, but also with a sense of themselves as researchers and agents of change. This is evidenced in the following passage from the conclusion of the Language Rights Group's report from the 2001 summer seminar:

> Engaging in a research project for the first time has allowed us to grow in astounding ways. None of us had ever conducted actual critical research before, so this project was very empowering. We have gained knowledge both as students and as researchers. As a group we have built upon the skills for social understanding and looking beyond what a person says. With the experience we have gained in doing research we can look at another author's research, synthesize it critically and sum the findings. We can now confidently use the knowledge that we have constructed to make sense of the inequalities that we see in society. Reading the word has enabled us to read the world.

Conclusion

I would argue that the most powerful tools for advocacy and change are students themselves. This change in outlook and practice is documented in the writings of students in the seminar and the numerous correspondences with students after leaving the seminar. For example, in a recent seminar, we invited past alumni to speak to the current crop of critical researchers. Each of the young women on the panel had created an organization dedicated to the struggle for educational justice. One young woman had organized a club on her college campus for undocumented students, like herself, who were being denied services on campus. Another had created a support group for entering students of color at her campus. Yet another had organized high school students enrolled in a continuation school.

The impact of the panel's presentations led me to do more checking on the social action projects of the seminar alumni. One young woman had traveled to Brazil to work with young people in the *favelas* (Portuguese for "slums"). Another had worked with kids in inner-city Boston. Three had traveled to New York City to work with high school students in their inaugural summer seminar. According to the program's director, they played a major role in making the project a success.

I fully expect that many of these students will become teachers, researchers, and organizers for educational change, engaging in a trying but rewarding struggle that will last a lifetime. As I have implied throughout this chapter, many of these young women and men are already involved in these activities. The short-term successes lead me to be much more optimistic about the impact of the seminar on the life chances of students than I am about necessarily transforming urban schools. That journey will be much longer, much tougher, and filled with more disappointments than successes. However, I am continually reminded by these powerful young women and men why it is so necessary to continue this struggle and why it is paramount to involve them in the struggle.

The policy implications of this work for me are quite clear. Local, state, and national policy-making bodies must find ways to set aside resources that grant young people (in school and out of school) opportunities to develop the skills they need to engage in research for advocacy and social change. School district officials, for example, can make space inside of classrooms so that young people can be sanctioned as participants in community-based research. District officials can also create programs for teachers to help in developing their capacity to incorporate the acquisition of these skills into the core courses of language arts, social studies, math, and science. I have observed several powerful examples in the Los Angeles schools of teachers who were able to use the platform of youth advocacy for social justice to teach valuable academic skills across subject matter. School and district officials can also set aside funds and open up spaces for after-school and summer enrichment programs that allow students to participate in communities of practice similar to those associated with the summer seminar.

Citywide, officials who control youth development funds can incorporate activities that develop research faculties. Sports and arts programs are essential to the development of our youth, but these programs can and should be complemented by community-centered programs that teach students literacy and leadership skills. Cities can also provide grants to community-based organizations that show initiative and success in creating these types of programs. As an example, I can point to a Los Angeles–area, community-based organization that received city funds to establish a leadership development program for current and former gang members. The intervention continues to be highly successful.

State-level policy makers can continue to offer incentives to public universities to create programs such as the summer seminar. The seminars, for example, were originally funded through state monies targeted at school districts that were underrepresented at the elite public universities. These universities, in turn, were provided with outreach funds to develop programs to attract high school students attending these underperforming schools. State departments of education can also set aside monies for grants that allow schools and community-based organizations to create innovative projects for developing skilled and highly literate youth advocates for social change. The most beneficial state-level policy, however, would be to radically alter funding structures, giving schools the resources they need to provide a high quality education for all students. It may require a revolution to institute this type of policy change, but I am not above advocating for revolution in academic book chapters!

National-level policy makers can also create grant initiatives that encourage the development of youth-focused programs and research agendas to evaluate the impact of these programs on youth identity development and the acquisition of academic and advocacy skills. Policy makers can also provide money to schools that are showing innovative ways to develop youth as leaders and advocates. National policy makers also play a significant role in setting the national educational goals. I would charge these policy makers to use their influence to promote an educational agenda that values the development of youth leadership abilities. As with the state-level policy makers, however, I would urge our nation's leaders to decide that we were no longer going to have subpar schools with inadequate resources. I might ask them to consider why the wealthiest nation in the history of the planet has schools without heating, air conditioning, sanitation, books, or technology. Some of the problems we face in education are quite complicated, but we would be mistaken were we to make calculus out of what is really a simple equation. Give the schools a lot more money—a whole lot more money!

The bottom line is that policy makers at every level are urged to devote attention and resources to invest in the capital of urban youth as future intellectuals and engaged citizens. The most pressing areas of financial need are still related to improving material conditions in urban education; but those types of structural remedies also need to be complemented by programs that develop the capacity of youth to be researchers, leaders, and agents of change in the struggle for social and educational justice. The motivation, compassion, and energy of these young people toward their schools and communities are unsurpassed. Their brilliance and potential are without bounds. Their vantage point is critical, and their insight invaluable. And it is not insignificant that their presence provides us who are only young at heart with a sense of conviction, a tremendous amount of joy, and, even in our most cynical moments, a large dose of hope.

Note

1. The state mandates that each school develop and provide an SARC that includes required elements (e.g., standardized test scores, teacher certification information, etc.), but that can also be supplemented with locally generated information.

References

Cole, M. (1996). *Cultural psychology: A once and future discipline.* Cambridge: Cambridge University Press.

Denzin, N. (1997). *Interpretive ethnography: Ethnographic practices for the twenty-first century.* Thousand Oaks, CA: Sage.

Fine, M. (1991). *Framing dropouts: Notes on the politics of an urban public high school.* Albany: State University of New York Press.

Foucault, M. (1972). The *archaeology of knowledge* (transl. by A. M. Sheridan Smith). New York: Pantheon Books.

Gramsci, A. (1971). *Selections from the prison notebooks of Antonio Gramsci* (edited and transl. by Quintin Hoare and Geoffrey Nowell Smith). New York: International Publishers.

Horkheimer, M. (2002). Traditional and critical theory (original work published 1937). In C. J. Calhoun, J. Gerteis, J. Moody, S. Pfaff, K. Schmidt, & I. Virk (Eds.), *Classical sociological theory* (304–318). Malden, MA: Blackwell.

Kincheloe, J. L., & McLaren, P. (1998). Rethinking critical qualitative research. In N. Denzin & Y. Lincoln (Eds.), *The landscape of qualitative research: Theories and issues* (pp. 260–299). Thousand Oaks, CA: Sage.

Kozol, J. (1992). *Savage inequalities: Children in America's schools.* New York: Perennial.

Ladson-Billings, G. (1994). *The dreamkeepers: Successful teachers of African-American children.* San Francisco: Jossey-Bass.

Lave, J. (1996). Teaching, as learning, in practice. *Mind, culture and activity, 3*(3), 149–164.

Lave, J., & Wenger, E. (1991). *Situated learning: Legitimate peripheral participation.* Cambridge: Cambridge University Press.

Merriam, S. B. (1998). *Qualitative research and case study applications in education.* San Francisco: Jossey-Bass.

Morrell, E. (2004). *Becoming critical researchers: Literacy and empowerment for urban youth.* New York: Peter Lang.

Noguera, P. (2003). *City schools and the American dream: Reclaiming the promise of public education.* New York: Teachers College Press.

Oakes, J., & Lipton, M. (2003). *Teaching to change the world.* Boston: McGraw-Hill.

Orfield, G., & Eaton, S. E. (1997). *Dismantling desegregation: The quiet reversal of Brown v. Board of Education.* New York: New Press.

Rogoff, B. (1990). *Apprenticeship in thinking: Cognitive development in social context.* New York: Oxford University Press.

Valenzuela, A. (1999). *Subtractive schooling: U.S.-Mexican youth and the politics of caring.* Albany: State University of New York Press.

Vygotsky, L. (1978). *Mind in society.* Cambridge, MA: Harvard University Press.

Wenger, E. (1998). *Communities of practice.* Cambridge: Cambridge University Press.

CHAPTER 8

"The Best of Both Worlds": Youth Poetry as Social Critique and Form of Empowerment

KORINA M. JOCSON

Rage consumes me
As the noose of past generations
Is tightened around my neck...

— Poetry for the People alumnus, 2000

I can whisper
I can whisper sweet nothings
Only loud enough for hearts to hear...

— Poetry for the People alumnus, 2002

For youth whose voices and experiences have been largely ignored in the schooling process, poetry acts as a site for critical transitions. It promotes a space for recognizing silenced voices (Weis & Fine, 1993) and a place for writing selves within an "aesthetic safety zone" (McCormick, 2000) to claim and develop a sense of being. In the past decade, poetry intervention programs in the form of classroom or after-school writing workshops have shown innovative ways of engaging adolescents' interest in poetry-related activities (e.g., Fisher, 2005; Jocson, 2004; Mahiri & Sablo, 1996; Morrell & Duncan-Andrade, 2002; Weiss & Herndon, 2001). Despite this trend, however, more research is needed to deepen our understanding of young people's abilities to write in relation to their literacy and social development. The purpose of this chapter is to provide a glimpse of urban high school youth's experience within a unique program called Poetry for the People (P4P), and identify some of the ways in which this experience was valuable in gaining writing skills, confidence in learning, and self- and social awareness. The import of poetry for young people's identities—in particular, emerging identities as empowered citizens—examined within the context of P4P advances current perspectives on how poetry can be used for effective writing instruction in and out of schools. P4P is one instantiation of space and time, a contemporary reminder of what American Third World writers and poets in the civil rights era demonstrated in combining creative writing and political activism to struggle against everyday inequities. For the present volume it is a reminder of the importance of creating learning contexts that assist young people in developing critical literacies—that is, gaining socially conscious perspectives through reading and writing poetry (of their own and of others).

Poetry as Empowerment In and Out of Schools

The late African American poet and activist June Jordan established P4P at the University of California–Berkeley in 1991. With its current program director, P4P maintains a strong political stance in democratizing how "the people" are conceptualized and represented in works of poetry. The program uses poetry to shape the level of sociopolitical consciousness and actions of historically marginalized populations, including the poor, homeless, prisoners, youth, and people of color, among others. P4P has been involved in various community projects and partnerships that primarily serve these populations outside the university campus; one of these partnerships is with an urban high school in Northern California. With an educational social justice agenda, P4P uses poetry as an empowering critical medium to move "the people" toward social transformation. This move, according to Jordan (1985), is an important one in order to advance poetry as a "conscious"-raising tool, "comprehensible" and "not hidden away from ordinary people" (p. 13). In P4P's current work with urban schools, "the people" refers to high school youth.

Poetry in the context of P4P (as part of Jordan's vision) is and has been treated as a tool for political and artistic empowerment. Within this framework, poetry is regarded as (1) a medium for telling the "truth," (2) reaching for maximal impact through the use of a minimal number of words, and (3) demanding utmost precision word by word (Muller & the Poetry for the People Blueprint Collective, 1995, p. 36). According to P4P's writing guidelines, that painstaking "precision" delivers the intensity as well as density of language that separates poetry from prose. The lesson that students in the P4P program are expected to come away with is that poetry should be based on one's lived experiences (truth), be purposeful (impact), and be attentive to language (precision). Students are generally provided TIP—truth, impact, precision—as a point of reference (and also a mnemonic device) for exploring P4P's approach to poetry. These guidelines, as centered on TIP, come into play in all P4P writing instruction and group workshops. College student-teacher-poets (STPs) in the university program use them to provide constructive feedback and assist students in what I argue as a process of "becoming critical poets." It is a process of apprenticeship between college and high school poets—to build on the knowledge of the former to guide the construction and understanding of poetry of the latter and, ultimately, vice versa.

As an STP for several years (2000–2003), I collaborated with undergraduate and graduate students from UC-Berkeley in extending the university work to other learning settings. I also held membership among a group of emergent activist poets (in age ranging from their 20s to 30s) as a consequence of P4P to facilitate poetry discussions, readings, and writing workshops at different levels and locations. Our collective efforts included working with high school students through a collaborative and pedagogical intervention inside several English classrooms (see Jocson, 2005). What follows is an investigation of high school students' participation in P4P, with emphasis on their production of poetry as a transformative act. For the purpose of this volume, I focus on the social meanings and contexts that led to the construction of students' poems, while highlighting P4P's influence on students' writing processes. Using textual and content analyses, I specifically draw out connections between these youth's exposure to provocative writing topics and the salience of such topics in exploring their complex identities. As I will illustrate, these topics shaped the aesthetics of their poetry, tapped into their abilities as writers/poets, and molded perceptions of themselves as urban youth of color *and* as members of society. "Profiling" poems (based on race, class, gender, and sexuality) as one of the topics, for example, provided an important lens into students' perceptions of themselves—who they are, what they do, and who and what they want to become. Such are perceptions or individual complexities in their lives that were reified in the form of poetry. A close examination of students' actual poems offers one way of understanding how marginalized youth name and shape their social worlds—worlds that are often pathologized or hidden from public view. This examination also offers some understanding of how poetry writing validates youth's varying identities, both emerging and existing within larger sociocultural and political contexts.

Poetry in this light serves as a form of cultural politics. Congruent with several themes in this book, it reveals the power of words as one means for youth to make sense of their lives and, for some more than others, to begin to imagine their agentive roles in their communities and society at large. The epigraphs above remind and call upon us as educators and researchers to be more attentive to the "noose of past generations" and to lend our ears to the "whisper … / Only loud enough for hearts to hear." In the following sections, the discussion of students' poems can help us to rethink the potential of poetry for classroom practice and literacy learning. First, I locate poetry using a theoretical framework within literacy education.

Theoretical Framework

Texts such as *Getting the Knack* (Dunning & Stafford, 1992), *Sandra Cisneros in the Classroom* (Jago, 2002), *Risking Intensity* (Michaels, 1999), *Studying Literature* (Moon, 2001), and *Teaching Poetry in High School* (Somers, 1999) have been resources for teachers interested in "new" poetry exercises and activities to expand their repertoire of practices and strategies for teaching English. However, much of contemporary discourse on writing instruction does not tell us how poetry is linked to literacy development in the lives of urban youth. In this chapter, I build upon works within new literacy studies that employ a sociocultural framework of literacy (Dyson, 1997; Gee, 1996; Street, 1984, 1993), focusing on poetry as a literate practice among urban youth of color.

Instrumental is Mahiri and Sablo's research (1996) on the nonschool literacy of African American youth. In this work they found that poetry, rap lyrics, and other forms of writing play an important role in the out-of-school lives of their students. They point out that these youth voluntarily engage in literate behaviors that are often not valued or acknowledged in school. In addition, they assert that these youth use complex ways of making sense of their social surroundings, and that their nonschool-based writing becomes a "refuge" to speak about experiences related to poverty, violence, crime, and drugs. In their analysis, Mahiri and Sablo call our attention to the disparity in students' attitudes about school-based (nonvoluntary) and nonschool-based (voluntary) writing, and how this disparity is a consequence of both pedagogical strategies in the classroom as well as the overall "silencing" inside school. Thus, by focusing on urban young people's experiences outside of school, Mahiri and Sablo make relevant students' cultural knowledge in their learning process and literacy development. Because themes and writing topics are provocative from the start, they claim that student writings can act as pretexts to conversations and other types of dialogue inside the classroom—not just among friends and family on the outside. Though its emphasis is on nonschool-based literacy and assumes a false binary between *school* and *nonschool*, Mahiri and Sablo's work offers us a sophisticated conceptualization of poetry in the lives of urban youth. Elsewhere Mahiri (2004) expands the relevance of such literacies across contexts.

Drawing upon their own experiences as urban high school teachers, Morrell & Duncan-Andrade (2002) contend that nonschool-based literacies and knowledge of cultural forms not only have a place in classroom learning, but also must be integrated in language arts curricula to innovate teaching as well as further students' literacy development. Similar to Mahiri and Sablo, they build on the notion of culturally relevant teaching and use students' knowledge of youth and popular culture as a bridge in engaging traditional "canonical" texts, including poetry (see also Morrell, 2004). In line with this kind of culturally relevant practice, Weiss and Herndon (2001) have devised a five-week "Youth Speaks" guide to assist English and language arts teachers in using spoken-word poetry in the classroom—from mapping a kind of pedagogical space, to crafting thematic poems, to delivering them in a culminating public event. Designed as a springboard to innovate classroom teaching, their work complicates our understanding of what it takes to create dynamic learning environments while enabling young people to grow as writers/artists.

In addressing similar concerns in literacy education, McCormick (2000) offers insight into the role of poetry in teenage youth's lives by identifying poetry as a potential site for constructing self. In her work she uses a broader sociological approach to investigate poetry as an "aesthetic safety zone" for youth who undergo daily surveillance at one urban high school. McCormick explains, through a close examination of students' work, how poetry becomes a "sanctuary within, a place to play out conflict and imagine multiple possibilities for identity" (p. 194). She notes that the young women of color in her study not only struggle against but also challenge objectified representations of self within the context of school as a contested site that both limits and expands notions of self-perception. These young women, according to McCormick, claim a space for individual expression, a space where they can shape their representation of self based on what they see and experience everyday—both physically (in the classroom) and aesthetically (through writing). As I will argue throughout this chapter, it is in these safe, rich-in-possibility spaces, whether physical or symbolic, that poetry can become relevant to literacy learning.

Data Collection and Analysis

The site for this study is Bellevue, a racially diverse, comprehensive high school in the San Francisco East Bay Area. Because of its proximity to the university, Bellevue has served as the premier school site for P4P's growing educational outreach in the community. A school-university partnership began in 1996 and has grown to include several collaborators, such as high school English teachers as hosts, college STPs as facilitators/mentors, high school students as apprentices/mentees, and other P4P staff as coordinators. The partnership has provided 9th- to 12th-grade students the kind of personal attention as any writing workshop. One difference between this partnership's and other poetry organizations' efforts in serving students is its pedagogical site, being present *inside* English classrooms *during* school hours. In other words, P4P "takes over" the class for the entire period and for approximately three days each week. In this four- to six-week period of what I call a "collaborative intervention" (Jocson, 2005), teachers, students, and STPs work toward the critical consumption, production, and dissemination of poetry. The final week is typically set aside for preparing students' work for publication in the form of a class anthology and performance in the form of a public reading. The duration of each collaborative intervention depends on host teachers' curricular schedules in a given semester; each is also planned to correspond with college STPs' semester (course) schedules.

Data collection for this 30-month research began through a pilot study in the fall of 2000. Several methods were employed including survey, interview, participant observation, collection of poetry and poetry-related artifacts, and official documentation. Out of 40 students in the initial survey, 7 focal students were purposely selected with regard to consent, availability, ethnicity, gender, grade level, grade point average, and year(s) of participation in P4P. All 7 were students of color (3 female, 4 male) with an overall grade point average ranging from 1.3 to 3.0; 3 students were in the 12th grade, 1 in the 11th, and 2 had recently graduated. One common thread among these focal students was that they all participated in the P4P program at one point or another during high school; 5 students were one-time and 2 were two-time participants. Notable in the selection of focal students is that 4 of them represented an underserved student population in one of Bellevue's small learning communities. In the context of a two-tiered or bimodal school that prides itself on "diversity" and integration, students of this small learning community were generally unrecognized for their talent and intelligence within the larger school. To illuminate such experiences, the two students whose poems are analyzed in this chapter were members of this small learning community.

To collect data, I conducted two formal in-depth interviews with each focal student to gain more understanding of the high school experience. I also encountered numerous informal conversations and interactions before, during, and after particular school and nonschool events. I used field notes and audio- and videotapes to document students' literacy practices occurring in and outside of classrooms. I also interviewed English teachers whose classrooms served as sites for the collaborative intervention, as well as other teachers in the school and parents of focal students. More important, for this chapter, I gathered students' past and current poetry and other poetry-related literacy artifacts, including notebooks, written drafts, and portfolios. My dual role as researcher and participant in the development of the study allowed me access into different classrooms and knowledge of students' whereabouts both on and off campus.

To analyze data, I used a framework called PPP—poetry as *practice, process,* and *product*—to make sense of the patterns developing in students' personal narratives, writings, and performances. These patterns led to overlapping categories that consisted of in- and out-of-school literacy practices, poetry production and its writing processes, and the purposes of poetry in students' lives; this in turn became integral to the organization, description, and assessment of the meanings, identities, and experiences of focal students. For the purposes of this chapter, however, I highlight only two students, Damon and Jaime, and their poems to show P4P's influence on their writing process.

Damon and Jaime are both young men of color who participated in P4P in the 2000–2001 academic year; at that time, Damon was in the 10th grade and Jaime was in the 11th. The latter had me as his STP during the writing group workshop. Given the nation's politics that year, it was timely for P4P to raise issues related to democracy because of the said "stolen election" of 2000. Both Damon and Jaime were first-time participants in P4P as well as first-time poetry writers. Although they had not thought of themselves as poets or writers, they attributed their continued interest in poetry writing in subsequent years to that initial experience in P4P. In part, Damon and Jaime as novice poets provide a unique perspective on youth poetry and demonstrate in their work their emergent identities as critical writers; they began to see the power of words, and how poetry can be used as a medium for social critique and as a form of empowerment. Their experiences and poems produced in the context of P4P serve as examples of the possibilities of critical writing and bring to light the role of P4P's pedagogy and curriculum in promoting democratic ideals and social justice. To understand Damon's and Jaime's emergent identities as critical writers is first to understand the nature of their participation in P4P.

Writing as Critical Youth Poets

In the course of the P4P intervention, students encountered a new topic each week—from self-affirmation, profiling, to love and urgent poetry (not limited to this order). These weekly topics were introduced on the first day of class and appeared in the P4P reader by section. Depending on the participant structure(s) used during class time, these topics served as points of instruction during large group discussions, lectures, and/or small group workshops. They also served as a thematic guide for students' own individual readings of poems for class and homework. Printed readers containing poems grouped under weekly topics were made available to every student. From my observations as an STP, I noticed that poems in printed readers were carefully selected to serve as examples of "good" poetry because of thematic content, strong imagery, consistent rhythm, and/or clear purpose. A mixture of popularly known and-not-so-known poets, including Sandra Cisneros, Martin Espada, Ruth Forman, June Jordan, Li Young Lee, E. Ethelbert Miller, Janice Mirikitani, Haas Mroue, and Naomi Shihab Nye (among others), provided the necessary pretexts for students and STPs to engage in conversations about particular themes (Mahiri & Sablo, 1996). These poems were integral to instructional and discursive moments, particularly in inciting dialogue across contexts, histories, and time. Many of the discussions and, thus, eventual writings about or responses to such poems revolved around broad notions of race, class, age, gender, sexuality, and culture as relevant to students' lives. Notable in these poems were identifiable cultural referents, themes relevant to urban adolescent youth, and illustrative techniques consistent with P4P's guidelines to create "maximal impact" and "precision" in poetry.

Typically, after rounds of discussion and other activities, students were asked to respond to a particular topic (depending on the week) and write a poem as part of their class assignment. Students' subjective readings and interpretations of other people's poetry—often ranging from seasoned poets to college STPs-turned-authors, novice STPs, and high school students themselves—served as departure points in carrying out the writing assignments. To better illustrate this process, below is a close examination of writings that Damon and Jaime had identified as poems they "remember the most from their participation in P4P." I turn to them now to explicate (1) how P4P's writing topics shaped Damon's and Jaime's response to the assignment, (2) what meanings each of them attempted to convey in their actual poems, and (3) why it was necessary for youth like Damon and Jaime to write poems in the manner that they did.

"The Best of Both Worlds": Rewriting Misperceptions About Biraciality

Damon, a biracial Filipino African American, was 17 years old and a senior in high school at the time of the study. He had a 3.0 overall grade point average and was interested in pursuing business, if not attending a culinary school, upon graduation. He first encountered poetry as a member of a 10th-grade world literature class in the fall of 2000. This class, in which a six-week collaborative intervention with P4P took place, looked at such topics as "bringing it home," "love," "racial profiling," "every word counts," and "rhyme and rhythm." Each topic was covered for a week (in that order); the first had students explore various meanings of *community* and *family*, key terms central to the ensuing whole and small group discussions about the notion of "home" (i.e., what they look like for different people and in different places). For instance, Haas Mroue's (1993) poem "Voyeur," about his Lebanese war-torn home, served as a pretext for discussion and, soon after, a template for a poetry writing exercise on "where I'm from." An excerpt from this poem reads:

> *I need to write about*
> *How a stray bullet chooses a neck, a temple*
> *And buries itself in gut*
> *How a mother waits in the dark*
> *For her son—fifty pieces in a sack*
> *Delivered to her doorstep*
> *How toes curl unto themselves*
> *and skin hardens and turns coarse*
> *like burnt sugar... (p. 27)*

Students were asked to write a poem by drawing on Mroue's style (i.e., the use of language, tone, rhythm, and other poetic devices). Damon did exactly that and, as he noted, "represented where [he is] from" and the community in which he felt he as a high school student was a member of. The following is the first poem he ever wrote in P4P and the first ever as a student in any class. His illustration of a common occurrence for students on their way to school or returning from lunch conveys the irony in his narrative. To secure this community's anonymity, "B'Town" is used as a pseudonym here.

A Sunny Day in B'Town

1   *It's a nice day outside dog all sun and no fog*
Let's hurry I just heard the bell
Don't forget to hit a right at the Original Mel's

In a hurry ya dig we didn't notice that
5   *B'Town Police Dept. Pig*

I felt like I was being nabbed cause the next
Thing I know my arm was being grabbed

What the hell are you messing wit me for
It's simple freedom that I adore
10   *This is suppose to be America*
Home of the free and all that B.S.
Pigs do a good job
To make others feel they're less
Helpless I seemed until I flipped out
15   *And turned bold and mean*
You can throw me in a paddy wagon
Wit cuffs as a restraint
They told me to shut up and wait
You wanna beat me like Rodney King
20   *I'll strike back wit a fist that holds my bling bling*
I don't give a damn what you got to say
Cause I'm
In B'Town on a sunny day

For Damon, this poem depicts the presence of police or "pigs" who monitor the streets in his community. The irony in "all that B.S." for the "good job" (lines 11–12) the police do is posed against how they actually "make others feel like they're less ... / Wit cuffs as restraint / ... to shut up and wait" (lines 13–18). To summon Rodney King's name calls out in similar fashion what youth in B'Town experience with the "Police Dept. Pig" on a daily basis while, as Damon points out, reserving the right to resist or "strike back wit a fist" (line 20). Noteworthy in this depiction is also Damon's poetic license to enclose the irony within another irony captured by the opening and closing lines, that is, how such bleak events unfolded on "a nice day outside dog all sun and no fog ... in B'Town on a sunny day." According to Damon, this poem is a significant one not only because it represents a personal experience that he and many of his peers often talked about and critiqued, but also because it demonstrates his humble beginnings as a poet. He revealed that he deliberately used a random rhyme scheme and experimented with line breaks. He chose this work to be published among the dozen or so poems he produced in P4P that year. "A Sunny Day in B'Town" appeared in the fall 2000 anthology.

Following this exercise on "where I'm from," students were then asked to read and examine other poems from the reader to prepare for the next assignment on "self-affirmation." Poems in this section of the reader included titles such as "Hanging Fire" (Audre Lorde), "Half-breed" (Cherríe Moraga), and "The Things in Black Men's Closets" (E. Ethelbert Miller), among others. To complete the assignment, Damon wrote "identity." It is a poem in which he asserts his biracial background as a response to a world that challenges who he is and what he looks like. In B'Town, according to him, "there are other biracial people like me ... but there are always stares and questions ... people always want to know what I am, like I'm from another planet or something ... so I wrote it."

identity
1   half and half
    since the start of my path
    mixed wit the best of both worlds
    genetics turned my naps into curls
5   hated on by many
    despite my friendly personality
    i'm not the conceited type
    i'm not the stuck up treatin others
    the way they treat me
10 i look deeper than the surface
    because i was not
    put on this earth to harm one soul
    i have no problems
    cause i was
15 put here to contribute
    slice through edge of happiness
    and i ain't close to done

Notable in this second poem, compared to his first, are the shifts in tone and Damon's interest in the writing workshop. According to Damon, it was an opportunity to "voice out some things that went unsaid about my dealings with people." Writing the poem went beyond "the feeling of just doing the assignment"; it became a declaration, a rewriting of common misperceptions about being black and Filipino, a place to construct self (McCormick, 2000). It was also an opportunity to take seriously his likened response to poetry writing and, in turn, his emerging identity as a writer/poet. For example, with his definitive stance on biraciality, Damon used such writing devices as parallel structure ("i'm not ... i'm not" in lines 7–8) to affirm what he is not—a "conceited" biracial person. According to him in an interview, having "good hair or mixed skin tone" was often the basis for these types of misperceptions.[1] He pointed to physical features ("genetics turned my naps into curls," in line 4) to assert that there is more to him than looks, playing down his apparent difference and, conversely, playing up his inner character. By comparing his personality to others ("i look deeper than the surface," in line 10), he was suggesting how people have treated and continue to treat him as a biracial person and how he would rather, in his words "contribute / slice through edge of happiness" (lines 15–16) than be "seen as one with problems." Not only was Damon attempting to reverse common misconceptions about "mixed children as confused" beings, but he also took an agentive stance through his writing about the complexities of his racial identity, which to him should neither be questioned nor condemned. Similarly, the final line in the poem ("and i ain't close to done") was an allusion to Damon's willingness to "make the world a better place to live in," for himself, his siblings, and other bi-/multiracial people. Damon noted line by line the meanings behind his words and reinforced the value of poetry in creating possibilities to change the nature of his surroundings and the relationships existing in them.

In addition to rewriting social perceptions, another notable aspect in Damon's writing process was his appreciation for the act of rewriting itself. Damon explained, for example, that "identity" was originally written in several short pages in his miniature poetry notebook. While participating in P4P, he transferred his original work to a larger college notebook containing more polished versions of his poems. Then, through additional revisions at home and during group writing workshop, Damon reduced the entire length of the original to a shorter two-page version, which again was revised at a later time. According to him, he took out specific verses that "just seemed too much" and extensively cut the poem down from its original five pages, to 49 lines. Not too long after that, Damon once again made changes and finally reduced "identity" to a crisp half page, 16-line poem.

During the intervention Damon admitted learning certain techniques and applying P4P guidelines to improve his poem, with emphasis on precision and word choice. He revealed in one interview some feelings he had about writing workshops, particularly in relation to how P4P began to change that.

> I've never really been in a workshop, like that. I mean, people always try to tell me that I'm a good writer ... but I mean, I never really took their advice until *this* time, when I *had* to.... I was happy I did.

Damon revealed gaining more confidence about his writing and producing several short book(s) of poems related to both school and nonschool activities *after* his P4P experience. Part of gaining this confidence came from his own recognition of his ability to write and, thus, greater appreciation for the revision phase of the writing process. He said:

I actually go over my work now. I rewrite to rewrite ... four to five times.... [For example, my] vocabulary.... Instead of using just certain words, I think about using the thesaurus.... 'Cause I'll put a word down, and then look at it for a second time, and I *know* there's a better word....

Rewriting became a significant and normalized practice for Damon. "Rewrite to rewrite" had become an important strategy, a kind of rewriting that is partly a consequence of the socializing learning context previously provided by P4P's collaborative intervention and writing guidelines. The other is an emergent identity and changing self-perception as a critical poet.

"Jus because": Resisting surveillance and police harassment

Jaime, a Chilean Peruvian American, was 18 years old and in his first year of college at the time of the study. He entered the university with an overall 2.9 high school grade point average and was interested in computer science and engineering. Jaime was a member of a six-week collaborative intervention in an 11th-grade American literature class in the spring of 2001. This class had topics similar to those in Damon's class, including "democracy," "racial profiling," "haiku/every word counts," "love/rhythm and rhyme," and "ode/revering in the small things" (in that order). The sixth week also closed out with performance and preparation for the final reading. In this collaborative intervention, however, political issues surrounding the "stolen" election of 2000 narrowed the focus of the curriculum to the meanings of *democracy*. Furthermore, current events such as Amadou Diallo's murder in New York and Wen Ho Lee's removal from office exemplified the notion behind a "hidden" democracy and unequal treatment of racialized people of color in the U.S.[2] These topics shaped class discussions about poetry and assignments that followed. One of them was "profiling."

In addition to a skit and interactive lecture performed by STPs, poems in the reader were used during class discussions and group workshops to illuminate experiences beyond self and connect with students' communities. Poems in this section of the reader included "The Wrong Street" (Cornelius Eady), "Recipe for Round Eyes" (Janice Mirikitani), and "Governor Wilson of California Talks in His Sleep" (Martin Espada), among others. These preselected works represented certain sociopolitical situations or conditions that related to students' lives. They also served as exemplary poems, highlighting the strong use of language and inclusion of specific details. Some of these poems caught students' attention more than others. For example, among the favorites was a poignant account of profiling along racial and gender lines, written by Uchechi Kalu, a former STP in 1998, a published poet and an aspiring teacher. It reads:

Poem for Anyone Who Thinks I'm Not African Enough
Sorry
I forgot
My spear
At home

Though more fitting in the "every word counts" section, this poem was primarily used to help explore the "profiling" topic (at least in this intervention). Students were asked to visualize short poems outside the haiku form and discuss the meaning of poems with "minimal words" with "maximal impact." From a collective reading of Kalu's poem, students recognized immediately the length of the title versus the length of the entire poem (i.e., nine versus seven words). This observation, for many, became an invitation to probe the depth of the poem's message as it related to the larger discussion on profiling, distinguishing the deliberate use of one- or two-word lines to convey it.

To complete the exercise, Jaime chose to write a descriptive poem about a specific racial profiling incident associated with the police. The incident happened after watching a World Cup soccer game, on his way home with a couple of friends in the East Bay area. His poem as it appears in the anthology is as follows:

Los Pacos Gringos
1 *We was only walkin down a block or 2*
   We was hella rowdy / because Chile tied Italy 2–2
   We all like each other's jersey
   Each one bright red with different shields
5 *Mine was the one with 11 on it*
   and a whole, proud shield
   We was only walkin
   When 5–0 showed up on us / ¡¡Que Wea!!
   There were three of them / one was really skinny
10 *He tried to have a deep voice*
   They pinned us up on the wall / and gave us a pat down
   but all they found was wallets and mini flags
   and some keys in some of us
   ¡Que mierda quieren!
15 *We had no idea*
   "where you guys goin"
   We was only walkin
   to Micky D's for those / 89 cent sandwiches
   A group of gringos with US jerseys
20 *All white and so clean*
   Past behind us with ease, staring at us
   ¡Anda por la ramputa que los repario! ¡Mierda!

> *We was asked these incredibly stupid ?'s*
> *How old we are / Where we live*
> 25 *Some of us didn't want to say shit*
> *And they threatened to arrest us*
> *¡¿No les tengo miedo a los milicos de mi país y te voy tener a bo?!*
> *Thank you for your cooperation*
> *cooperation my ass*
> 30 *¡Que se vayan por la conche su madre!*
> *All of this happened*
> *jus because we was only walkin*

According to Jaime, the profiling assignment served as a way to speak out about a particular frustrating day and incorporate a Chilean way of talking. For example, rather than use *carabinero* (the formal word for police), Jaime chose *pacos* (loosely translated as "pigs" in an American context) to represent everyday people's talk.[3] He did not hold his tongue and used a narrative style to describe a sequence of events that took place that day.

> I wanted to be clear [about the purpose of the poem] ... so I put a translation for each Spanish phrase. Most are cuss words ... maybe they're too much for people, but oh well. That's what I felt. I just put them on the bottom of the page.

Shifting from one language to another, Jaime demonstrated in his writing how linguistic and cultural hybridity played out in his life. He pointed out that the Spanish words and sayings (i.e., "que wea" in line 8—short for "que quevada," meaning, "what the fuck?") in the poem represent the kinds of thoughts that ran through his mind the moment he and his friends were being questioned and harassed by the police. For Jaime it was important to name the incident and the emotions that accompanied it. Conscious of his color-coded realities, Jaime pointed out metaphorically that (in line 4) "bright red"-jerseyed youth like him and his peers are more than likely to be racially targeted when compared to, say, their "all white"-jerseyed counterparts (in lines 19 and 20).

Additionally, Jaime appropriated African American vernacular English to signify the hybrid cultural context of which he considered himself a part both in school and in his neighborhood.[4] For instance, Jaime noted beginning and concluding his poem with the phrase "we was only walkin" to situate the mundaneness of racial profiling, that it could affront something as mundane as a simple walk down the street. He also used this phrase as a technique to repeat lines and further suggest the perpetuation of acts of profiling no matter the time and place (see lines 7 and 17). Interestingly, he closed with the line "jus because we was *only* walkin" (emphasis added) to reiterate the underlying message about his dealings with "Los Pacos Gringos," white police officers stopping him and his peers, as he put it, "for no reason, no reason at all." As he reflected on this moment during an interview, Jaime shared what was most compelling about the irony in the situation.

> Before, I knew all this stuff, like social justice, like racial profiling was there. I just didn't think... like I didn't think it's just me.... it's like it happens to <u>eevvverybody</u>. What would it matter if I would've said little old me got jumped by the police?

Jaime expressed in his poem the answer to this revelatory question, detailing a complex momentary reaction with a high level of sophistication. Though upset at the time of the police query, Jaime had to appear calm so as not to further agitate an already inappropriate line of questioning. He revealed that he thought it best "not to self-incriminate ... [and be charged with] police assault"; instead, he registered in his head "what I really wanted to say ... (and) cooperated with the police" to avoid prolonging the embarrassment and fright on his (and his friends') part. This strategy suggests a subtle form of resistance and shows how writing poetry acted as a refuge or sanctuary to speak openly about his experiences (Mahiri & Sablo, 1996; McCormick, 2000).

Jaime's anger and frustration—registered metacognitively—were the basis for his use of profanity and Spanish in his poem. As part of P4P's guidelines in connection to precision, students were instructed that any use of profanity in one's writing must be justified. Jaime knew about these guidelines and applied them in critical ways. His insertion of Spanish words like *mierda, ramputa,* and *conche* unmistakingly encapsulated part of his rage (see lines 14, 22, and 30).[5] Since he knew that he couldn't enact profane thoughts without facing more serious consequences during the police query, he let his anger surface all throughout his poetic narrative, intentionally using a different language to represent them. Further, part of the sophistication of his language as he explained it depends on *dichos*, or sayings, that he grew up hearing in his household. For instance, "¡¿No les tengo miedo a los milicos de mi pais y te voy tener a bo?!" (I am not scared of the military of my own country and you think I'm going to be scared of you?!) in line 27 was a dicho that he heard many times from his mother who experienced the military occupation in Chile during the regime of Augusto Pinochet.[6] This dicho appears in his poem exactly as he remembered it. Apparently, what was appropriate for his mother to say in/about Chile was also appropriate for him to say in/about the United States, a type of heteroglossic adaptation that shaped the meanings he imparts in his poem (Bakhtin, 1981). The strength behind these words reflected Jaime's sociopolitical stance on profiling and classified police harassment in his present day community as a kind of transplanted, if not new form of, military occupation. Jaime attributed this current stance to his former participation in P4P, revealing that it made him "more aware and critical" as a young person.

When you guys came in, you said, Write a poem, add detail, all this crazy stuff.... that kind of, you know, brought it [the police incident] back from the back of my brain to the front...ever since, I've been thinking about that...in class and everything.

At the end of the intervention in May 2001, Jaime's poem appeared in the Poetry for the People anthology. Jaime was also present at the final reading that took place at a community cultural center, where parents, teachers, students, STPs, and other supporters filled the room and celebrated youth poetry. It was, in his words, "the most memorable reading.... 'Pacos Gringos' (was) the first poem I've ever written ... and the first poem I've ever recited." For Jaime (as it was for Damon in the previous semester), reading in front of a large audience was exciting and, even though nerve-wracking, was the best part of his P4P experience because it was an opportunity to—*literally*—speak out and be heard. And admittedly, writing about a profiling incident was a crucial part in beginning to see himself as both a critical person and a critical poet.

Implications and Conclusion

The urban youth presented in this chapter created poems not just for poetry's sake, but also for life's meanings. Damon and Jaime, as participants in P4P, tackled complex social, cultural, and political issues related to forms of present-day racism, interpretations of history, and notions of race, culture, and class. They responded to highly charged writing topics and demonstrated their writing abilities within particular writing guidelines and spatial conditions set forth by the P4P program. Their work exemplified what some marginalized urban youth face as they confront realities in their homes, schools, neighborhoods, and places in between. Such were the realities that informed their cultural knowledge (Morrell & Duncan-Andrade, 2002) and served as pretexts for their writings (Mahiri & Sablo, 1996).

For Damon and Jaime (as well as other focal students in the larger study), poetry became a vehicle for expressing and exposing their lived realities, which are often hidden from public view. Poetry served as an "aesthetic safety zone" through which they could construct different selves (McCormick, 2000) and a medium to explore their identities as biracial and multilingual youth. It was a place to speak openly about the everyday complexities of what it means to be an urban youth of color. Through a closer examination of their most remembered poems, it became apparent how meanings derived in the production of poetry helped them to better imagine themselves as critical poets and as potential agents of social change. For Damon, writing about "identity" and bi-/multiraciality served as a pathway toward contributing to a more diverse world; for Jaime, writing about police harassment became a tool for resistance and a potential mechanism for social action. P4P's weekly topics and assignments provided the space for these students to explore such possibilities in learning about self and what it might mean to be a critically engaged citizen in the larger society. Additionally, P4P's writing guidelines, including the use of model poems by both seasoned and novice poets, pushed focal students to produce sophisticated poems and develop strategies for improving their writing skills. For example, Damon used the thesaurus at his leisure and revised regularly to help polish his writing, what initially was a poetry-based practice that later transferred to essays and other types of writing. Despite the push to revise, what remained at the center was the experimental nature of composing poetry or, as illustrated in both Damon's and Jaime's work, the unlimited ways of using free verse poetry as a medium to relate their experiences—whether in narrative, descriptive, or some other form.

There is no doubt that P4P occurring in the context of school served as a stepping stone to explore relevant issues often untapped by the larger school culture. P4P's pedagogy (i.e., poetry as political and artistic empowerment) and curriculum (i.e., development of weekly provocative topics and assignments) became integral in what took place inside teachers' respective classrooms. Though not by choice (because the intervention took place in a predetermined space, in an English class in school), Damon's and Jaime's participation provide evidence that, for some students, what took place in and through P4P was a unique and self-empowering experience. It was for the most part a beginning and, as other data across contexts further complicates (see Jocson, 2004), a continuing form of practice that did not end during the final reading event.

Youth poetry in this light tells us much about a different approach to incorporating poetry in various classroom and other learning contexts. As suggested throughout the analysis, poetry helped to shape the construction of selves integral to both "schooling" and being/becoming good writers. Poetry as seen here affirms the salience of students' voices and experiences in their writing as well as learning process. It shows how the acknowledgment of students' interests in and abilities to produce sophisticated poems create different possibilities for literacy learning. The lesson here, then, is to see poetry beyond a "unit" or "genre" to be explored momentarily; to recognize students for their intelligence, wisdom, and accomplishment; and to understand that poetry requires skills, planning, and practice, the way other valued "academic" endeavors do. To the extent that students develop such nuanced and precise vocabulary from drafting to revising poetry, for example, should directly help them on things like the SAT or ACT verbal sections for college. What is clear from the experiences of Damon and Jaime is the value of the written word for conveying ideas, deep analysis, and addressing different audiences for different purposes. For educators and advocates of youth, the study as presented in this chapter strongly suggests that it is important to (1) design assignments that are meaningful and relevant to students, and (2) carve out a caring and critical space where students can be themselves and talk about matters most important to them. It is also just as important to be more open to the use of provocative topics for writing instruction and/or discursive purposes. Indeed, poetry can serve as a safe space for students' convictions, experiences, and imaginations in charting new learning terrains. Poetry, with its potential to tap into certain intimations, can lead us one step closer to improving teaching and learning in order to serve all students.

Notes

I would like to thank Damon, Jaime, peer reviewers, and the editors of this volume for their feedback on earlier drafts of this chapter. Special thanks are due to the University of California All-Campus Consortium for Research on Diversity (UC ACCORD) for providing dissertation-year funding in support of this study.

1. Here Damon was referring to an ongoing biologically based debate about "good" versus "bad" hair that has been consistent with racist notions about beauty (see, for example, Banks, 2001). Damon expressed his own notions that "good" hair means having hair that is easily combed, in comparison to hair that is densely thick and nappy, which for him are one in the same.
2. In February 1999, four white New York police officers shot at unarmed West African immigrant Diallo 41 times, hitting him 19 times (for more information, see http://www.amadoudiallofoundation.org). A year later, they were all acquitted. In 1999, Dr. Wen Ho Lee, a Los Alamos National Laboratory scientist, was arrested by the FBI on espionage charges—stealing U.S. nuclear weapons secrets for China—and found not guilty after months in solitary confinement.
3. Jaime added that *paco* is considered a pejorative slur in Chile. Further, to address a police officer there as paco would lead to imprisonment.
4. African American vernacular English denotes the use of singular past tense copula for plural subjects, as in "we was," and the phonological rule relating to the deletion of consonant pairs as in "walkin" and "jus" (see Rickford, 2000; Smitherman, 1986).
5. In the translation section of Jaime's poem, *mierda* means "shit," *ramputa* means "motherfuckers," and *conche* means (loosely) "fuck."
6. In 1973 General Pinochet led a military coup ousting former president Salvador Allende's socialist government and reign over the Chilean popular masses (Cockcroft, 2000). Many Chileans in support of the latter were murdered or placed in concentration camps. According to Jaime, others fled the country, including his mother, who "in danger of being killed" left Chile and emigrated to the United States in the early 1980s.

References

Bakhtin, M. (1981). *The dialogic imagination: Four essays by M. M. Bakhtin* (C. Emerson & M. Holquist, Trans.). Austin: University of Texas Press. (Original work published 1935).

Banks, I. (2001). *Hair matters: Beauty, power, and black women's consciousness.* New York: New York University Press.

Cockcroft, J. D. (Ed.). (2000). *The Salvador Allende reader: Chile's voice of democracy.* New York: Ocean.

Dunning, S., & Stafford, W. (1992). *Getting the knack: Twenty poetry writing exercises.* Urbana, IL: National Council of Teachers of English.

Dyson, A. H. (1997). *Writing superheroes: Contemporary childhood, popular culture, and classroom literacy.* New York: Teachers College.

Fisher, M. (2005). From the coffee house to the school house: The promise and potential of spoken word poetry in school contexts. *English Education, 37*(2), 115–131.

Gee, J. (1996). Social linguistics and literacies: Ideology in discourses (2nd ed.). Bristol, PA: Taylor & Francis.

Jago, C. (2002). *Sandra Cisneros in the classroom: "Do not forget to reach."* Urbana, IL: National Council of Teachers of English.

Jocson, K. (2004). Urban youth as agents in creating community through poetry. *California English, 10*(1), 20–23.

Jocson, K. (2005). "Taking it to the mic": Pedagogy of June Jordan's Poetry for the People and partnership with an urban high school. *English Education, 37*(2), 132–148.

Jordan, J. (1985). *On call: Political essays.* Boston: South End.

Mahiri, J., & Sablo, S. (1996). Writing for their lives: The non-school literacy of California's urban African American youth. *Journal of Negro Education, 65*(2), 164–180.

Mahiri, J. (Ed.). (2004). *What they don't learn in school: Literacy in the lives of urban youth.* New York: Peter Lang.

McCormick, J. (2000). Aesthetic safety zones: Surveillance and sanctuary in poetry by young women. In L. Weis & M. Fine (Eds.), *Construction sites: Excavating race, class, and gender among urban youth* (pp. 180–195). New York: Teachers College Press.

Michaels, J. (1999). *Risking intensity: Reading and writing poetry with high school students.* Urbana, IL: National Council of Teachers of English.

Moon, B. (2001). *Studying literature: New approaches to poetry and fiction.* Urbana, IL: National Council of Teachers of English.

Morrell, E. (2004). *Linking literacy and popular culture: Finding connections for lifelong learning.* Norwood, MA: Christopher-Gordon.

Morrell, E., & Duncan-Andrade, J. (2002). Promoting academic literacy with urban youth through engaging hip-hop culture. *English Journal, 91*(6), 88–92.

Mroue, H. (1993). *Beirut seizures.* Berkeley: New Earth.

Muller, L., & Poetry for the People Blueprint Collective (Eds.). (1995). *June Jordan's Poetry for the People: A revolutionary blueprint.* New York: Routledge.

Rickford, J. (2000). *African American vernacular English: Features, evolution, and educational implications.* Malden, MA: Blackwell.

Smitherman, G. (1986). *Talkin and testifyin: The language of black America.* Detroit: Wayne State University Press.

Somers, A. (1999). *Teaching poetry in high school.* Urbana, IL: National Council of Teachers of English.

Street, B. (1984). *Literacy in theory and practice.* Cambridge: Cambridge University Press.

Street, B. (Ed.). (1993). *Cross-cultural approaches to literacy.* Cambridge: Cambridge University Press.

Weis, L., & Fine, M. (Eds.). (1993). *Beyond silenced voices: Class, race, and gender in United States schools.* Albany: State University of New York Press.

Weiss, J., & Herndon, S. (2001). *Brave new voices: The Youth Speaks guide to teaching spoken word poetry.* Portsmouth, NH: Heinemann.

CHAPTER 9

Urban Youth, Media Literacy, and Increased Critical Civic Participation

JEFFREY DUNCAN-ANDRADE

Introduction

Recent studies of youth and the media (Goodman, 2003; Nielson Media Research, 2000) indicate that the hours spent with electronic media (i.e., television, movies, video games) are highest among poor students of color, exceeding six and one-half hours per day. This intense investment in electronic media by urban youth has led the American Academy of Pediatricians (2001) to issue a policy statement encouraging schools to develop a media literacy curriculum; it has also led scholars to call for a critical media literacy pedagogy that empowers urban youth to deconstruct dominant media narratives, develop much-needed academic and critical literacies, and create their own counternarratives to those of the media, which largely are negative depictions of urban youth and their communities (Duncan-Andrade, 2004; Duncan-Andrade & Morrell, 2005; Goodman, 2003; Grossberg, 1994).

This chapter will focus primarily on the latter of these pedagogical strategies; that is, it will highlight the type of work students can do when teachers use pedagogical practices that encourage and develop urban youth as producers of media texts. Given the level of investment youth are making in media, these sites of production are potentially powerful places for them to put forth critique and analysis of urban social inequality, as well as to posit potential solutions to these problems. Access to this type of literacy pedagogy can positively impact the development of critical civic literacy, civic awareness, and civic participation among urban youth.

Drawing from an increasing body of research that suggests schools can and should more heavily invest in media literacy and production, this chapter will posit the argument that this pedagogical approach presents powerful pathways to the development of student agency against conditions of urban social inequality. This argument will be made using analysis of a university-based summer research seminar that uses critical media pedagogy to help urban high school students to research, analyze, and critique urban schooling inequality. The chapter concludes with a discussion of the implications of 21st century media texts for educators and policy makers and a call for their strategic use in schools.

Media as Critical Text: Analysis, Production and Civic Engagement

New literacy theorists recognize electronic media literacies (i.e., television, video games, and movies) as significant in the development of literacy, particularly among urban youth (Duncan-Andrade, 2004; Gee, 2004; Kress, 2003; Mahiri, 2004; Morrell, 2004b). As they argue to expand the definition of literacy to incorporate media texts, more attention must be paid to the implications of this argument for literacy pedagogy and production in schools. To begin addressing this need, this section draws from educational theory to provide a framework for urban youth media literacy pedagogy and production. Special attention is paid to defining media texts and the literacy events that occur within them, and their potential to develop critical sensibilities for increased school and civic engagement.

Media Analysis

For the past two decades, one of the most popular solutions to the perceived illiteracy of urban youth has been the development and implementation of a more culturally relevant curriculum (Banks, 1994; Ladson-Billings, 1994; Moll, Amanti, Neff, & Gonzalez, 1992). This has often been interpreted as a call for increased inclusion of authors of color and women authors in the curriculum. To be sure, there has been and remains a need for increased representation of the voices of the marginalized in traditional school texts. However, the multicultural education movement has not produced significant gains in the academic achievement of urban youth. While there are a variety of systemic and institutional factors that contribute to this ongoing failure, the multicultural literacy movement could be more effective if it drew from media texts to engage young people in culturally relevant instruction.

What is a media text? The problem with answering this question lies in the traditional interpretations of the word *text*. The term conjures notions of paper and print, an outmoded perception of the ways in which text is produced and disseminated in the 21st century. As the printing press takes a back seat to electronic forms of textual production, media texts are rapidly becoming the dominant form of communication. These forms of text defy the limits of print, appearing in seemingly ever-increasing forms (radio, billboards, television, movies, videos, video games). For youth, the inundation of their lives with media texts has resulted in a rapidly expanding gap between the texts in their lives outside of school and the textual interactions that are promoted inside of school.

When I refer to media as text, I am not only referencing the times when printed words appear in the media. I am also arguing that the images present in television, on the Internet, in video games, and conjured through oration on the radio, CDs, and MP3s are all forms of text that are worthy of scholarly analysis. The images, narratives, and themes that they produce offer material to critically examine virtually any of the topics that can be explored through traditional texts. There is research evidence that this approach to literacy instruction is an effective scaffolding tool into more traditional forms of text, and more engaging for urban youth (Lee, 2004; Morrell & Duncan-Andrade, 2003). Equally as important is research that suggests this pedagogical strategy can be used to help urban youth develop a sense of agency and critical civic engagement (Goodman, 2003; Morrell, 2004a).

Pushing Pedagogy That Promotes Change

Freire (1970) insists that pedagogy and curriculum for social justice must foreground a critical analysis of the material conditions of the poor. He contends that this focus on the tangible conditions of poverty and marginalization are central to the development of an educational program that works to empower historically disenfranchised groups:

> To surmount the situation of oppression, people must first critically recognize its causes, so that through transforming action they can create a new situation, one which makes possible a fuller humanity. But the struggle to be more fully human has already begun in the authentic struggle to transform the situation.... The pedagogy of the oppressed, which is the pedagogy of people engaged in the fight for their own liberation, has its roots here. (pp. 29–35)

For Freire, pedagogy for critical literacy is the most powerful tool for delivering on this project of social justice. His "pedagogy of the oppressed" challenges traditional concepts of literacy that largely exclude cultural literacies that are outside the mainstream. These more traditional forms of literacy pedagogy tend toward the implementation of a technical literacy for the poor that prescribes them into social, political, and economic marginalization. To alter the resultant social reproduction of this approach to education, Freire suggests pedagogies that develop a "reading of the word and the world" (Freire & Macedo, 1987). In this pedagogical approach, the teacher embraces and draws upon the cultural literacies that students bring with them to the school—their reading of the world. These skills are used to develop more traditional literacy skills with the explicit aim of using these literacy skills for socioeconomic and political mobilization for the individual and the community.

As theorizing about social justice pedagogy has expanded, too little attention has been paid to putting it into operation with children. Questions remain as to what these ideas about pedagogy look like in practice with urban youth. Do they produce the increased sense of agency and critical civic engagement that they promise? Teachers attempting to answer these questions must employ a pedagogy that draws from the path young people have already chosen, which would certainly include attention to media literacy.

Educators like New York's Steven Goodman have embraced this pedagogical route for their work with urban youth and have borne witness to the genius that urban schools are failing to capture. Goodman (2003) describes urban youth as capable rather than deficient. He depicts urban youth as possessors of analytical skills that map onto poignant analyses of the conditions in their communities, schools, and the larger society. Educators like Goodman experience what too many urban educators can only lay claim to with rhetoric: the capacity of every student to learn and to show products that reflect that learning.

Summer Seminar: Putting Critical Pedagogy into Practice

The remainder of this chapter examines ethnographic data from a summer program in which these principles of critical pedagogy and media literacy were used. Examination of video documentation, field notes, and student work products, collected over six weeks of participant observation in the seminar, will be used to guide the discussion.

Research Site: Summer Seminar 2004

Hosted by the University of California–Los Angeles's Institute for Democracy, Education, and Access (IDEA), this summer program met five days per week for six hours each day, engaging Los Angeles 11th-graders in a qualitative research study of local youth civic participation. Four Los Angeles teachers with reputations for commitment to issues of educational justice were asked to invite student participants, and acted as group leaders. All of the students selected were either black or Latino, and had grade point averages ranging from 1.5 to 3.8 on a 4.0 scale. The six-week seminar split 26 participants into four groups, each focused on a local geographic area. These groups researched the roles of schools and communities in the development of civically engaged youth.

Before doing their field research, students discussed readings on social theory (MacLeod, 1987; Oakes & Lipton, 2001), civic participation (Westheimer & Kahne, 2002), critical literacy (Finn, 1999; Freire & Macedo, 1987), and qualitative research methods (Berg, 2004). These readings generated discussions about social inequality in Los Angeles. Particular attention was paid to the role that schools play in perpetuating inequality in urban settings. The fact that 85% of the participants attend severely underperforming schools—the other 15% attend racially mixed schools with high failure rates for African Americans and Latinos—fueled intense discussions. Students were encouraged to write, share, and explore their own experiences with social inequality as a staging ground for researching those inequalities in the weeks to come.

Community Research, Video Production, and Youth Voices for Change

Knowing that many of the issues raised in sociocritical texts can be disheartening, the seminar instructors were careful to encourage students to respond from the position of agents of social change. One strategy to inculcate these feelings of agency was the use of narratives about youth organizing and youth activism against oppressive conditions in urban Los Angeles. These came in the forms of a video documentary (*Chicano!*), readings, and panels of community activists.

These counternarratives engendered feelings of possibility that were acted upon in the form of community case studies in four Los Angeles communities (Santa Monica, Watts, and South Central and East Los Angeles). In these studies, the youth researchers examined three central questions:

1. What does it mean for Los Angeles youth to participate powerfully in civic life?
2. How can these youth learn to participate in powerful ways?
3. What civic lessons do young people currently learn in and outside of Los Angeles–area schools?

Students spent a minimum of two days a week for the middle four weeks of the seminar in their respective focal communities. These days were used to conduct interviews with students, administrators, teachers, and community members, to take observational field notes, and to collect video footage of these activities. The sixth and final week was spent compiling this data into a written research report and a presentation. On the final day of the seminar, each research team made PowerPoint presentations to demonstrate the findings of their report at a forum attended by university faculty, state and local officials, community members, media, school officials, and teachers. After each PowerPoint presentation, the groups showed their video documentary to conclude their findings.

There are many stories of discovery emerging from the seminar over its six years of existence (Morrell, 2004a), and the 2004 summer seminar space was no exception. Undoubtedly, the readings and activity systems are deserving of more study, as they laid an important foundation for the community research that students did in weeks 2 through 5. However, the remainder of this chapter will focus on perhaps the most impactful activity system—the use of digital video equipment to capture and render critical narratives about the conditions of the schools, communities and lives that were being studied. As Miguel, a student in the South Central research group explained,

> If a picture is worth a thousand words, then one minute of footage with 1800 frames is worth 18 hundred thousand words. The use of the camera was invaluable. It allowed us to capture images that could only be expressed through live footage. These images not only helped supplement our data with concrete evidence, but allowed us to bring forth a world most people are blind to.

To more completely understand Miguel's sentiments and the potential of media texts to develop and represent youth critical civic literacy, this chapter turns now to an examination of the video product of the group studying the South Central School District of Los Angeles.

South Central Group: Using Media to Study a Community in Distress

The first time the South Central group set foot in the community, it was clear that there was a moving story waiting to be told. The area high school and surrounding community had been in the city's headlines with relative frequency leading up to the group's visit. In late February, a police officer was killed by a local resident less than 10 blocks from the school. Within minutes of the shooting, the community was flooded with over 100 police officers, a command center was set up in the middle of a major street, and house-to-house searches for the suspect began.[1] Eight helicopters hovered overhead for hours, providing live television coverage of the event on all major television networks. The high school was locked down, preventing students from leaving their classrooms. The manhunt and the community lockdown continued into the evening, when the suspect was finally apprehended while hiding in the trunk of his own car. He died 48 hours later after hanging himself while in the custody of the Los Angeles County Corrections Department.

This shooting served as further justification for a 2003 gang injunction issued for that area of South Central Los Angeles. The injunction legalizes the use of racial profiling techniques in the area and has dramatically heightened tensions between young men and the police. These tensions exploded again in late June 2004 when the police department used clubs and mace to subdue a local community activist and South Central High School parent at a birthday party. The beating of the parent was captured on home video and broadcast on major news stations around the country.

Aware of this very public community history, the students arrived at South Central High on July 6, 2004, in time for the end of a summer school day. Their plan was to interview students and teachers regarding their thoughts about youth civic participation in the community. While they were conducting their first interview with students in the front of the school, three police cars sped in front of them and screeched to a halt. Officers jumped out of their cars and chased down two students, apprehending them and placing them in handcuffs. The seminar students stopped the interview to capture the police activity on tape.

For Miguel, a Latino student from a more affluent high school, the events were both distressing and eye opening:

> I never knew stuff like that happened. I mean I did, I mean I've heard about it and seen stuff like that on TV, but to have it happening right before me and to watch it all through the lens of the camera ... that made me feel like I was doing something important, like I had a responsibility to let other people know what is happening in communities like this one.

For Tanya, a student at South Central High, her sense of responsibility was narrated a bit differently:

> Man, people just don't know—that's everyday around here. You just get to thinking that that's normal, even though inside you know it's not right. But, the more I think about it, I know it's not right ... maybe I'm supposed to do something about that.

Although Miguel and Tanya come from different parts of the city, they both understood the significance of the events they witnessed and the importance of having captured them within their research. At the end of the four weeks in the field, they volunteered to produce the group's final video. The visual text they created represents the best of the civic capacities among urban youth. It is filled with critique of the circumstances they witness and endure on a regular basis and optimism about the possibility of change.

Power and Pedagogy for the People The video begins with the title *Power and Pedagogy for the People* transposed on top of the image of a community mural. The mural is of several members of the Black Panthers, each clad entirely in black and holding up a clenched fist. The member in the center of the mural is a woman wearing dark glasses and holding a shotgun. In the background "Why? (What's Goin' On?)," a track from rap group The Roots' latest album plays, repeating the title of the song to the beat of heavy bass and symbols. As the soundtrack rolls, the images on screen switch to establishing shots of the community surrounding the high school. These images present their own critiques, which are made even more dramatic by the driving bass and a woman's melodic voice repeating the question, "Why?"

The establishing shots begin with running footage of a street sign of the renowned, and sometimes infamous, Crenshaw Boulevard and high school students sitting in front of a boarded-up house covered with graffiti. From there, different still images of billboards in the community appear with each beat of the bass drum: The Liquor Bank, 888-Get-Money, Housewives 98 Cent

Store, Hustler Casino. The still shots give way to images of the front of the high school as students pour out at the end of a school day.

As the camera moves to footage of students inside the school, the lyrics make a poignant critique of the sociopolitical climate in urban centers:

I'm kinda gettin' a little tired of always hittin'
That's the reason I'm gonna speak my mind
To keep from goin' insane...
We in the last innin'
The world keeps spinnin'
My people steady losin'
While the rich keep winnin'
It's like we never smilin'
And the devil steady grinnin'
Killin' what we representin'
Even our children and women'
[Video cuts to images of students leaving school.]
Young teens join the Marines
So they can die for the cause
Inducted up into the government's war
In the land full of money
Aint it funny
How none of it's yours

—The Roots, 2004, track 10

As the song's lyrics fade out, the beat continues as a black title screen appears with the words "September 1998," and then a second screen with the words, "817 9th Graders enroll at South Central High School." These titles transition into a poem performed by Xzavion, a 2004 South Central High graduate, who raps,

Being a brother every day is a struggle
That's why we hustle
And pack heat instead of muscle
And blast instead of tussle
Keep your head up
Because one day the storm will let up
And we'll finally all be able to get up
But you must pray upon the cross
Because most of our souls is lost

As Xzavion's voice and image fade out, they are replaced by new title screens that read "June 2003," then "Out of the 817 9th graders only 445 students graduate," then, "Student Disappearance Rate = 46%," and finally, "WHY?"

In the first 90 seconds of the video, students have drawn from popular music and still images, establishing shots, live interview footage, poetry, rap, and school demographic data to make a statement about the larger social context of urban schools and also the local context of South Central High School. This multilayered use of media texts to engage in social commentary is a profoundly literate activity. It is also a powerful example of the capacity of young people to speak critically about the conditions in their communities.

Having drawn from the canvas of the South Central community to establish the need for critical inquiry and analysis, the students then split the video into a series of sections. Each section begins with a topic title and is used to expand on the critical commentary, as well as to provide solutions for improving conditions in schools and the community.

"Citizenship and Authority." The first of these sections addresses youth and community perspectives on the relationship between citizenship and authority.[2] The section begins with an interview with South Central High's Assistant Principal, Mr. Nathan. As Nathan makes the claim that "we have our citizenship, we just don't know how to use it," the film cuts away from him to the live footage of the police arresting students and taking them away in handcuffs—the aforementioned footage from the research group's first day on campus. As one handcuffed black male youth is led away by a police officer, Nathan's voice is replaced by rap group Dead Prez's "They Schools":

> *I got my diploma from a school called Rickers*
> *Full of teenage mothers and drug dealin' niggas*
> *In the hallways the popo [police] was always present*
> *Search through niggas' possessions for dope and weapons*

> —Dead Prez, 2000, track 3

With these lyrics in the background, the image transitions from the student being taken away to footage the documentarians collected while inside the school. This footage is of two police officers walking through the breezeways of the school twirling their nightsticks and striking plastic garbage cans with them.

From the images of the police presence on campus, the video jumps to a lengthy interview piece with Aida, a Latina and South Central senior. Aida, having witnessed the police wandering through the breezeways, opens her interview by saying, "you have just witnessed what we go through everyday." Her testimonial is convincing as she stares straight at the camera, hands on her hips, head bobbing for attitude affect, lecturing the camera about the conditions South Central students endure:

We have to go to class with cops behind us.... sometimes we're on lockdown. Do you know what a lockdown is? A lockdown is when you're afraid you're gonna get shot if you get outside your classroom. They

keep you in a classroom for four and a half hours. They don't let you
out; not even to go to the restroom unless you're escorted.

This section reveals again the power of critical media as a tool of social
critique. The students are able to use a composite of various data sources to
construct a critical commentary about the increasing militarization of urban
school campuses. The blending of interviews with live footage of the overbear-
ing police presence on the school campus paints a disturbing but poignant
picture of the conditions of the urban school climate.

"Where Do We Go from Here?" Having painted a somewhat bleak picture of
the conditions facing youth in the South Central community, the next section
of the documentary brings forth the students' sense of hope. The section
begins with the question, "Where do we go from here?" This suggests that
while these students are aware that these conditions are not socially just, they
also understand that the response to these conditions remains an open-ended
question. Taking this as an opportunity to exert their agency, they spend the
remainder of the documentary discussing potential forms of individual and
institutional agency that are available toward enacting social change.

The students' approach to discussing agency begins with a counternarrative
to mainstream narratives of urban communities. They challenge deficit models of a culture of poverty and its pursuant claims of social apathy, laziness,
and listlessness. They begin this counternarrative by revisiting their interview
with the assistant principal, Mr. Nathan, who posits, "If people can spend time
at home, with their children, with their family, then they probably will have a
better situation. But, when you got to work four and five jobs just to make
ends meet … that's hell."

The students draw from Mr. Nathan's critique of the low-wage, service-
based economy that dominates South Central Los Angeles to challenge
popular notions that the problems of the urban family are due to social
deviance. Their use of Mr. Nathan's commentary suggests an understanding
that the absence of a just economic pay structure results in a disintegrating
family structure and the pursuant disintegrating social structure necessary
for widespread community success. They further their critique by inserting
Mr. Nathan's stock advice for students facing these challenges: "Understand
two words: "educate yourself." These words are often the only solution offered
to urban youth. However, this promise of the self-made individual, the
Horatio Alger parable, is a bankrupt promise in the eyes of urban youth who
find schools and the lessons taught in them increasingly less relevant to their
survival in the world. The students interpret Nathan's comments to be an
endorsement for education, and more specifically for attending school and
doing well there. To highlight the hollowness of this solution, they spring into
an examination of the massive inequalities present in the curriculum and
pedagogy at South Central High.

"Educate Yourself: Where Should We Start?" This section of the documentary returns to Aida, whose earlier critique of the militarized conditions at South Central is replaced by a more subdued stance and tone. Aida suggests that students and parents can turn to the school board to address school conditions: "The school board is there for students to voice their opinions ... that's basically the best you can do. Go out to these meetings ... go out with your group of supporters. Go out and petition. Basically, become an activist."

The video's use of Aida's duplicitous position shows the students' understanding of the double bind facing urban youth. Aida is both highly critical of the unjust conditions at her school, but trapped in the logic of turning to the very system she critiques for answers. The students respond to Aida's suggestions by inserting footage from their visit to the school board.

During the second week of the seminar, all of the research teams attended a group interview session with the representatives of several school board members. At the interview, one student asked what the school board planned to do about the low college going rates at most city center schools in Los Angeles. The representative for the South Central District responded, "We definitely have to do a better job with the secondary curriculum, so we've been focusing on the secondary literacy program."

As a response to both Aida and the representative, the video fades out of the promise of an improved secondary literacy program to images of Language!—the six-million-dollar literacy program that the Los Angeles Unified School District recently purchased for its secondary schools.

While running images of Language! the video plays a segment of rap group Dead Prez's song "They Schools" in the background. On this portion of the audio track, Dead Prez has sampled a scolding man's voice that asks, "Why haven't you learned anything?" Following the man's question is the voice of M-1, a member of Dead Prez, speaking over an eerie synthetic beat, mixed with acoustic piano:

Man, that school shit is a joke
The same people that control the school system
control the prison system
and the whole social system
Ever since slavery.

—Dead Prez, 2000, track 3

As this commentary plays, the documentary runs footage of the Language! textbooks being used to remediate Los Angeles's lowest achieving students. This footage begins with establishing shots of the books themselves, showing the books stacked on a desk and revealing the title of the literacy program splayed across all the primers. The camera then moves to a tight shot of an open textbook, revealing early elementary level text featuring cartooned, over-sized pictures of a cat next to the phrase, "A fat cat." Gliding across the desk, the camera moves to the next textbook, which uses an entire page to display an image of a boy swinging a bat, with large and boldface text that reads, "Thad is at bat. Wham! Bam! Thin Thad can hit it to the rim! Thad can dash. Thad has a big win!"

The images of this literacy program end with a shot of another textbook chapter titled "The Hat." On the chapter's title page, there is a cartooned image of a boy wearing a sombrero. Pages of the book are turned to reveal another cartooned, oversized image of this same boy asleep under a tree with the sombrero pulled over his face. The text next to the image reads, "Al can nap. The pal can nap." This segment ends with the camera moving in for a tight shot of this deeply disturbing image, which evokes racist popularized images of the lazy Mexican. Dead Prez's music is replaced by the school board representative's voice echoing, "literacy program, literacy program, literacy program" while an all-black title screen with the question "WHY?" appears.

This portion of the documentary reveals a variety of creatively critical responses to the conditions in schools. The seamlessness of the multi-layered critique in this segment of the video is profound. The students are able to move through at least three layers of critique, from (1) Aida's suggestion of turning to the school board, to (2) actual footage of commentary by the school board on their most recent major curriculum policy, to (3) footage of some of the material consequences of that policy. Even more could be made of the students' use of sound and image to critique the implementation of a dumbed-down and culturally irrelevant literacy program and its latent racialized images in the lowest-performing secondary schools districtwide.

From the school board, the video moves to an interview with Khalil, the South Central community member and middle-aged black parent beaten by the police mentioned earlier in this chapter. Khalil, answering the students' questions about what young people can do to become more civically engaged, responds almost as though he is speaking directly to the school board:

> You're dealing with folks who are not like-minded and that don't appreciate your values, or your understanding of what it is that you're trying to deal with…. You know, people just make remarks without thinking. That just goes to show you that people are not taking the time out to think before they act or say. So, that's where you know, you have to sit back and learn, well, okay, I'm not gonna do that.

Khalil's comments are used by the students to accomplish two things: first, they act as a response to the school board's track record of insensitive and misguided policies for increased policing and uncaring curriculum; second, they act as impetus for urban youth and communities to look inward for answers. This second use makes room for transition from a largely critical analysis of the conditions in schools and the community to the second portion of the video, which explores the possibilities for change.

"Turning to Self and Community for Answers." The students use this section of the video to represent the voices of the community as they speak out about what they want and need from elected officials and teachers. This begins with an extended interview with two recent South Central High School graduates:

Josh: They need to come make a visit instead of just being way up in Sacramento, talking about it on the news, talking about what they gonna do. They need to actually come down here and take some action. They need to come down here—

Mia: —and see what we need.

J: —and walk down the street with me. Walk around, talk to people. Talk to some of these crack heads that's out here. 'Cause they have stuff to say too, they done been through a whole lot.

M: Arnold Schwarzenegger went to everywhere else but here. I don't understand how ...

J (interjecting): Yeah. They go to all the nice neighborhoods.

M: I was just sayin' last night, 'cause of this Democratic Convention thing, and they travellin' around and campaigning. They should do that throughout the whole course of their time as president, or whatever their position is, they should come and talk to the people. If we vote for you guys, then they just sell us all these lies. I can't vote yet, but they sell all these people that vote all these lies and they don't live up to any of the stuff they s'posed to be doin'. And now we have this major budget crisis and that's effecting my education.

The inclusion of these two voices dispels myths of civically disinterested urban youth. What is captured here are voices of urban young people that are aware of the politics of campaigning, current political events, and the disinvestment of elected officials in the interests of urban communities. Both Josh and Mia are calling for an accountability from their elected officials that requires those officials to experience the lived conditions and voices of all the walks of urban life—from crackheads to gang members to college students.

The students return to the interview with community leader and parent Khalil, to display potential strategies for creating this sort of accountability:

> We need to confront our leaders, as young people, even myself. Confront them and ask them, where are they going and what do they want to do? And from there, I think we can establish with our own young generation of what we want to do from there. That gives us an idea of what's already been done and what we need to do from there.

As with Josh and Mia, Khalil is also calling for accountability from leaders. They want all generations to confront leaders and demand a plan from them for how they expect to address the needs of the community. The students' choice to include these voices is a call for increased critical civic engagement from urban youth; one that demands action from leaders while also expecting young people to hold leaders accountable.

From elected officials, the discussion turns to the role of educators for improving conditions in urban communities. For answers about what young people want out of the curriculum and teachers more generally, the video returns to the interview with Josh:

> Teachers need to talk about more realistic things than just going by what the book is telling you to teach us. You need to really reach out to people. Talk about real situations that people are really going through. 'Cause most of the time when the teacher is up there talkin' about all that other stuff, you not thinkin' about that, you're thinkin' about your situation that you're goin' through.

Although Josh wishes his teachers would connect with him on a more personal level, this logic is not always lost on adults. Sadly, some of the adults that understand this basic principle of being an educator are not given the opportunity to be in front of kids on a daily basis. Instead, those who come from the community and often have the most grounded understanding of the needs of the young people there are positioned outside of the classroom. To drive this point home, the video turns to a separate interview with Eleanor, a South Central High School custodian:

> People need to get more involved with the students as far as talkin' to them on a one to one basis, seein', you know, what's on their mind. These are things that I do. I'm not sayin' that everybody has to do them, but that's something that I do.

Eleanor's comments clearly reflect the same sensibilities that Josh is hoping for from teachers. From Eleanor, the video returns to Josh and Mia to expand on what it means to have teachers with sensibilities like Eleanor's.

> Josh: You'll be in a zone thinkin' about your own problems and stuff that's happenin' out in the streets and stuff ...

Mia [*speaking over Josh*]: Uh-huh … that doesn't matter …

J: that doesn't really concern you. But when the teacher hops on your level then you can really open up, like, dang! and get stuff off your chest. It might help solve problems that you're goin' through.

M [*referring to Mr. Cam, her favorite teacher*]: He asks questions.

J [*speaking over Mia*]: Yeah, he asks questions.

M: He asks, like, What's goin' on in you guys's lives, and do you have any experiences that relate to our lesson?

J: Most of these teachers they livin' way out here in Beverley Hills and the Valley, North Hollywood …

M: … and they teachin' us through their stereotypes.

J: Keep it real. Mr. Cam is the only teacher that I know that stay in the 'hood. Where I done been walkin' down the street and just seen Mr. Cam: "Oh, what's up?" So, he knows what goes on around here.

M: A lot of teachers, they teach us about out here through their stereotypes. So, it's hard for us to respect them because they lookin' at it negatively, and we lookin' like [*imitating a dialogue with a teacher*], "Well, I live here and it's not as bad as you think. Where do you stay?"

M: And once we find out they don't live out here, or they live in a better area, it's like, I can't honor the things that you sayin'. Because number one, you're down-talking me. You're down-talking my environment, which means you're basically disrespecting my whole history because everybody that I know has been livin' out here. So, that causes a problem as well.

It should not be surprising that in its effort to raise the critical voices of the community, the video draws most heavily from other young people and a community activist like Khalil. They seem keenly in tune with the fact that these voices can best represent the critical perspectives and agency needed for healing urban communities like South Central. By drawing so heavily upon those voices in the video, they also issue a not-so-tacit critique of the fact that these voices are all but absent in the mainstream discourse about what is needed in urban communities. In keeping with this pattern of giving voice to the margins, the video concludes with a series of recommendations about pro-active steps that can be taken by urban community members.

"Know Your History: Claim Control of (Y)Our Future." The title of this final section reflects the students' sense of the interconnectedness of the past with the present and the individual with the collective. By harkening on the importance of knowing one's history, the video insists that these conditions did not come to pass by accident, and neither should it be forgotten that there is a long and proud history of resistance among marginalized groups. The second part of the title reflects their sense that the word *your* cannot be spelled without including *our*, showing the connection between the individual and the collective. The video allows these ideas to be narrated in much the way the video began—that is, laying multiple media over one another to represent a complex idea.

The image moves quickly from footage of the interview with Khalil to footage of the South Central mural that began the video. Initially, Khalil is speaking in the background as the video scrolls through the mural's timeline of black history:

History is our greatest teacher. [*Camera cuts away to image of Malcolm X.*] And I think even right now, we need to start incorporating more of our histories. [*Camera cuts to image of Native Africans with drums.*] You know, black ... [*camera scrolls onto image of Mayan civilization*] ... and brown. One, to get an understanding of where we come from and where we can go with our potential. [*Camera scrolls to images of slave ships, graphic lettering of the word STOLEN, and images of African slaves in chains landing on Western shores.*] And two, to give ourselves a base, an understanding of faith, something to believe in. So that when there are disappointing times, or we have setbacks, it's not so devastating, we don't give up.

As Khalil finishes speaking, rapper Tupac's "Thugz Mansion" emerges as the soundtrack for the mural A camera scrolls across mural image of slaves being led in chains by a slave master to the auction block as Tupac raps,

I hear the gunshots
Nobody cares, see the politicians ban us
They'd rather see us locked in chains
Please explain why they can't stand us.
[Camera cuts to mural image of a slave with a hammer, breaking his chains off.]
Is there a way for me to change
Or am I just a victim of things I did to maintain?
[Camera cuts to mural images of Frederick Douglass, a black Civil War soldier, and a black Vietnam War soldier, and then scrolls to an image of Sojourner Truth holding a scroll that reads "All Men Are Created Equal."]
I need a place to rest my head

With the little bit of homeboys that remain
'Cause all the rest dead
Is there a spot for us to grow?
If ya find it, I'll be right behind ya
Show me and I'll go.

—Tupac, 2002, Disk 2, track 2

With Tupac's beat fading out, the video cuts to an interview with Gerard, a South Central community member in his early twenties, who says, "If we can just together, and establish something, it can happen." Gerard's comments here extend the video's challenge to stereotypes of the apathetic and hopeless young black man, presenting another piece of the group's critical counternarrative.

The tapestry woven by the video gets its final threads from Chisom, a 2004 South Central High graduate, who concludes the video by reading a poem she wrote:

While there's hope
We still have no clue
What they system's lies is doin' to you
Keepin' you from the most important thing you need: school
How many boys and girls don't graduate each year?
How many mothers' high hopes turn to fear?
If learning the truth is a battle
And this simplicity has you rattled
Then your life has chose its path

To conclude, the video cuts away from Chisom and back to the image of the Black Panthers from the video's opening title screen. Here the students added an echo effect to Chisom's reading of her final lines, resulting in the first four lines repeating twice and overlapping with the next line. The echoing of her voice becomes the backdrop for the still image of the Panthers with their fists raised in the air:

One thought [echoing:] One thought
Turns into one fist [echoing:] Turns into one fist
Multiplied by millions [echoing:] Multiplied by millions
Who choose to rise and resist [echoing:] Who choose to rise and resist
That's what's real
That's real
And, that's how we feel

Chisom's voice fades into a Tupac rap as the credits scroll against a black title screen. Tupac's widely recognizable voice allows the video to make one last statement to its viewers. Against the melody of an acoustic piano and a driving bass drum, he raps from "Me Against the World":

Scared of revolution
But I ain't givin' up on the hood
'Cuz I'd rather die

—Tupac, 1998, track 3

The video then cuts to Tupac's *"Me against the world."*

I'm losin' my homies in a hurry
They relocatin' to the cemetery
Don't wanna make excuses
'cause this is how it is
What's the use
Unless we shootin'
No one notices the youth
It's just me against the world.

—Tupac, 1998, track 3

Implications

The summer seminar was transformative for participants in several ways. It allowed them to develop and represent critical literacy through examinations of Los Angeles's schools and communities; it also allowed them to engage in multiple forms of social action. The act of doing socially responsible research in their communities is the most obvious form of their social action. However, their research findings have also been used in teacher education programs and educational research conferences around the nation. Finally, their documentation of the conditions in their communities and their proposed solutions to these conditions (in short, "rise and resist") are also forms of social action.

The students' video is a powerful example of social action on multiple levels. It is powerful as an example of the critical capacity and agency of urban youth. It is powerful as a counternarrative to the stories of apathetic and disengaged urban communities. It is powerful as a critique of the conditions of urban schools and communities. It is powerful as a tool that gives voice to a community that screams everyday but is seldom heard. It is powerful because it represents the expansive and wonderful abilities of urban students to contribute to the dialogue about social justice in ways that no standardized test could purport to measure. It is powerful because it exemplifies the types of complex and critical literacy skills made possible by giving students access to a postcolonial pedagogy—an "empowering education." It is powerful because, as Miguel put it, "having the cameras ... forced [us] to open our eyes to the inequities that we had not taken notice of before; we effectively became aware citizens."

The South Central group was not unique in their production of a powerful video documentary. The other three research groups also worked tirelessly to create moving videos based on their research. One group brought overnight wear and sleeping bags, staying all night on the university campus to finish their video in time for the final presentation. Another group stayed until 3:00 A.M. before rushing home to change clothes in time for the presentation. Tanya, a South Central High School student and member of the South Central research group, commented on the dramatic change she witnessed in one of her schoolmates that worked on the video for the East Los Angeles research group: I've never seen Keith this excited about doing work," she said. "Never. For him to stay up here till all hours of the morning to do some work on a project? Nope. Never."

Keith agreed, adding,

Man, school should be like this. If school was like this students would be way more willing to work. I mean, it's like it's not even really work. You can't even really call it that because it's fun and it's important.

The majority of the summer seminar participants were like Tanya and Keith, who are like most students in urban schools. They are not considered college material by their schools and their low grades and frequent disinvestment in school reflect those expectations. However, what Tanya's and Keith's comments make clear is the potential of the right pedagogical approach to recapture the interest and commitment of America's most disenfranchised young people.

Urban youth bring unique and important insight to the dialogue about social justice. They experience the material conditions of urban poverty in visceral ways that cannot be captured through adult lenses. Sadly, schools and the larger society have failed to create avenues with which youth can discuss their understandings of the problems and conditions facing urban centers. The absence of these narratives has not only meant the increasing marginalization of urban youth, but also that insight into solutions to these problems have been overlooked.

The challenge facing schools is to make use of pedagogical approaches that link literacy to social action and civic participation. If urban school leaders and teachers can muster the courage to be responsive to the sharp and critical insights of the students they serve, these kinds of educational endeavors can help schools connect more deeply with the communities they are serving. By allowing for pedagogy that uses literacy development to address the most immediate concerns in the lives of young people, schools will also have access to commissioned self-studies. The feedback made available in these studies can provide schools with valuable insights into how to more effectively serve their students.

The implications of this study are clear for anyone seeking to tap into the potential of urban youth as partners in addressing the educational opportunity gap. Administrators, teachers, teacher educators, and policy makers should pay heed, not only to the critique presented in the students' video, but in their comments about the process of building that critique. Student work products like this make it clear that it is the adults that are failing, not the kids. It is the 21st century, and it is high time that pedagogy and curriculum catch up with that fact by tapping into the new century's literacies and the capacity of urban youth to use those literacies to critically read and respond to their world.

Notes

1. The author lives in the South Central community and was witness to these series of events.
2. Each of this article's subsequent section titles are in quotation marks because they are the subsection titles used in the documentary.

References

Banks, J. A. (1994). Ethnicity, class, cognitive, and motivational styles: Research and teaching implications. In J. Kretovicks & E. J. Nussel (Eds.), *Transforming urban education* (pp. 277–290). Boston: Allyn & Bacon.

Berg, B. L. (2004). *Qualitative research methods for social sciences*. New York: Allyn & Bacon.

Dead Prez. (2000). *Let's get free*. Santa Monica, CA: Relativity Records.

Duncan-Andrade, J. (2004). Your best friend or your worst enemy: Youth popular culture, pedagogy and curriculum at the dawn of the 21st century. *Review of Education, Pedagogy and Cultural Studies, 26*(4), 313–337.

Duncan-Andrade, J., & Morrell, E. (2005). Turn up that radio, teacher: Popular cultural pedagogy in new century urban schools. *Journal of School Leadership, 15*, 284–304.

Finn, P. (1999). *Literacy with an attitude: Educating working-class children in their own self interest*. Albany: State University of New York Press.

Freire, P., & Macedo, D. (1987). *Literacy: Reading the word and the world*. South Hadley, MA: Bergin and Garvey.

Gee, J. (2004). *What video games have to teach us about learning and literacy*. New York: Palgrave.

Goodman, S. (2003). *Teaching youth media: A critical guide to literacy, video production, and social change*. New York: Teachers College Press.

Grossberg, L. (1994). Bringin' it all back home: Pedagogy and cultural studies. In H. Giroux & P. McLaren (Eds.), *Between borders: Pedagogy and the politics of cultural studies*. New York: Routledge.

Kress, G. (2003). *Literacy in the new media age*. New York: Routledge.

Ladson-Billings, G. (1994). *The dreamkeepers: Successful teachers of African American children*. San Francisco: Jossey-Bass.

Lee, C. (2004). Literacy in the academic disciplines and the needs of adolescent struggling readers. *Adolescent Literacy*, Issue 3, 14–25.

MacLeod, J. (1987). *Ain't no makin' it: Aspirations and attainment in a low-income neighborhood*. San Francisco: Westview.

Mahiri, J. (2004). *What they don't learn in school: Literacy in the lives of urban youth*. New York: Peter Lang.

Moll, L., Amanti, C., Neff, D., & Gonzalez, N. (1992). Funds of knowledge for teaching: Using a qualitative approach to connect homes and classrooms. *Theory into Practice, 31*, 132–141.

Morrell, E. (2004a). *Becoming critical researchers: Literacy and empowerment for urban youth*. New York: Peter Lang.

Morrell, E. (2004b). *Linking literacy and popular culture: Finding connections for lifelong learning*. Norwood, MA: Christopher-Gordon.

Morrell, E., & Duncan-Andrade, J. (2003). What youth do learn in school: Using hip hop as a bridge to canonical poetry. In J. Mahiri (Ed.), *What they don't learn in school: Literacy in the lives of urban youth.* New York: Peter Lang.

Oakes, J., & Lipton, M. (2001). *Teaching to change the world.* Boston: McGraw-Hill.

The Roots (2004). *Tipping point.* Santa Monica, CA: Geffen Records.

Solorzano, D., & Delgado-Bernal, D. (2001). Examining transformational resistance through a critical race and latcrit theory framework: Chicana and Chicano students in an urban context. *Urban Education, 36*(3), 308–342.

Tupac (1998). *Me against the world.* Jive Records.

Tupac (2002). *Better dayz.* Santa Monica, CA: Interscope Records. Disc 2, track 2.

Westheimer, J., & Kahne, J. (2002). What kind of citizen? The politics of educating for democracy. *American Educational Research Journal, 41*(2), 237–269.

Section III
Street Corner Democracy: Youth, Civil Society, and Community Change

The very idea of education cannot be adequately understood without attention to the meaning of democracy. Questions regarding what it means to be educated, the purpose and function of education, and what it means to be a citizen in America are questions that lie at the heart of democratic ideas and the educational process. For years, scholars have agreed that one of the central purposes of education is to promote democratic ideals required for effective citizenry. However, race, class, and gender have always complicated access to democratic participation in America. Similarly, public education also has grappled with questions regarding who should be educated, and this has presented serious challenges to democratic engagement. Decades of racial exclusion from quality education have undoubtedly created two educational realities within black and Latino communities. For some, education is a vehicle for democratic participation and social change; for others, education can serve as a tool to reproduce social inequality and foster apathy for civic affairs. If schools play a central role in preparing young people for democratic participation, how does life outside of schools promote or inhibit civic participation among youth of color from low-income communities?

The chapters in this section grapple with a set of complex questions regarding youth, civil society, and democratic engagement. How can civic engagement in the community shape young people's political identity and consciousness? How is space created in which to sustain political consciousness in community settings? How can local policy expand the grassroots activities reported on in this volume? Addressing these questions, the authors of the following chapters illustrate how social, political, and economic conditions promote institutional failure such as failing schools, environmental degradation, and gentrification while vastly diminishing the living standards for youth and their families.

These forces also severely inhibit young people from expressing their concerns and collectively responding in ways that improve community conditions. In other words, there is no formal democratic process with which young people might voice their concerns about policies that have a negative influence on their lives. Thus, the chapters in this section focus on how young people create the spaces—in conditions where there aren't any established spaces—where they can engage their communities and promote social justice. In chapter 10 Flores-González, Rodríguez, and Rodríguez-Muñiz illustrate the extent that community-based organizations and after-school programs represent that space for young people to express their political needs. These authors demonstrate how local youth can create space to voice their frustrations and transform their anger into community action by using Latino hip-hop culture to raise awareness of social problems, and as a magnet to attract other youth to fight for social justice. Strobel, Osberg, and McLaughlin explore in chapter 11 the contexts that allow youth to examine community and social issues that impact their lives. Drawing on data from an after-school program in the San Francisco Bay Area, the authors identify important features of an after-school advocacy program that enable youth to engage effectively in social change. In chapter 12, Soo Ah Kwon investigates a multiracial coalition of Asian and Pacific Islander youth in the Northern California Bay Area who successfully organized a campaign to stop the expansion of the juvenile hall in their community known as the Super Jail. Kwon illustrates how a collective panethnic identity was developed in resistance to the social, political, and economic marginalization of racial minority youth. Although these spaces may be minuscule in comparison to the size of space controlled by the dominant interest in their communities, they symbolically represent huge areas in which young people can devote attention to certain underdeveloped aspects of their own consciousness. Building from chapter 12, O'Donoghue examines in chapter 13 the relationship between space and public efficacy among youth activist organizations and illustrates how organizations facilitate activism among young people. In chapter 14, Aguilar-San Juan argues that youth organizing and youth activism must confront issues of racism and white privilege. By centering her discussion on the Twin Cities, Aguilar-San Juan provides an insightful discussion about the tensions that exist for youth activists of color in predominately white communities.

The chapters in this section are emblematic of the complex relationships among youth, civil society, and democratic engagement. By critically addressing problems of social inequality, the youth represented here evolve through several levels of awareness. First, they see themselves as members of a particular group that shares common cultural or social identities as well as experiences of injustice. Second, they are presented with an opportunity to understand the political economic exigencies that impede their ability to contribute to the development of their communities in ways that meet their needs. And third, some youth recognize that others, beside themselves, suffer from unfair conditions and that they have a stake in transforming the experiences of those who have different identities from them (see Flores-González, Rodríguez, & Rodríguez-Muñiz, chapter 10). In many ways, the chapters provide concrete examples of social justice youth development (Ginwright & Cammarota, 2002) and the levels of awareness that help young people attain an empowered and healthy sense of themselves. Two chapters (see Kwon, chapter 12, and Flores-González, Rodríguez, & Rodríguez-Muñiz, chapter 10) use the social justice youth development (SJYD) framework to analyze the actions of the young people they studied and/or worked with. Although the other chapters apply different theoretical lenses for analysis, they nevertheless touch upon aspects of youth consciousness that relate to the SJYD model.

These spaces come in variety of different forms, but there seems to be a grassroots or organic quality to most—originating from the devotion and hard commitment of the "people," yet outside the purview of the state. It is precisely the ability of these collective bodies of youth "to cultivate and sustain what Melucci called 'submerged networks' of everyday political life where actors produce and practice alternative frameworks of meaning, social relations, and collective identity below the horizon of established or officially recognized institutions" (Gregory, 1998, p. 152; see also Melucci, 1988). Therefore, an effective SJYD policy would not only attend to the political economic conditions fomenting harsh conditions for young people but also support the grassroots, community-based initiatives that expand their democratic participation.

CHAPTER 10

From Hip-Hop to Humanization: Batey Urbano as a Space for Latino Youth Culture and Community Action

NILDA FLORES-GONZÁLEZ, MATTHEW RODRÍGUEZ,
AND MICHAEL RODRÍGUEZ-MUÑIZ

Introduction

The work that we do ... is really more about a process of humanization, rather than automatically the Batey becoming a site, let's say, for organizing around a particular policy.... It's really more based on ... how these youth ... become part of building this community. And from there, sometimes it does mean that we get involved in different policy, maybe we'll go to Springfield, you know to support undocumented issues, and things like that.... The space is decolonizing, and that takes time, and that takes a series of discussions and dialogues, and it takes struggling things out, and it takes not being judgmental with youth, but being a space where they can come together and they can learn, and they can critique, and they can challenge.

—Roberto, founding member of Batey Urbano

The youth at the Batey Urbano stand in sharp contrast to the image most Chicagoans have of the Puerto Rican barrio youth. Humboldt Park has been home to Chicago's Puerto Rican community since the 1950s. Since the 1970s, the young residents of Humboldt Park have been criminalized by the media as gang bangers, dropouts, and teenage mothers. The local high school has been called a "Teenage Cabrini Green," after the infamous Chicago public housing project, and its students have been labeled as "predators." This labeling garnered the public support needed to implement zero tolerance policies in the streets, such as the Anti-Loitering Ordinance, as well as paving the way for the reduction of almost half of the student population at the local high school (Flores-González 2002a).

Accelerated gentrification in the Puerto Rican community since the 1990s has propelled youth to join the struggle to preserve their community. Targeted by police, school officials, and the punitive "low-tolerance" measures that accompany gentrification, they resist and challenge unjust practices through hip-hop, dialogue, and civic participation. Through the Batey Urbano, local youth can voice their frustrations and transform their anger into community action for social justice. They use urban Latino hip-hop culture as the means of communication, as a tool to raise awareness of social problems, and as a magnet to attract other youth to fight for social justice. This chapter discusses how Puerto Rican/Latino youth culture can lead to political transformation, youth organizing, and civic engagement. It also shows the importance of owning a social and physical space for this transformation to happen. Some of the questions this chapter addresses are: (1) how the Batey Urbano uses Latino youth culture to raise self, social and global awareness among youth, (2) how it engages and mobilizes youth to work for social justice, and (3) how it builds on its relationship with adult allies.

The Social Justice Youth Development Model

Ginwright and Cammarota (2002) argue that for youth to truly transform their lives, they need to develop a critical consciousness or understanding of the larger forces that oppress them, their communities, and other oppressed people, to effectively engage in social action to fight oppression. In a continual process of reflection and action, youth become increasingly aware of injustices committed against others and become increasingly committed to fighting for social justice. Ginwright and Cammarota formulated the Social Justice Youth Development model to explicate how youth can move from awareness of, and social action against, their own oppression to awareness of, and action against, the oppression of others. According to Ginwright and Cammarota, youth must progress through three levels of awareness. First, youth must develop self-awareness, or a critical understanding of who they are and how social forces shape their racial, class, gender, and sexual identities. Second, they must develop social awareness, or a critical understanding of how social forces shape inequality and how this affects their communities. Finally, youth must achieve global awareness, and a critical understanding of and a connection with other people's struggles against oppression. It is at this point that they understand oppression and the ways it is manifested around the world: in capitalism, colonialism, racism, and patriarchy. Because of their own and their community's oppression, they can understand, and identify with, other oppressed people and join in social action to fight oppression. Ginwright and

Cammarota add that fighting for social justice becomes a lifestyle that is fueled by their belief that social action will lead to change.

Ginwright and Cammarota (2002) assert that progressive hip-hop, with its critique of capitalism, colonialism, racism, and patriarchy, creates awareness of social problems and politicize youth into taking social action.

> At the self-awareness level, young people use hip-hop culture to express pain, anger, and the frustration of oppression through rap, song, and poetry, or the spoken work. At the level of social awareness, they use hip-hop culture to organize, inform, and politicize at the community level…. At the global awareness level, hip-hop culture carries some possibility to unite youth through common experiences of suffering and common struggles of resistance. (Ginwright & Cammarota, 2002, pp. 91–92)

Ginwright (2004) adds that hip-hop has an immense potential for transforming the educational experience of African American youth.

> I have found that hip-hop culture is a highly effective vehicle for engaging black youth in learning. Music, language, style of dress, poetry, and art can all be effective cultural vehicles to educate youth who have not responded to traditional ethnicity-based multicultural curriculum…. Hip-hop culture can encourage black youth to change their thinking about community problems and act toward creating a more equitable world. (Ginwright, 2004, p. 132)

In this chapter, we provide an example of a youth organization that uses Puerto Rican/Latino youth culture to create political awareness and engage young people in civic actions to improve their community. Using Ginwright and Cammarota's Social Justice Youth Development framework, we show how Batey Urbano uses hip-hop to develop self-awareness, social awareness, and global awareness among marginalized youth in the Puerto Rican barrio. However, this framework offers a linear analysis of progression when, in fact, what we have found in the Batey is that the three stages are in a continuous process of being realized, reformulated, and developed simultaneously. Thus, boundaries among self-awareness, social awareness, and global awareness are not clearly marked. Rather, these three stages of awareness exist along a continuum, with youth moving back and forth along it. What this means is that self awareness leads to social and/or global awareness, social awareness leads to self- and/or global awareness, and global awareness leads to self- and/or social awareness. We also found that at Batey, the youth's ownership of a social and physical space is crucial for the development of self-awareness, social awareness, and global awareness among its youth. For Batey youth, having their own space is not only symbolic but liberating, as it gives them the freedom to speak up and make decisions without the interference of adults. Keeping in mind the fluidity of the process and the importance of owning a space, the social justice youth development framework provides a useful way to show how the Batey helps youth achieve these three levels of awareness.

From Hip-Hop to the Political Transformation of Youth

Youth culture is singled out as proof of youth's destructiveness. While heavy metal music is vilified for its lyrics and negative messages for white youth, the most virulent attacks are deployed against hip-hop and particularly rap music (Binder, 1993). However, the public's views on urban youth are formed largely by the lyrics and the visual images of commercialized gangsta rap, which idolizes the gang banger lifestyle and devalues women as sexual objects. Researchers argue that "progressive" (also called "real" or "authentic") hip-hop speaks to the reality of life in inner-city neighborhoods without glamorizing the gang banger lifestyle (Bynoe, 2004; Kitwana, 2002; Rivera, 2004; Rose, 1994). Instead, it is the media, and in particular the record industry, that has crafted this erroneous image of hip-hop. Besides, there is much more to hip-hop than rap music.

Progressive hip-hop, the one that is created and re-created daily in inner-city streets and from which commercialized gangsta rap emerged, is far from this commercialized form. Hip-hop began in the 1970s, among African American and Puerto Rican youth in New York City, and soon became "the cultural and political voice of an entire generation of youth" (Stapleton, 1998). It emerged as an outlet for the frustration engendered by the social and economic marginalization of inner-city youth. Through its four forms or "elements"—break dancing, graffiti, MCing, and DJing—young people seek to tell their stories of marginalization and strategies for resistance. Hip-hop uses words, symbols, music, and movement to narrate the reality of inner-city life and to protest the social injustice inflicted on African American and Latino youth. Graffiti artists use symbols to tell their stories by painting designs on buildings and trains while b-boys or break dancers' intricate body movements vent their frustration. DJs produce new music styles with their innovative use of turntables, while MCs use rhymes and words to tell their stories.

Hip-hop has become for urban youth a means of communicating who they are and what their experiences have been growing up in the inner-city. Oftentimes, that is the extent of youth involvement with hip-hop: just a way to tell one's personal story. That is also what commercialized rap does and sells for entertainment: telling individual stories of hardships or exploits (drugs, sex, and crime), some of which are based in reality while others are made up. But "progressive" hip-hop, while still entertaining, is a way of expression that has a transformative dimension that leads to collective engagement and action. As such, hip-hop is not only a catalyst of individual experiences, but also a forum where youth become aware of community problems and understand the political, economic, and social forces that create these problems (Ginwright, 2004). Only then can they effectively question and challenge such forces and transform not only their lives but their communities (Ginwright, 2004). As Tony, one of Batey's leaders and a founding member, says,

> Spoken word is more part of the performance, and part of the way that your voice is used, the way that your body is used, the emotions in your face. And again, historically, Latinos and blacks have used voice and poetry in forms of communications, and transforming situations into something that's real, and to the youth, poetry and hip-hop, particularly Spoken Word, has a way to deal with reality, has a way to transform, transfer information to one another, and a way to tell stories and just be human.

> —Tony, founding member

Methods

This project is not conventional because it is not based on a strict methodology that separates the investigator from the participants. Rather, this is a participatory action research that is being carried out collaboratively between a university professor, two graduate students who were members of the Batey Urbano leadership, and members of the Batey Urbano Collective. And while this article lists three authors, members of the Batey Urbano helped by conducting interviews and providing feedback on drafts of this chapter. This ongoing study started as a small summer research project and has grown into a long-term project. The data presented here was mostly compiled in the summer of 2004, with some follow-up interviews in the fall of 2004. Because of the collaboration of Batey Urbano members in this project, most of the data reported here comes from three sources. First, we examined archival material including fliers, reports, and publications in local newsletters. Second, we included actual observations, recorded (audio, video, and photos) observations, and recollected observations (Batey members recounted their observations) of events and programs. Third, we conducted individual interviews with 12 members of Batey Urbano. While the data presented here borrows from the 12 participants, only seven of them are quoted. Tony, Roberto, and Javier are founding members of the Batey, and they are older than most members. Now past their mid-20s and working full-time, Tony, Roberto, and Javier are in the process of "retiring" from the Batey leadership to make room for younger people. Tere, a member of the Batey coordinating collective, and Miriam, who is not in a leadership position, just graduated from college. Alex, who is in his early 20s, has begun to assume more responsibilities and leadership. And Yolanda, who has not reached 20 yet, participates in various Batey programs. The other participants vary in their degree and length of involvement with Batey.

Batey as a Space in Which to Fight Gentrification

It is tough growing up in Humboldt Park, especially now that gentrification is encroaching on the community. Children must contend with poverty, street gangs, "failing" schools, and the lack of after-school programs that characterize inner cities. But they also face the threat of losing their homes and being separated from relatives and friends as more property is bought out to make way for high-priced condos (Alicea, 2002). They also must contend with an antagonistic police force called on to impose repressive ordinances against youth. Some Humboldt Park youth say that police brutality is increasing as gentrification continues to grow. By the 1950s, there was a sizeable Puerto Rican population in Chicago but they were dispersed in different neighborhoods. As urban renewal unfolded in the 1960s, many of the early communities disappeared as Puerto Ricans were forced to move because of rising property taxes and rental costs as well as suspicious fires that left many families homeless (Alicea, 2002; Padilla, 1987; Perez, 2004; Ramos-Zayas, 2003). Most moved to West Town, Humboldt Park, and Logan Square in the near northwest side of the city, where the Puerto Rican community has thrived for the past 40 years or more. In the last decade, West Town and Logan Square have undergone incredible transformation as they have fallen prey to gentrification. As gentrification creeps into Humboldt Park, the Puerto Rican community is facing again the threat of displacement. Different from 40 years ago, Puerto Ricans have launched a full-scale campaign to save their community (Flores-González 2002). This campaign encompasses a comprehensive plan that includes housing, business, education, and cultural development in the community. Spearheaded by the local alderman, the campaign involves over 100 community organizations including elected officials, non-for-profit organizations, churches, and businesses. Batey Urbano is one of the organizations that have joined forces to stop gentrification in the Puerto Rican barrio.

This is not the first time that a Puerto Rican youth organization has become active around the issue of displacement. In the 1960s, the Young Lords was founded in Chicago by a group of Puerto Rican gang members turned activists (Padilla, 1987). This organization later expanded to other cities like New York and Philadelphia. What started as a fight against displacement quickly expanded to other social issues such as affordable housing and day care. The Young Lords protested, disrupted meetings, and even occupied a church to demand social justice. Almost four decades later, Puerto Rican youth at Batey Urbano have organized to fight displacement, but this time they are not going at it alone, as they are part of a larger community effort. This time, they are using Puerto Rican/Latino youth culture to encourage youth to tell their stories and transform their frustration into a fight against gentrification.

Batey, as its members call it, was founded in March 2002 by a group of college students from Northeastern Illinois University, the University of Chicago, and the University of Illinois at Chicago. It is affiliated with the Juan Antonio Corretjer Puerto Rican Cultural Center (PRCC), a non-profit community-based organization that runs diverse programs in Humboldt Park. The PRCC is built on the principles of a "philosophy of self-determination, a methodology of self-actualization and critical thought, and an ethics of self-reliance best expressed in the motto 'To Live and Help To Live'" (PRCC, 2005, web page). According to its website, Batey's objectives are

(1) to provide a space for meaningful and purposeful representation of young Latinos' cultural experience, (2) to promote the skilled development of young Latino artists and cultural workers through forums, workshops, video presentations, etc., (3) to build a bridge between the Latino youth at the universities and in the community through the enhancement and/or development of campus newsletters, and (4) to support the organizing efforts of the community through a cultural and youth activists dimension. (www.bateyurbano.org, 2005)

Batey serves youth between the ages of 12 and 27. It is run by a coordinating collective, which is made up of college-age youths, mostly students at local universities. The collective, which meets at least once a week, is responsible for the operations, management, and programming of Batey. There is also a youth collective, comprised of students from seven surrounding high schools, ranging in age from 12 to 17 (some youth are still in elementary school and others remain part of the youth collective until they go to college). The Youth Collective also meets weekly, as Roberto explains, to "discuss what they want to do for the month, and our job, as [the] Batey [Coordinating] Collective is to facilitate students having those opportunities" (Roberto, Batey founding member). In addition to the collectives, there are different ways for youth to become involved in Batey. Some youths are "partners," who despite having no official vote or direct participation in decision making assist in the coordination of programs and general operations of Batey. Miriam, a college student and Partner, explains that Batey is an inclusive space where "I'm not worried about not being part of the collective because I do not feel excluded from the process." Other youth become "supporters" by participating as the audience or performers who make small monetary donations at the door. Finally, others may become "affiliates," who do not routinely participate in programs but may contribute human and financial resources to Batey.

Although Batey had its first month of rent and the cost of its outdoor sign funded by the PRCC, it quickly became an autonomous program that makes its own decisions and is self-sufficient financially. Most of its funding comes from the proceeds of the "Collection Basket" $3–$5 suggested donations that are collected during events, donations from other community organizations, and small grants written jointly with other organizations.

Batey challenges the popular notions of urban Puerto Rican/Latino youth culture as a negative influence on youth. At Batey youth can listen, write, perform, and ultimately shape what their culture is as Puerto Ricans and as Latinos. It is a space where young people can listen, discuss, and reflect on pressing social issues affecting them and their communities. It is also a space where young people learn to use words to communicate their feelings and thoughts in writing, and where they can speak up about them publicly. There, they can also learn valuable computer skills while doing hip-hop. The remainder of this chapter shows how Batey uses Puerto Rican/Latino youth culture to develop self-awareness, social awareness, and global awareness among the youth in the Humboldt Park neighborhood.

"This space here, it seems pretty small, but it's huge": From Hip-Hop to Humanization

> *This space here, it seems pretty small, but it's huge. It's huge in its nature, it's huge in the global processes and the way that it allows for us to connect. … So if you take the [Batey] with you wherever you go, then that becomes part of your experience…. And like I said, taking it outside, outside of the space, taking it outside of here, and really representing what the Batey is, what Batey represents. And I think that ultimately that's the meaning of the space.*

> —Miriam, Batey Urbano member

To an outsider, Batey may appear as a small storefront youth organization dedicated to progressive hip-hop. But Batey Urbano is more; it is a space for critical expression through spoken word, poetry, dancing, music, painting, and writing. It is, according to founding member Javier, "a space in the community for youth to be able to come and express themselves through expressions of … poetry, hip-hop, and other forms of Puerto Rican expressions." On most weekends, there is good poetry, rap, and music. The message carried by the verses and lyrics speaks of the pain and the joy of growing up in the Puerto Rican barrio. Most of the performances are good because they are authentic and come from lived experiences and are delivered from the heart. Some are simply extraordinary masterpieces that have little to envy, to the work of better-known performers. If one sticks around long enough, Batey takes on a different meaning, and it indeed becomes a much larger space that transcends its physical space; it is a space that takes youth from self-discovery to humanity. The extraordinary performances fade into the background, and what becomes fascinating is the political work going on there. Batey is much more than about helping youth discover their voices. It is about helping youth hear other voices. It is about helping youth unite their voices. Ultimately, Batey is all about transforming youth's voice into social action. What happens at Batey clearly shows how hip-hop and its message of social justice can be used to mobilize young people to engage in civic action to better their communities. As Tony explains,

> I mean, we're activists, that's what we do; we actively attack the system from within, and any means that we can use, as far as legally, and as far

as what we do, and sometimes, whether it's civil disobedience, whether it's strategies to address policy, or whether it's actually just building with young people and getting the needs of the community, and organizing a community to be able to determine itself on every level. We use the art forms to try to address that, [and] also to teach students skills, whether its media—to control our own media—to be able to have access to those things and those skills, and to really be able to start processing and determining our futures on every level.

—Tony, Batey founding member

"Hip-hop moves my soul": Batey as a Space for Self-Awareness

I think hip-hop is a series of expressions having to do with your inner self. I think hip-hop is who you are, what you live through. Hip-hop is a way of living, a way of life. When I think about hip-hop, I think of all the experiences that I have, I think of all the experiences that I want to have in life. So, I really think that hip-hop is life for me. Life in the sense that I love music, and music moves my soul, so hip-hop moves my soul. So I think it is part of my mind-set to live in a way what I think. I think hip-hop really moves me in a way that other types of music wouldn't be able to.

—Alex, Batey Urbano Coordinating Collective member

Hip-hop moves the soul of many urban youths, making it particularly suitable for raising awareness of social issues. Hip-hop moves the soul because the rhythms, lyrics, and body movements speak directly to the experiences of urban youth in Humboldt Park. The founders of Batey knew that "youth are attracted to rhyme" and that through hip-hop they would be able to find the path to self-awareness. In fact, the core of Batey and what generates the greatest following are its Three Nights of Expression, when youth can come to watch, listen to, and perform hip-hop. Thursday Nights are reserved for Poetry w/ Purpose, and youth can read their own or someone else's poetry. Typically, the night starts with an open mic (where poets can sign up to read their work), followed by a discussion of the poetry, and closing with a featured local poet. Friday Nights are set aside for the Five Elements of Hip-Hop and "battles" are often hosted, as well as featured performances of local talent. Mostly attended by high school students, these nights are loud and energetic, with the sounds produced by DJs, the improvised lyrics of the MCs, the beats of "human beat-boxers," and the exhilarating moves of the B-boys. Saturday Nights are set aside for Cultural Engagement, and are dedicated to Puerto Rican and Latino cultural affirmation through art exhibits, movies, speakers, live musical performances of the dance and music styles of Bonba y Plena, and other forms of Latino cultural expression.

Batey attracts youth who simply want to "listen to the music," but it also attracts youth who want to speak up. It provides the space, while hip-hop gives them a voice and a language through which to explore and make sense of who they are and how they fit in this world. Furthermore, Batey is a space where they can claim an ethnic identity that is devalued by society. In fact, the issue of identity is the most recurrent theme that emerges in performances. As Roberto explains, Batey is all about

> questioning identity and what it means ... and there's also this realiza-
> tion that the youth go into high school and they never learn about being
> Puerto Rican. I was never taught that there was a value in being Puerto
> Rican, or in being Mexican and things like that. So, it's also how to be
> retrained [in an] identity that for all their life has meant nothing. And
> so you see that being a topic, a recurring topic that they are taking own-
> ership; "I'm Puerto Rican and that's something. That means something.
> I'm somebody."
>
> —Roberto, Batey founding member

These youth have been subjected to what Valenzuela (1999, p. 3) calls *subtractive schooling,* the process by which a school "divests these youth of important social and cultural resources." Not only do the schools systemati-cally devalue the students' national, cultural, and linguistic backgrounds, but any display of urban youth culture, particularly in their dress, demeanor, and speech style, is interpreted as a sign that they are unintelligent low achievers and that they do not care about school (Valenzuela, 1999). By contrast, Batey is an *additive* space where youth can find their voice and a way of communi-cating with others without having to subscribe to conventional standards. At Batey, youth are free to be who they are and to express themselves and, more importantly, Tony notes, it "allows the students to say it's okay to be Puerto Rican. And that doesn't mean that you take yourself out of humanity, but you add yourself [to humanity]" (Tony, Batey founding member). Batey offers a space where youth are taken seriously, where they are valued and where they have something to contribute. And through hip-hop, youth explore who they are, discover their talents, and can engage in profound discussions about what is happening in their community. As Roberto sees it,

> [I] ... and if you see how much pride there exists in these Puerto Rican
> youth when they start rapping about their beliefs, they start kind of
> owning the skills of freestyle and things like that, you can see how much
> confidence it builds on them to talk about their experience, to be able to
> talk about who they are, and the childhood that they've gone through,
> and I think that we don't see music as an organizing tool, but it's a way
> to communicate, it's a way to share experiences, maybe as a beginning
> common ground that we can use....
>
> —Roberto, Batey founding member

This process is empowering, builds their self-esteem, and leads youth on the path to self-awareness.

Besides giving youth a space in which to express themselves, Batey also helps youth become self-aware of their strengths and how to develop their potential. For instance, Batey cultivates and fosters local talent and offers an alternative venue for artists who are not given a chance in mainstream venues. At Batey, young Latinos find a place that welcomes and celebrates their diverse art styles. Most importantly, Batey is a Puerto Rican/Latino youth culture space, and Batey members have been careful not to allow it to become a "Cotton Club." According to Tony,

> We didn't want to become the space that white folks would come to see us and watch us all perform and talk about who we are and get entertainment out of it. ... [In] other places in Chicago ... you'll have really white audiences kind of defining a space, or you'll have all black performers, and you find that the organizer of the event is white and it's like "come look at the natives," in a sense. . . . And so we created this space ... where we perform art for our own people ...
>
> —Tony, Batey founding member

Batey also seeks to provide youth who have been written off by the schools with practical skills such as literacy and technology. Through its Hip-hop Writing Workshops, youth learn to write. For many youth, this is the first time in their lives that they put their feelings on paper. These workshops contrast sharply with the youth's writing experience at school. Alex relates his experience:

> I came to the Batey Urbano, and we had writing lessons and stuff, and he [Tony, a Batey founding member] taught me how to write properly, and in the form of hip-hop. ... So basically I learned how to write in the Batey, with the people from the Batey when I was about 20 years old.
>
> —Alex, Coordinating Collective member

For Alex, taking a hip-hop writing workshop not only taught him how to write, but he has also learned how to teach writing to others, and this has opened up a whole new world of possibilities for him.

> I'm teaching poetry and stuff, and I like it a lot because it is an experience. So ultimately [I want to] become a teacher in the future, and it is kind of like paving the road, you know, so I can set those goals. It is kind of like opening up those roads.
>
> —Alex, Coordinating Collective member

Batey also uses technology, and particularly technology that is related to hip-hop. For instance, two of Batey's programs use hip-hop to prepare youth for the demands of an increasingly technological society. With few Humboldt Park families able to afford a computer, the "digital divide" is widening and further marginalizing community youth from a job market that increasingly relies on computer literacy. Batey Tech is an after-school program that connects academic preparation with computer skills. During Batey Tech, youth can get help doing homework or learning to use a computer. Over the summer, the Batey Tech program shifts gears, allowing for youth to expand their technological skills. One summer, students produced a CD, named *Project Humbodt Park*, learning on the way how to produce a hip-hop CD from its recording to its editing, layout, design, and marketing. The success of these workshops led to the redesigning of Batey's space to better build its capabilities for making CDs, publications, and even an Internet radio station.

Batey is a space where young people can come to enjoy themselves, discover their talents, speak up, and develop new skills. While hip-hop culture is used, the goal of Batey is to help young Puerto Ricans and Latinos understand who they are as individuals and as a community, to help them cope with their own and their community problems, and to motivate them to take action to transform their lives and their community. It is in the process of listening or performing hip-hop, or of attending writing or computer workshops, that many youths begin to understand how this form of expression and these activities are connected to a history of struggle. In turn, these youths become aware of who they are as Puerto Ricans and as Latinos and what it means to claim and define their identity within a community context. Notes Tony,

> I think it is giving a space ... [for] dealing with their culture and their identity, because their culture is denied, every aspect of who they are. ... We use different forms of youth culture, like hip-hop and poetry, to engage students and get their interest, but in the end, it has to do with engaging them with their identity, who they are, whether that be their ethnicity, nationality, or their background, their historical experience, and using that to build, and really using that to expand what they already know, and use their experiences ...
>
> —Tony, Batey founding member

"... We Organize Around Community Issues": Batey as a Space for Social Awareness

> So they constantly start seeing themselves, and they situate themselves, in the context of the community and that's one of the things that cements people. Because it is not just this personal realization.... [It] is coupled with their community and their people, [and] their history.
>
> —Roberto, Batey founding member

While discovering, claiming, and expressing one's identity—and particularly one's ethnic identity—is at the core of self-awareness, realizing that others share that identity leads to social awareness. At Batey, young people connect with each other through hip-hop. In telling about their lives, they begin to find common themes in their stories and realize that their experiences are part of larger social issues plaguing their community. Besides identity, many of their stories deal with gentrification and sexism. Although few initially use the term *gentrification*, stories of neighborhood change, forced displacement and residential relocation, and police harassment and brutality abound in their stories. Batey facilitates the discussion and analysis of these issues, helping youth understand what these issues mean as well as the social conditions that create and maintain them. Furthermore, Batey provides opportunities for youth to do something about these issues by engaging them in social action to improve their community.

Batey has laid out some fundamental ground rules of respect for self and others to foster understanding and facilitate dialogue through hip-hop. It has strict rules against drug and alcohol intoxication and no tolerance for dehumanizing language. Individuals who are or appear to be intoxicated are not allowed on the premises. Also, a poster reading No Racist, Sexist, or Homophobic Language is prominently displayed on the stage wall, and these rules are spelled out clearly at the beginning of all Batey events. Invariably, these rules are broken from time to time, particularly by high school students performing on Hip-hop Nights. This is understandable given the strong influence of commercial rap, with its use of obscene and derogatory language. When someone breaks the rules, they are given a verbal warning and if they continue to use derogatory language, they are not allowed to continue performing that night. Such occasions are used by Collective members to engage those present in a discussion on the connotations and implications of such language. However, this is not easy, especially for Batey female members who may call on the problematic language or behavior of high school boys who will not accept their authority. As Batey member Miriam explains,

> I think it's part of taking ownership of the space ourselves ... to say, "Hey, what you said is inappropriate, and it's wrong and this is why." And you know, there have been challenges. ... Sometimes we have to tell the young men several times, "You can't do that in here," or, "You can't hang out in the front," and it won't be until a man [from the Collective] comes out there and says, "Get inside. They told you get inside" that they come inside.
>
> —Miriam, Batey member

Contending with sexism is not limited to performances and events, nor to high school students. Batey members contend with sexism in their own day-to-day interactions at Batey and elsewhere. They are aware of the ingrained patterns that rule gender relations, and work hard at breaking these patterns. Even with this understanding, Collective female members say that these patterns affect relationships between men and women in Batey. The women feel that a lot of times when things are being discussed, you have to say, "Listen to me!" to the men in the Collective. Yet they also appreciate that, and often "they [the men] will 'call themselves out,' too," and that women in Batey feel they can confront and challenge men in a meaningful way that leads to a real dialogue. The women say that they are not "going to find another space where this is happening." This "head-on" approach to dealing with conflict leads Batey members to challenge ingrained notions about race/ethnicity, gender, and sexual orientation, but also gossip, disagreements, and misunderstandings among members. As Batey Coordinating Collective member Tere explains,

> If somebody has an issue, we'll encourage [her] to call it out, to talk about it, discuss it, and back it up. ... It's just, if we were going to say something behind someone else's back ... it's just better to talk about it.
>
> —Tere, Coordinating Collective member

While Batey makes a marked point of challenging sexism, gentrification is its main organizing issue. The members believe that focusing on conventional youth issues such as gangs and violence would only single out gang members and hide the root of inner-city youth problems. Pointing fingers at gang members would also pit community members against each other. By contrast, gentrification is an issue that affects all community residents and that threatens to destroy the community. For youth, the meaning of gentrification is easy to grasp because, according to Roberto,

> Some of them have actually been told, "You have to leave. We're going to build a condo where you live" ... and so they've seen changes happening, they see condos going up, they see that the block has changed character ... some of the youth remember going down on Division Street a lot further east, and that being part of this community. ...
>
> —Roberto, Batey founding member

Besides, they insist that gentrification is a youth issue and they offer as proof over a dozen youth who make references to displacement in their poetry and rap lyrics. Youth in Humboldt Park worry about gentrification, and—explains Tony—"not [everybody knows what gentrification is] ...

> [you] may see a condo go up next to your house, and you know that condo isn't for you, or you know that the area has changed, but people may not know that there is a word that explains that process.
>
> —Tony

Because their experiences are validated, these youth feel connected to Batey and to the community, and begin to participate more and more in Batey activities and not only in the performance nights. As they become more involved at Batey, they begin to participate in efforts to improve the community. Through their involvement at Batey, youth develop social awareness and a sense of ownership over the community and begin to search for alternatives and solutions to community problems. Through its programs, Batey offers youth opportunities to engage in social action to transform their community. Roberto explains,

> They perceive gentrification as being a threat to Batey, and to our flags [the Puerto Rican flags that mark Paseo Boricua, the name for Division Street in the area] and all the things that they have [at Paseo Boricua], and which they're now a part of. ... [For that reason] they're going to be involved in whatever process can slow it down and deal with it. Because they're beginning to ... want to be part of something. And they're seeing that there is a possibility, an effort being made that they will have a future here.
>
> —Roberto, Batey founding member

The most ambitious social action program is the Humboldt Park Participatory Democracy Project (PDP). This project is one of the most hands-on ways that youth and other members of the community can take part in the active resistance to gentrification. It is a project that grows from a philosophy rooted on the belief that the transformation of our community has to be defined and given life by the community members themselves. In other words, people must take ownership of their living conditions, and in the process take responsibility for their lives and their community through civic engagement and active participation in community building. Notes Roberto,

> Participatory democracy [is] a genuine form of democracy that has to do with people really being participants, not just voters, that they are engaged in where their community is going, and that they are part of building the future of their community. Regular representative democracy, the type of democracy their we see when we go out to vote in the United States ... is a limitation [because it is] giving one's power to an elected official. ...
>
> —Roberto, Batey founding member

What started as a group of youth walking the electoral precincts to register people to vote became a 10 week program that has trained over 50 youths to conduct door-to-door visits, their purpose being "(1) to assess and address community needs by linking residents to existing community service programs, (2) to build relationships with residents in order to dialogue about community life, and (3) to foster and nurture spaces for community members to participate in community development" (Rodriguez-Muñiz, 2004, p. 6). Miriam describes the experience:

> A typical Saturday afternoon, door knocking in my precinct, I look forward to going to a couple of houses that I already know ... with a couple of residents we've developed relationships. ... We get to talk, to have real conversation, other than just knocking on the door, like maybe, sitting down and talking to four people—where you come in and sit down and have coffee. Other than that you get to talk to like fifteen or eighteen.
>
> —Miriam, Batey member

PDP is now an ongoing program as participants continue to walk their precincts every Saturday.

Walking the precincts has made the extent of gentrification real for Batey youth. They were stunned by the rapid proliferation of condos in the community and the increasing number of whites who owned and lived in them. While this is something that they knew and spoke about, it was not until they walked house by house that they realized the magnitude of this problem. As a result, they launched the Return to the Barrio campaign in the summer of 2004 as a call to Puerto Ricans who had moved out of Humboldt Park to come back and invest in the community. Taking advantage of the Puerto Rican parades in June (one downtown and the other one in the community), Batey youth decorated a float with the theme Return to El Barrio, which displayed a large "Condo monster" devouring homes. What is amazing is that the design and construction of the float was implemented by high school students who participated in, and who were transformed by, the Participatory Democracy Program. Roberto explains,

> [They] did everything from building huge puppets to making signs, posters, decorating floats, getting flags, inviting and organizing other Puerto Ricans to be part of it. In about three weeks they were able to carry out an incredible amount of work. They put together an addition, *La Voz de Paseo Boricua* [*The Voice of Paseo Boricua*, a newsletter]. ... A lot of the youth internalized a lot of the importance of this community, and they also saw that they had a role to play and that they could really be instrumental to change, which a lot of times as youth, as colonized youth, [they] really don't see.... I think that's another example of how the Batey opens up spaces for youth to really believe in themselves, but also to believe in the community ... [they] see that they can carry out that work.
>
> —Roberto, Batey founding member

The summer campaign, as well as other projects—such as "Street Cleaning with DSBDA [2003]," a beautification and street-cleaning program along Paseo Boricua, "Haunted Paseo Boricua," where Puerto Rican folktales are used for Halloween festivities, and Three Kings Day, when Batey youth participate in the distribution of "Toys for Tots" gifts to children in the community, with the participation of close to 50 youths. For these youth, these programs involve them directly with the community and offer them the opportunity to engage in social action to improve their community.

"I learned what self-determination means for other people": Batey as a Space for Global Awareness

I have learned a lot of stuff about politics and everything else.... I learned what self determination means for other people, and what it means to me....

—Yolanda, Batey Urbano member

Batey youth are well aware of the problems that besiege their community and are taking direct action to challenge them. While engaging in Batey programs and community action, they also become exposed to other people of color. These interactions give them an understanding of other oppressed people and help them develop global awareness, leading them to build solidarity with other groups and to become involved in social action beyond their community.

Participating in Batey programs brings youth into contact with young people from other communities. As discussed earlier, Batey is not only a space for Puerto Rican and Latino youth, it is also a space that attracts and welcomes all youth of color. At Batey, notes Tony, "you'll have black performers as well as other Latino performers, and even recently a Native American performer ... it's always been a space that allows people to affirm who they are" (Tony, Batey founding member). In addition, Batey youth frequently take their performances to other communities in Chicago and in other states. This gives them the opportunity to tell their stories as well as to hear the stories of other youth of color, giving them an understanding of other people's struggles. The Batey was involved with the beginning stages of El Zócalo Urbano (2005), a Mexican youth space on the near west side of Chicago. On several occasions the youth from both spaces have collaborated to plan events, prepare for demonstrations by making signs and huge puppets, and to discuss the importance of Latino unity.

Through their association with other organizations, and most notably the Puerto Rican Cultural Center, Batey youth are also exposed to and join in the struggles of other communities. For instance, they participate in rallies and marches to defend undocumented immigrant rights with local Mexican organizations. They also participate in antiwar rallies and numerous other protests, marches, and rallies in Chicago.

While most of their efforts are local, Batey youth have also joined national efforts to fight injustice. Most notably is their involvement in Puerto Rican issues. In October 2002, Batey sent a delegation to help on a voter registration drive in Orlando, Florida, the city with the fastest growing Puerto Rican population in the U.S. In May 2004, they participated in the Encuentro Boricua, a Puerto Rican National Initiative, where national Puerto Rican leaders from around the country gathered in New York City to set forth a Puerto Rican agenda. Batey was in charge of organizing and running a panel for high school and college students at the Encuentro. Batey youth have also been involved in demanding that the U.S. Navy clean up the contamination that they left in Vieques, a small town of Puerto Rico that was used by the U.S. Navy for target practice for the last six decades. Finally, Batey youth support the self-determination of Puerto Rico and the inalienable right of a nation to determine its political status.

Batey's efforts for social justice include other Latino issues, and most notably amnesty for undocumented migrants. They are also part of a coalition of progressive organizations that seeks to advance a Latino national agenda. Batey's participation in this agenda includes recruiting and organizing youth, and attending national events such as the Democratic National Convention, where they blitzed the premises with flyers in an effort to advocate for a progressive Latino agenda.

More recently, they have become involved in international issues such as supporting the government of Hugo Chavez in Venezuela. Batey youth, explains Roberto, are impressed with the participatory democracy projects that are happening there.

> … kind of democratic initiatives happening [in Venezuela], about all levels of society, [from] the barrio all the way up to the government … you see oppressed communities resisting political globalization…. Our understanding is that gentrification is a first world manifestation of the undergoing globalization.
>
> —Roberto, Batey founding member

Recently they had the opportunity to meet with the Venezuelan Ambassador to the United States on his visit to the Puerto Rican community in Chicago, and "soon we'll be able to organize a delegation of youth to go there [to Venezuela]," explains Tony (Tony, Batey founding member).

Although Batey youth concentrate their efforts locally, particularly in fighting gentrification in their community, their involvement with Batey has clearly exposed them to other social problems that they knew little about. This exposure has made them aware of other people's struggles, to which they can relate, and has led them to support and work on behalf of these causes. What may have begun with a poetry night cosponsored with another youth organization has led to the organization of youth to fight for justice. Batey youth clearly see their role as organizers of youth and use Puerto Rican/Latino youth culture to foster dialogue and create awareness among young people in their community, in Chicago, and nationwide.

The Role of the "Elders": Batey as a Space for Intergenerational Dialogue

The fact that there has been an incredible amount of intergenerational space ... those of us, who are a lot younger in some respects, that are in our 20s or even in high school, that there is a certain level of communication you don't find in a lot of places ... and also from those different generations, and build something that is intergenerational, and is respectful of the experience that people have learned and gotten in the course of the many years of struggle, but also that there is something very important to take from the youth, and people who are younger, new ways of looking at things, different perspectives, sensibilities to things that are important. So this work is in a continuous path of continuity, I think what you see is pretty incredible. Bringing people together from these different age groups.

—Roberto, Batey founding member

Many people would be skeptical to believe that Batey youth have achieved so much without the intervention of adults, and would probably wonder if adults are "running the show" behind the scenes. There are some adults who provide support, experience, and guidance and give a push but they step back to let Batey youth make their own decisions. While there are a number of adults who help them, three people, all members of the Puerto Rican Cultural Center, provide constant support to Batey youth. Explains Roberto,

Luis has played a role of kind of facilitating, and overseeing the different projects that we've tried to begin, regarding technology, helping us out with really getting together things that might sound simple, such as getting Internet up in a space like this, put wiring. And Luis has really been overseeing that type of work, making sure that we were up to date and helping out with all of our technology questions. ... Ernesto, he has a wealth of experience working in this community, and building grassroots organizations, and has been an example to the Collective on how to operate, and how to struggle for things, and basically carry out the work that needs to be done. ... Maria has been helping organize ways that the Batey Tech could be successful, that the programs can match, and that the youth that participate at the high school will have the opportunity to feel that the Batey is part of their educational experience, but also part of their community experience.

—Roberto, Batey founding member

These adult allies are leaders in the community who have been involved in community struggles for most of their lives. Roberto notes that in those especially from "the [Puerto Rican] Cultural Center, what you can see is an incredible amount of work coming from people who've been working and been in the struggle for thirty plus years, with people who have made this community" (Roberto). Through their example, these individuals teach Batey youth an invaluable lesson of perseverance, respect for others, and integrity in one's ideals. Roberto continues: "In general, I would say that the elders of the Puerto Rican Cultural Center have all been instrumental in some way or another [that] the Batey exists" (Roberto, Batey founding member).

Batey members maintain their independence from the "elders" by seeking advice but retreating to make their decisions on their own. The Batey Coordinating Collective has weekly meetings that are off-limits to the elders. In writing this paper, Batey members have been eager to give their impressions about Batey, yet, they never allowed one of the authors, a university professor with years of community involvement, to attend any of the Collective's meetings. This strategy works and gives them the space in which to discuss issues without seeking the approval of or being pushed by elders. And while Batey participates in an intergenerational dialogue with its parent organization, the Puerto Rican Cultural Center, they maintain their autonomy. Even with the guidance of elders, Batey is an organization *for* youth run *by* youth.

Implications: Batey as a Space for Social Justice

Batey stands as an example of the social justice youth development model formulated by Ginwright and Cammarota (2002). Using Puerto Rican/Latino youth culture, and specifically hip-hop, Batey raises self-awareness among youth, who then begin to understanding who they are and how social forces shape their racial, class, gender, and sexual identities. As youth hear each other's voices and realize that their experiences are similar, they reach social awareness, an understanding of how social forces shape inequality and how this affects their communities. Gaining a sense of community, they join the struggle to fight oppression and improve their community. Batey youth have rallied around the fight against gentrification and have taken concrete action to prevent the displacement of the Puerto Rican community. Batey also helps youth achieve global awareness. Through hip-hop and community work, they realize, and connect with, other people's struggles against oppression. Batey has been particularly active in issues that affect Puerto Ricans as well as other marginalized groups in Chicago. This new understanding of oppression has effected drastic change in the lives of Batey youth as they come to understand themselves and their community better. Inspired by the example of "the elders" who have dedicated their lives to fighting for self-determination, Batey youth are making the commitment to be the next generation of social activists. Batey is all about humanizing disenfranchised youth and giving them hope and the tools to change the world. As Tony notes,

I think that they become human in a sense. That once you can realize that you can steer the ship and you can direct where it is going, it is a very strong and humanizing process that happens. So I think that these young people that really do get involved internalize the work, realize that they have a voice, they have a say, and they have the ability to change things, as opposed to just being audience members on the side and watching what goes on. They become active members, and actors, and in the work that we do. And they become in the process the agents of change that are necessary to change any society.

—Tony, Batey founding member

The success of Batey in attracting youth and engaging them in social action has not gone unnoticed by other youth in Chicago. Many Latino youth, especially Mexican college students, became involved with Batey, and while they felt welcome there, they also felt the need to have their own space. In February 2005, a group of Mexican youth opened El Zócalo Urbano in Pilsen, a predominantly immigrant Mexican neighborhood. While Zócalo is similar to the Batey, it is a separate youth organization with programs that are tailored to the needs of Mexican youth. The members of Batey and Zócalo interact frequently and work together in initiatives of interest to Latino youth. El Zócalo is a project of the Centro Sin Fronteras (Center Without Frontiers), an organization that focuses on the rights of immigrants, which the Centro has provided them with a space and other resources, but has left them alone to make decisions and run their organization.

Batey Urbano represents the will of youth of color to take responsibility, to be included in decision making, and to work toward change in their community. Batey is not only changing the way that Humboldt Park youth are viewed by the public, but it is also changing the way they are viewed by elected officials and policy makers. Batey youth are not shy about approaching elected officials and demanding social justice for their community. The political work done at Batey shows the potential of youth of color as political actors and as a major electoral power in large cities. Batey's political potential also lies in its role in the development of future leaders who, as they graduate from college and take on full-time jobs, will have the social, economic, and political power to transform not only their community but also the city and beyond.

References

Alicea, M. (2002). "Cuando nosotros viviamos ... ": Stories of displacement and settlement in Puerto Rican Chicago. *Centro: Journal of the Center for Puerto Rican Studies, 13*(2), 166–195.

Binder, A. (1993). Constructing racial rhetoric: Media depictions of harm in heavy metal and rap music. *American Sociological Review, 58,* 753–767.

Bynoe, Y. (2004). *Stand & deliver: Political activism, leadership, and hip-hop culture.* Brooklyn, NY: Soft Skull Press.

El Batey Urbano. (2005). Retrieved 2005 from http://www.bateyurbano.org.

Flores-González, N. (2002a). *School kids/street kids: Identity development in Latino students.* New York: Teachers College Press.

Flores-González, N. (2002b). Paseo Boricua: Claiming a Puerto Rican space in Chicago. *Centro: Journal of the Center for Puerto Rican Studies, 13*(2), 6–23.

Ginwright, S. (2004). *Black in school: Afrocentric reform, urban youth, and the promise of hip-hop culture.* New York: Teachers College Press.

Ginwright, S., & Cammarota, J. (2002). New terrain in youth development: The promise of a social justice approach. *Social Justice, 29*(4), 82–95.

Kitwana, B. (2002). *The hip-hop generation.* New York: Basic Books.

Padilla, F. M. (1987). *Puerto Rican Chicago.* Notre Dame, IN: University of Notre Dame.

Perez, G. (2004). *The near northwest side story.* Berkeley and Los Angeles: University of California Press.

PRCC [Puerto Rican Cultural Center]. (2005). Mission statement. Retrieved 2005 from http://www.prcc-chgo.org/prcc_mission.htm.

Ramos-Zayas, A. Y. (2003). *National performances: The politics of class, race, and space in Puerto Rican Chicago.* Chicago: University of Chicago Press.

Rivera, R. Z. (2004). *New York Ricans from the hip-hop zone.* NY: Palgrave Macmillian.

Rodríguez-Muñíz, M. (2004). Exercises in self-determination: The Humboldt Park experience. *Que Ondee Sola, 32*(4), 4–10.

Rose, T. (1994). *Black noise: Rap music and black culture in contemporary America.* Hanover, NH: Wesleyan University Press.

Stapleton, K. R. (1998). From the margins to the mainstream: The political power of hip-hop. *Media, Culture, & Society, 20*, 219–234.

Valenzuela, A. (1999). *Subtractive schooling: U.S.-Mexican youth and the politics of caring.* Albany, NY: State University of New York Press.

CHAPTER 11

Participation in Social Change: Shifting Adolescents' Developmental Pathways

KAREN STROBEL, JERUSHA OSBERG, AND MILBREY McLAUGHLIN

Engaging youth in social change efforts yields demonstrable benefits to both young people and their communities (Hart, 1992; Irby, Ferber, Pittman, Tolman, & Yohalem, 2001; Mitra, 2004; O'Donoghue & Kirshner, 2003; Zeldin, McDaniel, Topitzes, & Calvert, 2001). Youth who are engaged in programs that address neighborhood, school, or community issues develop feelings of social responsibility, a sense of connectedness to their community, improved self-esteem, and an increased understanding of social issues (see Yates & Youniss, 1996). Despite emerging interest in such benefits, researchers have not sufficiently explored the full range of positive developmental outcomes. Rather than focus primarily on youths' civic development, it is important to consider the ways in which involvement in social change affects multiple areas of young people's lives, including academic, interpersonal, and civic domains. Additionally, the benefits to communities that result from youth engagement in reform efforts remain relatively unexamined.

Such broad-reaching outcomes are most important to consider for those youth and communities that have access to the fewest resources. Urban youth of color encounter obstacles depriving them of knowledge about their communities or access to opportunities to participate (Atkins & Hart, 1992; McLaughlin, 1993). In this chapter, we draw on the experiences of urban youth of color who are participating in an after-school community research and advocacy program. Through our analyses of this particular program, we identify multiple developmental shifts associated with youth participation. Although we are not testing a particular theory, our embedded case study approach allows us to unpack the concept of youth involvement in social change so we can more effectively study, understand, and promote youth engagement.

Literature Review

The concept of social change appears to be subsumed into studies of civic engagement. Developmental psychologists present youth civic engagement as a task of adolescence involving elements of moral and cognitive development. Ideals of democratic citizenship and tenets of tolerance of and responsibility to others are examples of moral outcomes. Cognitive development in the civic engagement literature has often focused on the critical thinking and reasoning skills required in order to understand complex social issues as well as potential solutions (Larson & Hansen, 2004). Additionally, youth who participate in school and community reform learn how to analyze problems that they experience in their everyday lives (Ginwright & James, 2002).

While some researchers look for benefits associated with youth engagement, policy analysts and theorists focus on the costs of youth disengagement. Youth who are not interested in devising solutions to societal problems are likely to develop into adults who do not feel any sense of responsibility or obligation to the broader society (Youniss, McLellan, & Yates, 1997). Moreover, little exposure to social change efforts in youth limits the knowledge and skills that a young person can draw on upon reaching adulthood. In contrast, youth who participate in community-based youth organizations that train them in forms of social action are likely to feel more knowledgeable about and efficacious toward future efforts to bring about change in their community or society more generally (O'Donoghue & Kirshner, 2003; O'Donoghue & Strobel, 2003).

The way in which youth learn about social issues and their role in addressing those issues may be the critical link to broader developmental benefits. Therefore, the training context is an important focal point for understanding benefits derived from youth participation in social change. Programs that successfully motivate youth to pursue thoughtful strategies for social change may simultaneously empower youth to view themselves and their personal life trajectories differently. Learning contexts in which youth are granted a sense of autonomy, a sense of belonging, and a range of success experiences are more likely to maintain their interest in a topic and belief in their ability to constructively address the targeted social issue (Deci & Ryan, 1985; Eccles, 1983; Eccles, Wigfield, & Schiefele, 1998; Goodenow, 1993; Pintrich & Schunk, 1996). Furthermore, contexts that allow youth to examine issues that impact their lives and implicate their developing conceptions of justice and equity may promote sustained engagement in a campaign.

In this chapter we draw upon data from an after-school program to explore the following questions:

What features of an after-school community research and advocacy program enable youth to engage effectively in social change?

What does such engagement look like?

How is youth engagement in social change related to youth development in other domains?

The Research Site

An after-school program operating in two communities, the Youth Engaged in Leadership and Learning (YELL) program provides the context for this chapter. In YELL, cohorts of 15 to 20 youth are trained to use social science research techniques to study an issue of concern to them and to use their findings to formulate policy recommendations. YELL is based at a high school in West Oakland, California, and a middle school in Redwood City, California. The high school site serves a population of primarily African American and Asian American youth from low-income families who would be classified as living in high poverty, and the middle school site serves a population of primarily Mexican American students from low-income families who would be classified as working poor.

In addition to demographic differences between the two program sites, Redwood City and West Oakland differ in terms of their political contexts and social change processes. Ethnic and class stratification is easy to observe in Redwood City's neighborhoods and schools. Low-income Mexican American families live on one side of the city, and their children account for 61% of public school students. Issues of documentation status and second-language learning limit educational and career options for both youth and adults. Stratification is magnified among elected officials. As of 2001, only 5% of political leaders in Redwood City were Latino. Change in Redwood City happens from the top of the system down, facilitated by various bureaucratic structures, but historically, Latinos in Redwood City have not participated in the political structures within the community.

In contrast, West Oakland is a predominantly African American community steeped in a long tradition of grassroots social change. However, the residents of West Oakland are currently confronting the challenges of decades of severe poverty. Joblessness and displacement plague the adults, and youth are actively disengaged from underresourced schools. Among youth and adults alike, a sense of powerlessness dominates. In both communities the YELL program takes the youth through the same fundamental steps of identifying a problem, collecting data about key stakeholders' opinions, and developing recommendations; nevertheless, the political conditions of the community have the potential to create very different experiences in nearly every step of the process.

Methodology: Data Sources

Data for this study comes from multiple sources including field notes, interviews, and school record data. Field notes document the activities that transpired in each of the 90-minute YELL sessions, attending particularly to participant engagement and interactions. Notes were taken by trained participant observers and were supplemented by program directors. Interviews were conducted with all YELL participants and program directors. Youth were asked about their experiences in their school, community, and the after-school program. They were also asked to share their future goals and describe their personal roles in addressing community issues.

Over the past four years, 62 youth have participated in the YELL program in Redwood City, and in the past three years, 53 youth have been involved with YELL in West Oakland. For the purpose of this chapter we selected 4 youth who represent the experiences of typical youth who remain involved in the program beyond their first year of participation. The youth we selected for this chapter joined YELL in different years—therefore, our data for some youth spans up to four years, while our data for other youth is limited to a little over one year. For all of the youth we describe in this chapter, we have a minimum of two interviews. During their first year of involvement in YELL, the participants were interviewed once in the fall as they entered the program and once in the spring after YELL sessions ended. Returning youth are interviewed once each year.

The program directors were asked to describe the case study youth with regard to any personal, social, or academic changes they had noticed. They were also asked to share their insights about these youths' school experiences, home environments, and social networks.

In the next section we begin with an analysis of YELL as a context designed to train youth to participate in social change. We then describe trends we noticed among the youth most engaged in this program—that is, their tendency to adopt one of three different approaches to social change. As we discuss these approaches, we link them to opportunities afforded by the core program structures of YELL. Finally, we use four case-study youth to illustrate these findings, and to explore the developmental shifts experienced by youth in YELL who demonstrate a sustained commitment to school and community reform.

Promoting Participation in Social Change

Core Program Structures

By design, the YELL program continually makes adjustments according to school, community, and youth needs. Nevertheless, a number of core program structures exemplify YELL's innovative context for learning and development. Youth-led research accompanied by an action focus, a connection to host schools, and opportunities for prolonged involvement in the program and in the community all contribute to the distinct opportunities YELL affords.

Youth-Led Research. YELL is a youth-led program insofar as the youth choose the issue to explore, the research methods they will use, and the forms their recommendations will take. In past years, participants have developed campaigns around such issues as school safety, the media's negative portrayal of youth from a particularly stigmatized community, and the affordability of bus passes for students who depend on public transportation to get to school. Because YELL youth are often concerned by the inequities they confront in their schools and communities and because the YELL curriculum encourages them to talk and think about these challenges, they tend to target issues of social justice in their campaigns. The decision-making power youth are granted in YELL affords them a sense of ownership of the program.

The Action Focus. YELL uses an empowerment framework to engage young people in learning about their communities and sharing what they have learned. Although YELL does not train youth in direct action, it is an action-oriented program in that it involves participants in seeking and producing knowledge about a particular social problem or issue that interests them. Each year, depending on the campaign topic pursued, the youth have opportunities to share their ideas with relevant audiences. For example, in both communities, youth have presented their research-based recommendations to their school faculties. In addition, they have been invited to conversations with City Council members in Redwood City and have organized community forums in West Oakland. The different audiences and action strategies that youth develop reflect the traditional change processes in their respective communities.

The Connection to School. Because YELL is housed at school sites, academic support can easily be integrated into the program's operations. For instance, in West Oakland, the program director asks to see students' report cards each quarter, and she also provides after-school tutoring when YELL is not in session. In addition, she has arranged college visits for the students. In Redwood City, program directors have set aside YELL sessions to familiarize students with the requirements for college admission, and they have sat in on suspension hearings and meetings with school guidance counselors.

Additionally, the YELL directors have gradually become integral members of their host school faculties. Because the project is physically located at the school, and the YELL directors spend their working days primarily at the school, youth have the opportunity to stop by, seeking academic advice or personal support. Familiarity with the school context allows the adult YELL staff to better understand the school-related issues of concern to individual youth participants. Moreover, YELL directors' regular interaction with teachers means that the school faculty better understand the range of impacts the YELL program can have on specific youth as well as the school in general.

Opportunities for Continued Involvement. YELL is designed to support youth involvement over multiple years through a "ladder of opportunity." In Redwood City, returning youth can "graduate" from researchers to mentors. As mentors they facilitate discussions, offer insights based on their experiences in the program, and help support the new cohort of researchers. Mentors also help the program staff to build a cohesive and supportive group culture in which leadership is distributed and collective efforts take center stage. West Oakland youth have somewhat parallel opportunities, but are referred to as youth staff, demarcating their role as session leaders. Adult staff in West Oakland provide support to their youth staff through preparatory meetings and postsession debriefings; however, during the actual sessions, the youth are in charge.

Young people in both communities also have the option of becoming YELL ambassadors, who participate on panels or help to plan and lead workshops at local as well as national conferences. As mentors, youth staff, or ambassadors, the youth serve as resources, sharing their expertise and knowledge with others—be they younger students or adults.

YELL directors at both sites frequently apprise the youth of other opportunities to become involved in effecting social change, to represent the youth perspective, or to cultivate leadership skills. For instance, in Redwood City, at the behest of a past program director, some YELL participants joined the city's Teen Advisory Board, and they have since returned to YELL each year to recruit new members. In West Oakland, the high school that houses YELL has developed a leadership council of teachers, administrators, and students, and one or two seats each year are reserved for YELL participants.

The introduction to social change that YELL provides and the deliberate links YELL staff have forged with other youth development organizations and opportunities work together to inspire and enable many of the participants to continue to serve as committed civic actors in a variety of capacities.

A Typology of Youth Involvement in Social Change

As students developed within the context of YELL, we noticed significant differences in their interpretations of their tasks and in their contributions as agents of change. The combination of young people's descriptions of themselves, their activity choices, and comments from program directors directed our attention to a range of approaches to social change that youth participating in YELL tend to adopt. Based on this data, we have constructed a typology of three roles in approaches to social change: advocate, activist, and educator.

The Advocate. An advocate is distinguished by her commitment to a particular cause. While many youth articulate a vague interest in "making the world a better place," an advocate demonstrates her commitment to a specific issue. An advocate may devote herself to creating a safer school or to protecting her community from environmental pollution and degradation.

The youth-led research component of YELL may contribute to youth's commitment to the advocacy approach. Having the opportunities to select a campaign topic and to research that topic from the perspectives of different stakeholders exposes youth to a relatively broad conceptualization of an issue, its root causes, and possible solutions. Rather than mobilizing youth to rally for an assigned cause, the program gives them a chance to identify problems, concerns, or issues that matter to them. Many young people continue to care about these issues even after their YELL campaign concludes.

The Activist. Where an advocate has a cause and is focused on the ends, the activist is more interested in the means. Rather than attach himself to a particular issue, an activist seeks to take action as frequently as possible with the general goal of helping his school or community. Some activists may align themselves with a particular strategy, such as picketing, while others are satisfied with any form of direct action.

YELL does not train youth in direct action, yet it attracts youth who seek to take action. The program's emphasis on community knowledge and research, coupled with the ladder of opportunities, encourages youth to consider strategic action. In both West Oakland and Redwood City, the programs have responded to participants' interest in taking action by piloting new opportunities for YELL graduates to focus on the strategies for addressing the policy responses they had recommended. Yet, YELL still distinguishes itself by permitting youth to craft their own social change strategies.

The Educator. Where an activist concentrates on certain tasks or strategies, an educator concentrates on certain people. In our model, an educator assumes responsibility for supporting, helping, mentoring, or empowering a particular population—typically a marginalized group.

According to our typology, an educator does not necessarily need to work directly with others. Instead, it is possible to identify with the empowerment goals of an educator but look to a program or institution as the content provider. In the role of indirect educators, youth believe wholeheartedly in a program or an organization that empowers others, and the educators strive to ensure its continuation. They may serve as key players in the daily running of the program, or they may assume a backstage role, championing the program to others. Because YELL encourages participants to return after their first year in the program to serve as mentors or youth staff, there is a natural overlap between the direct, interactive educator and the indirect educator role of institutional supporter.

By placing youth in visible leadership roles within the program, YELL directors encourage youth to think of themselves as resources to one another. Opportunities to serve as mentors, youth staff, and ambassadors explicitly position youth as educators. For some youth, accepting the responsibility of educating others may seem overwhelming or beyond their reach. Before they see their individual potential to educate, some youth tend to focus on supporting and defending the caring and meaningful context that the program has created. For a typology of youth involvement in social change, see Table 11.1.

Table 11.1 A Typology of Youth Involvement in Social Change

Social Change Approach	Distinguishing Commitment	Program Feature
Advocate	To a cause	Youth-led: youth-driven campaign
Activist	To the process of making a change	Action-oriented: youth-defined action strategy Ladder of opportunities: multiple venues for action
Educator	To the goal of empowering others	Youth-led: decision-making, facilitation Ladder of opportunities: mentor and youth staff position youth as resources

Note: We noticed a few distinct trends in the formation of these approaches within YELL. Some youth came in with no real commitment to or understanding of either social change efforts or their potential role therein. Other youth came in with a certain belief system or track record that aligned them with a particular approach to social change. While the youth without prior commitments to an approach could come to acquire one, the youth with baseline commitments could either further develop this approach, or construct additional or alternative approaches.

Profiles of Youth Committed to Social Change

The four young people discussed in this section were chosen because they represent different cohorts, communities, and personal histories (see Table 11.2). Most important, they are representative of YELL youth who have demonstrated a commitment to the program. Although there certainly are members of YELL who do not develop a strong attachment to the program, we chose to study these four cases because they provide useful illustrations of the processes by which youth can become engaged and invested in social change efforts. In this section we introduce the youth, describe their participation in YELL, note their particular approach to social change, and consider evidence of developmental shifts. More specifically, for each youth we explore changes in their participation in YELL over time, in their academic performance and goals, and in their social interactions with their peers and with adults.

Julia. A guidance counselor at the Redwood City school site referred Julia, then an 8th-grader, to YELL. The counselor feared that Julia was on the path toward teen pregnancy and gang involvement. A Chicana, Julia lived with her single mother in a particularly dangerous part of town. Her grades were poor, and she seemed to have little sense of connection to school. After her first year of involvement in YELL, Julia returned to the program to serve as a mentor during her freshman year in high school. As a youth ambassador, she also attended and spoke at conferences. She continued in these capacities as a sophomore, but as a junior, she became more involved in facilitating a

Table 11.2 Description of Youth Cases

Name	Gender	Ethnicity	Grade Entered YELL	Length of Involement*	Community
Julia	Female	Mexican American	8th	4 years	Redwood City
Desiree	Female	Mexican American	8th	3 years	Redwood City
Jason	Male	Cambodian American	11th	2 years	West Oakland
Maya	Female	African American	9th	2 years	West Oakland

*Note: All of the case study youth are committed to YELL for another academic year.

transition-to-high-school workshop and a Latina support group—both off-shoots of YELL that she had helped to create. For her senior year of high school she planned to return to her role as a mentor.

By taking advantage of the entire gamut of opportunities offered through YELL, Julia appeared to be experimenting with different approaches to social change. At the end of her first year in YELL, Julia showed characteristics of an advocate dedicating her efforts to the specific issue of equity in education. During her first three years of high school she invested her extracurricular time in activities related to the educational futures of low-income Latino youth.

Over time, Julia also seemed to develop into an educator because she focused on enabling a specific population of Latino youth to recognize their potential. For example, she played an integral role in creating a workshop for 8th-grade youth with the goal of impressing upon the students the importance of graduation and college eligibility requirements. She sees herself as a teacher, as someone who can share her own experiences with younger students, offering them guidance as well as support. In explaining why she decided to return to YELL as a mentor, Julia said,

> It would help me, 'cause then I'll feel good with myself in knowing that I helped them be what they are or, you know, helped them. Just like, it's some kind of a way to lead them to something good. I just feel good about it.

As Julia continued in YELL she experienced a dramatic shift in her academic performance. She began 8th grade on the verge of dropping out of school, and over the course of her first year of participation in the project, her grades improved significantly. Julia credits her academic success to the opportunity that YELL provided her—namely, the opportunity to think about the problems in her community and how important it was for her to contribute to the solutions. At the end of her 8th-grade year, we asked Julia, "Are there ways you've changed since you joined YELL?" She replied,

> Yes. [Now] I'm a serious person ... when I got in YELL, I started to think a little bit better about who I am and what I want.... [E]verything used to be like all blank. I just acted ... I didn't even know what I was doing. And I used to get in a lot of trouble. And one day [my science teacher said to the principal], I want to show you the star of my class. And [the principal] just looked at me and he said, "Oh, wow!"

While YELL did not help Julia with her schoolwork directly, the experience seemed to contribute to her sense of commitment to her education as well as her belief in her ability to succeed academically.

Julia's emergent commitment to education prompted not only her teachers but also her peers to see and treat her differently. In her sophomore year of high school, Julia again credited YELL with helping her to effect this transition in her academic and social domains:

> If I didn't keep going to YELL I would be a totally different person right now. My 6th-grade year I was a little troublemaker in school, I would always be in fights with other people—all through 6th and 7th grade. Girls and guys too; I got in a fight with this guy, he pushed me and I slapped him in the face.

As a junior she again observed that YELL helped her to recognize and navigate a different life trajectory, and she contrasts herself with her friends from middle school: "I have a lot of friends who are in jail, some of my friends are pregnant and they have babies, some are married already." These were the life courses Julia's middle school guidance counselor foresaw when she first steered Julia toward YELL.

Over the years, Julia has learned to trust in her strengths as well as the messages conveyed through her multiple leadership experiences. She has had opportunities to advise on citywide grant-making decisions, consult with university professors, teach middle school students, make presentations to college students, and plan programs side by side with her old teachers from middle school. It seems that through those experiences (and many more like them), she has learned that she is a valuable resource to the community, and she seems to enjoy the process of watching adults now come to that same realization.

Desiree. When she joined the Redwood City YELL as an 8th-grader, Desiree's loud appearance, pink hair, and dramatic accessories clashed with her quiet demeanor. YELL marked her first extracurricular involvement, and she was content initially to assume a backseat role in the group, whispering her ideas and comments to her small group of friends in the program. During her freshman year in high school, Desiree returned to YELL as a mentor. She also participated in some of YELL's satellite programs, such as the transition-to-high-school workshop. In her sophomore year, Desiree again served as a mentor, but she now assumed the role of a very active, visible, and vocal member of the YELL community. As a sophomore, she also became involved with the same Latina support group Julia had joined, and with other social change programs in her community.

According to our typology, by her third year in YELL, Desiree would be considered an activist. As she made clear in an application she wrote for a leadership class, she now believes strongly in the importance of taking action:

> When I think of a leader not only do important legendary figures come to mind, but also normal everyday people like you or me. Everyone complains, but only a handful of people do anything about their complaints. I have decided that I will be one of those in the handful.

When Desiree entered YELL, she was a fair student, but she was frequently teased and bullied by peers. Upon transitioning to high school, her grades dropped, and her struggle to fit in socially intensified. Since then, Desiree has rebounded and has put herself squarely on a path toward college. It was during her third year of participation in YELL that Desiree first voiced her goal to attend a "good college." As the first to go to college in her family, she admitted to being scared and torn about going far away from her family and from the community that she has worked hard to improve, but she also expressed determination to make the most of her educational opportunities.

Participating in YELL and related activities has allowed Desiree not only to imagine new possibilities for her future, but also to keep negative possible selves at bay. Desiree explains,

> I like keeping myself busy because ... I have this idea that I think that people just do drugs or just illegal stuff because they're bored and they just have nothing to do. So they just go drink. And then I think it kind of helps me because then I'm just like, "Oh, I have to do this, I have to do that"—so, it's just keeping busy—and I just don't have extra time to go and cause trouble somewhere.

Like Julia, Desiree observes that her involvement in YELL has caused adults to see her differently. She feels that adults respect her for her efforts on behalf of her community. During a panel presentation, she comments, "Teachers will listen to someone that does their work." She also recalls an incident in which she was complimented by a teacher: "Yeah, ... I ran into an old teacher and he said that I had all grown up, but I didn't think that he knew me, but I guess because of YELL..." YELL enabled Desiree to experiment with a new identity, that of leader and social reformer. In embracing this identity, Desiree began to recognize new opportunities for herself academically and socially.

Jason. Jason's early experiences in school with teasing and bullying run somewhat parallel to those of Desiree. An Asian American youth of Cambodian descent, Jason initially saw the West Oakland YELL as a refuge or safe haven. He joined the program as a high school junior. Shy and easily flustered, he struggled to express himself verbally; however, he loved to write, and he was involved with the school's journalism program. As a senior, Jason returned to YELL to assume the role of youth staff member. After graduating from high school the following year, Jason continued to remain involved in the program as a staff member.

Over his time in YELL, Jason accepted the mantle of educator. After his first year in YELL, he was asked, "In your future, do you think you'll want to be involved in any community related work?" He responded enthusiastically, "Oh, yeah! I will still volunteer to work with youth and others because I want to help out, teach them what I've learned and teach them what they can do for their future." The following year, when he returned as a youth staff member, he was asked about this role. He explained that he saw his main charge as trying "to help support the youth leaders to be engaged," and he considered it his responsibility "to maintain a good purpose for the leaders and the youth [in this]." Jason's continued involvement in YELL, even after high school, reflects his interest in supporting, teaching, and sharing his experience and insights with younger youth.

Early in his involvement with YELL, Jason was frequently discouraged and frustrated by his performance in classes. Nonetheless, he took his schoolwork seriously, and he frequently attended the after-school tutoring sessions offered by the YELL director. Upon his graduation from high school, Jason credited YELL for his academic progress. He attributed his success to the structure and explicit support for academics he received in YELL. When asked how he would have been different had he not been involved in YELL, Jason recalls,

> The way I think about it, if I didn't join YELL, I probably wouldn't graduate from high school.
> Why?
> They also have a tutoring program, so yeah, thank God for that.
> What else about YELL made you graduate?
> Set a timeline to do what you've got to do for your work. A timeline to schedule your time to know when you're going to do this and when you're going to do that.

Jason had always wanted to follow in his sister's footsteps by attending college. YELL served as an alternative learning space in which he could work toward this important academic goal, and Jason is now enrolled in a local community college.

Socially, YELL also provided an important sense of belonging for Jason. He describes YELL as his "special place." In his second year, when asked why he has returned, he says, "It just feels like home. Just, I get to have someone to talk to and spend time with." In response to a question about what he is most proud of in YELL, he comments, "To have everyone who understands me in YELL, glad to have friends in YELL … yeah, that's it." The director of YELL observed that at first Jason sought YELL as a refuge; in school he had been teased by some and ignored by others. Gradually he learned not only to work with, but to trust, his peers. The YELL director reflected,

> I think he just developed a stronger … he wasn't so alienated and isolated in school any more. I think he felt like he was really on the outside for a long time, and I think that he started to feel a definite connection to YELL, and being someone in YELL, and then how that kind of trans-lated back to being a [West Oakland] student.

Maya. An African American, Maya joined the West Oakland YELL program as a freshman, with a range of other leadership experiences already under her belt. An eager, passionate contributor, she was also engaged in other aspects of school life, including cheerleading and her school's equivalent of student council. However, Maya struggled academically, and her social life was marked by the reputation of some of her family members as among the most notori-ous street fighters in the city. Maya eventually left her home, and has since bounced back and forth between group homes and foster care placements. Amid all of these changes in her home life, her involvement in YELL has remained steady. She returned to the program as a sophomore, and has served as a committed youth staff member. She also plans to remain actively involved in YELL now that she is a junior.

Her initial record of involvement in YELL, and in her school, positions Maya as the quintessential activist. When asked what she usually does when something in her school or community bothers her, she responds that she either tries to fix it or tries "to find something else that I can change that would help that other thing in the long run." Maya plans to continue to be involved in YELL because "I felt like I got a lot accomplished and I'm saying, if I can get all that done in one year, I'm just trying to imagine what I can do in four." She regards YELL as a program that "show[s] the youth that, you know, change starts with us."

Though she joined YELL with a general interest in "fixing things," over the two years of her involvement, Maya seems to have gradually become focused on a cause. Currently, she might be characterized as an emerging advocate. Toward the end of her second year of participation, Maya took an interest in the topic of youth voice in politics. She has been researching the topic and decided to participate in a trip to Washington State to register young voters.

While Maya joined YELL as a freshman with a desire to attend college and become a lawyer, it wasn't until her second year in the program that she began to take her schoolwork seriously. She came into the program every Monday and Wednesday to do her homework and she concentrated on developing better study skills. At the beginning of her second year in the program, she set the goal of attaining a 4.0, and she worked assiduously toward it.

YELL has also helped Maya to see herself in a positive light, offering an alternative social identity to the one that her siblings have followed and that she felt many of her peers expected of her. Like Desiree and Julia, who used YELL as an alternative to getting into trouble, Maya explained that YELL is, "just like something positive to do basically so I won't have time to be out on the streets or anywhere." At one point in her sophomore year, Maya was challenged to a fight. Rather than engage, Maya went to YELL, where she received support from both peers and adults for her decision to walk away. As it was for Jason, YELL became a sort of social safe haven for Maya, a place where she could develop the inner resources and the social supports necessary for successfully navigating the pressures of her social world.

As the above profiles illustrate, these young people sought YELL for a range of reasons, and they entered with various attitudes, beliefs, backgrounds, and experiences. Nonetheless, all were able to find something in the program with which they could connect, something that prompted them to return for another year, something that served as a platform from which they could discover or grow into themselves.

Summary of Developmental Shifts Associated with Participation in YELL

Among the case study youth, we observed shifts in their descriptions of themselves academically as well as socially. Academically, some of the youth began to improve their grades and their performance, while others showed more dramatic shifts in their general attitudes toward their education and their educational goals. Socially, all of the youth discuss a shift in their peer group, their opinions about how they are perceived by adults, and their attitudes toward their spare time. It is interesting to note that the developmental shifts do not seem to be correlated with a specific social change approach. Instead, it seems that these shifts are possible as long as youth are committed to one approach to social change. Although we did not study the experiences of YELL youth who did not develop strong commitments to social change, we surmised from conversations with YELL staff that these youth did not experience similarly profound shifts in academic or social domains. The patterns we noted are correlational, rather than causal, but these young people's own words suggest a powerful synergy exists between forming a commitment to a social change approach and experiencing personal change along other dimensions.

Conclusions

Our analysis suggests that there are concomitant advantages to developing a commitment to a particular social change approach. As youth emerge on the community stage as advocates, activists, or educators, they may come to see themselves differently in other venues as well—for instance, at school and among peers. Furthermore, because each of these approaches is associated with a certain kind of civic action, at the same time that the youth benefit personally, socially, or scholastically from their newfound sense of self their communities also profit from their efforts and accomplishments. In Redwood City, for instance, a youth educator is working to support and encourage her peers to stay in school. In West Oakland, an advocate met with her district superintendent to argue against the closure of her school and to propose ideas for improving the quality of the education it offers. By exploring the various ripple effects of social change commitments, we have identified implications for practice, policy, and research that can serve as channel markers for future efforts to realize the benefits to individuals and to communities that surface when youth are supported in effecting social change.

Implications for Practice

The attention that YELL directors and staff pay to the whole person may have facilitated the academic and social shifts we noted above. In other words, because practitioners in YELL keep abreast of participants' performance and engagement in school, because they offer after-school tutoring sessions, and because they make efforts to get to know participants' families and friends, they know the youth well. This personal knowledge of youth, in conjunction with YELL's youth-led structure, creates a distinct developmental space for youth. Similar to the "free spaces" and "counterpublics" that O'Donoghue describes (Evans & Boyte, 1992, and Fraser, 1992, respectively; both cited in O'Donoghue, chapter 13, this volume), YELL has become a space in which marginalized urban youth have input, ownership, and control. Within the program, participants are able to revise their image of themselves as "at-risk youth" into new identities as valuable civic actors. If they are to help marginalized youth achieve valued developmental outcomes, practitioners should work to create spaces dedicated to repositioning youth as active agents in their own lives and in their surrounding contexts.

In addition to being mindful of the various contexts participants negotiate, practitioners profit from awareness of the range of opportunities that exist in the community for youth involvement in social change work. This knowledge will enable them to steer youth toward appropriate spaces for either exploring alternative approaches or developing a nascent social change commitment more fully. In YELL, program staff take interested youth to rallies and to conferences, where the youth can experiment with activist and educator approaches. The program directors also forge partnerships with other youth programs and community organizations, such as a City Teen Advisory Board and a grassroots advocacy organization, which they encourage YELL participants to join. Learning about these opportunities allows youth to become more knowledgeable about the myriad ways in which they can contribute to their communities and also enables them to find a "fit" based on their talents and affinities.

Implications for Policy

The benefits to youth described in this chapter came about when social criticism was connected to active and constructive problem solving. Through participation in YELL, youth become increasingly aware of issues of inequity and injustice in their communities. Divorced from the YELL context, critical awareness alone has the potential to frustrate youth and contribute to a sense of alienation and powerlessness. However, when young people explore and engage in strategic action, those who have been most marginalized by public institutions and social systems begin to view themselves as effective participants and thoughtful contributors to the civic life of their communities (Ginwright & Cammarota, 2002). By introducing youth to different avenues for enacting change, the YELL program grants youth multiple opportunities to engage in social action and actively shift their developmental pathways.

Bridging after-school programs and school sites also appears to be a promising strategy for realizing the range of benefits of such programs to both youth and their communities. Schools occupy an important position in the community as nexuses in which diverse resources and opportunities for positive youth development can be concentrated. When such supports and services are clustered, communication can occur across groups. Counselors, teachers, parents, and program directors can all share their concerns about and hopes for individual youth. Such opportunities for sharing perspectives and strategies will enable adults not only to have a richer, fuller understanding of the youth with whom they work, but also to communicate clear and consistent messages to these youth about their assets and their potential.

Implications for Research

Although we believe that the typology we sketched will hold true across social change efforts, we suspect that the social, academic, and personal changes we noticed in the youth we studied may have been a function of the particular program sites and communities in which we based our inquiry. Future research could usefully attend to the mechanisms that enable such transfers of agency from one domain to another. In particular, the interplay between individual and contextual factors needs further examination. Participants' educational backgrounds, connection to particular campaign topics, relationships with program adults and peers, and family situations may all have a hand in determining which social change approach, if any, they adopt. Similarly, community demographics, political processes, problems, and opportunities may also influence the choices young people make and the trajectories they follow.

A particularly rich area for further inquiry, we believe, addresses the role of mentoring and modeling. As youth develop a commitment to social change, to what extent are they emulating or seeking to please the adults who have supported and inspired them? And at what point do these youth come to recognize themselves as mentors and role models to others? How do such realizations shape their commitment to a cause, a strategy, a population, a task, or a program? Exploring such questions will help us further understand the processes by which youth develop as agents of social change and as successful, efficacious young people.

Note

We thank Ben Kirshner for comments on this manuscript. In addition, we acknowledge Yolanda Anyon, Maria Fernandez, and Mary Hofstedt for their contribution to this work.

References

Atkins, R., & Hart, D. (2002). Civic identity in urban youth. Paper presented at the Thrive Conference, Pasadena, CA.

Deci, E. L., & Ryan, R. M. (1985). *Intrinsic motivation and self-determination in human behavior.* New York: Plenum.

Eccles, J. (1983). Expectancies, values and academic behaviors. In J. T. Spence (Ed.), *Achievement and achievement motivation* (pp. 75–146). San Francisco: Freeman.

Eccles, J. S., Wigfield, A., & Schiefele, U. (1998). Motivation to succeed. In W. Damon (Ed.), *Handbook of child psychology, Vol. 3. Social, emotional and personality development* (pp. 1017–1094). Hoboken, NJ: John Wiley & Sons.

Ginwright, S., & Cammarota, J. (2002). New terrain in youth development: The promise of a social justice approach. *Social Justice, 29,* 82–95.

Ginwright, S., & James, T. (2002). From assets to agents of change. *New Directions for Youth Development, 96*(1), 27–46.

Glaser, B. (1969). The constant comparative method of qualitative analysis. In G. McCall & J. Simmons (Eds.), *Issues in participant observation* (pp. 216–227). Reading, MA: Addison-Wesley.

Goodenow, C. (1993). Classroom belonging among early adolescent students: Relationships to motivation and achievement. *Journal of Early Adolescence, 13*(1), 21–43.

Hart, R. A. (1992). *Children's participation: From tokenism to citizenship.* Florence, Italy: UNICEF International Child Development Center.

Irby, M., Ferber, T., Pittman, K., with Tolman, J., & Yohalem, N. (2001). *Youth action: Youth contributing to communities, communities supporting youth.* Community and Youth Development Series (Vol. 6). Takoma Park, MD: Forum for Youth Investment/International Youth Foundation.

Larson, R. W., & Hansen, D. (2004, March). The development of strategic thinking: Learning to impact human systems in a youth activism program. Paper presented at the biannual meeting for the Society of Research on Adolescence. Baltimore.

McLaughlin, M. (1993). Embedded identities: Enabling balance in urban contexts. In S. B. Heath & M. McLaughlin (Eds.), *Identity and inner-city youth.* New York: Teachers College Press.

McLaughlin, M. W. (2000). *Community counts: How youth organizations matter for youth development.* Washington, DC: Public Education Network.

Mitra, D. L. (2003). Student voice in school reform: Reframing student-teacher relationships. *McGill Journal of Education, 38,* 289–304.

O'Donoghue, J., & Kirshner, B. (2003, November). Urban youth's civic development in community-based youth organizations. Paper presented at the International Conference on Civic Education Research, New Orleans.

O'Donoghue, J. L., & Strobel, K. R. (2003, November). *Directivity and freedom: The role of adults in youth civic empowerment.* Paper presented at the International Conference on Civic Education Research, New Orleans.

Perkins, D., Borden, L., Keith, J., Hoppe-Rooney, T., & Villarruel, F. (2003). Community youth development: Partnership creating a positive world. In F. A. Villarruel, D. F. Perkins, L. M. Borden, & J. G. Keith (Eds.), *Community youth development: Programs, policies and practices.* Thousand Oaks, CA: Sage.

Pintrich, P. R., & Schunk, D. H. (1996). *Motivation in education: Theory, research, and applications.* Englewood Cliffs, NJ: Merrill.

Yates, M., & Youniss, J. (1996). A developmental perspective on community service and adolescence. *Social Development, 5,* 85–111.

Youniss, J., McLellan, J. A., & Yates, M. (1997). What we know about generating civic identity. *American Behavioral Scientist, 40,* 620–631.

Zeldin, S., McDaniel, A., Topitzes, D., & Calvert, M. (2001). *Youth in decision-making: A study on the impacts of youth on adults and organizations.* Chevy Chase, MD: National 4-H Council.

CHAPTER 12

Youth of Color Organizing
for Juvenile Justice

SOO AH KWON

From 2001 to 2003, a multiracial coalition of Asian and Pacific Islander youth in Alameda County in the Northern California Bay Area, along with hundreds of other youth of color, engaged in a successful youth organizing campaign to stop the expansion of the juvenile hall in their community known as the Super Jail. This chapter examines the factors that attributed to the success of the anti–Super Jail campaign, as well as its limitation in illuminating how young people are actively shaping social policies that have real material effects on their lives. Here I will show how young people organized collectively under a politicized "youth of color" identity, a collective panethnic identity that was developed in resistance to youth criminalization—the social, political, and economic marginalization of racial minority youth. Young people's involvement and investment in the campaign were closely tied to their personal experiences with youth criminalization and incarceration. I will argue that the success of the campaign was in part due to a collective effort by a multiracial coalition to organize under a panethnic youth of color identity, although it was not without its limitations. My purpose is to explicate what policy makers, practitioners, activists, and scholars can learn about youth political activism from this youth organizing case study.

Specifically, I explore the participation of a diverse group of Asian and Pacific Islander youth in the anti–Super Jail campaign who are part of Asian and Pacific Islander Youth Promoting Advocacy and Leadership (AYPAL). AYPAL is a panethnic community-based youth organizing collaborative that draws youth (ages 14 to 18) from second-generation and immigrant Cambodian, Chinese, Filipino, Korean, Laotian, Mien, Samoan, Tongan, and

Vietnamese communities in Oakland, California. AYPAL follows three basic guiding principles: youth ownership, community involvement, and promoting social justice by engaging young people in youth organizing campaigns. My analysis of the anti–Super Jail campaign stems from an ethnographic study I conducted of AYPAL from 2001 to 2004. I engaged in participant observation of the everyday practices of youth in numerous settings, including youth group meetings, cultural art classes, workshops, schools, homes, political rallies and protests, community forums, and meetings with elected officials. I conducted extensive personal interviews with over 20 youth (which include oral histories of their families) and all adult AYPAL staff members. In addition, I conducted 15 youth focus-group interviews, totaling over 100 youth. As both an ethnographer and youth organizer, I was in a unique position to closely examine the diverse experiences of second-generation Asian and Pacific Islander youth.

In the following sections, I will provide a brief background of the anti–Super Jail campaign. I will examine the repressive social and political climate that served as the breeding ground for a politicized youth of color identity, and then delineate three factors that attributed to the success of young people's activism against the expansion of the juvenile hall, and one significant challenge. Finally, I describe the policy implications of building a youth organizing movement among young people for social justice.

The Campaign

"Alameda County doesn't need a bigger juvy [juvenile hall]! What we need is schools in our community! Books, not bars! Schools, not jails!" chanted a group of more than 100 youth activists as they marched three blocks from the Lake Merritt transit station in Oakland to the Alameda County Administration Building to demand a meeting with a member of the Alameda County Board of Supervisors, Alice Lai-Bitker. The young people carried signs that read EXPAND MINDS, NOT PRISONS and BOOKS NOT BARS, JUSTICE FOR ALL. After listening to speeches about the injustices of the juvenile system, they tried to gain access to the building. The supervisor had refused to meet with them during previous attempts and they were denied admittance once again. Undeterred, their voices grew louder as they marched in circles in front of the building, chanting, "Come on Alice, do what's right!" and "We're not leaving till we get a meeting!" Unfortunately, the supervisor snuck out the back entrance; but the demonstration generated television and newspaper coverage and started a public conversation around the issue of youth incarceration.

This is a glimpse of the efforts of a diverse group of youth of color, including AYPAL youth, to stop the expansion of the juvenile hall in their community. Two youth activist groups in the Bay Area—Youth Force Coalition and the Books Not Bars project of the Ella Baker Center for Human Rights—led the anti–Super Jail campaign. Youth Force Coalition is a Bay Area youth collaborative made up of more than 20 local youth organizing groups, including

AYPAL. The Ella Baker Center for Human Rights is a national organization that challenges human rights abuses in the U.S. criminal justice system, and the Books Not Bars project specifically addresses the growing prison industry in California.[1]

Although the success of the anti–Super Jail campaign depended on the organizing efforts of hundreds of youth of color, the participation of Asian and Pacific Islander youth of AYPAL was critical for the campaign's outcome. AYPAL was a prominent organizational partner within the Youth Force Coalition, and two AYPAL staff members were part of the tactical strategy team, the decision-making core of the anti–Super Jail campaign. AYPAL youth were a large and visible force (often making up more than half of the participants) at anti–Super Jail organizing actions, and pictures of AYPAL youth frequently adorned the front pages of local newspapers during the campaign.[2] They participated in many protest rallies, attended numerous Alameda County Board of Supervisors meetings, traveled to California Board of Corrections meetings in San Diego and Sacramento, pressured elected officials who supported the expansion with phone calls and public demonstrations, and informed the public about the expansion in a grassroots campaign of door-to-door visits.

The anti–Super Jail campaign started in the spring of 2001 after Alameda County's probation department requested a total of $54 million from the California State Board of Corrections to build a larger juvenile hall. To secure funds for the expansion, the probation department released inaccurate figures about youth violence, claiming an increase by 64% in 1999 when, in fact, crimes by young people had decreased by 27% (Horowitz, 2001). The department later admitted the mistake. Outraged by the news, a local youth media council organized a press conference to call attention to this matter. These young people, who understood firsthand the distortion of data by city officials to criminalize youth, joined the movement to stop the Super Jail. This critical consciousness among young people about the juvenile *injustice* system called many into action.

Throughout the two-year struggle, which was followed closely in local newspapers, the anti–Super Jail campaign took many twists and turns before the coalition won its demands. In May 2003, the coalition members' hard work paid off when the Alameda County Board of Supervisors voted for a smaller juvenile hall (from an original proposal of 540 beds to 330), to be located closer to the city of Oakland (where two-thirds of those detained lived), and to seek programs that promoted alternatives to incarceration.[3]

The Criminalization of Youth of Color

In the late 1980s and 1990s, young people faced a barrage of repressive national and local policies that sought to "control" youth behavior and rising youth crime, although statistical trends showed a steady decrease in youth delinquency and crime (Collins & Kearns, 2001; Males, 1999; Pintado-Vertner & Chang, 2000), curfews were imposed, antigang task forces were instituted, and police officers were assigned to schools. This troubling trend arose from a general social and political climate that targeted poor minority people of color. Daniel HoSang (2003) describes President Ronald Reagan's administration's attack on social services for low-income communities in the 1980s and its campaign to shift the blame for destitution to the breakdown of poor, racial minority families. Such effects have trickled down to youth. HoSang comments, "From this perspective, 'youth' itself became a pejorative identity, emblematic of the failure of family, values, and nation" (p. 4). Today, youth have become increasingly associated with violence and crime. Sensationalized media stories about youth violence—like those of the infamous Columbine High School shootings in Littleton, Colorado; the prevalence of urban youth crime; and racial minority teenage gangs—have helped demonize and criminalize young people. At the same time, they triggered a campaign for policies to control youth. Bernadine Dohrn (2000) writes, "A major consequence of the tidal wave of fear, violence, and terror associated with children has been adult legislative and policy decisions to criminalize vast sectors of youth behavior" (pp. 160–161).

In California, specifically, poor minority youth, their families, and their communities have been affected by a series of repressive voter initiatives. Proposition 184 (passed in 1994) instituted the nation's harshest "three strikes" law; Proposition 187 (passed in 1994) curtailed health and educational rights for undocumented immigrants; Proposition 209 (passed in 1996) outlawed affirmative action; and Proposition 227 (passed in 1998) ended bilingual education. In 2000, Proposition 21, the get-tough "Gang Violence and Juvenile Crime Prevention Act" often declared a war on youth of color, sought more severe penalties for gang-related crimes, and proposed that children as young as 14 be subject to trial as adults.

In tandem with this need to control youth behavior was a push in the 1990s to direct federal and state funds for law enforcement to the construction of adult and juvenile prisons nationwide. In California, for example, correctional costs have increased by 230%, and the state has built 21 new prisons since 1980 (Martin, 2004). In 1994, President Bill Clinton approved a motion to build new juvenile facilities and expand existing ones across the United States. A report by the National Council on Crime and Delinquency (NCCD) describes the effect, particularly in California:

> Across the state of California, there has been a juvenile detention facility construction boom. California already has one of the highest incarceration rates in the country. Now, the Legislature through the Board of Corrections has provided construction grants for new juvenile facilities in 40 of the 58 counties. California is increasing its capacity to detain youth by 50 percent, adding 3,150 new beds, in addition to replacing 1,300 existing detention beds. (Wordes, Krisberg, & Barry, 2001, p. 1)

Yet as the juvenile hall construction boom closely paralleled higher juvenile arrests rates, spending on education, school scholarships, and child protection services declined (Dohrn, 2000). California ranked 41st nationally in educational spending in 2000 (Martinez, 2000). This trend points to the direct relationship between the expansion of the youth criminal justice system and the criminalization of youth.

Such trends are troubling because youth criminal statistics point to a decrease in youth crime by 43% nationally in the last two decades. In *Framing Youth: Ten Myths about the Next Generation*, Mike Males (1999) debunks dominant representations of youth as violent, criminal, and lazy through statistical evidence. Males shows that negative claims about youth are biased, unfounded, and based on media coverage that falsely depicts young people, especially young people of color, as the source and center of societal ills. Although evidence points to a decline in youth crime, the juvenile criminal justice system continues to expand. The NCCD reports, "The growth in detention is fueled by old crime trends when the number of juvenile arrests were at their peak. In the past ten years, felony juvenile arrests in California declined by 45 percent" (Wordes et al., 2001, p. 1).

Even more troubling is the fact that minority youth are disproportionately affected by the increase in youth incarceration. African Americans, American Indians, Latinos, and a growing number of Asian and Pacific Islanders make up the majority of young people locked up in juvenile hall. In the 1980s, racial minority youth made up three-fourths of incarcerated youth; confinement of minority youth increased by 80% in the last decade (Office of Juvenile Justice and Delinquency Prevention, 1999). In Alameda County, the overrepresentation of incarcerated African Americans is even more pronounced. The NCCD reports that "89 percent of the youth admitted to the Alameda County juvenile hall are children of color" (Wordes et al., 2001, p. 1). In Alameda County, juvenile arrest rates for Asian and Pacific Islander youth rose 44.1% from 1991 to 2000. In particular, Samoan and Southeast Asian youth—especially Cambodian, Laotian, and Vietnamese—have the highest arrest rates and recidivism among Asian and Pacific Islander groups. In Alameda County, arrest rates for Samoan and Vietnamese male youth surpass rates for all other ethnic groups, including African Americans and Latinos (Le, Arifuku, Louis, Krisberg, & Tang, 2001). Moreover, racial biases are rampant in all aspects of the juvenile hall system (Butterfield, 2000).

The dramatic growth of juvenile hall facilities and youth incarceration rates in the past 20 years—a period during which youth crime has decreased—points to the negative effect of the process of youth criminalization, particularly as it affects youth of color. Males (1999) blames this process on news media outlets and politicians, whom he accuses of scapegoating youth. As evidence, he asserts that newspapers are three times more likely to report stories of youth homicide than adult homicide.

The Political Youth of Color Identity

Participants in the anti–Super Jail campaign organized under a shared political panethnic youth of color identity that was in resistance to the criminalization of racial minority youth. Elizabeth Martinez (2000) describes the burgeoning youth activism in the Bay Area as a "new civil rights movement," a movement that is in resistance to the social and political conditions that limit young people's opportunities. HoSang (2003) argues that this repressive political environment serves as a breeding ground for young people's oppositional consciousness and activism. He notes that this hostility "created the conditions for the emergence of 'youth' as a *political identity*, a shared world view that provided the basis for collective action" (p. 5). Laura Pulido (1996) discusses the development of a people of color identity in the environmental justice movement among African Americans, American Indians, Asian Americans and Pacific Islanders, and Latinos. She describes this identity as political; it is linked to resistance and activism and triggered by a common history of racism and oppression that people of color have experienced. A youth of color identity can be viewed as part of a larger multiethnic organizing movement among people of color around the United States.

The young people who fought against the Super Jail were keenly aware of the effects of youth criminalization. They understood the inequity of the county's attempt to direct funds to increase youth incarceration while young people were left to feel the social effects wrought by racism, poverty, unemployment, and failing schools in their lives and their communities. In Oakland for example, the 2000 census reported almost 20% of the general Oakland population living below the poverty line.[4] Yet the mean household income for white people nearly doubled that of African Americans between 1980 and 1990.[5] The immigrant population also disproportionately suffers from poverty. AYPAL youth understood the popular media representations of youth of color as dangerous and violent as a process of youth criminalization, and refused to succumb to this dominant discourse. Rather, they identified youth incarceration as a *social problem* and exhibited a strong political consciousness against a political system that sought to punish youth of color. They developed a sense of youth political agency and power in collective activism. In the following, I describe the factors that contributed to the success of the anti–Super Jail campaign and show how youth organizing is a powerful social change strategy among young people. I also describe a limitation in the campaign.

Issues That Matter

On November 15, 2001, about 200 young people staged a protest action in a parking lot in Sacramento after they were denied admission to a private meeting between the California Board of Corrections and the Alameda County Board of Supervisors. Danny,[6] an AYPAL member, was one of the many high school students who opted to skip school to join the protest. He spoke to the crowd through a bullhorn:

If you guys are asking, "Why are we here? Why aren't we at school?" That's because there are some things more important than school—like freedom. Our freedom is more important than our education. And California ranks Number 1 in jails, and 41st in education, so why should we go to school? What we want is more money to be spent in schools, not in jails. Locking us up in jails, what will that do? You will take away our futures. You should spend that money on schools instead.

Danny's comment reveals his critical stance toward a political system that places emphasis on incarcerating rather than educating youth. Young people in the crowd exhibited similar oppositional consciousness as they carried banners that read, DON'T BLAME THE YOUTH, BLAME THE SYSTEM and $ FOR PREVENTION, NOT INCARCERATION.

Alex and Johnny, two Mien (Southeast Asian) AYPAL members, were also stirred by a similar oppositional consciousness. They felt compelled to participate in the anti–Super Jail campaign because they have friends in the juvenile hall. Asian and Pacific Islanders are often overlooked in discussions of youth of color affected by the juvenile justice system, although arrest rates for Asian and Pacific Islander youth have increased dramatically while national arrest rates for African American and white youth have declined in the past 20 years (Le, 2002).

Alex, Johnny, and their friends were familiar with run-ins with police officers who often stopped them on the streets as they walked home to accuse them of being gang members. Such experiences, common among youth of color living in inner-city neighborhoods, add to their understanding of the link between police harassment and youth criminalization. And as the prison industry continues to grow nationally, larger numbers of youth come into direct contact with the effects of prison expansion. It is evident that as minority youth who are directly affected by the processes that criminalize youth of color, some AYPAL youth understand the link between youth criminalization and youth incarceration. Their critical consciousness is the result of both a self- and social awareness of youth incarceration as a social problem (see Ginwright & Cammarota, 2002). This political identity is a rearticulation of negative images of youth of color into a positive identity. Shawn Ginwright and Julio Cammarota (2002) describe the importance of a "social justice youth development" that "pays attention to the relationship between critical consciousness and social action" (p. 87). Alex was able to identify the need to halt the Super Jail because it has real potential material consequences in his everyday life and that of his friends: "It's important to us because it affects us! And we don't like it—the way they are expanding the jail and putting us inside it!"

Altering Relationships of Power in Collective Youth Organizing

For many *AYPAL* youth, anti–Super Jail rallies served as a source of political power and as a location in which they could develop an oppositional consciousness toward youth criminalization and youth incarceration. In the physical act of organizing, youth gained a sense of political agency—a belief that change *is* possible through collective youth organizing. They spoke about their experiences in a focus group interview.

Jay: I love going to rallies.

Kat: I love going to rallies, because you really get empowered.

Kila: [And you can] yell at them.

Clarence: That's when you feel like …

Kila: [*singing*] I've got the power.

Clarence: Especially when we win with some of them.

Kat: Yeah, that makes us feel much better…. Like they are really listening, but when we don't get things that we really need, it just gets us really frustrated and we just want to go back and start fighting over and over again until we get it.

Clarence: Like if they hear what we are saying and they start agreeing with us. Like that one in Sacramento. We went out there, it felt like they felt us, how we felt.

Matt: When you are at those places, there are actually people there who want to listen to what you gotta say, you know. They won't just say oh that's not right, or that's just ridiculous, they listen.

For other young people, protest actions provided them with the opportunity to teach their peers about the anti–Super Jail campaign and share their concerns about youth incarceration:

Alex: It's very fun and like, when you go, you bring, like, people that you know. And there, you know it's going to be fun because you get to talk to the people about what's going on, and what has happened, and to change what is about to happen.

Julie: You have fun, but while you have fun you are changing something.

May: Also you're learning, too … changing something, making a difference, right? When you go to rallies, we get to show people your power. Like my sister, after she went to a rally she told me that she wanted to go back tomorrow.

These voices articulate young people's political agency and their sense of the power gained through collective action (see Fantasia, 1998). These rallies provide young people the space to develop a critical analysis of youth criminalization.

Community Organizations Supporting Youth Organizing

In part, the success of the anti–Super Jail campaign depended on politicized youth who were involved in community-based organizations that supported youth organizing. Community-based organizations such as AYPAL provide young people with important social, cultural, and political space in fostering youth activism. Community-based organizations also serve as critical socio-cultural spaces for positive youth development (Flores-González, Rodríguez, & Rodríguez-Muñiz, chapter 10, this volume; McLaughlin, Irby, & Langman, 1994; O'Donoghue, chapter 13, this volume). In a study of second-generation youth, Ruben Rumbaut and Alejandro Portes (2001) note the importance of ethnic communities and ethnic organizations in providing supportive cultural and political environments, resources, and networks that allow young people to maintain a positive sense of self and ethnic identity while they negotiate dominant society. Peter Kiang (2001) looks specifically at Asian and Pacific American political participation and points to local community organizations as sites for political development: "The domain of community can represent a significant site of learning for Asian Pacific American young people as a struggle to understand the broader context of power, democracy and inequality" (p. 250).

For many Asian and Pacific Islander youth in Oakland, AYPAL is a culturally appropriate space where young people's racial identities and cultural heritage are recognized. As a panethnic youth organizing collaborative that attracts young people in ethnic-specific groups, AYPAL pays attention to the importance of young people's multiple identities. Moreover, they are supported and mentored by adult staff members who reflect the racial backgrounds of the young people. But AYPAL is a more than a space for identity confirmation. Young people also learn how to engage in youth organizing campaigns to solve problems in their communities. They learn to express their individual experiences with social injustice, and translate those experiences into a critique of collective social inequalities through political workshops and direct youth organizing campaigns like the anti–Super Jail campaign. Additional examples of AYPAL youth organizing campaigns include pressuring their school superintendent to make districtwide policy changes that were unfair to students; instituting an ethnic studies curriculum in their high schools; convincing the Oakland City Council to increase programming and staff at neighborhood recreation centers; and garnering congressional support to stop deportations of immigrants convicted of minor and/or nonviolent crimes.

Challenges of Panethnic Organizing: Are Asians Youth of Color, Too?

In their participation in the protests against the Super Jail, AYPAL youth dispelled dominant ideologies of youth of color deviance and specifically challenged representations of Asian and Pacific Islanders as the "apolitical model minority" (Kim, 2004). Claire Jean Kim (1999) claims that Asian Americans are racially triangulated vis-à-vis African Americans and Whites in a field of

U.S. racial positions that depicts Asian Americans (the "model minority") as "superior" to African Americans (the "underclass"), but "inferior" to Whites because of Asians' seemingly permanent foreignness. Historical constructions of Asians and Asian Americans in the United States as perpetual foreigners were manifested through various immigration policies that kept Asians as aliens, preventing them from full assimilation into U.S. life and full participation in U.S. democracy (Gotanda, 2001; Lowe, 1996; Palumbo-Liu, 1999). Kim (2004) describes how the model minority paradigm allows Asian Americans economic and academic success but blocks political agency to create the "apolitical model minority."

AYPAL youth made their activism plainly visible at protest actions, as pictures that accompanied local newspaper articles on the campaign attest. On July 2, 2001, for example, the front page of the *Oakland Tribune* featured a photograph of two AYPAL members carrying an AYPAL banner at a community education and outreach event, Not Down with the Lockdown, that drew more than 1,000 protestors. In the same newspaper on November 12, 2001, an article about a protest action against supervisor Lai-Bitker was printed next to a photograph of Kathy, a sign-carrying AYPAL member.

AYPAL youth even caught the attention of Alameda County Board of Supervisors' Nathan Miley, who made an unexpected visit to an AYPAL meeting so that he could, in his words, "meet and talk with the youth who had been so instrumental in the fight against the Super Jail." This visit demonstrates the visibility of AYPAL youth in the community and their influence in political organizing at a local level. Supervisor Miley's visit is significant in that as a politician he went out of his way to visit a group of constituents who have no voting power; this underscores the impression they left on him.

Yet despite the visibility of AYPAL members in local media and their recognition by politicians, the persistence of the model minority myth that identifies Asians as academic do-gooders unaffected by crime, youth incarceration, and violence pervaded even progressive multiracial collaborative efforts. Marie, one of the adult coordinators who represented AYPAL on the tactical strategy team for the campaign, constantly reminded others in the coalition that Asian and Pacific Islander youth also are affected by incarceration. She comments,

> As far as, like, being an Asian group, I think that sometimes the people of the coalition see things more in terms of black and white. And even though they do have APIs [Asian and Pacific Islanders] involved they don't talk as much about the Asian experience in juvy. And also, like, they'll forget, they'll say it's a black and Latino thing when they are on the radio, which is incorrect.

AYPAL youth also criticized other members in the coalition for not crediting AYPAL's importance to the anti–Super Jail campaign. Three youth spoke to the issue.

May: They use our pictures and stuff but they don't put our names on it though! ... They only say stuff about the Youth Force Coalition, and we know that we are part of it, but they don't mention, like, which youth programs are in there.

Kathy: Like the media, the newspaper and media: every time they say something about the rallies, they don't usually include AYPAL even though it's most of us out there.

Julie: Or if they do then they spell it [our names] wrong.

The overlooking of AYPAL youth's presence in the anti–Super Jail campaign reflects the tenacity of the model minority myth. Representations of Asian youth as studious bookworms also enveloped non–Asian and Pacific Islander coalition members, to make them think that Asian and Pacific Islander youth were not affected by the same systems of racial oppression that targeted other youth of color. Rather, it was a "black or brown" issue, and AYPAL youth did not fit the bill. Kim (2004) describes the persistent ambiguity surrounding Asian American political identity. Questions such as where Asian Americans fit into the racial order, where they stand politically, and whether they are really "people of color" act as significant barriers in building and sustaining cross-racial alliances. As Karin Aguilar-San Juan (1994) posits,

> The notion that we are the nation's "model minority" unfortunately pervades even so-called progressive establishments. Frequently white activists tell me they don't know any Asian activists and ask me perhaps somewhat anxiously to provide them with names. The leftist Asians and other people of color also reproduce the myth that we shun political work. (p. 4)

She continues, "Myths about Asian Americans belittle the damage done by discrimination we face, obscure the complexity of our experience, and make our contributions to the struggle against racism invisible" (p. 4). To combat the erasure of Asian and Pacific Islander youth caught up in the juvenile system, AYPAL youth created a giant Southeast Asian puppet with the words "Southeast Asian Youth Say No to Super Jail" written across its chest; they have taken the puppet to many anti–Super Jail protests.

The failure by anti–Super Jail coalition members to recognize that AYPAL youth share similar forms of oppression as other youth of color points to the dominance of defining racial politics within a static black and white paradigm in the United States. The fiery activism by African Americans, Asian and Pacific Islanders, and Latinos to stop the expansion of the Super Jail reveals the determination of young people to *counter* criminalization.

The Implications of Youth of Color Organizing for Policy

The efforts by AYPAL youth and others in the Bay Area to stop the Super Jail is an example of how young people are engaging in youth organizing practices as a strategy to bring about social change in their communities. AYPAL youth's participation in the campaign highlights the construction of a political youth of color identity that was created in opposition to the criminalization of young people. The stories of these young people's political activism reveal the diversity of experiences they share as political activists and their feelings on the subject of youth incarceration, which are often embedded in their personal and social experiences of growing up as youth of color in Oakland. They articulate a sophisticated analysis of and an oppositional consciousness against a political system that seeks to increase measures to incarcerate youth of color, as opposed to policies that would invest in youth. As youth of color activists, these young people reframe the notion of youth, and youth of color, as a political identity—an identity that is rooted in an oppositional consciousness and tied to collective forms of action. Their efforts offer a powerful example of how racial discourses and representations of urban and minority youth can be altered by responsible and engaged political activists.

Policy measures must recognize young people's political subjectivity and political agency, as is shown in the anti–Super Jail campaign. Contrary to mainstream beliefs about urban minority youth, these young people are not to blame for social problems. Rather, they are finding solutions to these problems, and policy makers need to follow suit. These young people convinced Alameda Board of Supervisors that money directed toward juvenile expansion is better spent on programs promoting alternatives to youth incarceration. As such, others need to invest money for "schools, not jails."

In the fight to stop the expansion of the Super Jail, these youth also revealed that the processes of youth criminalization are tied to larger social ills of poverty, deteriorating schools, and voter initiatives that continue to cut services for poor minority communities. Hence, policy makers must also look for ways to tackle the larger systemic racial and economic inequalities that plague young people's lives and communities.

Finally, policy measures must recognize and support community-based organizations for young people. In particular, special attention must be given and serious investment made to develop community-based organizations and programs that recognize young people's social and political development. Youth organizing and social justice oriented community-based organizations, such as AYPAL, offer young people opportunities to participate and grow in spaces that are different from individually focused, "youth fixing" programs usually directed at curbing youth violence and preventing drug use. It is in these spaces they are given the support and guidance to exercise their democratic right to be active members of society.

Notes

1. For more on these organizations, see their websites (http://youthec.org/youthforce/index.htm and www.ellabakercenter.org).
2. See Horowitz (29 July, 2001 and 12 November, 2001) in *Oakland Tribune*.
3. For related articles, see Ashley, 2003; Holzmeister, 2003; and DelVecchio, 2003.
4. In general, the population of Oakland earns $7,438 below the California median household income. The median household income in California in 1999 was $47,493, whereas the median household income in Oakland was $40,055. (Source: U.S. Census 2000 Summary File 4 (SF4)—Sample Data. Retrieved July 14, 2004 from http://factfinder.census.gov/servlet/DTTtable?bm=y&context=dt&reg=Dec2005F4).
5. The mean household income for African Americans grew from $16,908 to $28,439, while for white Americans it rose from $27,534 to $48,097. See Younis, 1998, p. 229.
6. All names of AYPAL members given here are pseudonyms.

References

Aguilar-San Juan, K. (1994). Linking the issues: From identity to activism. In K. Aguilar-San Juan (Ed.), *The state of Asian America: Activism and resistance in the 1990s* (pp. 1–15). Cambridge, MA: South End.

Ashley, G. (2003). San Leandro juvenile hall plan is ahead. *Contra Costa Times*. Retrieved March 12, 2003 from http://www.bayarea.com/mid/cctimes/5338339.htm?template=content.

Butterfield, F. (2000, April 26). Race bias cited throughout juvenile justice system. *San Francisco Chronicle*, p. 1.

California Tomorrow. (2001). *School reform organizing in the San Francisco Bay Area and Los Angeles, California* [Report]. Oakland, CA: California Tomorrow.

Cervone, B. (2002). Taking democracy in hand: Youth action and change in the San Francisco Bay Area. Occasional paper by What Kids Can Do, Inc. and the Forum for Youth Investment. Retrieved March 24, 2003 from http://www.whatkidscando.org.

Collins, D., & Kearns, R. (2001). Under curfew and under seige? Legal geographies of young people. *Geoforum, 32*, 389–403.

DelVecchio, R. (2003). Alameda County supervisors OK new juvenile court, prison board drops plans for teen 'super jail.' *San Francisco Chronicle*. Retrieved May 7, 2003 from http://www.sfgate.com/cgi-bin/article.cgi?file=/chronicle/archive/200.

Dohrn, B. (2000). "Look out, kid, it's something you did": The criminalization of children," In V. Polakow (Ed.), *The public assault on America's children: Poverty, violence, and juvenile injustice* (pp. 157–187). New York: Teachers College Press.

Espiritu, Y. L. (1992). *Asian American panethnicity: Bridging institutions and identities.* Philadelphia: Temple University Press.

Fantasia, R. (1988). *Cultures of solidarity.* Berkeley and Los Angeles: University of California Press.

Ginwright, S., & Cammarota, J. (2002). New terrain in youth development: The promise of a social justice approach. *Social Justice, 29*(4), 82–96.

Gotanda, N. (2001). Citizenship nullification: The impossibility of Asian American politics. In G. Chang (Ed.), *Asian Americans and politics: Perspectives, experiences, prospects* (pp. 79–101). Stanford, CA: Stanford University Press.

Holzmeister, K. (2003, May 7). Juvenile hall will stay in San Leandro. Oakland Tribune. Retrieved May 7, 2003 from http://www.oaklandtribune.com/cda/article/print/0,1674,82%257E18.

Horowitz, D. (2001, March 9). Juvenile hall says it overstated youth violence. *Oakland Tribune*, p. B7.

Horowitz, D. (2001, July 29). 1,000 oppose size of county's new juvenile hall. *Oakland Tribune*, p. A1.

Horowitz, D. (2001, November 12). Board of Corrections refuses to hear critics of juvenile hall. *Oakland Tribune*, p. B1

HoSang, D. (2003). *Youth and community organizing.* Occasional Papers Series, no. 2. New York: Funder's Collaborative on Youth Organizing.

Kiang, P. (2001). Asian Pacific American youth: Pathways for political participation. In G. Chang (Ed.), *Asian Americans and politics: Perspectives, experiences, prospects* (pp. 230–257). Stanford, CA: Stanford University Press.

Kim, C. J. (2001). The racial triangulation of Asian Americans. In G. Chang (Ed.), *Asian Americans and politics: Perspectives, experiences, prospects* (pp. 39–78). Stanford: Stanford University Press.

Kim, C. J. (2004). Asian Americans are people of color, too … aren't they? *AAPI Nexus, 2*(1), 19–47.

Le, T. (2002). Delinquency among Asian/Pacific Islanders: Review of literature and research. *Justice Professional, 15*(1), 57–70.

Le, T., Arifuku, I., Louis C., Krisberg, M. & Tang, E. (2001, July). Not invisible: Asian and Pacific Islander Juvenile Arrests in Alameda County. Asian and Pacific Islander Youth Violence Prevention Center, National Council on Crime and Delinquency. Retrieved July 10, 2002 from http://www.apicenter.org/information_sharing.html.

Lowe, L. (1996). *Immigrant acts: On Asian American cultural politics.* Durham, NC: Duke University Press.

McLaughlin, M., Irby, M., & Langman, J. (1994). *Urban sanctuaries: Neighborhood organizations in the lives and futures of inner-city youth.* San Francisco: Jossey-Bass.

Males, M. (1999). Framing youth: Ten myths about the next generation. Monroe, ME: Common Courage Press.

Martin, M. (2004, January 5). Critics say new state prison defies logic. They point to huge state deficit, dwindling number of inmates. *San Francisco Chronicle.* Retrieved January 6, 2005 from http://sfgate.com/article.cgi?file=/chronicle/archive/2004/01/05/MNG2D43G871.DTL.

Martinez, E. (2000). The new youth movement in California. Retrieved June 19, 2001 from http://www.zmag.org/zmag/articles/martinezmay2000.htm.

Office of Juvenile Justice and Delinquency Prevention. (1999, December). *Juvenile Justice: A century of change.* Retrieved January 20, 2000 from http://ojjdp.ncjrs.org/publications/PubResults.asp#1999.

Palumbo-Liu, D. (1999). *Asian/American: Historical crossings of a racial frontier.* Stanford, CA: Stanford University Press.

Pintado-Vertner, R., & Chang, J. (2000). The war on youth. *ColorLines.* Retrieved February 13, 2001 from http://www.arc.org/C_Lines/CLArchive/story2_4_01.html.

Pulido, L. (1996). Development of the "people of color" identity in the environmental justice movement of the Southwestern United States. *Socialist Review, 26,* 145–180.

Rumbaut, R., & Portes, A. (2001). *Ethnicities: Children of immigrants in America.* Berkeley and Los Angeles: University of California Press.

Wordes, M., Krisberg, B., & Barry, G. (2001, November 29). Facing the Future: Juvenile Detention in Alameda County. National Council on Crime and Delinquency. Retrieved March 21, 2002 from http://www.nccd-crc.org/nccd/n_pubs_main.html.

Younis, M. (1998). San Antonio and Fruitvale. *Cityscape: A Journal of Policy Development and Research, 4*(2), 221–244.

CHAPTER 13

"Taking Their Own Power": Urban Youth, Community-Based Youth Organizations, and Public Efficacy

JENNIFER L. O'DONOGHUE

Recent years have witnessed increased marginalization of youth from participation in the public realm. Even in institutions created to "develop" youth, young people often face ambivalence from adults about their ability to participate in real-world decision making and action (Costello, Toles, Spielberger, & Wynn, 2000). Youth in urban contexts are further marginalized as rising poverty and inequality, increased isolation, and policies that view youth as objects rather than collective agents of community change decrease support from communities and public institutions and limit youth's opportunities to impact the world around them (Hart & Atkins, 2002; Hart, Daiute, & Iltus, 1997). Urban schools, for example, with an emphasis on hierarchical control and order, limited conceptions of citizenship, and "high-stakes" accountability policies often fail to provide empowering civic learning (Berman, 1997; Conover & Searing, 2000; Flanagan & Faison, 2001; Youniss, Bales, Christmas-Best, Diversi, McLaughlin, & Silbereisen, 2002). Similarly, service learning programs have been criticized for their inattention to issues of social justice and the inability to engage urban youth (Tolman & Pittman, 2001) or support them in addressing deep-seated problems in urban communities (Boyte, 1991).

Marginalized by broader society, urban youth may need to carve out alternative spaces where they are not assumed deficient, invisible, or hypervisible (Weis & Fine, 2000) or too young or inexperienced to take on real responsibilities and important issues. Community-based youth organizations (CBYOs) may hold the potential to create such "counterpublics" for urban youth (Hart et al., 1997; Flanagan & Faison, 2001; McLaughlin, 2000; Pittman, Ferber, & Irby, 2000; Weis & Fine, 2000). As alternative sites for civic development (O'Donoghue & Kirshner, 2003), CBYOs may represent contexts within which urban youth can transform themselves into powerful public actors and effect change on the very social, political, and economic contexts that contribute to their marginalization.

While there has been much discussion and anecdotal evidence about the potential of CBYOs, there exists little empirical research providing context-specific knowledge about the spaces where youth can develop a sense of agency, public power, and an understanding of themselves as public actors, both individually and collectively. This chapter seeks to address this gap, exploring the relationship between space and public efficacy, looking specifi-cally at the influence of (1) organizational *intentionality* around supporting youth voice and power; (2) *public concepts* that provide a framework through which youth understand their work; (3) youth participation in organizational *decision making;* (4) *content and pedagogy* that provide opportunities for criti-cal reflection and active participation; and (5) *macropolitical connections* that engage youth with community issues and action. I will conclude my discus-sion with implications for policy aimed at supporting "powerful spaces" for urban youth.

Conceptual Framing

The concept of "counterpublics" (Fraser, 1992) or "free spaces" (Evans & Boyte, 1992) offers insight into understanding the democratic empowerment of urban youth in CBYOs. In their work examining democratic movements in the United States, Sara Evans and Harry Boyte (1992) introduce the concept of "free spaces," public places in a community that allow marginalized people (women, people of color, workers groups, sexual or ethnic minorities) to "learn a new self-respect, a deeper and more assertive group identity, public skills, and values of cooperation and civic virtue" (p. 17). Located between private lives and large-scale institutions, these settings provide conceptual and physical space within which ordinary citizens can come together to engage in democratic action—to "critique what is, shelter themselves from what has been, redesign what might be, and/or imagine what could be" (Fine, Weis, Centrie, & Roberts, 2000).

Urban young people's experiences in community organizations can be seen as expressions of marginalized people within an alternative public. This repre-sentation is consistent with the words of young people in one CBYO who describe their organization as a place where "people aren't always on you," youth can "find themselves ... and learn about what they want," and young people can "have our ideas, express them, say them, and then do them."[1] Having a space of one's own can contribute to a sense of agency and control over the world around oneself. Furthermore, for marginalized urban youth, such counterpublics can provide the space needed for the development of critical consciousness and self-awareness that is at the heart of social justice youth development (Ginwright & Cammarota, 2002). Flores-González, Rodríguez, and Rodríguez-Muñiz (chapter 10, this volume), for example, describe how a community center became a space in which Puerto Rican youth could claim their ethnic identities, feel valued for their contributions to the community, and place their own struggles within a larger context of oppression. Through CBYOs, urban youth can find the space they need not only to become public actors, but also to transform their consciousness around their public efficacy.

The counterpublic concept points to the importance of looking at CBYOs as spaces, rather than simply places, for youth participation and learning. This understanding emphasizes the internal aspects of such organizations (mission and culture, participation practices, content and pedagogy), as well as the ways in which they link youth to broader publics (through their macropolitical connections) and engage them in work toward community change. To understand how CBYOs influence youth's public efficacy, I look across these varying components of space.

Methodology

Analysis relies on data gathered through qualitative case study research conducted over two years in two multiethnic CBYOs located in low-income, urban communities in the San Francisco Bay Area. Youth in these communities face a combination of repressive conditions that restrict space for youth democratic participation: growing income disparity and concentrated poverty, gentrification, legislation that restricts access to quality education and healthcare, and punitive policies that criminalize young people.

The CBYOs in this study emerged in an effort to counterbalance these political economic conditions. While specific missions varied, both organizations were aimed at engaging traditionally marginalized urban youth in community change. At Youth as Effective Citizens (YEC),[2] youth community projects have included the creation of a charter high school, a youth-run media studio, a youth employment program, a child care center, and a community garden. In addition, YEC youth organized community members to construct a skate park and a school, facilitated workshops around youth development and educational change, hosted candidate forums around elections, and made presentations to the school board and city council. The second organization, Youth Supporting Youth Change (YSYC), sought to make an impact by providing grant money to youth-driven community change projects. Grant decisions were made by YSYC board members, a group of 10 youth involved in community outreach, facilitating workshops for youth groups and providing ongoing support to grantees through orientations and follow-up meetings.

Data collection at both sites involved weekly observation of program activities and meetings as well as public events and performances. At YEC, I focused primarily on one group of older youth (ages 16–18), but also attended community-wide meetings of the entire organization. At YSYC, my focus was on the board members, whom I followed through weekly training and planning sessions, community events, and decision-making processes. Formal interviews were conducted at two points, with 17 youth participants of diverse ethnic and racial backgrounds, ranging in age from 14 to 19, and 7 adult staff members (see Table 13.1).

Data analysis was enriched by the participation of youth data analysts, a group of three young people from these organizations who were trained in qualitative data analysis techniques. They spent one summer working with me, reading field notes and interview transcripts and helping make meaning of young people's experiences.

Discussion of Findings

The analysis here uses an "empowerment" conception of public efficacy (Perkins & Miller, 2000, cited in Tolman & Pittman, 2001), defining public efficacy as the extent to which young people see themselves as capable of affecting or influencing both their CBYO and the broader community. Generally speaking, youth in both CBYOs articulated a strong sense of agency and power, feeling that their voices mattered and that they could make an impact on their communities. Public efficacy for these young people was a complex, often nonlinear phenomenon, with a range of interpretations (see O'Donoghue & Kirshner, 2003). Further, there was variation among youth, particularly in the

Table 13.1 Demographics of the Youth and Adults Interviewed

	Youth Interviewed (n = 17)	Staff Interviewed (n = 7)
Gender		
Female	12 (71%)	4 (57%)
Male	5 (29%)	3 (43%)
Race/Ethnicity*		
African American	6 (35%)	–
Asian	4 (24%)	2 (29%)
White	2 (12%)	5 (71%)
Filipino/Pacific Islander	5 (29%)	–
Latino	6 (35%)	1 (14%)
Multiracial	5 (29%)	1 (14%)
Native American	1 (6%)	–

*Note: Participants were allowed to select more than one option.

realm in which they felt most efficacious; these contrasts help to understand the impact of different organizational features.

Analysis of the data revealed multiple factors of these CBYOs that impacted youth's sense of public efficacy: (1) intentionality; (2) public concepts; (3) decision making; (4) content and pedagogy; and (5) macropolitical connections. While discussed separately below, these categories are not so discrete or rigid; for example, organizational intentionality influences opportunities for youth participation in decision making, and content is closely linked with public connections. Similarly, development of public efficacy is linked across categories; while it may be less supportive of efficacy not to have a say in organizational decision making, for example, being able to have an influence at the community level may offset that.

Intentionality

Intentionality refers to the ways in which organizational mission, goals, and culture support or hinder youth's developing sense of public efficacy. As described above, both organizations had similar missions around youth involvement in community change. The differences between these organizations were the ways in which that mission was interpreted by youth and adults, how it was enacted in the culture of the organization, and how that impacted young people's sense of public power.

At YEC, both youth and adults had a strong, coherent understanding of the purpose of the organization. As stated by one adult codirector, the core of YEC was to create opportunities for youth to learn and practice effective citizenship, defined as "knowing what you think, believe, and feel, and taking meaningful action on that" (field notes, 2/28/03). Youth echoed this, describing YEC as a space for personal reflection and growth, youth voice, and community change; as one put it, "[I]t's just like introducing people to what they didn't know they had inside of them, and it's like putting it out in the world" (YEC youth, 2/5/03). This understanding played out in the culture of the organization, which was described by youth and seen in observations to be a place where adults encouraged youth to see and take their own power, to share their voice, and to push themselves to reach higher standards.

Moreover, the organization maintained that youth (and adults) could only become effective in the broader public realm if they experienced the "messiness of democracy" within the organization. Adults and youth in the organization both believed that "anybody here, adult or youth—it doesn't matter what their role is—can have an impact if they want to" (YEC adult codirector, 2/12/03). In addition, the organization felt that youth would only feel more powerful if they worked with adults who were engaged in the same processes of learning and empowerment as youth were, that it would be useful "for kids to understand that the adults are developing too.... There's power in having that kind of modeling going on all the time" (YEC adult coach, 6/10/03).

At YSYC, there was less clarity about the organizational mission, with implications for organizational culture and young people's sense of power. The official mission of the organization was "to empower youth and engage them in community change efforts" (organizational documents, 1/03). When asked about their understanding of the organization, youth's responses were clear and coherent: youth helping youth to change their communities. They focused on the board and the grant decisions, describing the ways in which they felt greater efficacy because of their decision-making power and control over resources. The adult ally of their group also directed his attention toward the board, feeling his energy would be most effective there.

However, for the adult program director, YSYC was not primarily about developing the 10 board members, but instead about empowering the many more community youth grant seekers. "The YSYC structure tries to be good for youth in the city more broadly. And the program is structured around that, not just trying to figure out what the youth on the board want" (YSYC adult program director, 6/5/03).[3] This led to a culture that was less empowering of board members for several reasons. While initially youth described adults as encouraging youth voice and involvement, over the year they developed a sense that this was not really true (see "Decision Making," below). Program emphasis shifted away from providing opportunities for board members to grow and develop; instead, adults became more invested in program "success" (making timely grant decisions), which led youth to feel that they were simply filling a role in an already determined game. The youth data analysts picked up on this tension between "youth empowerment" goals and "task orientation" realities: "they need to keep that [empowerment mission] in mind.... I didn't see that emphasized a lot .... I saw it like we have a task to do and let's do it, that type of thing." (youth data analyst 1, 7/29/03) The push for program "success" at YSYC exacerbated time-crunch issues that resulted in less space for youth creation, participation, and ownership. In addition, because of the mismatch in priorities between the adult program director and the adult ally who worked most closely with the youth, program decisions started to be handed down in a hierarchical manner. As a result, the adult ally felt disempowered—a feeling he then transmitted to the youth.

Organizational intentionality around youth voice and power seems more supportive of youth efficacy. When that intentionality was absent or weaker, the result was a "shrinkage of vision" of youth power.[4] Young people in both YEC and YSYC raised important questions about the true purpose of the organization: Was it about sustaining the organization, or providing open opportunities for youth to do real work in the community? They pointed out that when accountability for program "success" lies externally or with adults, organizations become more focused on that success than on authentic youth participation or youth outcomes: "A lot of the stuff we do now is like just political moves to make the organization seem better, but we're not doing anything to help the organization stay true to what it is" (YEC youth, 10/23/02).

When youth felt accountability had been shifted to others, they wondered, "What's the point?" or felt that there were "prejudices about what youth can handle" (YSYC youth, 7/15/03 and 7/21/03).

Public Concepts

In his critique of community service, Harry Boyte (1991) points out that a primary weakness of such programs is their lack of a vocabulary or conceptual framework through which to view work in the public realm. This public vocabulary might include such public concepts as accountability, citizenship, democracy, justice, activism, organizing, politics, or power.

At YEC, there was a concerted effort to introduce youth to a common language around their work. Adults and youth worked over several years to uncover what seemed to be the core concepts of their work, "the five R's"—risk, rigor, real, relationships, and responsibility—found on posters on the walls and discussed with and among youth. In addition, observations found adults and youth continually debating the meaning of concepts like *citizenship, leadership,* and *power.* For example, one adult coach had youth analyze power and responsibility at YEC using Hart's (1992) Ladder of Young People's Participation as a guide (field notes, 10/9/02). Similarly, adults engaged youth in analyses of power dynamics involved in their community change efforts:

> Adult Coach: "Somebody mentioned they fear us. Why would they fear us?"
>
> Youth 1: "We have power."
>
> Youth 2: "We know how to organize."
>
> Youth 3: "They're afraid of kids being able to run a school."
>
> Adult Coach: "Take a moment to understand that. That 19 teenagers got the city, this huge corporation, and the school district all worried. You have to realize the power you have." (Field notes, 10/31/02)

Such efforts have given youth a common language, one that they use with each other. At one public event, the youth emcee introduced the next speaker, "one of the brightest upcoming leaders," who in turn described a third youth as "an impactful friend" (field notes, 6/12/03). At YSYC, youth were trained in community problem analysis and discussed the concept of "root causes." Discussion of public concepts was not explicit, although the adult ally described training as "implicitly" political, carrying messages about systems of oppression that he felt youth were picking up on. However, interviews with youth do not reflect the same use of public language or level of understanding of public concepts as expressed by the youth of YEC. Moreover, there was a lack of coherence around the understanding of citizenship and their own sense of power as citizens. Indeed, on the one occasion where the public concept of "activism" was raised by a youth, it was dismissed by the adult ally with no further discussion in the group:

Youth: Could we say, "Did it motivate you to continue your activism?"

Adult ally: I don't think every project can be characterized by activism, and not all people think of their involvement as that.

Youth: But the definition of activism is just being involved in something.

Adult ally: But the connotation is different...
Adult rewords question, using "active".... (field notes, 3/19/03)

At YEC, the organization's commitment to using public concepts provided youth a public language that served as a framework for youth to understand their experiences, place themselves within something larger, and view themselves differently. One adult coach described her role as providing youth "some kind of theoretical framework to feel powerful," which involved "being clear about my language and the things I say" (YEC adult coach, 8/5/03). There exists a risk that such language becomes jargon, but in general, youth seemed to use it with seriousness. Indeed, constant use of language like "effective citizenship" opened the door for youth to claim that for themselves; all of the young people interviewed at YEC felt they were or would be effective citizens. In contrast, YSYC youth seemed to lack a public language that may have helped them step into their power. Few youth at YSYC seemed comfortable talking about the idea of citizenship or had a strong understanding of themselves as powerful citizens. Moreover, by not discussing varied conceptions of terms like *citizenship*, youth at YSYC relied on more traditional models such as voting, which by definition excluded them from civic power.

Decision Making

Involving youth in substantive decisions that affect the organization is often the hardest aspect of fostering youth participation in community organizations (Costello et al., 2000). Yet participation in determining the structure and direction of the organization is held to be one of the defining characteristics of "free spaces" (Evans & Boyte, 1992; Weis & Fine, 2000). Youth in this study also pointed to the centrality of being able to impact the organization by having (or not having) a role in organizational decision making.

Youth involvement in decision making at YEC was a point of contention among youth throughout my research. For this analysis, I use the 2002–2003 time period. In the fall, youth continually expressed frustration that adults were "making all the decisions." "I felt like we didn't have a say or anything like that, said one. "We got to yell at them, but then that was about it. That didn't make anything" (YEC youth, 2/5/03). In their analysis of power and responsibility (described above), youth concluded that the organization lacked formal mechanisms for young people to get involved in decision making (field notes, 10/9/02). As a result, a group of youth worked to create the Youth-Adult (YA) Council, a collaborative group responsible for making organizational policy decisions. The council began meeting in the late fall and played a central role in a second formal effort to involve youth in decision making that winter, Decision Day, in which youth worked to develop a proposal for organizational restructuring. Throughout the spring, adults and youth continued to work together to bring more youth voice into decision making. By the end of the year, most youth reported that they had been involved in decision making in some way and that they felt young people were able to influence the organization; as one noted, "It's almost as if YEC could not run if some random [young person] wouldn't just get up and say what they thought was right. So, it's like the driving force of the whole, entire [organization]" (YEC youth, 6/9/03).

At YSYC, youth started out the year more optimistic about their level of involvement and influence on the organization, but ended feeling less powerful.[5] In midyear interviews, most said is was possible for them to have an influence because it was "obvious" that adults wanted them to be involved, to "step up to the plate" or "go through the process with them." However, like YEC in the fall, YSYC lacked any kind of structured or formal mechanisms for youth to get involved in decision making. As one youth pointed out,

> They say, "Oh, we can't call you in … can't have you come in for another day besides just two hours a week." So, I mean, they would definitely want us to be there, and the intent is to have as much of our input as possible. It just doesn't work that way. (YSYC youth, 3/5/03)

By year's end, youth felt less like their participation in decision making was something the organization wanted and expressed a strong lack of efficacy in terms of organizational influence:

> I just was more aware of it later, because I was understanding better how the organization functions …. I guess I was more idealistic about the fact that it was really youth-run, and I think later I just realized how much was controlled by the adults (YSYC youth, 7/21/03)

This feeling was expressed by the adults who worked most closely with youth as well: "[I]t's made very, very clear to [the youth] they don't actually have a whole lot to do with what the organization decides and how things go" (YSYC adult ally, 7/2/03), which was "very self-defeating for this whole program" (YSYC adult staff member, 6/5/03).

The experiences at both sites, though different, offer common lessons about aspects of powerful youth participation in decision making. First, the level of decision making matters. Although youth were involved in decisions around how to use their space or time (YEC) or making grants (YSYC), participation in organizational policy decisions took on a sense of larger import for young people.[6] Youth expressed a need to create something, to make an impact on the organization; one noted, "There's no way any of us ever get to create our own program or anything within YSYC, and it's just this program that's set and you just follow the lead, basically, so that's not very empowering" (YSYC youth, 7/15/03).

Second, youth need structured opportunities for participation; they cannot be expected to simply take on decision-making roles that they have not had before: "It's kind of hard to really realizing that we can step up to the plate and do what we can do" (YEC youth, 11/4/02). Mechanisms like the YA Council provide a space and the support for youth to take on meaningful roles. However, this carries other implications. The YA Council involved only 8 youth out of 80, raising questions about whether all youth can have high-level, intensive involvement in decision making. This research, however, found that in terms of efficacy, it may not be necessary for all youth to be involved so intensively. While youth who participated in the Y-A Council likely developed more skill at decision making, other youth at YEC expressed an increased sense of efficacy simply by seeing young people involved. Alternatively, at YSYC, youth expressed concern that the organization had few young people on staff or in positions of decision-making power (field notes, 5/21/03, 6/11/03). So a sense of youth voice and agency more collectively may develop from seeing others like oneself in positions of authority.

Third, to involve youth in authentic, real decision making, adults have to be open to what youth will bring. As one adult explained, YEC worked to make real space for youth voice:

> And it wasn't play. It wasn't, "Oh, you're going to give us your input, but we're not really going to take it." I think there's a real seriousness about [listening to what youth say].... And just to see, like, how kids carried themselves out of that [decision-making process], like, "You know what? My words count." (YEC adult codirector, 2/25/03)

Alternatively, when this space did not exist, youth noticed and ended up feeling more frustrated and less powerful. A youth at YSYC described how adults involved her in decision making:

> They were telling me what their plan is and whether it would work and how I would want to change it.... If you have no plan when you come into the meeting ... we're all feeling accountable that we need to create a plan by the end of this meeting. Do you know what I'm saying? So, when they come in with a plan, you know they have a plan, so what's the point? Might as well just kick back and do whatever. (YSYC youth, 7/15/03)

Finally, involving youth in meaningful decision making is tightly linked to the idea of organizational intentionality. It requires a commitment to creating spaces for youth participation even when that may not be the most efficient process. One of the youth data analysts pointed to a "times of crisis" yardstick for evaluating an organization's commitment to youth decision making: "when crisis comes, you really see what the organization's about, like, who gets to make the decisions." She noted that when a crisis point was reached at YSYC, the result was a decision-making hierarchy, with youth at the bottom: "Decisions are made all the way up over there with [the executive director] or whoever, and then here's the youth, and so it has to go in all these stages before it gets back down" (youth data analyst 3, 7/29/03).

Content and Pedagogy

The educative components of counterpublics are thought crucial for developing the skills and values needed for effective participation (Evans & Boyte, 1992). The content dimension here refers to both the explicit and the embedded curriculum (McLaughlin, 2000), as well as pedagogical practices that youth point to as influencing their agency as public actors.

Much of YEC's content was geared toward youth gaining public skills like facilitation, decision making, public speaking, evaluation, working with a team, holding others and oneself accountable, and learning to work with and through diversity. As one adult coach described, it is crucial to "recognize that if you want to be powerful and empowered, that you also need pretty hard skills" (8/5/03). In her work with youth, she emphasized reflection to first acknowledge what skills young people have, and then helped them develop plans for how they would gain needed skills. This skills development was most often learned through practice, embedded in a larger content; that is, through working on a project to develop a charter school, youth learned to facilitate meetings internally and with community members, made public presentations before the school board, used consensus decision-making techniques, and evaluated their work.

YEC placed equal emphasis on personal understanding and growth. Indeed, one adult coach stated she would know her work had been successful if youth left the organization with "a sense of who [they] are and where [they] stand" (8/5/03). Adults coached youth through these learning and growth processes, modeling or stepping in as youth requested or needed. In addition, other, more experienced or skilled youth often served as models, some even having positions as youth coaches. Youth at YEC reported a strong sense of efficacy coming from their skills development and personal growth. As one youth put it, they developed not only the "tools and skills to go out into the world and be effective," but also the self-reflection to know how to use their power positively (YEC youth, 6/9/03).

At YSYC, youth underwent an intensive round of public skills training at the beginning of the year in facilitation, decision making, public speaking, and group work, as well as more role-specific training around how to approach outreach or evaluate project proposals. In addition, youth received mini-trainings on specific topics throughout the year—what the adult ally described as "on the fly." Pedagogically, the adult ally at YSYC most often relied on lecture or sometimes discussion in the form of "15 to 20 minutes of condensed information delivery from one side to the other" (YSYC adult ally, 7/2/03). In addition to trainings, youth reported that their understanding of community problems and issues and their awareness of how to make change increased by attending presentations and reading applications of community youth groups.

Experiences at both YEC and YSYC point to features of content and pedagogy that influence the link between skills development and public efficacy. First, reflection was crucial. At YEC, youth engaged in formal and informal evaluation throughout the year that focused on personal as well as group and organizational issues. At YSYC, youth participated in a formal, structured reflection twice over the year that focused on organizational issues as well as personal performance and skills development. In both organizations, reflection allowed the young people to see skills that they had developed and was a point of assessment about what skills or knowledge they needed to work on in the future. In addition, youth at YEC described how reflection allowed them to develop an awareness of their personal power and influence.

Second, youth at both sites raised the need for relationship development as an intentional content feature. At YEC, while relationship development is core to the program, many of the upper-division youth felt that in their final year they had not spent enough time on it, and thus had not developed the relationships that encourage responsibility or create a safe space for personal reflection and change. Similarly, youth at YSYC described relationships as simply "cool," and wished for more organizational emphasis on this.

Third, pedagogy that allows for authentic practice and real room for youth voice is more empowering for young people.[7] Youth at YSYC describe how they were encouraged to participate: "[The adults] told us on the first day that, 'no, don't be shy and this and that when it comes to dealing with talking and showing yourself'" (YSYC youth, 2/25/03). Observation, however, saw little room for youth voice or ideas outside of grant decisions. The adult ally described how his hope had been to empower youth by modeling things like meeting facilitation or participation; because youth had become accustomed to adults doing things, however, "they let go of really wanting that responsibility or owning that" (YSYC adult ally, 7/2/03). This theme of open pedagogy was particularly strong in analysis done by the youth data analysts, who felt that youth were articulating a need to be able create things, to learn by doing, and to learn from their mistakes. For example, one youth analyst felt the decrease in youth engagement at YSYC came from a lack of space for creation:

You don't get to create anything. You're just pretty much doing, following orders, in a way.... And so when you don't create anything, your mind's kind of lazy, like, "Why do I need to do this?"... It's not empowering unless it's creative. (youth data analyst 3, 7/15/03)

It is important to note that the pedagogical piece is intertwined with other factors. The time crunch caused by the push for "success" at YSYC, for example, constrained the adult ally in terms of using a more open or youth-centered pedagogy. In addition, at both sites, there was constant tension around the question of who was responsible for youth participation; was it just a matter of adults making space, or did youth also need to "step up"? The youth data analysts talked of the need to provide skills, resources, and space for young people, especially youth who have less experience with more participatory pedagogies. They pointed to organizational intentionality and adult role: the culture needs to be supportive of authentic youth participation and adults have to *want* to give youth the space and the chance because the youth themselves may not always know what is possible (youth data analysts 1 and 2, 8/5/03).

Macropolitical Connections

In contrast to many CBYOs, a defining characteristic of counterpublics is held to be their "conversation" with the broader public sphere (Fraser, 1992). This definition "highlights the specifically public dimensions of settings which people own, where they become transformed from private actors ... to public agents, able to understand themselves in terms of their impact on the larger world" (Evans & Boyte, 1992, p. xiii).

At YEC, public connection was central to the definition of the organization as a place where youth could make change in their communities. Youth described how YEC allowed them to come together, discuss issues of concern, and then organize to make change. This was supported in observations, which found that the organization consistently provided space in which youth could connect with current issues and events in their world, from local city elections, to statewide education reform, to the war in Iraq. In recent years, however, youth have become critical, saying that less time has been spent engaged in public work and more on internal, organizational projects. They questioned YEC's goal of community work, calling it "just like a front" and said they were "not really in the community as much as [they] used to be" (YEC youth, 11/4/02 and 6/9/03). While youth felt able to impact their communities because of past experiences with the organization, the more recent lack of connection had negatively impacted some youth's sense of efficacy; one noted, "I feel like I haven't done as much as I could have to feel that kind of [public] power. I know I can do a lot of things, but I just, I haven't put that into work [this year]" (YEC youth, 6/9/03).

At YSYC, community connection was also at the core of the organization. Youth were engaged in outreach with, led workshops and orientations for, and provided follow-up support to community youth groups. It is interesting to note that although board youth were not directly involved (at least through YSYC) with community change efforts, by claiming ownership of the community projects they funded, all but one youth in the group articulated a strong sense of public impact: "When you're here, you're assisting in those [community] youth making a change, and even, like, helping them is sort of making that change, so you're sort of a part of that change" (YSYC youth, 6/17/03). Moreover, the awareness that board members gained of the work of community youth increased their own sense of efficacy as young people.

In addition, YSYC youth gained a sense of power through their control over resources—in this case, grant money. While power coming from money may be problematic, for these youth it represented a way in which they were enabled to support their communities and other youth. They saw the very fact of youth having control over resources as a type of community change:

> The power that we usually see the adults have more than kids, they're giving it to us now .... The responsibility, the big role of deciding who gets money and who doesn't .... Most of the time, especially when it's government funded, they want adults to deal with the money. They don't want little ratty kids from the streets. (YSYC youth, 7/2/03)

In YEC and YSYC, macropolitical connection was a central aspect of the young people's experience, leading them to articulate a strong sense of public agency. The experiences of these two organizations also point to aspects of macropolitical connections that are more (or less) supportive of efficacy. First, community work is closely linked with decision-making authority. Youth wanted to have a say in choosing what issues were important and what types of community involvement they wanted. Youth rebelled when asked to participate in ways they had not chosen themselves: "It's like they picked the project for us .... We never heard of it and never said that, like, 'Oh, this would be something we should take on'" (YEC youth, 10/23/02). One youth data analyst was similarly critical of what she saw as an adult-driven process for choosing community projects:

> It's just like, "Okay, so you [adults] decide what the community is about, what the community has been through, like what the community's struggles are, why they're like that, and what you can do about them. You make arrangements and then come and tell us [youth] exactly what we have to do." ... It's really just ridiculous. (Youth data analyst 3, 7/29/03)

Second, youth pointed to the importance of feedback from the community in strengthening their sense of efficacy. Those at YEC described how the most meaningful parts of their experience came through interactions with the public, when they saw or understood their community impact. For one youth, the importance of feedback was made startlingly clear. In our final interview, she said she had had no impact at all, even though she had been one of 10 young people who created the charter high school. However, at an event the next day she cried as she talked about how that feeling had changed:

> I didn't think I had [had any impact on the community] until today. This morning several youth said they wouldn't make it without this school, and I realized that I helped create that. I helped make it possible for them. (YEC youth, 6/12/03)

At YSYC, on the other hand, the youth ended the year frustrated when the adults decided to cancel their grantee follow-up event: "We didn't really have that concept of checking back in with groups and having a continued relationship, seeing what happened, what came out of that grant cycle" (YSYC youth, 5/28/03). Youth data analysts further linked this lack of macro connection with a lack of ownership on the part of the review board youth: "If they weren't here last year and they didn't do site visits or they didn't see the projects at work, so they don't have any reason to care about the projects" (youth data analyst 2, 7/29/03). Indeed, when asked for an example of their community impact, almost all YSYC youth mentioned a group they had funded whose project event they had attended. Concrete feedback led to a concrete sense of impact.

Conclusion and Policy Implications

Ginwright and Cammarota (Introduction, this volume) point to young people's right to be agents, actively participating in making the decisions and creating the policies that impact their lives. Often, the responsibility for "stepping up" is placed solely on youth. However, for youth to break out of traditional, marginalizing patterns and "take their own power" is not an easy task.[8] As one young person noted,

> I came here ... I was kind of looking for the same thing as in a traditional school, like a teacher to say, "Well, this is what's going to happen." So I think that at first it was kind of different for me because they used to always say, "Well, what do you think? What do you think?" And I kind of got angry because I thought, "It's not about what I think" ... because I was not used to having my opinions heard. (YEC youth, 6/3/02)

Community-based youth organizations can help young people by building organizational intentionality around youth voice, public language, participation in decision making, skills development, and public work. This means providing a balance of structured opportunities and openness for joint creation and accountability. It means presenting frameworks for youth to understand their experiences and reflection and feedback mechanisms to become aware of their power and influence. This chapter outlines organizational factors that influence youth's developing efficacy with the hope of informing thoughtful, intentional practice and policy.

This research carries several implications for policy. First, it highlights the concept of *space*. Social justice policy for youth must attend to the current lack of spaces that support young people's transformation into powerful, collective, public actors. This chapter hopes to broaden policy makers' understanding of educational sites for youth, highlighting crucial out-of-school developmental contexts. Second, it demonstrates that not all CBYOs are equal, and articulates the organizational factors that influence youth experience and development in these contexts.

Third, by developing an understanding of the aspects of CBYOs that influence urban young people's sense of public efficacy, it points to features of these organizations that may be imported into schools and other developmental contexts for urban youth. While many schools may have become "depleted sites for democracy,"[9] for urban youth, they are often the primary public institutions with which they have a connection—as important as they are, experiences in CBYOs are not the norm for urban young people (Flanagan & Faison, 2001). Thus, it becomes all the more important to understand how classrooms and schools could be restructured to be sites of power for young people instead of marginalization.

Notes

I would like to thank the members of the Youth, Communities, and Social Justice Project for helping push my thinking around these issues. In addition to the editors, particular thanks go to Michelle Fine, Ben Kirshner, Milbrey McLaughlin, and Maria Torre for their feedback on drafts of this chapter. Research for this chapter was supported by the Center for Information & Research on Civic Learning and Engagement.

1. These statements come from young people whom I interviewed on May 17, 2001, and June 6, 2001. Hereafter, interviews and excerpts from my field notes will be cited parenthetically in the text.
2. Organization names herein are pseudonyms.
3. It is important to note that my purpose is not to judge which focus is "better," more appropriate, or more effective. Rather, it is to outline the ways in which lack of clarity of focus impacted the board youth.
4. Thanks to Michelle Fine for providing this term to think about the ways in which adults became more invested in their own (or outside) definitions of success, thus shifting accountability and opportunity away from young people.
5. In my discussion of decision making at YSYC, I refer to decisions around organizational practices or policies, not to the grant-making decisions in which youth were deeply involved.
6. It should be noted that having decision-making power over grant monies gave youth an extremely strong sense of power. As one youth data analyst put it, the decision over what to do with $60,000 is completely different from the question of whether to "go bowling or not" (youth data analyst 3, 7/29/03). The important

point that youth expressed, however, is that power over grant decisions is power within a very structured, limited realm.

7. Kirshner (chapter 3, this volume), for example, provides a compelling description of how a "youth-centered" apprenticeship might work effectively.

8. This phrase, used here and in the title of this chapter, came from an interview with a young person who talked about how society views youth of color as "a very dispensable group of people that are not capable of really taking their own power and taking, like, the society into their own hands" (3/5/03).

9. I borrow this term from Michelle Fine.

References

Berman, S. (1997). Children's social consciousness and the development of social responsibility. Albany: State University of New York Press.

Boyte, H. (1991). Community service and civic education. *Phi Delta Kappan, 72*(10), 765–767.

Conover, P. J., & Searing, D. D. (2000). A political socialization perspective. In L. M. McDonnell, P. M. Timpane, & R. Benjamine (Eds.), *Rediscovering the democratic purposes of education* (pp. 91–124). Lawrence: University Press of Kansas.

Costello, J., Toles, M., Spielberger, J., & Wynn, J. (2000). History, ideology, and structure shape the organizations that shape youth. In *Youth development: Issues, challenges, and directions* (pp. 185–231). Philadelphia: Public/Private Ventures.

Evans, S., & Boyte, H. C. (1992). *Free spaces: The sources of democratic change in America.* Chicago: University of Chicago Press.

Fine, M., Weis, L., Centrie, C., & Roberts, R. (2000). Education beyond the borders of schooling. *Anthropology and Education Quarterly, 31*(2), 131–151.

Flanagan, C. A., & Faison, N. (2001). Youth civic development: Implications of research for social policy and programs. *Social Policy Report: Giving Child and Youth Development Knowledge Away, 15*(1), 1–15.

Fraser, N. (1992). Rethinking the public sphere: A contribution to the critique of actually existing democracy. In C. Calhoun (Ed.), *Habermas and the public sphere* (pp. 109–141). Cambridge, MA: MIT Press.

Ginwright, S. A., & Cammarota, J. (2002). New terrain in youth development: The promise of a social justice approach. *Social Justice, 29*(4), 82–95.

Hart, D., & Atkins, R. (2002). Civic competence in urban youth. *Applied Developmental Science, 6*(4), 227–236.

Hart, R. (1992). *Children's participation: From tokenism to citizenship.* Florence, Italy: UNICEF Innocenti Research Centre.

Hart, R., Daiute, C., & Iltus, S. (1997). Developmental theory and children's participation in community organizations. *Social Justice, 24*(3), 33–63.

McLaughlin, M. W. (2000). *Community counts: How youth organizations matter for youth development.* Washington, DC: Public Education Network.

O'Donoghue, J. L., & Kirshner, B. R. (2003, November). Urban youth's civic development in community-based youth organizations. Paper presented at the International Conference on Civic Education, New Orleans.

Pittman, K., Ferber, T., & Irby, M. (2000). *Youth as effective citizens.* Takoma Park, MD: International Youth Foundation.

Tolman, J., & Pittman, K. (2001). *Youth acts, community impacts: Stories of youth engagement with real results.* Community and Youth Development Series (Vol. 7). Takoma Park, MD: The Forum for Youth Investment, International Youth Foundation.

Weis, L., & Fine, M. (Eds.). (2000). *Construction sites: Excavating race, class, and gender among urban youth.* New York: Teachers College Press.

Youniss, J., Bales, S., Christmas-Best, V., Diversi, M., McLaughlin, M., & Silbereisen, R. (2002). Youth civic engagement in the twenty-first century. *Journal of Research on Adolescence, 12*(1), 121–148.

CHAPTER 14

Taking Charge in Lake Wobegon: Youth, Social Justice, and Antiracist Organizing in the Twin Cities

KARIN AGUILAR-SAN JUAN

Introduction

This chapter explores ongoing efforts to determine the meaning and potential impact of "youth organizing" in the Twin Cities of Minneapolis and St. Paul, Minnesota. Here, youth organizing is in a nascent, transitional stage focused primarily on youth service and youth development. This chapter will identify and analyze a small yet noticeable critical impulse toward empowering youth—particularly youth of color—to make institutional and structural change. While Minneapolis and St. Paul are two distinct urban areas containing their own unique histories and constellations of neighborhoods and communities, this chapter will consider the two cities together as a metropolitan region. In this region, as in other parts of the country, structural inequalities such as poverty, cutbacks in public schools, urban gentrification, suburban sprawl, criminalization, and incarceration have left many youth—particularly poor youth, immigrant youth, and youth of color—supermarginalized from power and resources in their neighborhoods.

The prevailing model of working with youth in the Twin Cities is top-down and service oriented. The concept of youth organizing as a youth-centered, community-based approach to social justice—one that is distinct from student organizing on college and university campuses—is not yet widely recognized, clearly articulated, or firmly rooted here. However, a small, energetic, and vocal group of youth and adults is engaging in youth organizing. Their youth organizing activities combine community organizing techniques and

247

perspectives with a race-cognizant and antiracist organizing agenda. I will argue here that antiracism should be central to youth organizing in this region. As youth organizing becomes a more trendy, fashionable, and well-funded approach to dealing with youth problems in the Twin Cities, practitioners must attend to the deeply entrenched causes and consequences of racial inequality within and across neighborhoods and communities. Without openly and actively addressing the impact of systems of racism and white privilege on the region's youth, the emergent model for youth organizing could turn into a model that empowers white, middle-class, and suburban youth at the expense of poor youth, immigrant youth, and youth of color.

Theories of Youth and Social Justice

In their insightful and timely analysis of youth and social justice, Shawn Ginwright and Julio Cammarota (Introduction, this volume) identify several reasons that youth—especially youth from working-poor, urban communities—are disenfranchised systematically from society. The bold strokes they paint about the patterns of marginalization among youth are disturbing. Even worse, they point out that youth are increasingly left out of the solutions to their own disenfranchisement. Because youth advocates have failed to conceptualize youth issues in a way that enables young people themselves to take center stage, youth advocacy, once part of the solution, has become part of the problem. As a theoretical corrective, the authors propose an alternative theoretical framework that emphasizes:

1. Youth action may be interpreted as a collective and rational response to state control and repression.
2. Youth action occurs in a community context in which youth exercise civil rights and act as members of communities.
3. Communities, especially place-based ones, provide opportunities and challenges to youth that are in turn shaped by larger economic, political, and social forces. A behavioral approach to youth issues will not take these forces into account.

By identifying these points, the authors outline a conceptual revolution in youth organizing. Their work builds on previous findings represented in a series of occasional papers published by the Funders' Collaborative on Youth Organizing (FCYO). By emphasizing that youth organizing is a "fusion of community organizing tactics and youth development outcomes," FCYO underscores the special role that youth can and do play in revitalizing and reenergizing communities across the nation (Ginwright, 2003, p. 2; see also HoSang, 2003).

This conceptual revolution reflects the ideas already put into action by young people at the grassroots level—organizers who have made it their job to improve their own lives and communities.[1] For many of these youth organizers, the link between the fate of individual youth and larger patterns of inequality in their communities is obvious. For example, YouthAction is a national intermediary for youth and community organizations based in Albuquerque, New Mexico. In their mission statement, the members of YouthAction name their constituencies plainly in terms of "communities of color, low-income communities, and LGBTQ [lesbian, gay, bisexual, transgender, and queer/questioning] communities." The fact that YouthAction identifies its base this way suggests that youth are working hard to build a sense of common cause across boundaries of race, ethnicity, culture, class, gender, and sexuality because they see their problems as rooted in something much more complex than just their own personal failures and differences as young people. Moreover, their spin on youth organizing—"Youth Organizing Components" (Youth Action, 2005) is a document available at their website—gives flesh and blood to the idea that youth can be agents, not just recipients, of social change.

To ground my interdisciplinary approach, epistemological assumptions, and political commitments to youth and social justice, I draw my cues from scholarship in racial formation/critical race theory, critical white studies, urban sociology, political economy, and social movement theory. Omi and Winant (1994) posit that ethnicity, nation, or class cannot explain away "race." More important, racial formations are produced from above by the state and challenged from below by social movements, which potentially include youth. In general, critical race theorists (Bell, 1995; West, 1999) similarly argue for the centrality of race in determining group access to legal, political, and economic resources. Key among these theorists, Crenshaw (1995) and Roberts (1995) call for a racial framework that centers the plight of women of color—instead of relegating them to the margins or ignoring them entirely. Recently, scholars from a variety of disciplines have produced a critical analysis of whiteness as "property" (Harris, 1995) and as a category with "cash value" (Lipsitz, 1998). Because of Minnesota's unique demographic and cultural context, these insights into whiteness cannot be overemphasized. Feminist scholarship brings into view the many ways that the contexts for social movements are informed by gender, along with racism and global capitalism (Naples, 1998). Although I do not comment on gender or sexuality in this chapter, my larger project treats race as deeply intertwined with gender and sexuality. Urban sociology, a well-established field that is currently reinvigorating itself by looking at the role of culture and identity in metropolitan regions, helps frame neighborhoods as places where families and children generate material and symbolic resources for community growth (Dreier, Mollenkopf, & Swanstrom, 2001; Medoff & Sklar, 1994). Political economy, tinged with cultural studies, emphasizes landscapes of power—and powerlessness (Zukin, 1993). Social movement theory looks at social change and public policy from the perspective of grassroots organizing, or what we might think of as "politics from below." These theories allow us to distinguish between nonprofit and grassroots organizations, and encourages us to identify and analyze the goals, strategies, and motivations behind movements for social change and social justice (McAdam, 1982; Scott, 1990; Tarrow, 1994; Young, 1995). Even as I seek to inform myself about the role of youth in social movement building, I worry seriously about my complicity in joining a circle of "experts" who are no longer youth themselves—and yet who claim to know what youth really need.

One of my underlying assumptions throughout this chapter is that the problems that youth face demand a community-based, historically grounded approach rather than a more narrow approach that focuses on individual deficiencies, culture, or behavioral traits. Framing youth this way is crucial to understanding the broader context in which youth are emerging as an exploited group and as a scapegoat for larger social and historical problems that, although they did not cause them, strike them the hardest. Youth organizing is potentially the most effective way to solve the problems facing youth because the youth-organizing concept frames what conservatives portray as only individual deficiencies or behavioral traits instead in terms that involve enduring and entrenched systems and structures. In this chapter, I will show that at least a handful of adults are beginning to understand that youth—especially poor youth, immigrant youth, and youth of color—can and do play a central role in community-based struggles for social justice, even in the far-flung land of "Lake Wobegon."

Methodological Considerations

This chapter highlights one aspect of my larger, ongoing, and comparative study of youth organizing for racial justice and democracy in three midsized metropolitan regions: Albuquerque, New Mexico; Detroit; and the Twin Cities. The larger study is designed to contextualize the differences and similarities in youth organizers' approach to racial identity, racial inequality, and racial justice with regard to specific place-based characteristics, histories, and changes. My inspiration for this project came first from my encounter with Grace Lee Boggs, an elder Chinese American activist and cofounder of Detroit Summer, a grassroots and youth-led initiative to "rebuild" and "respirit" Detroit. Later, through the Next Generation Leadership program of the Rockefeller Foundation,[2] I met four individuals whose experiences as and with youth organizers greatly impressed me: Taj James, now executive director of the Movement Strategy Center; Kim Miyoshi, founder of KidsFirst!; Hez Norton, founder of the North Carolina Lambda Youth Network; and Stephen Patrick, director of Youth and Emerging Initiatives, New Mexico Community Foundation, who introduced me to key contacts in Albuquerque. From them I learned to think about youth organizing in local and national terms. Eventually, I met three experts on youth organizing in the Twin Cities—Sarah Agaton-Howes, Brandon Lacy Campos, and Gunnar Liden—who became my friends and key contacts for this project. Nancy Naples, a professor of sociology and women's studies (University of Connecticut–Storrs), helped me to design this project and to develop and pursue my research questions (see also Naples, 2003).

For this examination of the relationship between youth organizing, social justice, and antiracism in the Twin Cities, I draw on several sources of information. Since 2001, I have informally interviewed a dozen adult organizers (ranging in age from 25 to 50) about the nature and scope of youth work in the Twin Cities. These unstructured conversations have provided me with valuable anecdotal information about the widely ranging goals, strategies, organizational structures, and personal motivations that shape the Twin Cities in terms of youth advocacy and youth service. In my notes from those conversations I discerned certain themes, issues, and problems that relate to youth organizing (as it has been defined above) and racial justice.

Those conversations served as the stepping stones upon which I subsequently entered the community of youth organizers as a participant-observer. I spearheaded a pilot project of the Twin Cities Youth Dialogue on Race and Cultural Diversity that took shape as three daylong workshops for 30 youth (ages 15–19) during the summer of 2003. To plan, design, and execute this pilot, I worked closely with a core group of 7 young adults who are professionally and personally committed to youth organizing. Taj James served as my outside consultant in planning this project. In the following nine months, I kept close ties with those adults and the youth with whom they work by talking and interacting with them in person, over the phone, and via e-mail. They helped me to define the mission of the Twin Cities Youth Dialogue as a "local intermediary" that keeps alive a network for youth organizing around racial justice.

For the present study I conducted in-depth, open-ended interviews with four adults who work within a youth-organizing frame. Because of a restrictive human subjects research protocol where I work, I have not yet conducted formal interviews with people under the age of 18. I do plan to conduct formal interviews with youth for the larger project of which this study is a part. The adults I interviewed range in age from mid-20s to late 40s; three of them have lived in Minnesota for most of their lives. In many important ways, their thoughts and experiences reflect their white, native, Latino, mixed-race, and queer communities. I selected these individuals on the basis of their ability to articulate the extent and significance of youth organizing in the Twin Cities today. In this regard, they are unusual informants whose insights are valuable precisely because they bring a critical perspective based in daily practice to the local conversation about youth. My interview questions sought to elicit their personal biographies; definitions of social change and social justice; motivations for working with youth and young people; relationships to youth and elders in their communities; experiences with racism and antiracist organizing; the significance of exposure to organizing networks outside of Minnesota; the relationship between place and community; and perspectives on local Minnesota culture.

The interviews lasted from one hour to three and one-half hours. I tape-recorded each interview and later coded them according to widely recognized principles of qualitative data analysis. I paid particular attention to definitions of "youth organizing" and to the factors that my contacts identify as promoting and supporting youth organizing. I was also very interested in the way the interviewees framed their relationships to various communities—whether place-based, identity-based, or both.

To supplement my interview data, I also consulted websites and paper documents (annual reports, neighborhood assessments, notes from meetings) generated by the organizations with which each interviewee works. In my twin roles as participant and as researcher, I attended many events: an antiracism workshop, a harvest festival, a spoken-word performance, and several youth-led discussion groups. I have worked closely with a handful of youth whom I plan to interview formally in the near future. To get a bigger picture of regional trends and the issues facing youth, I analyzed statistics on racial change and socioeconomic status across the state of Minnesota and in various neighborhoods in the Twin Cities. To get a sense of the extent to which poor youth and youth of color face more severe conditions than their white peers, I also examined statistics describing the population characteristics of youth in public schools, in correction facilities, and in crisis shelters. I present some of this data here.

My observations, interviews, and fieldwork suggest that one of the most important battles youth organizers face in the Twin Cities involves the enduring and invisible structures of racism and white privilege.[3] Youth are embedded in neighborhoods and communities whose histories and cultures have been distorted, objectified, ignored, or simply erased. To empower these youth requires much more adult guidance, peer support, and self-reflection than a midnight basketball game (to mention one popular notion of what "youth programming" means here) can offer. Even a program that puts youth in decision-making positions—but which does not deal with the devastating loss of history or culture in their communities—is likely to fall short in this context. A full-blown project for youth organizing in the Twin Cities needs to encompass an antiracist agenda, including education around history and culture, immediate survival needs, identity development, personal growth, leadership and organizing skills, and other community-related issues.

The Context for Youth Organizing in the Twin Cities

In Minnesota, whiteness is both everywhere—and nowhere to be seen. The popular myth of Lake Wobegon helps to reinforce the notion of Minnesota as a land of country bumpkins where time stands still—and nonwhite, indigenous people do not even exist. Garrison Keillor, the radio personality whose show *Prairie Home Companion* has a national following, created the myth of Lake Wobegon partly as a way to express his dislike for the conservative environment of small-town life here. The myth is so powerful that many people believe it is a real place. In *In Search of Lake Wobegon* (Olsenius and Keillor, 2001), documentary-style photographs of actual people living and working in rural Minnesota illustrate an essay by Keillor about his imaginary Minnesotan place; the result is a surreal, postmodern narrative about a myth that is evidently true! In a scholarly article titled "Minnesota: A Different America," geographer and native Minnesotan David Lanegran (2000) portrays the state as an unusual place with its own leisure culture and tradition of deer hunting and ice fishing. The article treats these as leisure activities that are normal and characteristic of Minnesotans, without recognizing how the very same activities might be viewed, for example, by native people.[4]

In myriad and complex ways, the myth of Lake Wobegon normalizes whiteness and simultaneously renders invisible the experiences and histories of racialized minority groups in Minnesota. This normalization of whiteness thus weighs heavily on attempts to organize among people of color here. The present study is not an adequate or appropriate venue for a full exploration of their marginalized experiences and histories. Instead, in order to give a sense of scale to the obstacles that confront youth organizers, I offer some statistical indicators. These indicators suggest that youth organizers face serious demographic and social challenges in this region, the most pressing of which is a lack of both conceptual and physical spaces in which to develop an alternative youth-oriented consciousness and political agenda.[5]

Youth organizing in the Twin Cities is emerging in a social, geographic, and historical context that is in many ways distinct from that of coastal regions or dense metropolitan areas that have experienced more racial diversity over a longer period of time. Minnesota's population is sparse; across the entire state there are only five million people. Of these, 89.4% are white, and the majority of these are of German, Swedish, or Norwegian background. When lumped together into a "minority" category, African Americans, American Indians, Asian Americans, Native Hawaiians, and Latinos (of any race) comprise just over 10% of the total state population. Coalitions among racialized minority groups are obviously necessary in a situation where sheer numbers are so small. But because each group's history and identity is often ignored or overlooked by the dominant culture, working across lines of race and culture is often difficult.

Minnesota's youth population exhibits greater diversity than the population at large. The number of minority children (nonwhite and Latino ethnicity combined) doubled between 1990 and 2000 from 9.8% to 18%. Immigration from outside the United States accounts for some of this increase: Minnesota is home to relatively large numbers of Ethiopians, Hmong, Mexicans, and Somalis who are younger and have more children than whites do. In general, families of color tend to have more children and higher fertility rates than do white families.

Racial diversity is concentrated in the Twin Cities, and racialized minority groups tend to be younger overall than whites. White students have fled the public schools, isolating themselves in better-off private and charter schools; consequently, African American, Asian Americans, Latinos, and American Indians now constitute the majority in the public school systems of St. Paul (71%) and Minneapolis (73%).[6] In 2004 and 2005, thousands of Hmong refugees from Thailand arrived in St. Paul, adding many new students to the public schools. While the median age of whites is 37.2 years old, minority groups have median ages of between 23 and 25.5 years old.

As in other regions of the country, in Minnesota poverty, homelessness, and school dropout rates show great disparities across race. Child poverty is relatively high in the counties containing St. Paul and Minneapolis: 15.7% in Ramsey County (St. Paul) and 10.5% in Hennepin County (Minneapolis) were poor. In 1999, 9.4% of white non-Latino children lived in poverty, compared to 30% for Latinos, 36.6% for Asians, 49.1% for African Americans, and a shocking 54.2% for American Indians.[7] African Americans, American Indians, and Latinos make up over half (57%) of the homeless youth population, although they represent only 6% of the total population of the state. In grades 7 to 12, the white population experienced a dropout rate of less than 2% in 2001–2002. Meanwhile, nearly 10% of Latinos and American Indians dropped out in that same period.

Given these terribly stark racial disparities, it is perhaps not surprising that a disproportionate number of juveniles in state correctional facilities are youth of color. For example, among the total (relatively small) population in the state's juvenile facility at Redwing during 2002, 14.3% were American Indian, 13.1% were African American, and 6% were Latino.[8] According to the Children's Report Card,[9] the rate of juvenile apprehensions rose steadily in the late 1990s, reaching a high of 63.1 per thousand in 1997.

Perhaps the people of Minnesota are not entirely unaware of or insensitive to the structural problems that are indicated by these numbers. According to the Metro Trend Watch (Wilder Research Institute, 2004b), most adults rate their quality of life as "good" or "outstanding." The report notes that "racial minorities, especially blacks, and people with incomes under $30,000" feel less positive about the situation. However, in an assessment of racism in three Minnesota counties in 2004, the Wilder Research Institute found that while people seemed aware of "racism" as a real issue, few define "racism" as institutional discrimination or bias (Wilder Research Institute, 2004a). Like most Americans, Minnesotans tend to consider racism—if they see racism at all—a matter of personal dislikes and intolerance. In disturbing ways, the triumph of neoconservative public policy shows itself in a declining ability of even the most educated people to connect their personal traumas to larger collective narratives—what C. Wright Mills called the "sociological imagination." The spread of liberal "color-blindness"—that is, a resistance to seeing racism—makes addressing the structural dimensions of racism even more difficult.[10] As far as I know, there is no similar survey of perceptions of racism among youth.

All of this is not to ignore or belittle Minnesota's long and remarkable tradition of "raising hell," embodied, for example, in the accomplishments of the late senator Paul Wellstone and his late wife Sheila.[11] For those readers especially on the East and West Coasts who imagine Minnesota as a cultural "Nowheresville," it might be surprising to know that radical politics have an admirable history here, though not without complex racial undertones. In *Making Minnesota Liberal*, historian Jennifer A. Delton emphasizes the importance of antiracism in shaping Minnesota's civic consciousness in the years just following World War II (Delton 2002, p. 40). Curiously absent from her important narrative, however, is any reference to the Duluth lynching of three black men falsely accused of rape in 1920.[12] This tragic incident occurred a decade before the election of Floyd B. Olson as the first governor to represent the Farmer-Labor Party; Olson became a populist of mythic stature who united farmers and laborers. Delton's history implies that Minnesota's progressive white residents organized mightily against economic injustice, but they might not have been paying attention to racism until the rise of Nazism in Germany, when taking a public stand against racism became an act of national pride.

Clearly, Minnesota's unique demographic, politicoeconomic, and cultural characteristics pose a number of challenges to poor communities and communities of color. For antiracist organizers of any age, the biggest obstacle may be the prevailing color-blind logic that makes it difficult for even self-proclaimed progressive organizations to name racism, or the privileges of whiteness, as a social and political reality. For that reason, definitions of youth organizing that prioritize structural change ("action") over cultural change (mere "talk") in more diverse metropolitan regions such as the San Francisco Bay Area or New York City need to be modified slightly in order to accommodate the specific context of the Twin Cities. Here, a certain amount of cultural change must precede or at least accompany structural change if communities of color, and youth, are to take charge of the future in Lake Wobegon.

Social Service Versus Social Justice in Youth Organizing

The Twin Cities boasts a huge number of organizations devoted to youth. Among these organizations, there is a correspondingly wide range of beliefs and philosophies about the best ways to involve youth in their own issues and in the issues facing their neighborhoods and communities. On June 21, 2004, the Center for Neighborhoods sponsored a dialogue focused on "youth civic engagement" attended by nearly 40 adults and some youth who represented nearly as many organizations in the Twin Cities. The meeting, held at the offices of a local philanthropic organization, brought grassroots organizations together to raise awareness and develop connections around "youth."

Susan Doherty, the facilitator of this dialogue, discussed the dialogue and youth organizing in general with me in one of my four long interviews. Dialogue participant Sarah Agaton-Howes, provided me with another of my long interviews. I also analyzed the official notes from the meeting. I conducted a third interview with Gunnar Liden, who was invited to the dialogue but was unable to attend. Together, the interviews and the notes provide a strong indication of the "spin" that key individuals and organizations in the Twin Cities put on their work with youth.

Susan is an educator who has trained youth leaders, helped teachers become effective advisors for youth, and led planning processes around school reform. From her perspective, the goal of the dialogue was to "increase awareness" about ways to involve youth and build youth leadership in communities. As part of the introduction to the dialogue, she presented a chart, courtesy of FCYO, titled "Youth Engagement Continuum." She brought the chart to the meeting because, in her words, "I want to see people understand the spectrum of ways to work with youth and the impact of involving youth as real partners in action." This chart was also printed as an attachment to the meeting minutes, which were distributed to all the participants. The facilitator made clear at the outset that the focus of the meeting was intended to be on youth organizing, that is—systemic change. During the dialogue participants did not actually discuss or debate the distinctions between the various models of youth engagement as outlined in the FCYO document, but they did mention the need to begin thinking in terms of these various models.

Participants received a printed agenda prior to the dialogue that listed questions for discussion. They were:

> What should happen as a result of youth civic engagement projects? In what ways could a neighborhood's quality of life be increased through the actions of youth?
> What is already happening to provide youth civic engagement opportunities?
> What are the gaps? Where should more efforts be made?
> What next steps should we take?

The three-hour dialogue was divided into these four sets of questions. Participants broke up into small groups and tackled each question in turn. The minutes present the results of the conversation under headings representing topics that arose during the discussion. For example, the first discussion about the ideal outcomes of youth civic engagement is summarized into a list with seven headings: decision making, diversity, education, intergenerational connections, safety, service, and youth action. The second discussion about what is currently happening to produce those outcomes is summarized under the same headings, with each participant contributing examples from his or her own organization. The third discussion produced a lengthy list broken down into two columns: the gap and what to do about it. The fourth discussion resulted in eight suggestions, ranging in scope from "mapping" the organizations and communities along a youth engagement continuum, to organizing an event with a speaker from a youth-led organization, to having a youth-planned, metro-wide youth summit.

The discussion on "what to do" about the gap between what should happen and what is already happening yielded the most interesting findings. The participants identified gaps in practical and concrete terms that point to practical and concrete steps. For example, the first gap noted is, "We need to change adults' attitudes about youth." The next column describes six actions that need to take place for attitudes to change. These include: trust youth enough to really be involved, train/challenge adults to make real room for youth, and screen carefully when hiring staff to work with young people. Another example is the second gap: "We need more opportunities for youth to be truly engaged as an integral part of the community." The participants came up with seven steps to deal with this problem, including: consider alternative ways to engage youth; address culture and values of youth people; train youth in skills needed for decision making, involve youth as facilitators at meetings like this; and look at informal learning times—all the time a young person has is worth something. The rest of the discussion picked up on the need for intergenerational relationships, cross-cultural connections, material support and networking, and a connection between "schools and the rest of the world."

The dialogue made evident a certain level of dissatisfaction that many youth advocates in the Twin Cities have with the traditional, service-oriented approaches to working with youth. The comments and suggestions that participants offered about how to address the gaps between what should happen and what is happening with regard to youth civic engagement indicate that many of the key ingredients needed to bring youth organizing to the Twin Cities are already present. One of those key ingredients is antiracism, or a race-cognizant perspective on youth and their communities.

Youth Organizing and Antiracism in the Twin Cities

If youth are truly meant to be at the center of youth organizing, then as a youth-organizing agenda becomes more prominent in the Twin Cities, poor youth, youth of color, and immigrant youth are likely to play leadership roles in youth work. But for youth in positions of social marginality—due to class, race, gender, sexuality, or other barriers—stepping up to the plate may require an extra-long and difficult process. At least in theory, youth who are marginalized for different reasons are often all in the same boat when it comes to surmounting daily crises, confronting adultism, and working toward personal development, internal reflection, skill acquisition, and leadership.

For Brandon Lacy Campos, Gunnar Liden, and Sarah Agaton-Howes, youth organizing and antiracism are both personal and professional projects. Brandon grew up in a multiracial family and attended public school in Minneapolis. His college years took him to the southern United States, where he took a job with a youth-led organization that provides resources and services for queer youth. Actively engaged in national LGBTQ and antiracist networks, he is now back in Minneapolis, where he is initiating the development of a youth-organizing program within an organization that serves homeless youth.

As a white student at the University of Minnesota, Gunnar became interested in community organizing and multiculturalism. He moved to the West Side of St. Paul and is now the program director for a youth-oriented community gardening enterprise that targets the environment, racism, and poverty. Sarah grew up on the Fond du Lac reservation near Duluth, Minnesota in a family that was very involved in tribal government and the American Indian Movement. After many years working in social services, she married a Filipino American who shares her involvement in antiracism projects, and together they came to the Twin Cities. At the time of this interview, she worked as the youth organizer for a national antiracist organization based in Minneapolis.

Working with youth in a community-based, historically grounded framework means not only that youth must lead, but that youth must work to discover the solutions to their own social problems. For Brandon, that means his organization must make a transition from a purely service-oriented approach to a youth-organizing approach. Within the past year, the conversation in his organization has moved gradually from "We really need to change the way that we're working here in terms that make sure that young people have at least some say in the way that program is developed, evaluated" to "We need to do youth leadership." Using materials from FCYO, Brandon pushed the conversation one level higher, to youth organizing, as he explained in our interview:

> Brandon Lacy Campos: And so after that meeting when I had that sort of backing—now the community has said, and we've agreed, that we need to do youth leadership, youth development, youth organizing work, or youth leadership work—is when I brought out the stuff from FCYO and said, Not only do we need to do youth leadership, we need to do youth organizing. And this is what youth organizing is, this is what it looks like, and this is how we'll have to change. And we had to stress to the managers that this will be a significant cultural shift in the organization that has to have board backing, that will take some really deep—like we'll need to hire consultants, we'll need to hire outside people to come in and teach us how to be adult allies. What ageism really means. How does it appear in our programming? While at the same time learning how to give up power to young people.

> Karin Aguilar-San Juan: What did you tell them are the rewards for doing this?

> BLC: Well, I think part of it is, that document was so well laid out that they were like, "Oh, we get it." I think the other piece was, I think once they already got the thought process, the thing I put through is, what we're doing is we need to continue the services that we doing. What we're doing is making sure that youth in crisis are getting their immediate

needs taken care of. But what happens after these immediate needs are taken care of? How are we teaching them, what are we teaching them about the reasons why youth homelessness exists? The reasons why the school districts set up youth of color for failure. Like how do they, and how do we teach them about that and how do we teach them to address those issues once they are made aware of them? I was like, "And that's what community organizing does and that's what youth organizing does." It takes the power out of a situation and puts it in the hands of people affected by it. And gives them the tools to then address those situations.

While the conceptual divide between social-service delivery and building real social change often seems very wide and high, this example suggests that in fact the two approaches are closely connected. Homeless youth in Minnesota need immediate assistance and guidance from adults. But once youth are on their feet, they need the tools and resources to deal with the larger systems that perpetuate homelessness. Having developed his own organizing skills over the years via youth-led and youth-oriented trainings and workshops, as a young adult Brandon appears to have convinced his organization that youth organizing is not only a reasonable approach but a necessary one.

Gunnar approaches his work with youth in what I see as a teacherly manner, although Gunnar declines to see himself as a teacher in the conventional sense. Side by side with youth in the gardens, he gets to know them as people. As he puts it, "There's a big difference between keeping them busy and building a relationship with them." In this, Gunnar echoes Susan's comment that mid-night basketball programs do not address deeper needs. The gardens are a site for the education of youth around the environment, racism, and poverty. Gunnar sees his job as a form of community organizing, pushing youth "past the surface" to arrive at bigger and deeper issues. Sometimes, he has to help youth see that things they don't like around them are connected to these issues, such as racism, which, he says, "for adults ... is so huge." Allowing the youth to identify their own concerns leads, perhaps inevitably, to discussions about history and culture. Many of the youth he works with are first- or sec-ond-generation immigrants from Mexico or Southeast Asia. When they finally said, "We wish we knew where we were from," Gunnar took that as a signal to create the Homeland Project. Two winters ago, Gunnar, along with two other adults, took five Southeast Asian girls, ranging in age from 13 to 17, to Laos and Thailand so they could learn about their roots as Hmong people. Before the trip, the girls were interviewed several times by the local media. After the trip, I invited the girls to speak in my college course called Asian American Community and Identity. The Homeland Project is an example of a youth-led initiative that addresses their vexed relationship to a land and culture of origin.

While this project does not generate "structural" change of the sort that youth organizing usually promotes, in order for Hmong youth in the Twin Cities to become integrated into or to lead antiracist social movements, they clearly need to step through a process of cultural inquiry and self-discovery. In certain ways, this process is made more difficult and more urgent because of Minnesota's cultural and political history. Yet, in other ways, it is a process whereby youth move from a heightened awareness of their personal histories to a heightened social awareness.

In more recent months, Gunnar has developed a core of older (16- to 18-year-old) youth who are involved in discussions about racism. The antiracism component of Gunnar's youth organizing was inspired by his participation in an antiracism workshop sponsored by Campus Compact. In the summer of 2004, as part of the Twin Cities Youth Dialogue on Race and Cultural Diversity, I worked closely with four youth (white, Mexican, and Hmong) to help them lead an antiracism workshop for 80 high-school students sponsored by the local YWCA. Their role as "guest speakers" who addressed the issue of race each from his or her own perspective allowed the workshop participants to see antiracist organizing as something youth can and must do. Again, discussion is a necessary prelude to action in the Twin Cities and, although the forms of action these youth might take are not yet clear, their impulse to see racism in structural, systemic terms is already a challenge to Minnesota's prevailing logic of individualistic color-blindness.

For Brandon and Gunnar, educating youth of color about racism is a task that emerges naturally out of an engagement with their communities. But just because you "do community organizing" does not mean that you understand the significance of racism, even if the communities you work with are racially marginalized. Sarah Agaton-Howes stresses that community organizing does not necessarily entail an antiracist framework. In her opinion, community organizers in the Twin Cities need to be more aware of the impact of racism.

Karin Aguilar-San Juan: So can you say a little bit about the difference between antiracist organizing and community organizing?

Sarah Agaton-Howes: I think that … community organizing can be just as racist as anything else if you don't look at race and racism, culture, history. Like, if you're not … looking at how history and culture plays into community, how are you really gonna organize that community to be powerful? You know, if you don't understand how they became disempowered, and you just come into a community and say, "Oh, well I think we'll organize around this, because this is what I think this community needs"—and you don't understand what's happening. You know what I mean? So I think to me the difference is, is that you, looking at those things ... and also with that, people of color need to be in leadership.

Just as youth organizing means putting youth at the center of the organizing project, so antiracist organizing means that people of color need to take control of their organizations and exercise meaningful, decision-making power. In a region where people of color hold only token positions in many organizations, moving forward with an antiracist agenda is no small task. Working with youth requires taking culture and history into consideration. In this observation, Sarah corroborates Gunnar's inclination to support his youth in their search for their histories and identities in Laos and Thailand:

Karin Aguilar-San Juan: Are young people different than adults in how they organize?

Sarah Agaton-Howes: Yes. It's different in different cultures too. The push in the history of white youth, young college organizing is we're building youth power and it's this young people's thing. And a sort of disconnection with older people and elders. Which I think is part of the problem with white culture ... they don't have a connection to their elders.

Sarah identifies a lack of connection with the past as a feature of white culture and history that youth organizers might not see or understand unless they already know how the cultural logic of racism operates. This comment suggests that in the context of the Twin Cities "youth organizing" without an explicit racial lens ends up being a model of working with youth that covertly revolves around white youth and the cultural and historical issues related to whiteness and white privilege. The comment also reinforces the distinction, made by many youth organizers, between community-based movements led by youth of color versus campus-based movements led by primarily white, middle-class students.

The methods with which Brandon, Gunnar, and Sarah have integrated antiracism into their youth organizing work vary widely. But these examples indicate that to proceed with a youth organizing agenda that does not somehow account for the racialized experiences of all youth—but particularly those of youth of color—is a dangerous proposition, one that perhaps we should avoid. Unfortunately, this chapter is not long enough for me to explore in any depth how youth organizing and antiracism actually go together in the Twin Cities, at least in its nascent forms.

Instead, this study emphasizes the impact of racism on youth in the Twin Cities. I do not intend to ignore or overlook the complex relationships between poverty and racism or, on the other side, between wealth and white privilege. Nor do I intend to diminish or overlook the significance of gender and sexual orientation in the lives of youth of color; indeed, in future research, I hope to look more closely at the leadership roles of queer youth of color. So far, however, racism and efforts to dismantle racism comprise salient themes in my interviews with youth organizers because the youth they work with often belong to nonwhite communities whose histories and cultures have been overlooked or dismissed by mainstream (read: white) society. In order to empower these youth, youth organizers have had to develop an awareness about race—what I term a *race-cognizant* framework—and a language the enables youth of all colors to participate as full members in building their communities and revitalizing their cities.

Implications for Policy

In many ways, the Twin Cities are just like any other U.S. metropolitan region in the sense that youth—particularly poor youth, youth of color, and immigrant youth—bear the brunt of structural inequities in housing, public schools, transportation, and the criminal justice system. Although the population of Minnesota is sparse, many of the same issues that face youth in other regions—especially adultism and the pressures of mass consumerism—are also present here.

However, Minnesota is also its own unique place with its own unusual sense of culture, history, and identity. Perhaps no written description can do justice to the actual experience of people of color who live, work, and organize here. In the semifictional land of Lake Wobegon, whiteness is omnipresent and invisible all at the same time. As the Twin Cities metropolitan area becomes more racially diverse due primarily to immigration from abroad, the cultural logic of whiteness and white privilege are more apt to be exposed and challenged. One of the ways that the white privilege is being exposed and challenged is in the discussions among community organizers about social service versus social change. When communities of color are only recipients of services and not also decision makers regarding the programs that serve them, questions about power, identity, and resources become sources of conflict and controversy in the community. Voicing these questions out loud is the first step toward reallocating their skewed distribution. Ultimately, of course, communities need to address systemic disparities that prevent people of color from accessing power and resources and from taking important leadership positions.

This study of youth organizing in the Twin Cities makes clear the need for certain explicitly antiracist frameworks, resources, and practices regarding youth and their communities. Youth of color, in particular, need to learn about their collective histories and cultures, in tandem with the skills all marginalized youth need to survive, grow, and work with others. But recognizing group cultures goes against the individualistic orientation of white, middle-class society and the prevailing "color-blind" approach to race and racism. A social-change framework that encourages youth to openly addresses structural racism and white privilege in their midst will also allow youth of all colors to situate themselves alongside their collective histories and cultures.

For youth advocates, the failures of traditional social service approaches are becoming ever more clear. Youth advocates seem to be hankering for alternatives to "helping" youth in a patronizing, missionary way. The youth organizing models promoted by FCYO and YouthAction in faraway New York City and Albuquerque have drifted all the way to the Great White North, where conversations about putting youth in the center are beginning to change the way some organizations and programs in the Twin Cities are managed. Talking is starting to generate real systemic change; for example, YouthLink has taken the first steps toward youth organizing actively against homelessness, instead of only passively receiving services. The question, as Susan Doherty puts it, is if organizers can garner the funding support to "take this to scale" beyond certain neighborhoods and into the larger metropolitan region of the Twin Cities. In an era of federal and state retrenchment, nonprofit organizations are frequently left to ponder such questions.

Moreover, the challenge of spurring youth organizing at the level of specific neighborhoods continues to push up against the idea that troubled youth just need to be "kept off the streets." This idea perpetuates the invisibility of broad social patterns, substituting instead a bootstraps mentality that essentially blames youth for their structural disadvantages. While playing basketball keeps poor youth of color off the streets, where they are perceived as threats to public safety, is anyone wondering why more affluent youth of color and white youth are so disciplined and dedicated to their homework and extracurricular activities, so mindful of public expectations, their sights set so clearly on higher goals? What explains their higher aspirations, and how can some or all of those factors be reproduced for disadvantaged youth? Youth organizers suggest that part of the solution lies in allowing youth to take charge of the larger project of building family and community resources. Validating and supporting youth in developing their connections to home and community—an area of special concern to youth of color—is a crucial step toward youth empowerment.

This study finds that in the Twin Cities, as in other regions of the country, "youth" are not a community unto themselves, but that they are embedded into their own communities to which particular histories, cultures, and identities are attached. Youth organizers need to adopt race-cognizant, antiracist approaches toward working with youth. All young people need adult role models; youth of color need to work with adults with whom they can identify in terms of race and in other ways. Communities of color need to have decision-making power in their own lives, so that youth can follow in their footsteps. For youth to really take charge in the Twin Cities, adults need to continue to pursue their own goals of social and racial justice.

Notes

I extend sincere thanks to my key contacts in the research field: Sarah Agaton-Howes, Brandon Lacy Campos, Susan Doherty, and Gunnar Liden. For his helpful comments on this chapter, thank you also to my friend and colleague, labor historian Peter Rachleff. I am grateful to the Woodrow Wilson National Fellowship Foundation and Macalester College for supporting me as I develop this new area of research.

1. For five fascinating profiles of youth-led and youth-driven organizations, see Youth Wisdom Project, 2004.
2. The Next Generational Leadership program is now affiliated with the Wagner Graduate School of Public Service at New York University.
3. Throughout the past five years of work and research in the Twin Cities, I have remained an outsider. My own tangled identities are mostly likely at play here: a brown-skinned lesbian feminist professor who teaches about white privilege at an elite private college is, for some Minnesotans, "different" (read: strange and unpleasant). The findings I offer in this study are thus presented merely as scholarly and sympathetic observations. Far be it for me to descend upon the Twin Cities—displacing decades of local knowledge—and declare these observations as "fact."
4. In this study, I refer to indigenous peoples as "Native" unless I am citing statistics from sources that use "American Indian." There is not enough room here to explain the difficulties of using the term "people of color" to refer to colonized indigenous peoples. I use the term provisionally with apologies to my indigenous comrades.
5. Although this chapter does not provide a theorization of "space" per se, the studies by O'Donoghue (chapter 13, this volume) and Flores-González, Rodríguez, and Rodríguez-Muñiz (chapter 10, this volume) provide fascinating and useful approaches to space in other regions.
6. These figures are from the websites of the St. Paul Public Schools (http://www.spps.org) and the Minneapolis Public Schools (http://www.mpls.k12mn.us); both retrieved February 22, 2005.
7. See Note 6. The figures for Asians, African Americans, and American Indians includes mixed-race children, by "race alone or in combination."
8. Redwing's population was 148 in 2002. See the Minnesota Department of Corrections website (http://www.corr.state.mn.us/facilities/redwing.htm); retrieved September 12, 2004.
9. See the Children's Report Card (http://server.admin.state.mn.us/children/indicator.html?Id=1081&G=31&CI=31); retrieved September 11, 2004.
10. For a blistering critique of neoconservative color-blindness, see Prashad, 2001.
11. For a narrative on Senator Wellstone's life and work see About.com's website (http://minneapolis.about.com/gi/dynamic/offsite.htm?site=http%3A%2F%2Fnews.mpr.org%2Fcollections%2Fcampaign2002%2Fsenate%2Fwellstone.shtml); retrieved September 12, 2004.
12. For more on the lynchings, see the Minnesota Historical Society website (http://collections.mnhs.org/duluthlynchings/); retrieved March 2, 2005.

References

Bell, D. (1995). Racial realism. In K. Crenshaw, N. Gotanda, G. Peller, & K. Thomas (Eds.), *Critical race theory: The key writings that formed the movement* (pp. 302–312). New York: New Press.

Crenshaw, K. W. (1995). Mapping the margins: Intersectionality, identity politics, and violence against women of color. In K. Crenshaw, N. Gotanda, G. Peller, & K. Thomas (Eds.), *Critical race theory: The key writings that formed the movement* (pp. 357–383). New York: New Press.

Delton, J. A. (2002). *Making Minnesota liberal: Civil rights and the transformation of the Democratic Party.* Minneapolis: University of Minnesota Press.

Dreier, P., Mollenkopf, J., & Swanstrom, T. (2001). *Place matters: Metropolitics for the twenty-first century.* Lawrence: University Press of Kansas.

Ginwright, S. A. (2003). *Youth organizing: Expanding possibilities for youth development.* New York: Funder's Collaborative on Youth Organizing.

Harris, C. (1995). Whiteness as property. In K. Crenshaw, N. Gotanda, G. Peller, & K. Thomas (Eds.), *Critical race theory: The key writings that formed the movement* (pp. 276–291). New York: New Press.

HoSang, D. (2003). *Youth and community organizing today.* Occasional Papers Series, New York: Funder's Collaborative on Youth Organizing.

Lanegran, D. A. (2000). Minnesota: Nature's playground. *Daedalus, 129,* 81–100.

Lipsitz, G. (1998). *The possessive investment in whiteness: How white people profit from identity politics.* Philadelphia: Temple University Press.

McAdam, D. (1982). *Political process and the development of black insurgency, 1930–1970.* Chicago: University of Chicago Press.

Medoff, P., & Sklar, H. (1994). *Streets of hope: The fall and rise of an urban neighborhood.* Boston: South End.

Naples, N. A. (1998). *Community activism and feminist politics: Organizing across race, class, and gender.* New York: Routledge.

Naples, N. A. (2003). *Feminism and method: Ethnography, discourse analysis, and activist research.* New York: Routledge.

Olsenius, R., & Keillor, G. (2001). *In search of Lake Wobegon.* New York: Viking Studio.

Omi, M. & Winant, H. (1994). *Racial formation in the United States: From the 1960s to the 1980s.* New York: Routledge.

Prashad, V. (2001). The problem of the 21st century is the problem of the colorblind. Retrieved March 2, 2005, from http://www.zmag.org/sustainers/content/2001-03/31prashad.htm

Roberts, D. (1997). *Killing the black body: Race, reproduction, and liberty.* New York: First Vintage.

Scott, A. (1990). *Ideology and the new social movements.* London: Unwin Hyman.

Tarrow, S. (1994). *Power in movement: Social movements, collective action, and politics.* New York: Cambridge University Press.

West, C. (1999). *The Cornel West reader.* New York: Basic Civitas.

Wilder Research Institute. (2004a, January). An assessment of racism in Dakota, Hennepin, and Ramsey Counties. Retrieved March 2, 2005, from http://www.wilder.org/research/reports.html?summary=1226.

Wilder Research Institute. (2004b). Metro trend watch 2004. Retrieved September 12, 2004, from http://www.metrotrendwatch.org/2004report.html.

Young, I. M. (1995). Social movements and the politics of difference. In J. Arthur and A. Shapiro (Eds.), *Campus wars: Multiculturalism and the politics of difference* (pp. 199–225). Boulder, CO: Westview.

YouthAction. (2005). Youth organizing components. Retrieved July 13, 2005 from http://www.youthaction.net/411youthcomponents.html.

Youth Wisdom Project [of the Movement Strategy Center]. (2004). Making space, making change. Retrieved July 13, 2005 from http://www.movementstrategycenter.org.

Zukin, S. (1993). *Landscapes of power.* Berkeley and Los Angeles: University of California Press.

Section IV
Perspectives on Youth Civic Engagement and Youth Policies

There is a reemerging interest in understanding how youth contribute to their communities. This interest has in part been encouraged by concerns raised by Putnam (2000), who believes that America is experiencing dangerously low levels of civic, community, and political participation. Civic engagement or civic participation can be described as a range of activities that strengthen social ties, build collective responsibility, and benefit society as a whole. Research suggests, however, that youth from low-income communities have fewer opportunities and are less likely to participate in civic and communities affairs (Hart & Atkins, 2002), and that traditional ways of conceptualizing civic participation (such as specific knowledge of the branches of government) may be inappropriate for assessing civic engagement among youth in poor communities (Lang, 1998; Sanchez-Jankowski, 2002). Youth who have histories of racial discrimination and exclusion from mainstream civic activities such as student government or citywide youth councils have different strategies for engagement that often are overlooked by social scientists. Often, civic participation among minority youth is reflected in activities that address quality-of-life issues they view most important in their lives, the lives of their families, and their respective communities. Such activities might include, addressing police harassment when coming and going from school, encouraging the school to purchase new heaters for their classrooms during cold winters, or advocating for free bus passes for transportation to and from school for students who receive public assistance.

But how do we as researchers, policy makers, and practitioners engage youth in meaningful civic decision making? How do we describe the nature of relationships among youth, adults, and civil society? The authors in this section address just such questions. In chapter 15, Torre and Fine argue that participatory action research is not simply an effective strategy to get youth engaged in social problem solving, but that it is young people's *right* to shape and challenge the policies that shape their lives; the authors illustrate how participatory action research is both rigorous and yields more effective policies for youth. Sherrod argues in chapter 16 that while our understanding of citizenship and engagement in civil society are vital to our democracy, very little attention has been given to the broad and diverse forms of youth civic participation. Situating our notions of youth activism within the context of ethnic, racial, class, sexual orientation, and disability status, Sherrod explores how political identity can be developed and sustained among diverse groups of young people. But how do we account for America's antiyouth culture? How are adult fears of young people reflected in public policy? In chapter 17, Males argues that social change, racial change, commodification of youth culture, and a social crisis among the adult baby boomer generation has contributed to an irrational national fear of youth. Using demographic techniques, Males's argument is clear, cogent, and concise: America's fear and repression of young people is a threat to social cohesion and a healthy democracy. To illustrate how young people are contributing to society, rather than shredding away America's social fabric, Checkoway and Richards-Schuster argue in chapter 18 that given institutional support, young people mend the ruptures in our society by confronting institutional failure in their schools; through their insightful discussion of the Lifting New Voices project, the authors illuminate the role of youth organizing in educational reform.

References

Carpini, M. X. D. (2000). Gen.com: Youth, civic engagement, and the new information environment. *Political Communication, 17,* 341–349.

Hart, D., & Atkins, R. (2002). Civic competence and urban youth." *Applied Developmental Science, 6*(4), 227–236.

Lang, C. (1998). Political/economic restructuring and the tasks of radical black youth. *Black Scholar, 28*(3–4), 30–37.

Putnam, R. D. (2000). *Bowling alone: The collapes and revival of American community.* New York: Simon and Schuster.

Sanchez-Jankowski, M. (2002). Minority youth and civic engagement: The impact of group relations. *Applied Developmental Science, 6*(4), 237–245.

CHAPTER 15

Researching and Resisting: Democratic Policy Research By and For Youth

MARIA TORRE AND MICHELLE FINE

Participation lies at the core of democracy and justice. We refer here to participation in decision making about our lives and communities, about the kind of world we want to live in, about the social policies and practices that govern our lives. Across contexts as varied as the workplace, public housing, and education, there is compelling evidence on the social psychological, political, and intellectual significance of democratic participation (Freire, 1982; Levin, 2004; Martín-Baró, 1994; Saegert & Winkle, 2004; Vanderslice, 1995). People's ability to "exercise their free agency and choose in an informed and participatory way," as political and economic theorist Amatrya Sen (2004) reminds us, is a necessary condition for democracy (p. 65). The United Nations has taken an even stronger position, declaring participation a fundamental human right in their Convention on the Rights of the Child. The convention, which has been endorsed by all nations *except* the United States and Somalia, states that children everywhere have basic human rights—including the right to participate fully in family, cultural, and social life (UNICEF, 1989). And so it seems clear: there must be adequate opportunity for adults and youth to help design, reflect upon, and challenge (as necessary) social policies of intimate impact. Democratic policy formulation insists upon deep participation—of rigorous investigation, dialogue, dissent, and public debate … *even in the United States.*

We construct this chapter to articulate the *how* of such participation by youth in policy research and development amid the neoliberal assault on poor and working-class youth in the United States. Across schools, communities, and prisons, in our participatory research projects with hundreds of youth from California, Delaware, Illinois, New York, and New Jersey, we have heard much about distributive, procedural, and inclusionary injustice, whereby youth are systematically denied access to goods, services, and opportunities; denied the opportunity to grieve or challenge this injustice; and seemingly exiled beyond the borders of a just community (Deutsch, 2004; Opotow, 2002). Poor and working-class youth of color are particularly enraged about the underfunding of their education and the simultaneous overfunding of their criminalization (see Kwon, chapter 12, this volume; Males, chapter 17, this volume). From the windows of their schools, these students watch as the long arms of the state— the prison industrial complex (the "bad" arm) and the military (the "good" arm)—reach deep into their communities, seducing and removing youth at alarming rates. While high stakes tests hasten their premature exit from high school, the economy remains hostile to young people without diplomas (Haney, 2002).

The cumulative consequences of these policies of injustice have been well documented: the finance inequities and inadequate school facilities (Fine, Burns, Payne, & Torre, 2004), the racialized enforcement of zero tolerance policies in schools (Ayers, Dorhn, & Jackson, 2001; Ruck, Smith, & Fine 2004), the spike in dropout rates due to high-stakes testing (Fine, 1991; Haney, 2002),[1] the reduction in financial aid for higher education (Bloom, 2005), the swelling of juvenile incarceration rates and sweep of juveniles of color into adult facilities (Males & Macallair, 2000; Poe-Yamagata & Jones, 2000), the aggressive military recruitment of poor youth and the Religious Right's assault on adolescent sexual freedoms (Delpit, 1995; Hilliard, 2002; Kohn, 2000). Across the nation, poor and working-class youth are being relocated from schools to the streets, from streets to prison, from colleges to the military. And all the while, advertising and media campaigns are designed toward diverting youth attention and desire, encouraging both private consumption for the middle and upper classes and military conscription for the working-class poor (Harris, 2004).

We have documented further, in both California and New York, students who have exercised their civic responsibilities and mustered the courage to bring their grievances to educators and policy makers, and who have too often been procedurally dismissed, ignored, or trivialized by government, community, and even educators (Fine, Roberts, & Torre, 2004). As a result, youth—poor and working-class youth, and youth of color in particular—logically conclude that in this nation, at this time, they are, through gentrification, being pushed out of the moral community of the deserving (Fallis & Opotow, 2003). Considered worthless, they nevertheless sustain, a neoliberal state built on their backs and cementing over their futures. In their eyes, and in the eyes of their more privileged peers (Burns, 2004), the richest country in the world seems determined, through policy and practice, to sacrifice their lives, minds, souls, and imaginations in our national quest for capital greed, military might, and global domination. For young people, the oxygen of freedom, opportunity, and justice is being depleted. It is no wonder that the UN Convention on the Rights of the Child hasn't been ratified here.

But reproduction is never complete. Oppression historically and reliably meets with resistance (Apple, 2001; Fanon, 1967; Smith, 1999). In the face of massive policy injustice youth, like adults, are neither simply passive nor compliant. Working with activists, scholars, foundations, community-based organizations, and progressive educators, youth are crafting participatory research projects that critically investigate the social policies that constrict and construct their lives; and they are examining and questioning the policies that ravage their communities and threaten their imaginations (Cahill, Arenas, Jiang, Rios-Moore, & Threatts, 2004; Social Justice Education Project, 2004; Kwon, chapter 12, this volume; Morrell, chapter 7, this volume). Throughout the country, in vibrant collectives that dot urban, suburban, and rural landscapes, we find cells of participatory youth research projects, bearing witness to the sacrifice and demanding radical reform. We use the remainder of this chapter to chronicle this subterranean movement of participatory action research projects by and for youth, and invoke it as an emergent strategy for a mass movement of youth documenting, challenging, resisting, and revising the social policies carved on their backs.

Participatory Action Research *with, by,* and *for* Youth

Youth participatory action research (PAR) projects typically center around issues of structural violence that intimately impact the lives of young people: educational justice; access to quality health care; the criminalization of youth; gang violence; police brutality; oppression based on race, gender, and sexuality; gentrification; and environmental issues. The goals extend from the exposition of local inequities with contextual specificity to broader coalition building with similarly situated youth both nationally and globally.

A methodological stance rooted in the belief that valid knowledge is produced only in collaboration and in action, PAR recognizes that those "studied" harbor critical social knowledge and must be repositioned as subjects and architects of research (Fals-Borda, 1979; Fine & Torre, 2004; Martín-Baró, 1994; Torre, 2005). Based largely on the theory and practice of Latino activist scholars, PAR scholars draw from neo-Marxist, feminist, queer, and critical race theorists (Anzaldúa, 1987; Apple, 2001; Crenshaw, 1995; Lykes, 2001; Matsuda, 1995; Weis & Fine, 2004; Williams, 1998) to articulate methods and ethics that have local integrity and stretch topographically to sight/cite global patterns of domination and resistance (Katz, 2004).

Enabling youth to interrogate and denaturalize the conditions of their everyday oppression inspires a process of community and knowledge building. As Paulo Freire (1982) has eloquently argued,

> The silenced are not just incidental to the curiosity of the researcher but are the masters of inquiry into the underlying causes of the events in their world. In this context research becomes a means of moving them beyond silence into a quest to proclaim the world.

Repositioning youth as researchers rather than as the researched shifts the practice of researching *on* youth to *with* youth—a position that stands in sharp contrast to the current neoliberal constructions of youth as dangerous, disengaged, blind consumers who lack any type of connection. Frustrated, alienated, and angry survivors of discrimination mature into active policy critics and agents engaged in conversation, confrontation, and reform. Legitimating democratic inquiry within institutions as well as outside, PAR excavates knowledge "at the bottom" and "at the margins" (Matsuda, 1995, p. 63), and signifies young people's fundamental right to question, investigate and contest policies that enforce injustice (Torre, 2005).

Our own PAR work, spanning the past decade, rests on our fundamental recognition that marginalized/oppressed youth carry sharp critique and knowledge about the very mortar of social formations, and that revealing and legitimating this knowledge significantly challenge existing forms of institutional and structural oppression that have been naturalized as inevitable. Building on prior research, we add a spirit of "radical inclusion" whereby, in our most recent project, relatively advantaged youth were invited to study social injustice alongside those who have historically been denied material opportunities. Using resources drawn from the academy, their communities, and personal experience, radically diverse youth collaboratively investigated the political biographies of privilege and oppression and unearthed the long-buried histories of resistance. We have found that with this practice, over time, coalitions of unsuspecting allies coalesce within the praxis of inquiry, documentation, speaking back, and the reimagining of policies for social justice (Burns, 2004; Guinier & Torres, 2004; Leach, Snider, & Iyer, 2004). When PAR collectives are organized as "contact zones"—that is, purposely diverse communities that explicitly acknowledge power and privilege within the group (see Pratt, 1992)—and then *use* these differences as resources to further the social justice agenda of the research, there is the potential to produce research that is optically and ethically layered, that addresses issues that otherwise might be left uninterrogated, that pushes boundaries considered comfortable, and explodes categories once thought to be "normal" (Torre, 2005).

We present here an example of one such PAR project. Crafted prior to, and in anticipation of, the 50th anniversary of the U.S. Supreme Court ruling on *Brown v. Board of Education*, this case encourages us to closely analyze the dynamics of policy-directed PAR with youth within schools and communities unfortunately committed to maintaining (elite, adult, and White) privilege while exercising a polite disregard for critical youth knowledge.

The Opportunity Gap Project and *Echoes of Brown*: Youth Engage in Participatory Action Research

In the Fall of 2001, a group of suburban school superintendents of desegregated districts gathered to discuss the disaggregated achievement gap data provided by the states of New Jersey and New York. As is true nationally, in these desegregated districts, the test score gaps across Asian American, White American, African American, and Latino students were disturbing. Eager to understand the roots and remedies for the gap, school superintendent Sherry King of Mamaroneck, New York, invited Michelle Fine and colleagues from The Graduate Center of the City University of New York (CUNY) to join the research team. We agreed, under the condition that we could collaborate with a broad range of students from suburban and urban schools, to create a multi-year participatory action research project. Over the course of two years of youth inquiry, more than 100 youth from urban and suburban high schools in New York and New Jersey joined researchers from The CUNY Graduate Center to study youth perspectives on race- and class-based (in)justice in schools and the nation. We worked in the schools, identifying core groups of youth researchers drawn from all corners of the school—from special education, English as a second language programs, gay/straight alliances, discipline rooms, student councils, and advanced placement (AP) classes. We designed a multigenerational, multidistrict, urban-suburban database of the experiences of youth and adults, tracing the history of struggle for desegregation from *Brown* to date, and social science evidence of contemporary educational opportunities and inequities analyzed by race, ethnicity, and class (see Fine, Bloom, Burns, et al., 2005).

At our first session, youth from six suburban high schools and three urban schools immediately challenged the frame of the research. One student noted, "When you call it an achievement gap, that means it's our fault. The real problem is an opportunity gap; let's place the responsibility where it belongs—in society and in the schools." And so we became the Opportunity Gap Project. Youth participated in a series of "research camps," each held for two days at a time in community and/or university settings. Immersed in methods training and social justice theory, together we deconstructed what constitutes research, who can do research, and who benefits from it. The students learned how to conduct interviews, focus groups, and participant observations, and how to design surveys and organize archival analyses. Many students received high school credits (when a course on participatory research was offered in their schools) and 42 received college credit for their research work.

Building on the central tenets of PAR we agreed that within our research collaborative:

- Each participant was understood to be a carrier of knowledge and history.
- Everyone must hold a sincere commitment to creating change for educational justice.
- Issues of power and difference were to be explicitly addressed and explored.

- Disagreements and disjunctures were to be excavated rather than smoothed over.
- Individuals and the group were understood to be "under construction" (i.e., that opinions, ideas and beliefs were expected to change and grow).
- Everyone was to be committed to a common goal of understanding, researching, and, ultimately, performing the history and contemporary politics of racial and class (in)justice in public education.

At the first research camp we designed a survey to assess high school students' views of race and class (in)justice in schools and the nation. The youth researchers were given a very rough "wrong" draft of the survey that they dedicated the weekend to its revising, inserting cartoons, open-ended questions such as "What's the most powerful thing a teacher said to you?" and sensitive Likert Scale items like "Sometimes I think I'll never make it" or "I would like to be in advanced classes, but I don't think I'm smart enough." Over the next few months, we translated the survey into Spanish, Haitian Creole, and braille, and distributed it to 9th- and 12th-graders in 13 urban and suburban districts. At the second and third camps, other groups of youth researchers from the same schools (with some overlap) analyzed the qualitative and quantitative data from 9,174 surveys, 24 focus groups, and 32 individual interviews with young people. In between the camps, youth cross-visited four urban and suburban schools to document the racialized impact of finance inequity and tracking on the structures, opportunities, social relations, and outcomes of public education. And as the data was analyzed, teams of youth and adult researchers fed back their school-specific data to varied groups of faculty, students, and community members.

Throughout 2003 we wrote scholarly and popular articles and together delivered professional and neighborhood talks.[2] As we traveled with the stories of our findings, however, we worried about the limits of talk. We saw most audiences nod in solidarity, but met far too many adults who refused to listen to young people's complex renderings of *Brown*'s victories and continuing struggles. We sat inside schools where it was clear that the achievement gap—the latest face of segregation—was built fundamentally into the structures, ideologies, and practices of these schools. We found ourselves trapped by obsessive questions pointing to poor youth and youth of color: What's wrong with them? Even in the same school building, we have a gap? If we stop tracking, how else can we teach students at their "natural" levels? We grew weary even as we watched audiences tear up, wondering if perhaps responsibility was being wiped away with a tissue.

And so, that summer, with the milestone anniversary of *Brown* approaching, we decided to shift to performance as public scholarship, and extend our social justice and social research camps into a social justice and the arts institute. We recruited another radically diverse group of young people, aged 13–21, who were interested in writing, performing, and/or social justice, and brought them together with community elders, social scientists, spoken word artists, dancers, choreographers, and a video crew to collectively pore over data from the Educational Opportunity Gap Project (Fine et al., 2005); to learn about the legal, social, and political history of segregation and integration of public schools; and to create *Echoes of Brown, 50 Years Later*, a performance of poetry and movement to contribute to the commemoratory conversation of the 50th anniversary of *Brown*. Together, we studied the history of *Brown*, Ella Baker, Bayard Rustin, and Emmett Till; finance inequity, tracking, battles over buses, and bilingualism; the unprecedented academic success of the small schools movement; what it means to have separate schools for lesbian, gay, bisexual, transgender, and queer/questioning (LGBTQ) students; and the joys, dangers, and "not yets" of integration. And in a scholarly and aesthetic experiment that challenged the boundaries of time, geography, generation, and discipline, we braided political history, personal experience, research and knowledge gathered from a generation living in the long shadow of *Brown*, producing a performance for 800 on May 17, 2004, as well as a DVD and book of the work, *Echoes of Brown: Youth Documenting and Performing the Legacy of Brown v. Board of Education* (Fine, Roberts, Torre, et al., 2004).

Participatory Methods for Heightened Validity and Accountability in the Creation of Socially Just Policies

In this next section of the chapter we raise a series of questions and give reflections on participatory action research with youth. We have gathered frequently asked questions with questions we wish were frequently asked; may they serve as practical templates that can be adapted to the social and political needs of educators, activists, and youth. We aim to demonstrate the possibilities of PAR, not only to substantiate the heightened claims to validity we believe derive from PAR done well, but also to reveal its potential for strengthening youth research and analytical skills and for building understanding and critique that bridges young people's local experience to larger social histories, policies, and practices.

Who Is in the Room? How Questions of Inclusion/Exclusion Frame Research

Throughout our work we have found it crucial to think through questions of inclusion/exclusion, presence/absence: Who is in the room when research questions are being framed? Who is missing? If everyone on the research team is in AP and honors classes, will the questions reach far enough to excavate issues important to the lives of those in special education? If the school principal or faculty handpicks the researchers, will all quarters of the school be heard? Will dropouts get a hearing? Will students who are angry and alienated? Recent immigrants? Have we heard from the outliers? The rebels? The quiet students filled with thoughts who sit mute and watch? And once a rich mix of students are present, how do we construct research teams able to probe the experiences of those *suffering* from unequal educational practices, as well investigate the experiences of those *benefiting* from them?

As we crafted the research design, we decided to have two kinds of research teams. The first was a set of local teams that were demographically homogeneous, savvy about local politics, and committed to local work. These teams served what theorist Adreanne Ormond has called "cultural incubators," providing spaces for validating and deepening understandings of both individual and commonly faced experiences, as well as for hard conversations about discrimination and injustice frequently derailed or silenced by members outside the group (Ormond, 2004). The second type was a set of cross-site camps/institutes that were intentionally diverse, committed to policy issues across settings, and drawn from divergent views of local policies and politics. These groups were useful in pushing research members to reposition their individual thoughts and experiences within a broader social context, specifically to understand the social construction of privilege as well as disadvantage. This commitment to groups organized around "sameness" and "difference" was an important methodological consideration, as each provided valuable contributions to the whole.

Bridging Selves and Experience with History and Policy

While we recruited for diversity, we took seriously the many identities and intersections each life carries (Crenshaw, 1995). That is, within the research team there was an understanding that we are all constructed of multiple selves and that in each of our bodies we hold identities that feel powerful in some spaces and powerless in others. By raising and addressing issues of power and privilege throughout our research practice, as well as structures and practices that maintain oppressive systems, an environment was created where we all (adults and youth) could reflect on our multiple identities and their varying relationships to privilege, oppression, and each other. As we moved through our work, youth were able to call on different aspects of their identities, to better understand material, or to move away from experiences that were too uncomfortable, or to make connections across seemingly different positions.

Emily Genao, for instance, wrote a spoken-word piece in response to some of the qualitative data we collected from high school students. When reviewing student responses to the question, "What do you believe are the causes of the achievement gap?" Emily found that all too many students responded, on the survey, "Blacks are genetically inferior," or something similar. Emily, like many of the youth researchers and performers, was visibly pained and angered by the revelation that her peers really believed in genetic inferiority. Her poem challenges the "science" of genetic inferiority and social categorizing, and in so doing it insists that the audience meet the multiple selves Emily carries:

You said some people are genetically less intelligent
Whose genetics exactly are inferior?

Whose genetics exactly are missing a few crossbars on the double helix?
Whose genetics are you examining though your microscope?
You don't need to specify
Since it is misconceived that those people are usually the ones
With the sun kissed skin
The doorman who suffers through the 2-hour train ride from Queens
The cleaning lady trying to hold down 2 jobs and a newborn at home
The kid who plays his Slipknot CD too loud
You wouldn't sit next to him anyway
When you slide my culture under your power magnification you see me:
A first generation college student
Actress who will transcend the role of rape victim, maid, gossiping neighbor
Poet whose grass roots are growing back in again
Dancer with salsa in her hips and azucar in her blood
Dreamer of Puerto Rican sunsets, Manhattan darkness, with a scar on her
Lower East Side
Only it isn't your microscope
It was passed on to you from your ancestral scientists
Now it's your turn
To look at everyone through the
Antiquated lens
Only you don't turn it on yourself
Because you didn't inherit inferior DNA

When designing our research camps, institutes, and school-based teams, we struggled with how to help youth open up critically to contextualize and historicize what feels like their "personal experience." We were not interested in simply producing a space for youth to produce spoken word pieces about their "individual" and "idiosyncratic" lives. We were committed, with the wisdom of historian Joan Scott (1990), to helping youth place their experience critically in a sea of knowledge drawn from history and contemporary politics. In doing so we witnessed the doubled impact of injecting social political history into research: how it validates individual experiences and places them in larger social contexts as well as offers a depersonalized space of analysis to cool down the rising emotions inherent in facing large-scale injustice. In the moments when the messy intersections of privilege and oppression became too difficult or personally painful, we witnessed how our practice of introducing an explicit language of power and structural relations allowed youth to distance themselves for a moment, readjust their researcher hats and reexamine the data before them, ultimately developing analyses that encouraged a fluidity between individual lives and structural critique.

In one of our conversations about the legacy of *Brown,* lawyer Carol Tracy helped us to see how the Supreme Court decision prompted a rethinking of civil rights, feminism, disability rights, and the gay liberation movement, opening doors for girls across racial/ethnic groups, for students with disabilities, and for LGBTQ students. A hot conversation ensued about new funding for the Harvey Milk School—with students pressing us: Is this progress … a school for lesbian and gay students? Or is this a step backward? The debate was fierce, with most of the young women agreeing that all schools should be working on issues of homophobia and that separating out queer students would simply be a throwback to the days of segregation. Then Amir Billops spoke up. Sharing his deep disappointment with the unrealized promises of his "integrated" high school, he connected the history we had been discussing, the experiences of LGBTQ youth at his school, and his own experiences of being an African American student in special education:

> When we were talking about the dancer [Kathryn Dunham] and how she walked off the stage in the South during the 1940s because Blacks were in the balcony, I realized that happens today, with me and my friends. At my high school they put the special education kids in the balcony, away from the "normal" kids. They [LGBTQ students] may need a separate school just to be free of the prejudice. Putting people in the same building doesn't automatically take care of the problem.

That night, Amir wrote "Classification":

> *Possessing this label they gave me,*
> *I swallowed the stigma and felt the pain*
> *of being seen in a room with six people.*
> *Yeah, it fell upon me and the pain was like stones raining down on me.*
> *From the day where school assemblies seemed segregated*
> *and I had to watch my girl Krystal from balconies …*
> *Away from the "normal" kids*
> *to the days where I found myself fulfilling self-fulfilled prophecies.*
>
> *See I received the label of "special education"*
> *and it sat on my back like a mountain being lifted by an ant—*
> *it just can't happen.*
> *It was my mind's master.*
> *It told me I was dumb, I didn't know how to act in a normal class.*
>
> *I needed two teachers to fully grasp the concepts touched upon in class,*
> *and my classification will never allow me to exceed track two.*
> *So what is it that I do—*
> *so many occasions when the classification caused me to break into tears?*
> *It was my frustration.*
> *My reaction to teachers speaking down to me saying I was classified*
> *and it was all my fault.*

Had me truly believing that inferiority was my classification.
Cause I still didn't know, and the pain WAS DEEP. The pain—OH GOD!
THE PAIN!
The ridicule, the constant taunting, laughing when they passed me by.

Amir drew on his experiences in special education classes to understand why having a separate school for LGBTQ youth might be necessary in a climate where the price of integration is paid in taunting and physical abuse. In taking a risk with the research team by sharing for the first time his experiences in special education, Amir repositioned himself from a student in need of special tutors to an experienced educator. He spoke eloquently to his co-researchers, complicating their notions of segregation, asserting that integration cannot insist on assimilation. Just as adults lose critical pieces of knowledge about young people's lives when young people are excluded from the research process, were it not for Emily and Amir our research team might have produced a simplistic understanding of categories of identity and the politics of integration.

Documenting the Topography of Oppression and Resistance: Searching for
Patterns and Pockets of Oxygen

We take seriously, when working with youth, the idea that our participatory research focuses on documenting historic and contemporary patterns of discrimination and injustice, and also on those historic and contemporary fissures in the system where social movements thrive, where struggles for justice begin to breath, where contestation and resistance are evident. We feel a moral obligation to help young people remember and imagine a time when movements of protest were alive, energized, and filled with a sense of possibility. We do not believe that youth grow depressed from studying oppression, but we do worry that they could become more demoralized if the study of oppression is decoupled from the history of resistance.

For this reason we added the elders component to the *Echoes* work, in which we interviewed a series of elders who dedicated their lives to racial, economic, and educational justice. Thus, for instance, the late lawyer Arthur Kinoy spoke to us about his work in the South:

In the airport I was met by four Black ministers, fine people, and they took me to the only place where Whites and Blacks could meet, legally—the Black church …. The next day I go down to the courtroom, and there are 200 or 300 African American people, all sitting in the back, the ones who had been arrested. And the judge says, "Who are you?" And I say, because we had a little law firm in those days, Kunstler, Kunstler, and Kinoy, "I'm from the new KKK!" I'll never forget, everyone started applauding. And that night, we had a wonderful celebration in Mississippi. We were drinking and eating, when my friend, Fannie Lou Hamer, pours out a little bourbon, throws her arms around me, raises her glass and shouts, "I want you to meet my people's lawyer! Power to the people!"

When youth are deprived of this critical history, they are bereft of images of protest of meaning, longevity, and victory. We consider it morally and intellectually crucial to include evidence of possibility (like the presence of the small schools in the opportunity gap survey) as we work with youth to map the contours of historic and contemporary oppression.

The Power of the Aggregate

Beginning locally, youth researchers in our project presented their findings back to their schools and communities. While some principals and superintendents welcomed the research, others tried to rationalize the data. One such example occurred at a "speak back" at a high school when Kareem Sergent, one of the youth researchers, was trying to detail the racialized patterns of school suspensions to his largely White teaching faculty:

> Now, I'd like you to look at the suspension data, and notice that Black males in high schools were twice as likely as White males to be suspended, and there are almost no differences between Black males and Black females. But for Whites, males are three times more likely to be suspended than females: 22% of Black males, 19% of Black females, 11% of White males and 4% of White females.

The educators, arms crossed, challenged the data. Kareem continued, "You know me, I spend a lot of time in the discipline room. It's really almost all Black males." Hesitant nods were followed by immediate explanations about how in June "it gets whiter," and "sometimes there are White kids, maybe when you're not there." Kareem turned to the charts projected on the screen, "You don't have to believe me, but I speak for the hundreds of Black males who filled out this survey. We have to do something about it."

While the session within the school was, perhaps predictably, filled with resistance, it revealed what we came to call the *power of the aggregate*. Youth researchers, like the rest of us, find comfort and power in the aggregate patterns that the survey and interview material provide. Frustrated with faculty unwilling to listen to his analysis of the discipline data, Kareem tried to use his "personal relationship" to the discipline room as a hook. When faculty resisted further, he took up the persona of the social scientist, reporting, simply, the evidence. He declared, calmly, that while they might choose to dismiss *his* particular case, they would nevertheless have to contend with hundreds of young African American men who completed the survey and told us the same. Kareem found confirmation and support in the aggregate data.

Designing for Tears and Outrage

Justice research is by nature a difficult task. Beyond the often daunting nature of entrenched social problems, facing the ugly realities of injustice can be painful. By no means does research introduce oppressive systems like racism or homophobia to youth researchers. However, the process of uncovering the degree to which racism or class discrimination has infected our society evokes emotional responses that need to be addressed. Consider the room's reaction as White, South African–Canadian–U.S. Kendra Urdang read a spoken-word piece about her desegregated high school:

> *And in the classrooms, the imbalance is subtle,*
> *undercurrents in hallways.*
> *AP classes on the top floor, special ed. in the basement.*
> *And although over half the faces in the yearbook*
> *are darker than mine,*
> *On the third floor, everyone looks like me.*
> *So it seems glass ceilings are often concrete.*
> *…*
> *So let's stay quiet, ride this pseudo-underground railroad,*
> *this free ticket to funding from the board of ed.*
> *Racism is only our problem if it makes the front page.*
>
> *Although brown faces fill the hallways,*
> *administrators don't know their names,*
> *they are just the free ticket to funding,*
> *and this is not their school.*

As Kendra welled up with emotion, so did others, surprised that a White girl "got it." This was typical in the camps and the institutes. In our work we now anticipate the emotions that may flood the rooms of participatory research. And we see these emotions as critical empirical material—as data. We have used field notes and "graffiti museums" to display and chronicle our frustration, anger, amazement and, at times, rage. Youth researchers used the floor-to-ceiling paper-covered walls of the graffiti museum to scrawl responses to the racist explanations of the achievement gap they encountered while coding the qualitative responses to the survey taken by 10,000 of their peers. Similarly, after cross-school visits where economic disparities—computer-filled rooms off shiny corridors versus broken-down gyms and no science labs—were so flagrant, that as youth researchers took copious field notes, they were encouraged to pay strict attention to the feelings and emotions attached to "We're going to have to compete with them in college?" and "They thought schools like mine only exist in the movies." Recognizing and reflecting on these feelings and emotions as data, rather than bias, informed our analysis and enabled the creation of more meaningful research products.

Anticipating the Resistance

As adults we bring a longer history of struggle to the table. We bring a familiarity with certain forms of resistance to particular lines of antagonistic critique. By preparing youth beforehand of a possibility, or processing a hostile response after the fact, we can add layers of understanding, create analytical tools and future strategy to the justified anger felt when justice research by youth is dismissed.

Kareem's story above is familiar. A young person of color dares to raise a question about local injustice and the audience freezes in denial. Refusing responsibility, they treat the young person as though he has made it all up or is exaggerating, not taking responsibility (now *there's* a projection!). This scene is so familiar as to be nauseating. And yet, in our work, as in the work of Jeanne Oakes and Julio Cammarota, we know that schools, public institutions, and boards of education do typically deflect the critical commentary youth have to offer. And so, with this wisdom we simply note that the adult research-ers have a responsibility to *find audiences of worth*—those who deserve to hear, who will respect and engage the brilliance and passion of youth researchers; work with youth researchers to anticipate the resistance and combat it; and ensure that we (the adults) are always more vulnerable than the youth, their educators, and their parents.

As with all research projects, participatory work with youth carries ques-tions of ethics, vulnerabilities, and negotiations of power. The dynamics vary based on the nature of the work, the situatedness of the struggle, and the launch site for the research. Methods and strategic moves differ when PAR emerges from within community organizing, where allies and targets are clear, than when PAR is launched from within inequitable (schools) or oppressive (prisons) social institutions. Depending on the project, youth may decide to work alone or with adults. They may design research that seeks to change local conditions, or simply expose injustice; they may seek to collaborate with representatives within the institution under scrutiny, or reveal the systemic inequities brewing within. As a result, research products may range from performance to scholarly documents; websites to organizing campaigns; 1–800 tell-all phone numbers to presentations at professional conferences. We leave you with the words of Tahani Salah, one of the youth researchers and per-formers who brought her Muslim, outspoken, passionate, brilliant self squarely into the center of the work when she pleaded with the audience:

> *Diversity is our beauty and integration our blood*
> *as it flows down the roads that we walk on screaming,*
> *The people united shall never be defeated.*
> *With reason centuries old*
> *It's now time for our revolution*
>
> *The children of today cannot love our tomorrow*
> *if the leaders of today do not.*

Regardless of setting, context, politics, and players, participatory action research readies the embers to ignite radical social change. With youth at the center, participatory action research builds skills, communities, organizing, and scholarship.

Notes

1. See the National Center for Fair and Open Testing website (http://www.fairtest.org); retrieved November 25, 2005.
2. Youth researchers took up (and published) research studies of finance inequity, tracking, community-based organizing for quality education, and the unprecedented success of the small schools movement. See Bloom & Chajet, 2003, and the website for the Brooklyn Rail (http://www.thebrooklynrail.org/poetry/fall02/moneyfornothing.html); retrieved November 25, 2005. http://www.thebrooklynrail.org/poetry/fall02/moneyfornothing.html.

References

Anzaldúa, G. (1987). *Borderlands/la frontera: The new meztiza.* San Francisco: Aunt Lute.

Apple, M. (2001). *Educating the "Right" way: Markets, standards, God, and inequality.* New York: Routlege/Falmer.

Ayers, R., Ayers, W., Dohrn, B., & Jackson, T. (2001). *Zero tolerance.* New York: New Press.

Bloom, J. (2005). The hollowed promise of higher education. In L. Weis & M. Fine (Eds.), *Beyond silenced voices: Class, race, and gender in United States schools* (pp. 63–81). Albany: State University of New York Press.

Bloom, J., & Chajet, L. (2003, fall). Urban students tackle research on inequality. Retrieved November 25, 2005 from http://www.rethinkingschools.org/archive/18_01/ineq181.shtml.

Burns, A. (2004). The racing of capability and culpability in desegregated schools: Discourses of merit and responsibility. In M. Fine, L. Weis, L. Pruitt, & A. Burns (Eds.), *Off white: Readings in race, power and privilege* (pp. 373–394). New York: Routledge.

Cahill, C., Arenas, E, Jiang, N, Rios-Moore, I., & Threatts, T. (2004). Speaking back: Voices of young urban women of color. Using participatory action research to challenge and complicate representations of young women. In A. Harris (Ed.), *All about the girl* (pp. 233–244.) New York: Routledge.

Crenshaw, K. (1995). Mapping the margins: Intersectionality, identity politics, and violence against women of color. In K. Crenshaw, N. Gotanda, G. Peller, & K. Thomas (Eds.), *Critical race theory: The key writings that formed the movement* (pp. 357–383). New York: New Press.

Delpit, L. (1995). *Other people's children: Cultural conflict in the classroom.* New York: New Press.

Deutsch, M. (2004, February). Oppression and conflict. Plenary address at the Conference on Interrupting Oppression and Sustaining Justice, Teachers College, Columbia University, New York.

Fallis, R. K., & Opotow, S. (2003). Are students failing schools or are schools failing students? Class cutting in high schools. *Journal of Social Issues, 59* (1), 103–120.

Fals-Borda, O. (1979). Investigating the reality in order to transform it: The Colombian experience. *Dialectical Anthropology, 4,* 33–55.

Fanon, F. (1967). *Black Skin, White Masks.* (C. Farrington, Trans.). New York: Grove.

Fine, M. (1991). *Framing dropouts: Notes on the politics of an urban high school.* Albany: State University of New York Press.

Fine, M., Bloom, J., Burns, A., Chajet, L., Guishard, M., Payne, Y., & Torre, M. E. (2005). Dear Zora: A letter to Zora Neal Hurston fifty years after *Brown*. *Teachers College Record*, *107*(3), 496–529.

Fine, M., Burns, A., Payne, Y., & Torre, M. E. (2004). Civics lessons: The color and class of betrayal. *Teachers College Record*, *106* (11), 2193–2223.

Fine, M., Roberts, R. A., & Torre, M. E., with Bloom, J., Burns, A., Chajet, L., Guishard, M., & Payne, Y. A. (2004). *Echoes of Brown: Youth documenting and performing the legacy of Brown v. Board of Education*. New York: Teachers College Press.

Fine, M., & Torre, M. E. (2004). Re-membering exclusions: Participatory action research in public institutions. *Qualitative Research in Psychology*, *1*, 15–37.

Freire, P. (1982). Creating alternative research methods. Learning to do it by doing it. In B. Hall, A. Gillette, & R. Tandon (Eds.), *Creating knowledge: A monopoly* (pp. 29–37). New Delhi: Society for Participatory Research in Asia.

Guinier, L., & Torres, G. (2004). Off-white: Whiteness of a different color? In M. Fine, L. Weis, L. Pruit, & A. Burns (Eds.), *Off-white: Readings in race, power and privilege*. New York: Routledge.

Haney, W. (2002, July 10). Ensuring failure: How a state's achievement test may be designed to do just that. *Education Week*, pp. 56–58.

Harris, A. (2004). *Future girl: Young women in the 21st century*. New York: Routledge.

Hilliard, A. G., III. (2002). Introduction. In V. G. Morris & C. L. Morris (Eds.), *The price they paid: Desegregation in an African American community* (pp. i–ix). New York: Teachers College Press.

Katz, C. (2004). *Growing up global: Economic restructuring and children's everyday lives*. Minneapolis: University of Minnesota Press.

Kohn, A. (2000). *The case against standardized testing: Raising the scores, ruining the schools*. Portsmouth, NH: Heinemann.

Leach, C., Snider, N., & Iyer, A. (2004). Poisoning the consciousness of the fortunate. In E. Walker & H. Smith (Eds.), *Relative deprivation: Specification, development, and integration*. Cambridge: Cambridge University Press, 136–163.

Levin, H. (2004, February). *Worker democracy: Is it feasible?* Paper presented at the Conference on Interrupting Oppression and Sustaining Justice, Teachers College, Columbia University, New York.

Lykes, M. B. (2001). Activist participatory research and the arts with rural Maya women: Interculturality and situated meaning making. In D. L. Tolman & M. Brydon-Miller (Eds.), *From subjects to subjectivities: A handbook of interpretive and participatory methods* (pp. 183–199). New York: New York University Press.

Males, M., and Macallair, D. (2000). *The color of justice*. Washington, DC: Building Blocks for Youth.

Martín-Baró, I. (1994). *Writings for a liberation psychology*. Cambridge, MA: Harvard University Press.

Matsuda, M. (1995). Looking to the bottom: Critical legal studies and reparations. In K. Crenshaw, N. Gotanda, G. Peller, & K. Thomas (Eds.), *Critical race theory: The key writings that formed the movement* (pp. 63–79). New York: New Press.

Opotow, S. (2002). Psychology of impunity and injustice: Implications for social reconciliation. In M. C. Bassiouni (Ed.), *Post conflict justice* (pp. 201–216). Ardsley, NY: Transnational.

Ormond, A. (2004). *The voices and silences of young Maori people: A world of (im)possibility*. Unpublished doctoral dissertation, University of Auckland, New Zealand.

Poe-Yamagata, E., & Jones, M. (2000). *And justice for some*. Washington DC: National Council on Crime and Delinquency.

Pratt, M. L. (1992). *Imperial eyes: Travel writing and transculturation*. New York: Routledge.

Ruck, M. D., Smith, K., & Fine, M. (2004). Resisting at the border: Warnings from the U.S. about zero tolerance. In B. Kidd & J. Phillips (Eds.), *From enforcement and prevention to civic engagement: Research on community safety* (pp. 203–214). Toronto: University of Toronto Centre of Criminology.

Saegert, S., & Winkle, G. (2004). Crime, social capital, and community participation. *American Journal of Community Psychology, 34*(3–4): 219–233.

Scott, J. (1990). *Domination and the art of resistance: Hidden transcripts.* New Haven, CT: Yale University Press.

Sen, A. (2004). How does culture matter? In V. Rao & M. Walton (Eds.), *Culture and public action* (pp. 37–58). Stanford, CA: Stanford University Press.

Smith, L. T. (1999). *Decolonizing methodologies: Research and indigenous peoples.* London: Zed.

Social Justice Education Project. (2004). *Listen and learn: Chicano/Latino high school students speak out about education.* Tucson: University of Arizona Mexican American Studies and Research Center.

Torre, M. E. (2005). The alchemy of integrated spaces: Youth participation in research collectives of difference. In L. Weis & M. Fine (Eds.), *Beyond silenced voices: Class, race, and gender in United States schools* (pp. 251–266). Albany: State University of New York Press.

Torre, M. E., & Fine, M. (2006). Activism, (out)rage and (in)justice: Participatory action research with youth on the politics of public schools. In L. Sherrod, C. Flanagan, & R. Kassimir (Eds.), *Youth activism: An international encyclopedia,* pp. 456–462. Westport, CT: Greenwood.

UNICEF (1989). United Nations Convention on the Rights of the Child. Retrieved November 25, 2005, from http://www.unicef.org/crc/crc.htm.

Vanderslice, V. (1995). Cooperation in a competitive context: Lessons from worker collectives. In B. B. Bunker & J. Z. Rubin (Eds.), *Conflict, cooperation and Justice: Essays inspired by the work of Morton Deutsch* (pp. 175–204). San Francisco: Jossey-Bass.

Weis, L., & Fine, M. (2004). *Working method: Social injustice and social research.* New York: Routledge.

Williams, P. J. (1998). *Seeing a colorblind future: The paradox of race.* New York: Farrar, Straus and Giroux.

CHAPTER 16

Promoting Citizenship and Activism in Today's Youth

LONNIE R. SHERROD

Introduction

In this chapter, I examine what we know about how young people grow into citizenship, the importance of promoting an activist orientation to citizenship in youth, and how society may need to attend to the development of citizenship if we are to successfully promote its growth in the diverse population that now defines youth in this country.

Youth is a somewhat elastic term; usually it means young people 15 to 25 years of age—that is, basically high school- and college-age youth (Flanagan & Bertelsen, 2005). One of my mantras is that "citizenship is as important a domain of adult responsibility as work or family, yet it has been the subject of far less research and program attention." Hence, research on civic engagement in youth is important, and it is especially important to attend to the broad diversity of youth in today's population, who vary across social class, ethnicity, immigrant status, religion, sexual orientation, and disability status.

A colleague has pointed out, in response to my mantra, that he considers work and family to be part of citizenship. Indeed, our surveys of young people about citizenship also make this point; working and being productive is one aspect of traditional views of citizenship, along with patriotism and respect for the flag; helping others is the complementary view of citizenship—the prosocial view (Bogard & Sherrod, 2005). In this chapter and elsewhere, I argue that an activist orientation is also a critical aspect of citizenship in a democracy (Sherrod, 2005; Sherrod, Flanagan, & Kassimir, 2005). One important aspect of research on civic engagement in youth is defining their views on citizenship, especially as these views may vary across the dimensions of diversity that define today's youth population.

Citizenship certainly involves a sense of allegiance to the nation or state, so patriotism reflects this aspect. But youth also appropriately have allegiances to family, school, and community, and these allegiances also relate to ideas about citizenship, both traditional and prosocial (Bogard & Sherrod, 2005). Allegiances are important because they represent the individual's investment in these social institutions and his or her willingness to protect them. Citizenship is important to societies because it involves beliefs and behaviors that contribute to the preservation of these societies. Voting in a democracy is one good example: if the majority of people do not vote in a democracy then the elected officials do not represent their full constituency.

I will use this chapter to explore what we mean by "civic engagement" in youth, and what we need to be doing to promote its development. The major components of the concept for this chapter provide the specifics around which I organize this study. I will explore identity, social justice, community, and neighborhood as ingredients of civic engagement. Finally, I consider the need for special attention to youth who may not enjoy the full benefits of citizenship. One key consideration is the policy supports for promoting civic engagement. One clear need in this regard is allowing such supports to be youth led.

A Brief History of Research on Civic Engagement

There has not been a lot of research on civic engagement in youth; this is one reason for the mantra I voice so often. There have been two major historical periods of research attention to the development of citizenship. The first, in the 1950s, reflected the developmental approach of that time and focused on early experience and socialization by the family. The second, during the 1970s, focused on social movements such as the civil rights movement and anti–Vietnam War protests. It therefore involved adolescents and youth but was not very developmental in orientation (Flanagan & Sherrod, 1998; Sherrod, 2005).

Research and program attention on the development of citizenship is, however, increasing, fueled in part by the writings of Robert Putnam (1996, 2000), who has argued that we face a crisis today in terms of young people's low levels of civic engagement. Putnam argues, using indicators such as newspaper readership, participation in organizations such as the Kiwanis Club, and voting, that civic engagement has been steadily declining across the past decades. Putnam's stance is controversial, as some authors argue that civic engagement has not declined but simply changed in nature (Youniss & Yates, 1997). For instance, whereas people are less likely to read newspapers, they may get news from other sources such as TV and the Internet (Peiser, 2000). Youth voting is low, but volunteerism is at an all-time high (McLeod, 2000).

This debate has fortunately sparked public interest, which has focused attention on civics education and has spurred new research and program development. A recent survey of public attitudes showed that the public believes that attention to citizenship should be one priority of schools (W. K. Kellogg Foundation, 2000). Numerous private foundations have launched initiatives aimed at youth civic engagement; the Carnegie Corporation, the Ford Foundation, the W. K. Kellogg Foundation, the Pew Charitable Trusts, and the William T. Grant Foundation are examples. And there have appeared three special issues of academic journals devoted to research on the topic (Flanagan & Sherrod, 1998; Niemi, 1999; Sherrod, Flanagan, & Youniss, 2002).

Nonetheless, we as a society are not attending to the development of citizenship as we should be. In particular, we are not exploring how we may promote the development of citizenship. In this chapter I will explore the need to promote the development of citizenship across the growing population diversity of youth in this country—in regard to ethnicity and culture, social class, religion, sexual orientation, and handicap status. Across these dimensions of variability, youth are not equal in their access to the rights and responsibilities of citizenship; for example, gay and lesbian youth are not afforded the right to marry. How does youth's experience of citizenship affect their views of it, and what implications do their views have for the ways society can promote the development of citizenship?

Young People's Civic or Political Identity

Adolescence and youth is a critical time for the development of a personal or individual identity. Erickson (1963) defined the process of developing an identity as the fifth stage of his eight-stage life-span model of development, and Marcia (1980) operationalized this development into four statuses and provided an empirical measure. Research has focused on gender identity, occupational identity, and, to a lesser extent, religious identity. There has, however, been little attention paid to political identity. Yet ideally we would like young people's sense of their political participation, as active or inactive, liberal or conservative, to be one aspect of their individual identity. But what are the dimensions of citizenship that might enter a young person's identity?

Citizenship clearly involves obeying laws, voting, following current events—generally taking an interest in and being involved in the larger, national interest or polity. However, one can be involved in one's community or devoted to a school or church and express some of those same behaviors but be oriented to institutions other than the nation-state. Furthermore, concern for others and altruism are also frequently viewed as components of citizenship. Yet one can be quite selfish and oriented entirely to one's own material or occupational success and still be involved with and committed to the nation-state, in regard to voting, campaigning, following news, and the like. Hence, citizenship is certainly multifaceted, if not a quite complex domain (Sherrod, Flanagan, & Youniss, 2002).

One clear component of the development of citizenship is youth's understanding of the rights and responsibilities that go with it. If scholars and practitioners who are experts on the topic acknowledge the complexity of conceptions of citizenship, it is perhaps not surprising that youth's views are also diverse. If you simply ask urban teenage youth (across a range of individual characteristics relating to ethnicity, social class, and religion) the question, "What is a good citizen?" they will most frequently report that citizenship is simply good behavior such as obeying laws; and they will rarely offer more than one such quality (Sherrod, 2003). If, however, you ask them specifically about specific possible aspects of citizenship, they offer more information.

Our empirical research program has examined political attitudes and ideas about citizenship in both high school and college-age young people. We give youth surveys listing various possible rights and responsibilities of citizenship. We have sampled a diverse array of youth across race, social class, academic orientation, and so forth, but all have been from an urban area and its surrounding suburbs. We ask the young people to rate on a five-point scale how important each right or responsibility is to citizenship. We then factor analyze the responses to see if a specific set of components emerge for youth's ideas about citizenship.

These factor analyses of youth's ratings of 15 to 20 qualities of citizenship generate two components to their sense of rights: entitlements, such as education and health care, and freedoms, such as freedom of speech and freedom of religion. Two components to responsibilities are generated: giving back to the community or helping other people, and typical political participation and patriotism (including working and being productive; Bogard & Sherrod, 2005; Bogard, Sherrod, & Davila, 2004; Sherrod, Bogard, & Davila, 2004).

Different youth, of course, see different components of citizenship as important. Immigrant youth, for example, are more likely to emphasize the traditional view of citizenship responsibilities; girls are more likely to emphasize the prosocial side (Baskir & Sherrod, 2005; Bogard & Sherrod, 2005). The point is that our empirical research examining young people's ideas about citizenship shows that by adolescence, their views of citizenship reflect the range of possible conceptions carried in adulthood.

An important next question for research is how young people's conceptions of rights and responsibilities relate to their developing sense of self as citizens. We have asked young people to rate on a five-point scale their sense of their own citizenship—being a very good, active citizen (5) versus being a bad, inactive citizen (1); not surprisingly, most report they are an average citizen (3). But what are the dimensions on which they base this appraisal? We would expect those youth who emphasize traditional views of citizenship to see themselves as good citizens if they vote, whereas those who value prosocial views should see themselves as good citizens if they do community service. A good citizen should be someone who exemplifies those behaviors that the young person considers to be key rights and responsibilities of citizenship. In general we find this to be the case, but this is a question for which more research is needed.

The important point is that in a democracy we want civic participation to be as much a part of youth's identity as their gender, sexual orientation, family loyalty, occupation, or religion. And we need to organize our efforts to promote civic engagement, such as civics education, to contribute to the development of clear ideas about the rights and responsibilities of citizenship that then are incorporated into the young person's political identity.

Social Justice as a Component of Good Citizenship

A concern for social justice should be one aspect of citizenship. An ability to recognize injustice and a willingness to act to correct it is a desirable trait for the citizens of any democracy. *Activism* is one term for such behavior. A commitment to obeying the law is one aspect of being a good citizen; otherwise there would be anarchy. However, a democracy also depends on citizens who make informed judgments about the fairness of existing laws and who at times object to policies and even (as in many movements for social justice) disobey unjust laws. Behavior that maintains order may be one aspect of citizenship, but so is activism or taking action to improve the nation-state; this activist behavior is frequently not considered to be good behavior because it can lead to disorder. However, the exercise of good judgment is a component of citizenship, and involves assessing when behavior is needed to maintain the status quo and when it is necessary to take action to change it (Sherrod, 2005).

Activism is also difficult to define. It is generally thought to include protest events and actions, advocacy for causes, and information dissemination to raise consciousness. In general, it is behavior to promote causes, to change the status quo. This is what distinguishes it from other civic behaviors such as voting. An aspect of activism on which there is disagreement is whether it is action to help oneself or only to help others (Sherrod, 2005).

Throughout history, youth have been the segment of the population most likely to refuse to accept the status quo and to act to change society for the better. The developmental nature of adolescents and youth make them particularly susceptible to adopting an activist orientation toward citizenship (Flanagan & Bertelsen, 2005). Teens experience cognitive changes that make them more open to new possibilities and lead them to look for utopian views of the world (Elkind, 1985). Youth search for an identity and explore who they want to be (Marcia, 1980). And youth are just starting out on their adult lives and thereby look for a better world; their adulthood is emerging (Arnett, 2004). For all these reasons, one would expect youth to be ripe for an activist orientation to citizenship. Indeed, numerous examples of youth activism can be found historically, and include activism for a variety of issues: child labor, environmental protection, animal rights, support for Palestine, and the condemnation of sweatshops. Historical examples include Nazi resistance, the civil rights mvement, and the anti–Vietnam War movement of the 1970s (Sherrod, Flanagan, & Kassimir, 2005).

Despite their age-related proneness toward activism and the numerous current and historical examples of youth activism, when in our research we ask youth about their ideas of citizenship, they almost never volunteer behaviors such as acting to change unjust laws as a responsibility of citizenship. One has to force a six-factor solution of the rankings of citizenship responsibilities, expanding the original two-factor solution described in the previous section, to see a factor emerge that relates to activism (Sherrod, Bogard, & Davila, 2004). In addition to *activism*, we use other terms in our surveys, so it is not just that the term itself may carry loaded meanings. Recognizing injustices and adopting behaviors to change them is not viewed by youth, or perhaps adults for that matter, as a desirable quality of citizenship—at least not in the United States. Why would this be the case? One reason may be the ways that society tries to promote the development of citizenship.

Families, Communities, and Neighborhoods

We would expect young people's ideas about citizenship—as well as their behavior—to be determined in part by the ways that we as a society try to promote the development of citizenship. Research has shown three categories of child and youth experience to relate to later civic engagement: civics education, youth involvement in school activities, and youth community service programs (Barber & Eccles, 1999; Kleimer & Chapman, 1999; Neimi & Junn, 2000; Sherrod, Flanagan, & Youniss, 2002). That is, three important correlates of later civic engagement in the form of behaviors such as voting are civic knowledge, which comes from civics education; school extracurricular activities, which give youth a chance to practice at being citizens; and community service, which also provides an occasion to work for one's community. This is not to say that other avenues for youth involvement—with their families or in religious activities—are not equally important, but they have not been the subject of as much research.

Civics education, school activities, and community service are the routes that research has shown serve to promote the development of citizenship. Yet these three mechanisms by no means would lead youth to adopt an activist orientation toward citizenship—to notice or be concerned about social justice. Civics education for the most part imparts constitutional law. It rarely even covers such social phenomena as the civil rights movement (Torney-Purta, 2002). Activities can serve to maintain the status quo in schools; activism is often frowned upon (Barber & Eccles, 1999). Community service can instill prosocial values, but it does not necessarily promote that social change is a route to helping people (Yates & Youniss, 1997). Hence, existing youth experiences that we know relate to the development of citizenship are not likely to promote an activist orientation.

Furthermore, individual variability or diversity is quite important to the promotion of citizenship in youth. Youth are not equal in terms of the opportunities available to them for learning about citizenship. Disadvantaged urban youth, ethnic minority youth, immigrant youth, and sexual minority youth represent the growing diversity of young people in this country today. To examine citizenship, it is essential to attend to such diversity. Yet such youth are both understudied and underrepresented in efforts to promote citizenship. The precursors that research has shown relate to later citizenship, such as civics education and community service, may not be equally available to or valuable to all youth (Hart & Atkins, 2002; Stepick & Stepick, 2002). Certainly we would expect diverse youth to follow diverse routes to citizenship, and existing research supports this notion (Sherrod, Flanagan, & Youniss, 2002). For example, boys and girls show different political views, and they participate in different school activities, which relate to their differing views (Sherrod & Baskir, 2005). Ethnic minority and immigrant youth also show allegiances to different social institutions—school, family, and community—and these different allegiances relate to different civic views (Bogard & Sherrod, 2005).

Civics education, school activities, and community service (in which you typically work outside your own community) are rather mainstream socialization experiences. In contrast, research shows that the social groups in which youth live—families, communities, and neighborhoods—to be important to their allegiances (Fulgini, Tseng, & Lam, 1999; Hart & Atkins, 2002; Tseng, 2004). As a result, these vehicles are also likely to be important to the development of citizenship in youth. If different youth experiences relate to later civic engagement in young people who vary across social dimensions such as class or race, then one might also surmise that the final state of citizenship may also look different in these youth. And research shows that ethnic minority and immigrant youth have different views of citizenship than European American youth born in this country (Bogard & Sherrod, 2005).

The Marginalization of Youth

All youth are to some extent marginalized in that they physically mature in their early teens but are not given any real adult responsibilities until a decade later, in their mid-20s. Certain youth are, however, especially marginalized in that they are not even given the opportunity to participate in activities that seem to put them on the road to adult responsibility (Hart & Atkins, 2002). Education, school activities, and community service, for example, offer mainstream youth the promise of later meaningful adult activities. If minority or disadvantaged youth participate less in these activities, then the road to adult responsibility may seem more remote to them.

Youth in general are also given a bad rap in the modern world, are feared and denigrated by adults (Gilliam & Bales, 2001). However, in recent years an important new approach to policy and research has arisen that confronts this negative view of youth. This approach is based on the recognition that the goal of youth policies and programs should be to promote positive development—not to prevent problems, as has been the approach for the past few decades of youth work. All youth have needs, and they differ in the extent to which their needs are met by the naturally occurring resources in the form of families, schools, and communities. From this perspective, one can then define internal and external assets available to youth, and research shows that the number of assets correlates with freedom from problems and with positive development in areas such as civic engagement (Benson, Leffert, Scales, & Blyth, 1998; Scales, Benson, Leffert, & Blyth, 2000).

One popular idea—that of resiliency or the ability to overcome risks—is not a useful concept from this perspective because it is based on differences among individuals. Instead we need to focus on differences between young people's environments and try to fix those environments instead of trying to fix youth (Benson et al., 1998; Larsen, 2000; Scales et al., 2000; Sherrod, Busch, & Fisher, 2004; Tolan, Sherrod, Gorman-Smith, & Henry, 2003).

Promoting positive development is an important idea in regard to the development of citizenship (Sherrod, 2004). We do not need to worry about apathy or lack of involvement in civics, as described by Putnam (1996, 2000). Instead we need to ask how we can promote the positive development of citizenship in youth, including how we may encourage them to adopt an activist orientation when needed. And it is especially important to attend to the development of citizenship in youth who may feel marginalized and hence see no reason to participate in civic life. One way of promoting civic engagement in youth is to give them some responsibility, to develop initiatives that are youth led.

Youth-Led Initiatives

Young people who do not enjoy the full array of citizenship rights and responsibilities should be more likely to take an activist orientation to citizenship. Some youth face prejudice and discrimination and may see fewer opportunities for success—or at least the road to success is more difficult for them. As a result they should be more likely to note social injustices, and faced with such injustice they should adopt an activist approach to citizenship. That is, privileged youth do not need to adopt an activist approach to citizenship in order to maintain or improve their well-being; in fact, their social privilege might lead them to be conservative. Youth who face disadvantage, discrimination, and injustice should be more likely to look to activism. And research shows that when different groups of young people are given a sense of empowerment, these youth are more likely to adopt such an orientation. This volume contains numerous examples (e.g., Torres and Fine, chapter 15, on participatory youth action research, or Jocson, chapter 8, on voices in poetry) in which diverse youth are given a voice or a means of action, and in all cases they demonstrate a willingness and capacity to take advantage of that opportunity.

The vehicles found to relate to later civic engagement—education, activities, and service—may not be the most effective vehicles for promoting citizenship in youth who may feel some disenfranchisement, who feel marginalized. For example, community-based programs that give youth a role in their communities may be more important to these youth than civics education, which may seem abstract and removed from their daily lives. Opportunities to act on behalf of their own communities through such youth programs may be more important than community service that involves helping someone outside one's community. We may need to develop different mechanisms for promoting the development of citizenship in diverse youth that tie into the social institutions in which they participate—their families, their own communities and neighborhoods, and maybe also their religions or ethnic heritages.

Hence, we are ignoring the development of citizenship in youth and particularly are not promoting an activist orientation to citizenship in our young people; yet, this is exactly the orientation needed in a democracy. However, by meeting youth on their own terms—that relate to family, community, and neighborhood instead of school activities or service—and by approaching youth from a perspective of positive development that empowers them, we offer a means of engaging them in our civic life.

Policy Supports for the Development of Citizenship in Today's Youth

Poor and minority youth and youth who feel marginalized often do not have the same opportunities as other young people to participate in school activities or to do community service, and their civic education, like the rest of their education, may be especially poor (Sherrod, Flanagan, & Youniss, 2002). Community-based youth programs may present a more promising way to promote civic engagement in poor and minority youth than school-based civic education, school activities, or community service. There are several general and specific examples of youth programs that can be described (Roach, Wheeler, & Sullivan, 1999).

One significant challenge for policy and the design of programs to promote civic engagement is recognizing the need for diversity in such policies and programs—to match the diversity found in today's youth. I have, in this chapter, emphasized diversity by social categories such as race or class, but individuals vary in lots of other ways. Unfortunately, one size does not fit all in regard to policies and programs. Recognizing and responding to diversity is one of the most serious challenges we face in promoting the development of young people. It is not clear how to adopt an approach in legislation or other vehicles for crafting policy and programs that accommodates the diversity of youth today (Sherrod, 1997). Hence, community service may work to promote civic engagement in some, but we may need other programs for others. Ideally, what we need to do is to make sure an array of development-promoting vehicles are available to serve the needs of a diverse population. I offer just two examples of possible approaches below.

Youth Governance

Giving youth a voice and some responsibility in governance is one particularly promising approach (Zeldin, Camino, & Calvert, 2003). The goal is to involve youth fully in settings of community decision making and action. These efforts aim to protect the rights of adolescents and to build civil society by promoting the civic development of youth. Youth participation in governance of organizations has positive influences on the young people themselves and on the organizations and communities involved. Zeldin et al. (2003) argue that positive impact on youth and on the organizations is most likely to occur when youth participation is characterized by five defining elements: meaningfulness, authenticity, the opportunity to have an impact on others, collaborative action, and partnerships with adults. Practices that support youth participation include strategies for sustaining the engagement of youth over time, creating a scaffolding of choice and opportunity for young people, building from the strengths of youth and adults, and facilitating power sharing among diverse stakeholders. The policies and norms of societal institutions in the United States tend to run counter to endorsement of youth participation; for example, the United States is only one of two countries that has yet to endorse the United Nations Convention on the Rights of Children. Nonetheless, youth participation is one critical approach to promoting the development of attitudes and skills that will make effective adult citizens.

Youthbuild

There are numerous other specific program examples. YouthBuild, one of the largest and most widely known (Stoneman, 2002), is a training and leadership program that employs out-of-school youth to rehabilitate housing in low-income areas. The program gives jobs to unemployed youth between the ages of 16 and 21; it is open to both young men and women but the nature of the work attracts more young men. Since the program started in 1993, more than 7000 units of low-income housing have been built by youth, and there are now 180 programs across the country. Nationwide, 89% of the students who enter the program get their high school diplomas and 86% go on to college or jobs paying an average of $7.61 per hour. Participants come from varied backgrounds but most (73%) are from low-income families, and 31% received public assistance prior to entering the program. The average cost per participant is $20,000 per year, including stipends; this is less than the military, prisons, boot camps, job corps, or most colleges. The success of YouthBuild is due to several qualities. Youth are connected to meaningful experiences, do something to help communities, develop relationships with building supervisors and peers, and learn practical as well as social skills. Many of the young people become so attached to the program that they move into management-level positions within the program after completing the initial experience. Participants have a strong commitment and connection to the program. It clearly instills a sense of civic pride, and youth are civically engaged, even though this is not necessarily an explicit goal of the program (Stoneman, 2002; Tolan et al., 2003).

Both forms of youth programming, governance and the specific example of YouthBuild, unlike either civics education or school activities, build in an orientation to activism and to changing the world for the better. And they tend to involve different youth than do community service or participating in school activities. There are numerous other examples across the nation, and our efforts to promote the development of citizenship needs to embrace these venues rather than looking to the traditional socialization vehicles of civics education, community service, and school activities.

Concluding Thoughts: Developmental Considerations in Regard to Promoting the Development of Citizenship

Young people are on the verge of exercising their citizenship by beginning to participate—as in voting, for example; for this reason, the youth phase may offer particular opportunities to promote the development of citizenship. Youth may be a sensitive time for promoting citizenship; we need more research to determine if this is the case. And one form of needed research is experimentation with diverse methods of promoting citizenship and, particularly, promoting an activist orientation to citizenship.

This chapter has focused on young people because the limited evidence available points to the youth period as an opportune time to promote citizenship. However, even if this is a sensitive stage in life for intervening to promote civic engagement, we still need to ask what forms of earlier intervention are also needed. We need research on possible precursors to later civic engagement before the youth period. Are there, for example, experiences in school-age or even preschool-age children that influence their later views of citizenship and their participation as citizens? We need research on a number of questions: Should Head Start and preschool begin to awaken children to citizenship? And how should it do so? The TV channel Nickelodeon has an election-year campaign for school-age children; how effective is it? There is little research and hence almost no guidance on how to promote citizenship in youth; there is virtually no research on the role played by the early years of development.

We need to develop research, policies, and programs oriented toward promoting the development of citizenship throughout adolescense. Citizenship is as important as any other area of adult endeavor, so development of it should be a national priority, like developing literacy, or math and science skills. And we need to worry about the development of citizenship in all youth.

Note

I wish to acknowledge the invaluable and varied assistance of my students: Lauren Baskir, Kimber Bogard, Carlos Davila, Ann Marie Hoxie, Omar Quiñones, and Christopher Smith. The research reported upon herein was supported in part by grants from the W. K. Kellogg Foundation and the William T. Grant Foundation.

References

Arnett, J. (2004). *Emerging adulthood: The winding road from the late teens through the twenties.* New York: Oxford University Press.

Barber, B. & Eccles, J. (1997, April). Student council, volunteering, basketball, or marching band: What kind of extracurricular involvement matters? Paper presented at a meeting of the Society for Research in Child Development, Washington D.C.

Benson, P., Leffert, N., Scales, P., & Blyth, D. (1998). Beyond the village rhetoric: Creating healthy communities for children and adolescents. *Applied Developmental Science, 2,* 138–159.

Bogard, K., & Sherrod, L. (2005). Allegiances and civic engagement in diverse youth. Manuscript submitted for publication.

Bogard, K., Sherrod, L., & Davila, C. (2004, July). *Ethnicity, allegiances, and civic attitudes.* Paper presented at a meeting of the International Society for the Study of Behavior Development, Ghent, Belgium.

Elkind, D. (1985). Egocentrism redux. *Developmental Review, 5,* 218–226.

Erickson, E. (1963). *Childhood and society.* New York: W. W. Norton.

Flanagan, C., & Bertelsen, A. (in press). In L. Sherrod, C. Flanagan, & R. Kassimir, (Eds.), *Youth activism: An international encyclopedia.* Westport, CT: Greenwood.

Flanagan, C., & Sherrod, L. (1998). Political development: Youth growing up in a global community. *Journal of Social Issues, 54*(3).

Fuligni, A. J., Tseng, V., & Lam, M. (1999). Attitudes toward family obligations among American adolescents from Asian, Latin American, and European backgrounds. *Child Development, 70,* 1030–1044.

Gilliam, F., & Bales, S. (2001). Strategic frame analysis: Reframing America's youth [Special issue]. *Social Policy Reports, 15*(3).

Hart, D., & Atkins, R. (2002). Civic competence in urban youth. *Applied Developmental Science, 6*(4), 246–257.

W. K. Kellogg Foundation. (2000). Retrieved from http://www.wkkf.org.

Larsen, R. (2000). Toward a psychology of positive youth development. *American Psychologist, 55,* 170–183.

Marcia, J. E. (1980). Identity development in adolescence. In J. Adelson (Ed.), *Handbook of adolescent psychology.* New York: Wiley.

McLeod, J. (2000). Media and civic socialization of youth. *Journal of Adolescent Health, 27,* 45–51.

Neimi, R. (1999). Editor's introduction. *Political Psychology, 20,* 471–476.

Neimi, R., & Junn, J. (2000). *Civic education: What makes students learn?* New Haven, CT: Yale University Press.

Peiser, W. (2000). Cohort replacement and the downward trend in newspaper reading. *Newspaper Research Journal, 21,* 11–23.

Putnam, R. (1996). The strange disappearance of civic America. *American Prospect, 7*(24), 34–48.

Putnam, R. (2000). *Bowling alone: The collapse and revival of American community.* New York: Simon and Schuster.

Roach, C., Sullivan, L., & Wheeler, W. (1999). *Youth leadership for development: Civic activism as a component of youth development programming.* Washington, D.C.: National 4-H Council.

Scales, P. C., Benson, P. L., Leffert, N., & Blyth, D. A. (2000). Contribution of developmental assets to the prediction of thriving among adolescents. *Applied Developmental Science, 4*(1), 27–46.

Sherrod, L. R. (1997). Promoting youth development through research-based policies. *Applied Developmental Science, 1*(1), 17–27.

Sherrod, L. R. (2003). Promoting the development of citizenship in diverse youth. *PS: Political Science and Politics, 36*(2), 287–292.

Sherrod, L. R. (2004, October). Civic engagement as an expression of positive develop-
   ment in youth. Paper presented at the International Conference on Applied
   Developmental Psychology, University of Jena, Weimar, Germany.
Sherrod, L. R. (in press). Youth activism and civic engagement. In L. Sherrod, C. Flanagan,
   & R. Kassimir (Eds.), *Youth activism: An international encyclopedia*. Westport, CT:
   Greenwood.
Sherrod, L. R., & Baskir, L. (in press). Gender differences in the political interests of
   U.S. teens. *Journal of Social Issues.*
Sherrod, L. R., Bogard, K., & Davila, C. (2004, March). The development of citizenship
   in diverse youth. Paper presented at Biennial Meeting of the Society for Research
   on Adolescent Development, Baltimore.
Sherrod, L. R., Busch, N., & Fisher, C. (2004). Applying developmental science: Methods,
   visions, and values. In R. Lerner & L. Steinberg (Eds.), *Handbook of adolescent
   psychology* (pp. 747–780). New York: Wiley.
Sherrod, L. R., Flanagan, C., & Kassimir, R. (Eds.) (in press). *Youth activism: An
   international encyclopedia.* Westport, CT: Greenwood.
Sherrod, L., Flanagan, C., & Youniss, J. (Eds.) (2002). Growing into citizenship: Multiple
   pathways and diverse influences [Special issue]. *Applied Developmental Science,
   6*(4).
Stoneman, D. (2002). The role of youth programming in the development of civic
   engagement. *Applied Developmental Science, 6*(4), 221–226.
Tolan, P. H., Sherrod, L. R., Gorman-Smith, D., & Henry, D. (2003). Building protection,
   support, and opportunity for inner-city children and youth and their families.
   In K. Maton, C. Schellenbach, & B. Leadbeater (Eds.), *Fostering resilient children,
   youth, families, and communities: Strength-based research and policy.* Washington
   DC: American Psychological Association.
Torney-Purta, J. (2002). The school's role in developing civic engagement: A study of
   adolescents in 28 countries. *Applied Developmental Science, 6*(4), 203–212.
Tseng, V. (2004). Family interdependence and academic adjustment in college: Youth
   from immigrant and U.S.-born families. *Child Development, 75*(3), 966–983.
Youniss, J., & Yates, M. (1997). What we know about engendering civic identity.
   American Behavioral Scientist, 40, 620–631.
Zeldin, S., Camino, L., & Calvert, M. (2003). Toward an understanding of youth in
   community governance: Policy priorities and research directions [Special issue].
   Social Policy Report, 17(3).

CHAPTER 17

Youth Policy and Institutional Change

MIKE MALES

The United States is the most anti-youth society on earth. This is not because American youth suffer absolute deprivations worse than youth of other nations (though the United States falls far short of the standards of health care, housing, economic support, and opportunity afforded youth in similarly affluent Western countries). What characterizes America's singular hostility is that youth here are worse off *relative to adults* than those of any other country for which we have reliable information.

In no country, rich or poor, other than the United States do we find youths two to three times more likely to live in poverty and destitution (in homes with incomes less than half of the poverty level) than middle-aged adults. In 2003, the U.S. Census Bureau reports, 18% of U.S. children and adolescents lived in poverty (in homes with annual incomes of less than $14,400 for a family of three), compared to 8% of middle-aged adults. Some six million children and teenagers live in destitution (in homes with annual incomes less than $7,200 for a family of three), 2.5 times the rate of middle-aged adults. Persons under the age of 20 comprise 40% of the nation's destitute (U. S. Bureau of the Census, 2004).

The United States also affords its young people fewer rights in relation to adults than any other country. America is the only country to impose curfews (literally, house arrest) on its youth, which, if adopted in daytime and nighttime form as recommended by the U.S. Department of Justice under both presidents Bill Clinton and George W. Bush, would allow persons under age 18 legally to be in public only a couple of hours most days of the year. The United States is the only country whose federal administration, both Democratic and Republican, has proposed mandatory, random drug testing of public school students. While many nations deny fundamental rights to their citizens of all ages, no country other than the United States permits its adults to exercise rights of free speech, expression, assembly, press, privacy, exemption from corporal and other cruel punishments, and use of alcohol and tobacco while subjecting its youth to such sweeping denial of those same rights.

On the basis of little more than authorities' whimsy, American youths suffer extensive and systematic censorship of expression (*Hazelwood School District v. Kuhlmeier*, 484 US 260, 1988); legal banishment from certain films, literature, and other "adult" culture; harsh and arbitrary policing; criminal sentences longer than adults receive for equivalent offenses (California Youth Authority, 2004); violent legal punishments even to the point of injury (*Ingraham v. Wright*, 430 US 651, 1977); forced childbearing if authorities deny consent for abortion (*Hodgson v. Minnesota*, 497 US 417, 1990); and draconian demands for absolute abstinence from use of alcohol and tobacco. Amnesty International (2004) reports the United States has conducted half the world's executions of persons for crimes committed as youths since 1990 (*Stanford v. Kentucky*, 492 US 361, 1989), outdoing even the world's most repressive regimes such as those of China, Iran, and Nigeria.

While other countries suffer intergenerational tensions and some impose mild and sporadic restrictions on youth, none—not even the United Kingdom, which seems to copy America's worst social policies—approaches the United States in subjecting youth to authoritarian controls in a society in which adults enjoy such broad freedoms. In rulings from 1980 to the present, the U.S. Supreme Court has declared children and youths have no constitutional rights whatsoever (see *Stanford v. Kentucky*)—not even the right to government protection from severely violent abuses of which the state is aware (*DeShaney v. Winnebago County Department of Social Services*, 489 US 189, 1989) or officials' inflicting of brutal punishments constitutionally banned even for *criminals* (*Ingraham v. Wright*).

For most American authorities, even this level of repression is insufficient. Demands for more restrictions on American youth abound, from banishment from all movies depicting cigarette smoking to 24-hour, 7-day-a-week adult supervision of teenagers through a panoptic network of school, after-school programs, and parents (Larner, 1999). The endless stream of vituperation and fear American interest groups and press stories *routinely* express toward young people—girl gangs, teen hookups, online peril, suburban heroin, school test cheating, date rape, "rave menace," "mean girl," athletes on steroids, suicide epidemics, drunken debauchery—would be branded hate speech if hurled at any other group.

Americans, in short, act as if we are enraged at our young. The United States is the only one of 194 nations that has failed to ratify the United Nations Convention on the Rights of the Child. Americans' flouting of the principles of decent treatment of children and youth that have been accepted by *every other nation* would place the country in immediate violation of the convention's requirement that government, commensurate with its resources, guarantee the young "the benefits of social security ... adequate nutrition, housing, recreation and medical services" and protections from "cruel, inhuman, or degrading treatment or punishment," including "capital punishment or life imprisonment for offenses committed by persons below the age of 18" (UNICEF, 2004). As all other nations submit detailed plans to UN agencies to comply with the convention's mandates, the United States engages in increasingly angry dismantling even of weak child welfare, health, and rights guarantees, evidenced most recently in the 1990s "welfare reform" and legal crackdowns.

America's policy of subjecting young people to high rates of poverty and repression cannot be said to "work." Just the opposite. The United States suffers far higher rates of murder, gun violence, violent deaths, drug addiction, drunken driving and other alcohol abuse, imprisonment, HIV and AIDS, unplanned pregnancy, homelessness, obesity, family breakup, urban decay, wealth concentration, and civic apathy among young and old alike than any other comparable Western country—worse, in fact, than most developing, and many Third World, nations. In no sense, except in its financial and military dominance, can the United States be called a successful, functioning society.

Anti-Youth Panics: Artifacts of Change, Adult Disarray

What accounts for the extraordinary hatred and panic Americans express toward their young? Not the behaviors of youths themselves, which (as will be shown) display healthy trends. This chapter will argue that four factors explain anti-youth anger:

1. *Social change.* As Margaret Mead (1970, 1978) predicted three decades ago, adults in modern societies undergoing rapid social change will come to fear their youth as harbingers of a baffling, and therefore menacing, future.

2. *Racial change.* Adult fear and rejection of youth are exacerbated in the United States, which, as the only racially diverse, affluent country, is experiencing *both social and demographic change.* The latest (2005) census estimates find 33% of the U.S. citizenry is Latino, African American, Asian, Native American, or other nonwhite race, compared to a 13% minority population in Canada, 8% in Australia, 4% in the United Kingdom, 2% in Germany, and 1% in Japan. America's racial split is along age lines: 40% of the population under age 20 is nonwhite, compared to just 24% of those over age 40. In major U.S. urban areas and states such as California, majority-white voters and hierarchies govern youth populations which are mostly of color. American whites and more affluent minorities feel no obligation to support younger populations from whom they feel alienated by racial makeup, social class, generational split, and the imagined menaces inherent in these divisions.

3. *Commodification.* The United States's lack of social cohesion, and particularly its absence of commitment to children and youth, renders collective

responsibility for each others' well-being an anathema. The mainstream American family is constantly depicted as besieged by outside forces threatening violence, drugs, and the corruption of children (Demos, 1979). Youth have become objects of fear, a menace to be contained, a commodity that interest groups on both the right and the left deploy standard advertising hyperbole to exploit in an increasingly privatized social-policy climate.

4. *Grownup deterioration.* In addition to the above strains, America's baby boom generation—now moving into positions of government, business, and institutional authority—is an extraordinarily troubled, self-centered cohort. Baby boomers (led by aging whites) suffer staggeringly higher levels of drug abuse, criminal arrest, imprisonment, family instability, and other difficulties than were known in any previous middle-aged population. Unfortunately, America's political tradition of blaming social problems on powerless minorities prevents the confrontation of spiraling middle-aged addiction, crime, AIDS, and imprisonment crises. Strenuous efforts by all sides to deny the fact that boomer troubles are driving America's most serious domestic problems have warped political and social science debates to the point of complete informational breakdown and generated a stampede to blame scapegoats—primarily the young and poor.

Can Wealthy Nations Handle Racial Diversity?

America's uniquely irrational panic and disownment toward its young—which not only threaten the viability of this society, but has worldwide implications—was forecast by anthropologist Mead in her final book, *Culture and Commitment* (1970, 1978). The modern trends prompting greater adult fear of youth today are progress and social change, effects of the supplanting of traditional postfigurative societies with modern prefigurative ones. In postfigurative cultures, which dominated human existence for hundreds of thousands of years, Mead wrote, change is slow and imperceptible; the older adult embodies what the culture was, is, and will be, its rituals and its wisdom. Since the lives of infants will resemble those of grandparents, the parents' task is to transmit the ancestral customs to their children.

In contrast, prefigurative societies are characterized by rapid, jolting social change. In such dynamic milieus, children become the symbols of the culture's future while confused adults find their experiences, traditions, and wisdom increasingly irrelevant. "There are no elders who know what those who have been reared within the last twenty years know about the world into which they were born," Mead notes. "It is not only that parents are no longer guides, but that there are no guides" (1970, p. 61).

Adult perceptions of social realities in recent decades, particularly as they apply to youths, are distorted by the newness of prefigurative societies. "The adult imagination, acting alone, remains fettered to the past," Mead warns

(1970, p. 73). Grownups yearn for a lost, idealized past in which life was simpler, more moral, less violent. (Such times did not exist, of course. Older adults' reconstituted memories of a crime-free Depression, for example, don't jibe with police reports showing crime and violence rampant in the 1930s—especially murder, which peaked in 1931 at levels not seen since.) Adults assert moral superiority, view social problems through old and unreliable lenses, imagine endless crises among the young, and implement misdirected, even dangerous, remedies.

Inevitably, adults come to misperceive that their society harbors "too many of the wrong kind of children" who seem fearsome and alien. The result is an elder society that no longer sees the young as "the sure symbol of continuity and hope," but of ominous discontinuity and change (Mead 1978, p. 128). Generational abandonment and societal disintegration then loom as real possibilities. Still, Mead remained optimistic that adult imagination would evolve to meet this new challenge, even to delight in the dynamic imagination of "rearing unknown children for an unknown world" (1970, p. 75).

Mead's optimism was partially vindicated by Europe's, Japan's, and Latin America's evolution from postfigurative to prefigurative cultures over the last century without arousing inordinate fear toward the young—though American-style random panics toward youth, especially in Japan and the United Kingdom, are rising. Why, then, did fear and anger against youth become so virulent in the United States? "I did not reckon heavily enough on the inevitable hostility that would accompany parents' alienation," Mead later lamented (1978, p. 127).

One major difference is that while European or Japanese children may seem to think differently than their elders, they at least *look* like their elders. In the multiracial United States, as noted, the growing diversity of the population has led to children and youth appearing to both *think* and *look* differently than their parents do. Thus, the diversity manifest in the young, the threat posed by youth of color and their diabolical corruption of white youth with base values, is increasingly imagined as the cause of society's imagined degeneration.

But *Aren't* Kids Getting Worse?

A major question in evaluating Americans' rampant fear of the young is whether it is rational. Are kids today dramatically more dangerous and endangered, as every source from popular media to august institutional "experts" tells us?

The answer is a resounding "No." Modern American youth trends demonstrate dramatically that evolution to a multicultural society can accompany positive changes. Two astonishing trends are evident. First, by most major indexes of behavior, American youth today, though generally poorer, have never acted better. Second, the timing and trajectory of youth improvements shows they are not related to crackdowns and other remedial policy efforts.

This analysis begins with California, the site of the nation's most rapid racial and social change—and, significantly, the nation's most profound improvements in youth behavior. The latest statistics show that as California's

Table 17.1 Improvements in California Teenagers' Behaviors Since the 1970s, by Race and Gender, 2003*

Behavior	Male, ages 10–19				Female, ages 10–19			
	White	Latino	Black	Asian	White	Latino	Black	Asian
Homicide arrest	−72%	−60%	−69%	+26%	−38%	−38%	−62%	n.a.
Felony arrest	−65	−60	−61	−43	−31	−35	−5	−15
Suicide	−37	−48	−28	+38	−62	−58	−81	−25
Violent death	−67	−85	−81	−64	−66	−86	−93	−32
Births		n.a.			−48	−22	−59	−61

Note: Change in rate of selected behaviors, adjusted for population changes. Earliest years for which statistics are available by race are 1975 (arrests), 1970 (deaths), and 1977 (births). Asian rates of homicide arrest and suicide for 1970s are based on few or no cases, making change calculations unreliable.
Sources: California Criminal Justice Statistics Center (1970–2003); Center for Health Statistics (1960–2003).

teen population evolved from 72% white in 1970 to 65% of color in 2005, teen problems of every kind plummeted (see Table 17.1). Youth homicide, felony, and total arrests are at their lowest levels since figures were first compiled in 1959; violent crime is at its lowest level since 1967. Teen suicide rates are at their lowest level since 1958 (a time when suicides were incompletely tabulated); drug abuse deaths are rarer than at any time since 1965; and violent deaths are at their lowest ebb since statistics have been kept. Births to teen mothers are rarer today than at any time since 1949; teenage HIV/AIDS infections have declined more rapidly than in any other age group over the last 15 years (California Criminal Justice Statistics Center, 1975–2003; Center for Health Statistics, 1960–2003).

In both California and nationally, youth school dropout rates are at historic lows: college enrollment and community volunteerism are at all-time highs. Major surveys such as Monitoring the Future (MTF) find students report less violence at school and more optimism in self-appraisals than students in the first survey 30 years ago. Contrary to incessant images of alienated, miserable, peer-tortured, consumer-driven adolescents presented by the media—both mainstream and alternative—and their "experts," only 1 in 10 teens in the most recent MTF survey reports a negative self-image, only 2% are dissatisfied with their friends (the aspect of life they rate most favorably), just 10% report negative peer pressures; 70% get along well with parents, and few covet more material possessions (Johnston, O'Malley, Bachman, & Schulenberg, 1975–2003). In addition, youths have shown moderating trends in many behaviors such as smoking, drinking, and drug use that have sharply reduced the risks suffered by past generations.

As Youth Get Better, Aging Baby Boomers Get Worse

These remarkable improvements in youth behavior, the most profound of any youth generation of which we have record, is all the more surprising given two serious, negative trends endured by young people. First, misbehavior has exploded in their parents' generation. Since 1970, both in California and nationally, middle-aged troubles have soared even as teens were moderating their own behavior. Nothing illustrates the diverging generational trends splitting youth (ages 10–19) from their baby boomer parents (ages roughly 30–59) more than changes in drug abuse deaths, felony arrest, and imprisonment over the last 25–30 years (see Table 17. 2). The long-term pattern, which holds consistent for other measures and comparison years, is one of massive intergenerational *improvement*. Huge declines in teenage drug abuse rates (reflected in deaths from illicit drugs) accompanied large declines in felony arrest rates and—astonishing in California, a state where prison populations have burgeoned under get-tough crime laws—an actual drop in juvenile imprisonment.

Meanwhile, baby boomer drug deaths have increased sharply, along with even larger increases in felony arrests and a gigantic surge in imprisonment (California Department of Corrections, 2004). In 1986, the violent crime arrest rates of Californians in their 30s soared past those of juvenile teens. By 2002, for the first time, 40-agers became more violence prone than adolescents. Today, a California middle-ager is nearly twice as likely to be arrested for a serious crime and seven times more likely to be imprisoned than his counterpart of 25 or 30 years ago.

California's most recent figures show drug overdose is now the state's second leading cause of premature death, exceeding suicide, homicide, gun killings, and AIDS. Illicit drug deaths by age in 2003 tell the story: ages 10–19, 51 deaths; 20–29; 323 deaths; 65 and older, 359 deaths; and, astonishingly, ages 30–59, 2,954 deaths (see California Criminal Justice Statistics Center, 1975–2003; Center for Health Statistics, 1960–2003). The highest rates are among middle-aged

Table 17.2 Intergenerational Changes, California Youth vs. Parent Population, 1970s–2002

	Youth (ages 10–19)			Parent (ages 30–59)		
	Drug Death	Felonies	Incarcerations	Drug Deaths	Felonies	Incarcerations
1970*	235	146,179	4,414	869	59,121	6,812
2003	51	105,892	4,067	2,954	229,353	104,820
Rate change**	–84%	–47%	–28%	+54%	+89%	+699%

Notes: *The table compares the latest (2003/04) figures to earliest 1970s figures available for California: 1970 for drug deaths; 1975 for felony; 1977 for prison populations. **Adjusted for population changes by year for each age group.

Sources: California Criminal Justice Statistics Center (1970–2003); Center for Health Statistics (1960–2003); California Department of Corrections (2004).

white and black Americans; the lowest are among young African Americans and Latinos, ages 15–29.

Nationally, the picture is much the same. In 1970, the National Center for Health Statistics tabulated 2,700 middle-aged deaths from drug overdoses; in 2002, that number was over 20,000. Today, persons over 35 comprise 75% of all deaths from methamphetamine, 80% from cocaine, and 85% from heroin. Adjusted for population increase, middle-aged drug overdose death rates increased by 400% (National Center for Health Statistics, 1960–2003). (In contrast, drug abuse death rates among teens and young adults fell from 1970 to 2003.) Hospital emergency treatments for illicit-drug abuse also show an escalating, rapidly aging drug abusing population now centered among those in their 40s (Drug Abuse Warning Network, 2002). Sociologist Erich Goode (whose *Drugs in American Society* is a standard college text), has declared, "taking psychoactive substances recreationally poses a much more serious health hazard to the middle-aged than to younger persons" (Goode 2005, p. 153).

The herculean resolve of federal drug war authorities—misled by the Office of National Drug Control Policy—and drug policy reform groups such as Marijuana Policy Project to ignore the middle-aged drug crisis has been disastrous. One of the few negative youth trends—the eruption in homicide among impoverished young inner-city men in the late 1980s and early 1990s, which has since abated—was fueled by conflict among drug gangs and dealers supplying soaring middle-aged addictions.

As in California, baby boomer drug abuse spawned burgeoning crime nationwide. In 1975, the FBI reported 70,000 Americans ages 35–59 arrested for violent felonies; by 2003 that rose to 175,000. Middle-aged property felony arrests rose from 135,000 in 1975 to 375,000 in 2003; drug arrests skyrocketed from 30,000 to 450,000. Relative to their population increase, middle-aged violent crime rates jumped 60%, property crime rates doubled, and drug offenses leapt 800% in one generation (Federal Bureau of Investigation, 1960–2003). (Meanwhile, arrest rates for these offenses among teens and young adults *fell* by 15%.) Reviewing the statistics, shocked U.S. Office of Juvenile Justice and Delinquency Prevention analysts noted that concern over "a new breed of middle-aged superpredator" was more justified than over the "myth" of juvenile superpredators (Snyder & Sickmund, 2000, pp. 130–31). That warning made no headlines.

The baby boom drug abuse and crime explosion is costly in human and monetary terms. In the 1970s, just one-third of new prison admittees were over age 30; today nearly 60% are. Contrary to the theories of liberal groups like the Sentencing Project, the increase in older offenders is not due to longer sentences, but to the massive growth in boomers' felony arrests and recidivism. Seven in ten parolees over age 30 are returned to custody for new offenses or violations within a year. In 2004, California spent $3 billion to imprison convicts over age 30 (an age group criminologists insist is immune to offending)—more than the state spends on its entire university system.

Baby boomers drive not only America's worst drug abuse, crime, and incarceration trends, but other social ills. Refuting official claims, the Centers for Disease Control (1993–2004) figures show a large majority of new HIV infectees are over age 30. In 1993, the first year the Centers for Disease Control's *HIV/AIDS Surveillance* tabulated new HIV infections, just one-third were in persons over 35. Today (as of 2003), nearly 60% are. New middle-aged HIV diagnoses have soared at triple the rate of persons under age 35.

Rising behavior crises have rendered a large share of middle-aged Americans too unstable to maintain healthy families, leading to an explosion in divorce and disruptions to the normal raising of children. Demand for foster care for teens whose parents can't or won't care for them has reached unmanageable peaks in nearly every state. New industries to manage, police, and remediate youths have arisen and now prosper by manufacturing endless panics over imaginary youth troubles.

From Scapegoating to Disowning Youth

The most shocking aspect of the baby boomer crisis (easily confirmed by examining FBI, National Center for Health Statistics, U.S. Census Bureau statistics, and similar standard references) is not that it happened. The disruptions of the 1960s and the inept, ideologically driven social and health policies of the 1980s and '90s predicted that boomer troubles would be large and unaddressed. What is beyond belief is the abject, unanimous denial—by interests on the left, in the center, and on the right, academic and popular, public and private—that any sort of middle-aged crisis exists. Check the websites of major interest groups, institutions, and media, regardless of their political orientation, public/private affiliation, academic/institutional nature, or mainstream/alternative bent, and you will discover that boomer drug, crime, and other ills are taboo topics. Nowhere are they mentioned.

Part of this denial is political. Boomers are America's most economically and politically prestigious demographic. Politicians and interests may benignly criticize middle-agers for failing to monitor or transmit values to their supposedly wayward kids, but they are loath to directly blame behavior, health, and moral crises on such a powerful, mainstream constituency that all profit from by flattering.

However, the larger denial goes beyond political expediency. The idea that boomers comprise our chief "problem population" and that young people represent considerable improvement deeply offends Americans' beliefs in the sanctity of adulthood, adult authority, and adult prerogatives pitted against the antisociality of adolescence. Surveys show that anger at and fear of youth is the only bigotry that crosses the political spectrum. Explicit defenses of grownups and a moralizing, degrading stance toward young people dominate leftist entities such as Alternet, Salon, the Media Education Foundation, and the MoveOn.org and centrist and right-wing sources such as Fox News, *Time* magazine, the *New York Times*, and the Manhattan Institute. This unanimity buttresses Mead's conclusion that adults' phobia toward modern youth results not from rational analysis, but from evolutionary atavisms that remain poorly understood.

Beyond boomer behavior crises, the second negative trend affecting youth is political: generational attrition. Parents and grandparents of the past (though acerbic at times) refrained from harshly condemning, punishing, and abandoning younger generations, Mead wrote, because they were "the comforting image of replication of themselves"; today's elders, however, "feel no such restraint when all the young, including their own children, have turned into strangers" (1978, p. 126). Hayes-Bautista, Schink, and Chapa (1988) have documented the "generational compact's" abrogation by the old. "When faced with a choice between pursuing an affluent, 'Yuppie' lifestyle that consumes many resources and deferring part of that gratification to invest in a younger generation that is very different ethnically," boomers were choosing themselves (p. 55). Yet, boomers will demand that these same young pay increasing shares of meager incomes for a growing elder population's social security.

Over the past three decades, both private and public investment in the young have deteriorated. California leads the abysmal trends. Today's young people will be the first in American history to be poorer than their parents. In 1965, the family income gap between 50-year-olds and 25-year-olds was just $16,000 in constant 2003 dollars; today, it tops $40,000 (U.S. Bureau of the Census, 2004). Boomers, the wealthiest and most tax-subsided generation ever, refuse to pay taxes to support younger cohorts. Older generations have enacted hefty 30% tax cuts over the last 25 years, benefiting themselves while forcing massively higher costs on young people. College tuitions have quadrupled in real dollars; the average student now carries $19,000 in education loans, constituting "unmanageable debt" for 4 out of 10, the U.S. Department of Education reports. "The world of middle age and power is like a world of childless property owners who resent the school taxes because they have no children of their own," Mead lamented a quarter century ago (1978, p. 127).

California's 2004–2005 budget declares open generational warfare, freezing or cutting taxes for richer, mostly older taxpayers while shoveling massively higher expenses (skyrocketing tuitions, $20 billion in bonded debt repayment, deferred spending obligations) onto future taxpayers. In one generation, boomers have reversed the principle that older generations pay for younger ones. We are now well on our way to making the young pay for the old.

Recognizing Youth Adaptability

How, then, have California's and America's increasingly diverse youth responded to the hostile conditions forced on them by angry, disarrayed elders? It is here that the emerging picture is most intriguing and encouraging.

First, teenagers have not returned grownups' hostility—yet. Public Agenda's 2000 survey found that while two-thirds of adults condemned youth in blanket pejoratives and feared the next generation will make society worse, teens rated adults as individuals—most good, a few rotten. The National Association of Secretaries of State (1999) reported that "youth volunteerism is on the rise," especially "in one-on-one settings such as soup kitchens, hospitals, and schools ... motivated by a young person's desire to help others in a personal way" (p. 3). As older voters support slashing schools and services for the young, polls show no favor among young people for cutting social security for the old. Interracial dating and marriage is much higher among today's teens than among previous generations, presaging a more truly integrative society. Clearly, young people's attitudes are far better adapted to the demands of tomorrow's multicultural, communitarian future than their elders' greedy, isolating, stereotypical mind-sets.

Second, youths are adopting new approaches to the risks that plagued their elders. Authorities' and interest groups' fixation on what percentages of teens report on "behavior risk" surveys that they drink, smoke, use drugs, have sex, and so on, is anachronistic. (In fact, my correlational analysis of 28 years of MTF reports shows that the more teens report using drugs, the fewer who suffer real-world risks such as violent death, homicide, suicide, criminal arrest, school dropout, and self-reported violence and delinquency.)

Overlooked is the fact that the major trend among youth is not abstinence, but moderation. Cigarette smoking is a telling example. MTF reports that while the proportion of teens and college students reporting smoking cigarettes has fallen only slightly in the last quarter century, heavy daily smoking has fallen by 40%. Among the 735 University of California–Santa Cruz students I've surveyed, 62% report smoking in the past year. This might seem disastrously high, especially for a modern, health-conscious California Bay Area population, until the details are analyzed. Of student smokers, one-third smoke less than once a month, another one-third smoke at least once a month but less than daily, just 1 in 10 (6% of all students) smoke at least a half pack every day. Further, two-thirds of smokers smoke less than the whole cigarette; "social smoking" involves passing a cigarette around a group, each taking only a few puffs. Contrary to health authorities who insist occasional "social smoking" is the precursor to addictive smoking, 90% of social smokers report they smoke the same or less than they did in the past.

These same trends show up for drugs and alcohol. While the *National Survey on Drug Use and Health* (Substance Abuse and Mental Health Services Administration, 2003) reports that 17-year-olds and 40-year-olds are equally likely to drink alcohol and to "binge drink" (consume five or more drinks on one occasion), the National Center for Health Statistics reports show 17-year-olds are only half as likely to drive drunk and kill or injure someone, and less than one-fifth as likely to die from an alcohol overdose. The management of both drinking and heavy drinking among today's young people is more advanced than among their middle-aged parents.

Another major curiosity (about which officials remain steadfastly uncurious) is why teens today are so unlikely to die from drugs. The remarkable mystery is most evident in coastal California and New York. In 1970, teens residing in the Los Angeles, San Francisco, and New York City's metropolitan regions were *six times* more likely to die from drugs than teens elsewhere, comprising 48% of the country's teenage drug deaths. Then, from 1970 to 2002, New York City's teenage drug toll fell from 136 deaths to 7; Los Angeles and San Francisco's, from 204 to 23—trends that accompanied large drops in suicide, violent death, and other ills. Today, New York, Los Angeles, and San Francisco teens are *less than half* as likely to die from drugs as teens elsewhere and comprise just 6% of all teen drug deaths. In these massive conurbations totaling 24 million people, just 30 teenagers died from illicit drugs (including overdoses, accidents, suicides, and other mishaps) in 2002. How did this happen? It is unlikely that coroners are overlooking teenage deaths; they're certified by federal drug authorities to provide accurate and complete investigations of drug mortality. Their toxicology equipment detected 3,100 adult deaths from illegal drugs in 2002. Nor are teens immune to drug overdose—370 teens died from drugs in these cities in 1970. Nor are teen addicts later dying in young adulthood: only 5% of these cities' drug decedents today are under age 25.

Yet teens today are not abstaining from drugs. In fact, MTF reports teens are twice as likely to use illicit drugs now than their counterparts of 1970. Why, then, the smaller death toll? Generations X and Y, especially in hard-hit areas like New York and coastal California, have benefited from three decades of society's exposure to hard drugs. They have seen the devastating toll of crack, methamphetamine, and heroin on adults and are choosing milder drugs instead. When I asked imprisoned Chicago youths why teens weren't overdosing (just 5 of the city's 865 illicit-drug deaths in 2000 were juveniles), the sum of the cacophony of shouts was, "Because you can't die from weed!"

A good example of the natural evolution of drug safety among modern youth occurred with Ecstasy. While Ecstasy is not the "crack cocaine of the '90s," as one widely quoted officer hysterically dubbed it, it is not harmless. Early in the drug's rave/club era, adverse reactions caused by dehydration, body temperature fluctuations, and (especially) contaminated drugs were clearly increasing. Groups such as Dancesafe quickly arose to provide free medical information, water, and drug testing at raves. In reports for 1999 and 2004 the Drug Abuse Warning Network (2000, 2004) found that despite rising millions of users, deaths and hospital emergency cases involving club drugs (Ecstasy, GHB, LSD, and ketamine) remained "very rare," accounting for fewer than 1% of drug-related emergency room cases, and death tolls too small to reliably tabulate.

Finally, another intriguing youth trend is the big increase in marriage among teenage boys, the only group to show an increase during the 1990s.

The decennial censuses report the percentage of married teen boys, on the decline for a century, suddenly doubled during the last decade. Why? And why did rising marriage accompany a massive decline in births? In 1990, 41% of married teen girls gave birth; in 2003 that number figure just 16%, accounting for nearly all the decline in births among teens during the period. A large majority of married teens told the 2000 census they don't live with their partners, yet remain happily married. What is the purpose of teen marriage (most of which, for both sexes, involves partners in their 20s) today? The old purposes—having or legitimating babies, forming separate households—evidently no longer apply.

These changes and moderations in youth behavior are not due to crackdowns and policies aimed at youth. In fact, "get tough" policies hamper the ongoing improvements in youth behavior that long predate them. The decline in teen drug deaths began in the late 1970s, well before the "war on drugs" was launched in the late 1980s. Similarly, consistent research "fails to support the argument that curfews reduce crime or criminal victimization," a 10-study review found (Adams, 2003; see also Reynolds, Seydlitz, & Jenkins, 2000). Systematic studies of school uniforms and "zero tolerance" policies by the Educational Testing Service (Wenglinksy, Coley, & Barton 1998) and by Notre Dame education faculty (Brunsma & Rockquemore, 1999) show they do not improve discipline, drug or alcohol violations, or attendance, and may negatively affect academic performance. MTF researchers' 900-school study in 2003 found that school drug-testing programs, whether applied to athletes or all students, have no effect on student drug use except a possible *increase* in use of drugs other than marijuana (Yamaguchi, Johnston, & O'Malley, 2003). Initial studies by advocates lauding "back to basics" schools that employed strict discipline and testing were shown to be questionable, even silly, by later analysis (Rothstein, 2004).

Efforts to criminalize youth for engaging in adult behaviors also look dubious as longer-term studies accumulate. A *New England Journal of Medicine* study found vigorous enforcement of laws criminalizing youth purchases of tobacco products was followed by significant increases in youth smoking (Rigotti et al., 1997). A Rutgers University economics department paper found laws criminalizing alcohol use by persons under age 21 slightly reduce fatal accidents among 18- to 20-year-olds but increase fatalities even more among 21- to 23-year-olds (Dee & Evans, 2001). In fact, the major improvement in teenage traffic safety over the last 25 years, including 50% declines in fatal crashes and drunken driving deaths, appears unrelated to policy changes (Dee & Evans, 2001). Boot camps, Scared Straight! programs, trying youths as adults, and other panaceas for which great claims of success in reducing juvenile crime were made consistently have been found ineffective, and often harmful, by research (Lundman, 2001; Bishop, Frazier, Lanza-Kaduce, & Winner, 1996). In contrast, cities that permit young people more freedoms and public access are better protected from crime and violence (Males, 2000; Males & Macallair, 1999).

None of these remarkable changes in youth behavior has been publicized or even officially noticed, except in the rare instances in which authorities seek undue credit for improvements or to deplore young people for not completely abstaining. In a society in which social policy is privatized and youth are mere commodities, the information all sides seek and exploit is not the most important (no matter how accurate and topical), but the most salable (no matter how distorted or even ridiculous).

If Not Countered, Anti-Youth Hostility Will Worsen

Mead's 1970s predictions appear more timely than ever as the 21st century unfolds. The gradual evolution of American youth attitudes and behaviors toward greater respect for diversity, moderation of risk, greater community responsibility, and compensation for the older generation's failings signal encouraging, prefigurative developments necessary to build tomorrow's multicultural society. Meanwhile, adults' rising fear and retreatism, our inability to see youth changes in anything except tones of panic and peril, represent the postfigurative retrogressions Mead warned would jeopardize society's continuity.

The demographic and political trends that spawned aging America's hostility against youth—social and racial changes, adult behavior and attitude deterioration, the privatization of social policy and commodification of youth by interest groups—will intensify as the younger population of color grows rapidly and the white population ages. By 2031, the U.S. Census Bureau predicts a majority of America's population under age 25 will be of color at the same time half of the still-dominant white population is over age 45. Unless the irrational sources of elder fears are recognized and reasonably rethought, adults in societies of rapid social and demographic change (of which California and the United States are harbingers) may be incapable of seeing youth and the future they represent as anything but menacing.

The final question, then, is what innovative policy framework might maximize the favorable trends among American youth that have accompanied social and demographic evolution and minimize the toxic attitudes and behaviors founded in grownups' failure to adapt to this evolution. Some intriguing possibilities emerged in the November 2004 U.S. presidential election, which brought a sharp increase in young-adult voting and the first signs of massive generational splits. Both mainstream and, unfortunately, progressive media have misrepresented trends in young adult voting, dismissing them as trivial ("Rock The Vote/Vote or Die: Failure," sniffed *CNN Headline News*, and it was a common sentiment) or as the modest product of traditional get-out-the-vote movements.

Neither is accurate. My analysis of *Los Angeles Times* exit polls and the Edison/Mitofsky National Election Poll of 76,000 voters in all 50 states and the District of Columbia (see also Center for Information and Research on Civic Learning and Engagement, 2005) revealed the increase in 2004's young voter participation (up six to eight million over 2000) is too large to credit merely to organizations' exhortations. Further, the chasms between young and old are too wide to dismiss as trivial. If voters under age 30 had prevailed, Democratic candidate John Kerry would have won by a 55% landslide, carrying 31 states with 376 electoral votes, and the U.S. Congress would be solidly Democratic. Younger voters disapproved of President Bush by a 14-point margin (older voters approved the president by 6 points), though Democrats have done little to deserve the support of young voters, either. In many states, younger and older voters seemed to come from different planets. Mississippians over the age of 30 endorsed Bush by a 26-point margin, while those under 30 rejected him by 14 points. In New York, 75% of the voters under 30 backed Kerry. Democrats' lead among young Californians was triple that among older ones. Young voters are twice as likely as older ones to support gay marriage and strongly believe "government should do more to solve problems"—a sentiment older voters reject (Lopez, Kirby, & Sagoff, 2005).

These striking differences between younger and older voters are founded in differing demographics, economic status, and experiences. Nearly 30% of 2004's voters under 30 were African American or Latino, and 6% identified themselves as gay or bisexual—double the proportions among voters over 30. Young voters are much less likely to be Protestants or gun owners, more likely to live in cities and to have suffered job losses, and more likely to see economic issues as a major concern. The youngest voters, aged 18 to 24, are even more forward thinking than 25- to 29-year-olds. These are encouraging developments, especially for California, where the 18- to 29-year-old population (70% of which is nonwhite) will grow by one million over the next decade while the archconservative, middle-aged Anglo population declines by half a million.

Progressive groups can promote youth ascendancy by jumping the baby boom ship—that is, by refusing to perpetuate the anachronistic politics of fear and repression that pander to aging, mostly white constituencies; by embracing a distinctly generational stance that publicizes the positive improvements among youth occurring in the context of a diversifying society; and by recognizing that concern for civil rights must expand to include youth and younger-generation rights as crucial new elements of the fight for racial and social justice. Youth participation in power is no longer a sappy slogan, but the most essential route to facilitating American society's adaptation to social change. As Mead affirmed, adults' rigid, fearful, backward-looking reaction to younger generations embodying vital social and racial transformation is not an inherent flaw in aging cognition, but a time-bound reaction against today's continuous social change, "a present for which none of us was prepared by our understanding of the past" (1970, p. 58).

American elders need not feel useless and menaced; our experiences and traditions offer much to inform discussions of managing change, and there is no evidence that younger generations manifest any ill intentions toward older ones à la *Wild in the Streets* or *Logan's Run*. History's wealthiest, most privileged grownups certainly possess the resources and capacities to reshape our institutions to welcome and channel change rather than futilely attempting to suppress it. The extreme irrationality of Americans' fear and repression toward the young and the shredding of America's social cohesion signal the urgency of fundamental shifts in our attitudes and institutions.

References

Adams, K. (2003). The effectiveness of juvenile curfews at crime prevention. *Annals of the American Academy of Political and Social Science, 587,* 136–159.

Amnesty International. (2004), Execution of child offenders since 1990. Retrieved February 8, 2005 from http://web.amnesty.org/pages/deathpenalty-children-stats-eng.

Bishop, D., Frazier, C., Lanza-Kaduce, L., & Winner, L. (1996). The transfer of juveniles to criminal court: Does it make a difference? *Crime & Delinquency, 42,* 171–191.

Brunsma, D. L., & Rockquemore, K. A. (1998). The effects of student uniforms on attendance, behavior problems, substance use, and academic achievement. *Journal of Education Research, 92,* 53–62.

California Criminal Justice Statistics Center. (1970–2003). *Crime and delinquency in California* [Annual reports]. With supplement, *California Criminal Justice Profiles, 1977–2003* [Annual reports]. Sacramento: California Department of Justice.

California Department of Corrections. (2004). Prisoners and Parolees 2002. Retrieved December 4, 2004 from http://www.corr.ca.gov/OffenderInfoServices/Reports/OffenderInformation.asp.

California Youth Authority. (1987–2003). *Length of institutional stay for first-time parole releases for the Department of Corrections and Youth Authority* [Annual reports]. Sacramento: California Youth Authority.

Center for Health Statistics. (1960–2003). *Vital Statistics of California* [Annual reports] and Birth Public Use File 2001–2002 [electronic data set]. Sacramento: California Department of Health Services.

Center for Health Statistics. (1965–2003). *Vital Statistics of California* [Annual reports] and Death Public Use File 2000–2002 [electronic data set]. Sacramento: California Department of Health Services.

Centers for Disease Control. (1990–2003). *HIV/AIDS Surveillance Report* [Annual reports]. Atlanta: Centers for Disease Control.

Dee T., & Evans, E. (2001). Behavioral policies and teen traffic safety. *AEA Papers and Proceedings, 91,* 91–96.

Demos, J. (1979). Images of the American family, then and now. In V. Tufte & B. Meyerhoff (Eds.), *The changing American family* (pp. 43–60). New Haven, CT: Yale University Press.

DeShaney v. Winnebago County Department of Social Services, 1989.

Drug Abuse Warning Network. (2002). *Annual Emergency Department Data, and Annual Medical Examiner Data* [Annual report]. Washington, DC: Substance Abuse and Mental Health Services Administration, U.S. Department of Health and Human Services.

Drug Abuse Warning Network. (2000). *Club Drugs: The DAWN Report.* Washington, DC: Substance Abuse and Mental Health Services Administration, U.S. Department of Health and Human Services.

Drug Abuse Warning Network. (2004). *Club Drugs: The DAWN Report.* Washington, DC: Substance Abuse and Mental Health Services Administration, U.S. Department of Health and Human Services.

Federal Bureau of Investigation. (1970–2003). *Uniform Crime Reports for the United States* [Annual reports]. Washington, DC: U.S. Department of Justice.

Goode, E. (2005). *Drugs in American society.* New York: McGraw-Hill.

Hayes-Bautista, D. E., Schinck, W. O., & Chapa, J. (1988). *The burden of support: Young Latinos in an aging society.* Stanford, CA: Stanford University Press.

Hazelwood School District v. Kuhlmeier, 1988.

Hodgson v. Minnesota, 1990.

Ingraham v. Wright, 1977.

Johnston L. D., O'Malley, P. M., Bachman, J. G., & Schulenberg, J. E. (1975–2004). *Monitoring the Future* [Annual reports]. Ann Arbor: University of Michigan Institute for Social Research.

Larner, M. B. (Ed.) (1999). When school is out [Special issue.] *The Future of Children, 9*(2). Retrieved October 15, 2004 from http://www.futureofchildren.org/pubs-info2825/pubs-info_show.htm?doc_id=71873.

Lopez, M. H., Kirby, E., & Sagoff, J. (2005). The youth vote, 2004. The Center for Information & Research on Civic Learning & Engagement. Retrieved June 12, 2005 from http://www.civicyouth.org/PopUps/FactSheets/FS_Youth_Voting_72-04.pdf.

Lundman, Richard (2001). *Prevention and control of juvenile delinquency* (3rd ed.). New York: Oxford University Press.

Males, M. (2000). Vernon, Connecticut's juvenile curfew: The circumstances of youths cited and effects on crime. *Criminal Justice Policy Review, 11,* 254–267.

Males, M., & Macallair, D. (1999). An analysis of curfew enforcement and juvenile crime in California. *Western Criminology Review, 1*(2). Retrieved June 1, 2002 from http://wcr.sonoma.edu/v1n2/males.html.

Mead, M. (1970). *Culture and commitment: A study of the generation gap.* New York: Doubleday.

Mead, M. (1978). *Culture and commitment: The new relationships between the generations in the 1970s* (Rev. ed.). New York: Columbia University Press.

National Association of Secretaries of State. (1999). Survey on youth attitudes: New millennium project. Washington, DC: National Association of Secretaries of State.

National Center for Health Statistics. (1960–2003). *Vital statistics of the United States, Part 1: Mortality* [Annual reports], and U.S. Mortality Detail File [electronic data set]. Washington, DC: U.S. Department of Health and Human Services.

National Institute on Drug Abuse. (1975–2003). *National household survey on drug abuse* [Annual reports]. Washington, DC: U.S. Department of Health and Human Services.

Office of Juvenile Justice and Delinquency Prevention. (2000). *Juvenile offenders and victims, 1999: National update.* Washington DC: U.S. Department of Justice.

Public Agenda. (2000). Kids these days '99: What Americans really think about the next generation. Retrieved August 1, 2001 from http://www.publicagenda.org/specials/kids/kids.htm.

Reynolds, M., Seydlitz, R., & Jenkins, P. (2000). Do juvenile curfew laws work? A time-series analysis of the New Orleans law. *Justice Quarterly, 17,* 205–220.

Rigotti, N. A., DiFranza, J. R., Chang, Y., Tisdale, T., Kemp, B., & Singer, D. E. (1997). The effect of enforcing tobacco-sales laws on adolescents' access to tobacco and smoking behavior. *New England Journal of Medicine, 337,* 1044–1051.

Rothstein, R. (2004). *Class and schools: Using social, economic, and educational reform to close the black-white achievement gap.* New York: Economic Policy Institute, Columbia University Teachers College.

Sanford v. Kentucky, 1989.

Substance Abuse and Mental Health Services Administration. (2003). *National survey on drug use and health.* Washington, DC: U.S. Department of Health and Human Services.

UNICEF. (2004). Convention on the Rights of a Child: Who Has Not Ratified, and Why Not? Retrieved XXXX from http://www.unicef.org/crc/faq.htm#009.

U.S. Bureau of the Census (2004). *Income, poverty, and health insurance coverage in the United States, 2003.* Washington, DC: U.S. Department of Commerce.

Wenglinsky, H., Coley, R., & Barton, P. (1998). *Order in the classroom: Violence, discipline, and student achievement.* Princeton, NJ: Educational Testing Service Policy Information Center.

Yamaguchi, R., Johnston, L., O'Malley, P. (2003). *Drug testing in schools: Policies, practices, and association with student drug use.* Ann Arbor, MI: Institute for Social Research, University of Michigan, 2003.

CHAPTER 18

Youth Participation for Educational Reform in Low-Income Communities of Color

BARRY CHECKOWAY AND KATIE RICHARDS-SCHUSTER

Young people should participate in educational reform, because their participation provides a legitimate source of information and ideas for making policy, planning, and program decisions. It prepares youth to exercise their political rights and to participate actively in a democratic society. It strengthens their social development, by increasing their individual involvement, organizational capacity, and ability to create community change (Hart, 1997; Johnson et al., 1998; Youniss & Yates, 1997).

Young people in low-income communities of color have a special stake in educational reform, because they experience disproportionate undereducation and have potential to create a new constituency for change—if their voices are heard. Yet although participation is increasing, most studies of youth in these areas focus on them as "troubled and troubling" rather than as competent citizens and community builders with a right to participate (Finn, 2001; Kurth-Schai, 1988).

Youth participation of this type challenges the usual role of young people as targets rather than as the agents of public policy, especially in low-income communities of color. Although young people are directly affected by educational policies, they are too often displaced and thus disengaged from the process. In contrast, our argument is that young people are willing and able to participate, and that if only a fraction of them were to increase their involvement, and if society were to view them as competent citizens, they might create a powerful new constituency for educational reform.

This chapter focuses on youth participation in educational reform in low-income communities of color. It draws on information from review of the limited literature and from Lifting New Voices (LNV), a national demonstration project to increase participation in organizational development and community change. This project provides perspectives on the ways in which young people frame the issues, the strategies and tactics they employ, and the lessons learned from empirically based practice. As such, it advances our argument and strengthens our belief that more knowledge of youth participation as a subject of study will contribute to its quality as a field of practice.

Perspectives on Participation

Youth participation in educational reform is a process of involving young people in the educational policy, planning, and program institutions and decisions that affect their lives. It includes youth-led, adult-led, or intergenerational initiatives by formal agencies to involve youth in their activities, or by young people to join together and take action of their own. It includes efforts that address both broad systemic issues related to discrimination and poverty and also everyday experiences with unsanitary toilets and inedible food (Cervone, 2002; Fletcher, 2003).

Youth participation in educational reform is increasing in communities nationwide. There are initiatives by people who mobilize around issues, organize action groups, and advocate their interests on school boards, city councils, and state legislatures (Colgan, 2002; Fletcher, 2003; Joiner, 2003). In California, they document inequities in school suspension policies and prevent cuts in youth services (Cervone, 2002). In Michigan, they conduct campaigns for new school curricula responsive to racial and ethnic diversity (Checkoway & Richards-Schuster, 2003). In Pennsylvania, they work to reduce class sizes and increase after-school programs, under the banner that "education is a right, not a privilege" (What Kids Can Do, 2001).

Youth participation of this type requires a shift in the view of the role of young people in society, which often ascribes authority to adult leaders who advocate for youth rather than enable them to organize on their behalf. However, these emergent initiatives represent both a view of "youth as citizens" (Dryfoos, 1990, 1998; Jarvis, Shear, & Hughes, 1997; Nixon, 1997) and also a "new politics" that is stirring, especially in communities that are traditionally underrepresented in voting and other mainstream forms of political participation (Hart, 1997; Johnson et al., 1998; Quinn, 1995). As the U.S. population changes and people of African, Asian, and Latino descent become the majority, these initiatives will have special significance for diverse democracy, and will benefit from more systematic study.

The present literature on community participation in educational reform is largely about adult initiatives. For example, there are studies of school officials to involve community members in order to build support for program implementation, or by interest groups to exercise influence in board elections, bond millages, and other school politics (Salisbury, 1980; Stone, Henig, Jones, & Pierannunzi, 2001). Other studies enable educators to formulate strategies for involving parents and families in community advisory councils and school-community partnerships that strengthen learning and improve schools (Epstein, 1995). Whatever their specific focus, such studies are largely about the participation of adults, rather than of young people (Gold, Simon, & Brown, 2002; Zachary & Olatoye, 2001).

Recent youth participation in educational reform has resulted in new studies of these phenomena. For example, Cervone (2002) documents youth efforts to "take democracy in hand" and influence educational change in the San Francisco Bay Area; Chow, Olsen, Lizardo, and Dowell (2001) document efforts in other California communities; and Mediratta and Fruchter (2001, 2002) map efforts in Baltimore, Chicago, Los Angeles, the Mississippi Delta, New York City, Philadelphia, San Francisco, and Washington, D.C.

In addition, the Cross City School Campaign for Urban School Reform, a national network of urban school reform leaders, reports efforts to involve youth on state boards in Maryland, California, and Vermont, and identifies community groups working on education organizing (Gold et al., 2002); Endo (2002) tallies hundreds of youth organizing efforts with approximately 75% focusing on education-related issues; and the Forum for Youth Investment (2004) and Yu (2003) compile bibliographies with secondary literature and case studies of youth and community.

Youth participation in educational reform can be expected to increase in the future. Private foundations provide program funding, and national organizations strengthen local capacity (Funders' Collaborative on Youth Organizing & Edward W. Hazen Foundation, 2003; McGillicuddy, 1997). What Kids Can Do provides a forum for youth-led research and youth organizing (Cervone, 2002); the Applied Research Center prepares youth to track institutional racism and issue racial justice report cards (Gordon, Della Piana, & Keleher, 2000).

We expect that future studies of youth participation in educational reform will assess activities and outcomes similar to other participation studies. For example, we expect studies that show that such participation provides a legitimate source of information and ideas for making policy, planning, and program decisions, for young people have everyday experiences that position them to "provide a different lens" (Noguera, 2003, p. 135).

We also expect studies that show that youth participation in educational reform prepares young people for active participation in a democratic society; strengthens their social development; and increases their individual involvement, organizational capacity, and ability to create community change. There has been no systematic study of youth participation at these multiple levels, but there is reason to expect that subsequent studies will substantiate its effects on such measures as personal confidence, social connectedness, civic competencies, and leadership development. At present, however, the benefits are not established by systematic research (Checkoway & Richards-Schuster, 2003).

We argue that more knowledge of youth participation as a subject of study will contribute to its quality as a field of practice, and draw upon Lifting New Voices as a national project addressing these phenomena.

Lifting New Voices

Lifting New Voices (LNV) was a national demonstration project designed to increase the participation of young people 15 to 21 years old in organizational development and community change. Coordinated by the Center for Community Change with funding from the W. K. Kellogg Foundation and the Ford Foundation, the project aimed to demonstrate what happens when community-based organizations try to enable young people to organize themselves, plan programs, and become more central to planning and decision-making (Checkoway & Richards-Schuster, 2003; Checkoway, Richards-Schuster, Abdullah, Aragon, Facio, Figueroa, et al., 2003).

Six community-based organizations were selected for participation in the project: Citizens for Community Improvement of Des Moines, Iowa; Direct Action for Rights and Equality of Providence, Rhode Island; People United for a Better Oakland (PUEBLO) of Oakland, California; Southern Echo of Jackson, Mississippi; the Southwest Organizing Project (SWOP) of Albuquerque, New Mexico; and Youth Force in the South Bronx, New York. Each organization formulated a plan, hired a youth organizer, and established a structure for implementation.

As expressions of participation, young people took initiative on numerous issues including their right to freely assemble in public places, resident control over public housing, gentrification in low-income neighborhoods, and portrayal of youth in the media. They employed several strategies to mobilize protest demonstrations, organize action groups, participate in public agency proceedings, and develop community-based services responsive to youth (Checkoway & Richards-Schuster, 2003).

LNV was evaluated by a participatory process that involved youth and adults in documenting their activities, assessing their outcomes, and using the information for improving their effectiveness. Each organization had a community-based evaluator who worked with an evaluation committee of youth and adults to facilitate the process. National evaluators analyzed activities across sites and assessed outcomes in terms of overall activities (Checkoway & Richards-Schuster, 2003).

Evaluators employed various methods for gathering information. They used methods that are standard among adults, such as observations, interviews, focus groups, and surveys. They also used methods deemed more age appropriate, such as involving youth in skits and sociodrama about neighborhood problems, compiling writings and photographs in a project scrapbook, and interviewing parents about the effects of the project on their children. These methods were chosen by and for young people.

Organizing around Educational Reform

School and school conditions were the most common issues around which LNV groups organized. This was not surprising, because schools are places where young people spend disproportionate time and too often experience inadequate services and unjust conditions. Young people used their experience and status as students to mobilize other youth and identify other issues for their organizing.

Academic and Curricular Reform

Young people organized around academic and curricular issues, such as racial tracking and culturally insensitive curricula. For example, young people in Oakland and Albuquerque organized against racial tracking in their schools. Working with the Applied Research Center's Racial Justice Report Card project, they analyzed school transcripts to determine the impacts of race on school tracking and graduation rates (Gordon & Della Piana, 1999). They held meetings with community leaders and school officials, demonstrated the prevalence of racial inequities, and used the findings for community organizing.

As young people became more conscious of these issues, they challenged teachers and administrators to change curricula and also devised curricula of their own. In the South Bronx, they criticized the lack of cultural content, created their own curriculum on Black and Latino social movements, and taught this curriculum in civics classes. In Mississippi, they sought to increase Black studies in the curriculum and, when school officials refused, they established their own class with cultural content about people of African descent.

In Providence, young people were frustrated with the lack of cultural curricula content and campaigned to change the high school curriculum. Twenty of them spent a year discussing what they wanted to learn, formulated action plans, organized other youth and parents, and testified at school board meetings. They worked with a curriculum specialist to design the program, which they presented to school administrators and board members, who supported their proposal and approved five new multicultural course electives which were implemented in the next school year.

School Conditions and Facilities

Young people organized around inadequate school conditions and institutional facilities. In Providence, for example, they held meetings with school officials about outdated books, filthy bathrooms without running water and toilet paper, and cafeteria food that was undercooked, unhealthy, and prepared in unsanitary kitchens. As a result, the superintendent created procedures for filing complaints and appointed students to food testing teams.

In Mississippi, young people confronted local officials about unsafe environmental conditions. They protested the location of schools near illegal hazardous waste sites in one area, and near cotton plantations where the spraying of chemical poisons caused dangerous fumes in another. Because of this, officials ordered waste site cleanups and a moratorium on aerial spraying near the schools.

In Iowa, young people organized a resident patrol to protect school grounds against crime and drug trafficking in a nearby neighborhood. They recruited parents and other adult volunteers for the patrol, monitored the streets, and assisted the students in safely getting to and from school. As a result, residents joined together in solidarity, police were more attentive, drug dealing decreased, and the youth felt safer.

School Policies and Practices

Young people protested school policies and practices that they considered unjust, and usually framed these in terms of discrimination against communities of color. In Des Moines, for example, they protested an attendance policy that expelled students with more than six unexcused absences in a year. They argued that the policy was not clearly communicated to those for whom English was not a native language, and that it discriminated against low-income families who lacked access to private or public transportation. They made specific recommendations to school officials, who accepted their proposals, made district policy changes, and provided special support to students whose absences were due to economic circumstances.

In Providence, young people protested a transportation policy under which students were ineligible for free transportation if they lived within three miles of school. They researched the issue and concluded that the policy was unfair to those who lacked private transportation and were necessarily forced to walk to school. They communicated with school administrators and then organized a protest demonstration in which students and parents marched 2.7 miles which represented the distance that many low-income students were required to walk daily.

In Albuquerque, young people worked with students and parents in a nearby town to change a dress code that was used to suspend and expel youth of color. They facilitated local meetings, conducted community surveys, organized a large rally, and asked school board members to change the policy. After their request was denied, young people held a sit-in at the superintendent's office to demand a meeting, and this too was denied.

The Criminalization of Young People

Young people organized around the increasing criminalization of youth through policies they viewed as school board attempts to stigmatize low-income youth of color and assure white middle-class residents that they were "getting tough on violence."

In Mississippi, for example, youth and adults joined a Schoolhouse 2 Jailhouse campaign that demonstrated the relationship between schools and prisons. They were aware that school dropouts, suspensions, and expulsions were increasing while more private prisons were under construction. They argued that school systems lacked adequate programs to keep students of color in the schools, and that the construction of new prisons took youth into the criminal justice system.

In Oakland, young people challenged a proposal by Mayor Jerry Brown to create a Military Charter School, which was viewed as a racist policy designed to remove youth of color from the public schools. Young people organized large rallies, conducted a petition drive against the proposal, and mobilized youth and adults around the issue. The campaign culminated when more than 100 youth and adults spoke out against the charter school at a meeting of the school board, whose members then rejected the charter school proposal. Although the mayor gained support for the proposal at the state level, youth claimed victory for challenging the mayor and sensitizing the community about the racist nature of the proposal (Aragon, 2001).

Young people in several communities protested policies of placing police in the schools, which they interpreted as both dangerous and racist. In Providence, for example, youth learned that school officials had allocated a large sum for police presence without any incidents to warrant them. They confronted the principal and demanded that the police be removed, but he refused to take action. They recruited more youth to the issue, collected petitions demanding the removal, and presented these to the principal, who again refused to take action. Young people rallied outside the building during school board budget discussions, and testified on the issue in public meetings. When school board members cut funds for police from the budget, they claimed victory for their campaign.

In the South Bronx, young people created the Cops Outta Schools campaign to protest police placement in the schools. When school board members transferred school security to the police department and proposed to arm the police and create a miniature police station in the local high school, students protested. They conducted surveys that documented youth experiences with police in the schools, held meetings with the chancellor, and demanded the removal of the police. As an organizer explained,

"This is just the beginning. Placing police in our schools is just a step toward our preparation as inmates to fill the cells. The more our schools look and act like prisons, the more prepared we will be for a life behind bars." (Checkoway et al., 2003)

Strategies and Tactics

Organizing around schools differed from one area to another, but generally included strategies not normally associated with young people. However, these youth articulated goals that emphasized class, race, discrimination, and oppression as forces in their lives. They identified issues that reached out to community constituencies who shared their goals, and employed various tactics or planned activities in ongoing campaigns. These included direct-action tactics, as follows.

Protest and Demonstrations

Some young people used high visibility forms of protest through public demonstrations. In the Oakland military charter school campaign, for example, they protested the mayor's proposal by marching outside the school board meeting, waiving signs and cardboard cutouts of the mayor's head in front of the television cameras, and chanting "Students, not soldiers!" In the campaign for freedom of assembly in Albuquerque, they held large-scale rallies, marched through the mall passing out brown imitation dollar bills to reflect the revenue generated by youth of color, and pressured store owners to make changes in the mall policy.

Civil Disobedience and Authority Challenges

Young people used forms of civil disobedience and noncooperation to challenge authority and amplify the issues, such as when Mississippi students organized a walkout to protest an unfair corporal disciplinary policy in one school, and in another questioned school policies on tardiness and suspension, organized fellow students to be late for school, and required the whole school to receive suspension. Other young people used nonviolent intervention through sit-ins and other challenges to authority, such as when Albuquerque youth organized a sit-in in the school superintendent's office until he agreed to a meeting to discuss the dress code.

Research and Evaluation

Young people conducted research and evaluation as part of their organizing for change. In response to the rising rates of school suspensions and expulsions, for example, PUEBLO youth organized a multiracial group of researchers, interviewed students who had been suspended, and conducted surveys in schools and the community. They concluded that the schools used suspension too often, that this compromised student learning, and that it criminalized male students of color and violated their due process rights. They prepared a report, produced a documentary, educated the community, and recommended steps for action on the issues.

Accountability Sessions

Other young people held accountability sessions with public officials as a tactic for organizing around issues. In the South Bronx, for example, they forced a meeting with the New York City chancellor of public education and other top administrators to protest the policy to place police and police mini-precincts in the schools. In Providence, they held sessions with the superintendent to protest school conditions and exact a commitment for change; with the deputy superintendent to demand multicultural curricular reform and a seat on the curriculum committee; and with food contractors to protest the quality of food served through the lunch program.

Public Proceedings

Youth also used public hearings and other public proceedings as a vehicle for organizing. In Oakland, for example, they organized around a series of school board hearings on the charter school proposal. At the preliminary hearing, they recruited youth groups to attend the proceeding and speak against the proposal. At the meeting at which board members would vote, they recruited youth and adult allies to demonstrate outside the building, more than 200 people to attend the meeting itself, and a long line of young people to speak against the proposal for more than five hours, after which board members voted against it (Aragon, 2001).

Action Coalitions

Other young people formed action coalitions in which groups joined together for a common cause. In these coalitions, young people built collective agency and developed new forms of social networking and civic capital. For example, Oakland youth brought together a number of other youth, adult, parent, and teacher groups in their campaign against the charter school. Mississippi youth and adults built a strong working group that provides education and training around school reform and has led successful campaigns to fight legislative education policy at the local and state levels.

South Bronx young people formed coalitions with organizational allies, contacted elected officials and political leaders, and tried to influence the outcomes of policy decisions. For example, they joined a coalition of 120 community organizations to advocate for public policies that address education and other issues through joint marches, rallies, letter-writing campaigns, and advocacy days at the city hall. They also worked with groups to engage young people and press public policy demands on educational reform issues in the state legislature (Checkoway et al., 2003).

Educational Programs of Their Own

As part of Lifting New Voices, young people exercised their rights to participate in educational reform, and also developed education and training programs of their own. For example, Southern Echo conducted residential training programs preparing young people with skills for bringing residents together around educational battlegrounds and organizing the community to stop the use of public education in suppressing the African-American community.

Also, SWOP conducted intensive training with cultural content on social movements against oppression and practical skills in community organizing, including internships in which they gained hands-on experience in youth-led campaigns. In a campaign against racist dress codes in a school district, interns recruited youth and adults, conducted community meetings, and organized rallies at the school board.

Youth Force conducted in-house training for youth leaders to develop political theories and practical skills, and a summer "boot camp" to train new community organizers for work in the schools and community. They established a "street university" as an area-wide educational program with a broad range of public workshops featuring content on organizational development and community change for young people. They also conducted research to develop knowledge for their organizing (Figueroa, Infante, & Serna, 2000; Scott, Leo, Ledesma, Diaz, & Jamesh, 1996).

Despite differences in their approaches, these efforts shared some similarities. They all provided political education about diverse democracy as a concept, and curricular content about specific population groups and their struggles to overcome oppression. They employed experiential learning and emphasized open talk of their social and cultural identities and class and race as forces in the community. They also provided practical skills in community organizing that are unavailable in the public schools, and information and ideas about policy issues that affect young people's everyday experiences, such as racial segregation and institutional inequalities, high-stakes testing, police presence, school violence, dress codes, disciplinary policies, and "schoolhouse to jailhouse."

These efforts enabled young people to develop their political efficacy and civic capacity for challenging educational policies and proposing reforms. In this way, organizing around schools and school reforms enabled them to advance a "new civics" for a "new politics" that will promote education for diverse democracy in the years ahead.

Toward a New Politics of Educational Reform

Young people are increasing their participation in educational reform in low-income communities of color, and their initiatives can be expected to increase in the years ahead. Because schools are where they spend a disproportionate amount of time and are especially problematic in economically disinvested areas, young people's issues grow from their everyday experiences, such as outdated books, inadequate facilities, and institutional policies that discriminate against their racial or ethnic groups.

When young people draw upon their own experience as students, they have potential to provide new information and ideas for educational reform. Endo (2002) describes this as an ability of youth to raise issues in school governance that might not have otherwise been on the radar of adults. In so doing, young people provide a legitimate source of information for making better decisions in the institutions that affect their lives.

Youth participation in educational reform enables young people to develop substantive knowledge, practical skills, and social attitudes conducive for democracy. At a time when there is concern about the civic disengagement of young people, these initiatives provide a vehicle for them to increase their public participation and civic engagement.

As such, youth participation provides what Giroux (2003, p. 25) describes as "a critical democratic education that encourages dialogue, critique, dissent, and social justice." In this way, it may enable young people to advance a "new civics" for a "new politics" that promotes education for diverse democracy.

Young people in these communities are ideally positioned for influencing public policy for future reform. These youth are usually portrayed as "troubled and troubling" rather than as competent citizens and community builders, and their positive participation can change their place in society and the policies that affect their lives. In educational reform, their participation may "pave the way for more effective school change" (Ginwright, 2004, p. 131).

These young people experience disproportionate undereducation, and have potential to create a new collective constituency for policy change. Too many policy makers have been conditioned to believe that these youth do not want to learn, but instead require punitive policies or remedial services. Yet, if young people started demanding what policy makers believe they do not want, and if this reengaged parents, teachers, and community leaders, it might cause policy makers to address youth issues.

Indeed, the failure of present policies to address issues of young people in low-income communities of color can be conceived as both cause and consequence of their nonparticipation in the formulation of the decisions that affect their lives. As these youth increase their participation, however, policies and the structures to support their participation can be expected to change.

More research is needed to address unanswered questions that arise with increasing initiatives. What are the major models and methods of participation? What are the short- and long-term impacts at the individual, organizational, and community levels? What are the factors that facilitate and limit effective practice? What types of knowledge and skills are needed by youth participants and adult allies? What are some strategies for sustaining the field? What kinds of support will be needed from private institutions and public agencies, and what are some ideas for making this happen? These are not the only questions arising, but they are among the important ones.

At present, however, youth participation in educational reform remains relatively undeveloped as a field of practice and subject of study. There are increasing initiatives, and increasing accounts of them, but they are few in number, and more work is needed. If the present chapter contributes to this, then its purpose will be served.

References

Aragon, M. (2001). *A long time coming: Oakland's victory over Jerry.* Oakland: People United for a Better Oakland.

Cervone, B. (2002). *Taking democracy in hand: Youth action for educational change in the San Francisco Bay Area.* Providence, RI: What Kids Can Do.

Checkoway, B. (1998). Involving young people in neighborhood development. *Children and Youth Services Review, 20,* 765–795.

Checkoway, B., & Richards-Schuster, K. (2001). Lifting new voices for socially just communities. *Community Youth Development, 2,* 32–37.

Checkoway, B., & Richards-Schuster, K. (2003). *Final evaluation of Lifting New Voices.* Ann Arbor: University of Michigan School of Social Work.

Checkoway, B., Richards-Schuster, K., Abdullah, S., Aragon, M., Facio, E., Figueroa, L., et al., (2003). Young people as competent citizens. *Community Development Journal, 38,* 298–309.

Chow, M., Olsen, L., Lizardo, R., & Dowell, C. (2001). *School reform organizing in the San Francisco Bay Area and Los Angeles, California.* Oakland: California Tomorrow.

Cook-Sather, A. (2002). Authorizing students perspectives: Toward trust, dialogue, and change in education. *Educational Researcher, 31,* 3–14.

Cushman, K. (2003). *Fire in the bathrooms: Advice for teachers from high school students.* New York: New Press.

Delgardo-Gaitan, C., & Treueba, E. (2001). *The power of the community: Mobilizing for family and schooling.* Lanham, MD: Rowman and Littlefield.

Dryfoos, J. (1990). *Adolescents at risk: Prevalence and prevention.* New York: Oxford University Press.

Dryfoos, J. (1998). *Safe passage: Making it through adolescence in a risky society.* New York: Oxford University Press.

Edwards, D., Johnson, N., and McGillicuddy, K. (2003). *An emerging model for working with youth: Community organizing + youth development = youth organizing.* New York: Funders' Collaborative on Youth Organizing.

Endo, T. (2002). *Youth engagement in community-driven school reform.* Oakland, CA: Social Policy Research Associates.

Epstein, J. (1995). School/family/community partnerships. *Phi Delta Kappan, 76,* 701.

Figueroa, L., Infante, P., & Serna, P., (2000). *In between the lines: How the New York Times frames youth.* New York: New York City Youth Media Watch.

Finn, J., & Checkoway, B. (1998). Young people as competent community builders: A challenge to social work. *Social Work, 43,* 335–345.

Finn, J. (2001). Text and turbulence: Representing adolescence as pathology in the human services. *Childhood, 8,* 167–192.

Fletcher, A. (2003). *Meaningful student involvement.* Olympia, WA: The Freechild Project.

Forum for Youth Investment. (2004). Youth action for educational change: A resource guide. Washington, D.C.: The Forum for Youth Investment, Impact Strategies, Inc.

Freudenberg, N., Roberts, L., Richie, B., Taylor, R., McGillicuddy, K., & Greene, M. (1999). Coming up in the boogie down: The role of violence in the lives of adolescents in the South Bronx. *Health Education and Behavior, 26,* 782–799.

Funders' Collaborative on Youth Organizing & Edward W. Hazen Foundation. (2003, Fall). Grantmakers for children, youth, and families. *Insight, 5*(1), 1–16.

Ginwright, S. (2003). *Youth organizing: Expanding possibilities for youth development.* New York: Funders' Collaborative on Youth Organizing.

Ginwright, S. (2004). *Black in school: Afrocentric reform, urban youth, and the promise of hip hop culture.* New York: Teachers College Press.

Giroux, H. (2003). *The abandoned generation: Democracy beyond the culture of fear.* New York: Palgrave-Macmillan.

Gold, E., Simon, E., & Brown, C. (2002). *Strong neighborhoods, strong schools: Successful community organizing for school reform.* Chicago: Cross City Campaign for Urban School Reform.

Gordon, R., Della Piana, L., & Keleher, T. (2000). *Making the grade: A racial justice report card.* Oakland, CA: Applied Research Center.

Gordon, R., & Della Piana, L. (1999). *No exit: Tracking students of color in the United States.* Oakland, CA: Applied Research Center.

Hart, R. (1997). *Children's participation: The theory and practice of involving young citizens in community development and environmental care.* London: Earthscan.

HoSang, D. (2003). *Youth and community organizing today.* New York: Funders' Collaborative on Youth Organizing.

Jarvis, S., Shear, L., & Hughes, D. (1997). Community youth development: Learning the new story. *Child Welfare, 76,* 719–741.

Johnson, V., Ivan-Smith, E., Gordon, G., Pridmore, P., & Scott, P. (1998). *Stepping forward: Children and young people's participation in the development process.* London: Intermediate Technology Publications.

Joiner, L. (2003). The student's voice. *American School Board Journal, 190.* Retrieved July 29, 2004 from http://www.asbj.com/2003/01/0103Coverstory.html, Vol. 1.

Kohn, A. (1993). Choices for children: Why and how to let the students decide. *Phi Delta Kappan,* September. Retrieved July 29, 2004 from http://www.alfiekohn.org/teaching/cfe.html, *75*(1), 8–20.

Kozol, J. (2000). *Ordinary insurrections: Children in the years of hope.* New York: Crown.

Kurth-Schai, R. (1988). The role of youth in society: A reconceptualization. *Educational Forum, 53,* 113–132.

Martinez, E. (n.d.). Community organizing: The new youth movement in California. Retrieved May 23, 2001, from http://www.schoolsnotjails.co/article.

Mediratta, K., & Fruchter, N. (2001). *Mapping the field of organizing for school improvement.* New York: Institute for Education and Social Policy.

Mediratta, K., & Fructer, N. (2002). *Organizing for school reform: How communities are finding their voices and reclaiming their public schools.* New York: Institute for Education and Social Policy.

McGillicuddy, K. (1997). *Funding youth organizing: Strategies for building power and youth leadership.* New York: Funders' Collaborative on Youth Organizing.

Nixon, R. (1997). What is positive youth development? *Child Welfare, 76,* 5.

Noguera, P. (2003). *City schools and the American dream: Reclaiming the promise of public education.* New York: Teachers College Press.

Salisbury, R. (1980). *Citizen participation in the public schools.* Lexington, KY: Lexington.

Scott, N., Leo, K., Ledesma, G., Diaz, H., & Jamesh, R. (1996). *Jail Logic.* New York: Youth Force.

Shirley, D. (1997). *Community organizing for urban school reform.* Austin: University of Texas Press.

Stone, C., Henig, J., Jones, B., & Pierannunzi, C. (2001). *Building civic capacity: The politics of reforming urban schools.* Lawrence: University Press of Kansas.

Welsh, M. (2001). *CCI resident patrol case study.* Ann Arbor: Lifting New Voices/University of Michigan School of Social Work.

What Kids Can Do. (2001). More than service: Philadelphia students join a union to improve their schools. *Making Youth Known, 1,* 4.

Youniss, J., & Yates, M. (1997). *Community service and social responsibility in youth.* Chicago: University of Chicago Press.

Youth United for Change. (n.d.). Youth platform: education is a right, not a privilege! Retrieved December 5, 2001 from http://www.epopleaders.org/yucplat1.html.

Yu, H. C. (2003). *An annotated bibliography on youth organizing.* New York: Funders' Collaborative on Youth Organizing.

Zachary, E., & Olatoye, S. (2001). *Community organizing for school improvement in the South Bronx.* New York: Institute for Education and Social Policy.

Conclusion
Youth Agency, Resistance, and Civic Activism: The Public Commitment to Social Justice

PEDRO NOGUERA AND CHIARA M. CANNELLA

The child should be fully prepared to live an individual life in society and brought up in the spirit of ... peace, dignity, tolerance, freedom, equality and solidarity.

—UNICEF, Convention on the Rights of the Child

Each of the chapters in this book shows in different ways that despite a relative lack of power and despite the ways in which young people are often marginalized and maligned, youth—even those who are poor and disadvantaged—have the potential to take action upon the forces that oppress, constrain, and limit their lives. The authors remind us that this is possible even for young people deemed to be "at risk," who have low skills, who have been written off as unemployable and uneducable. Despite the odds against them, under the right circumstances they have the ability to critique the situations that restrict their lives, to articulate that critique in verbal, written, and artistic form, and to move beyond critique by taking action to assert and affirm their interests as individuals and as members of families and communities. This volume documents the ways that youth are redefining what constitutes civic engagement, as they create and assume powerful roles as individuals and as members of families and communities. Given that young people in urban areas are too often unfairly characterized as undisciplined and unmotivated—or even worse, as delinquent, menacing and insolent—this may come as a revelation to many readers.

To the extent that we are able to see beyond the stereotypes and distortions that are perpetrated through the one-dimensional portraits of urban youth frequently found in the media, then perhaps such a revelation may also elicit a different set of perspectives on how to relate and respond to youth when they act. Rather than responding to young people's attempts to be heard and taken seriously with fear, contempt, or condescension, more adults, particularly those with power and authority, may find it possible to see in youth agency the kernels of our future democracy. And this is not the type of democracy that is limited to voting on designated dates, but the kind of democratic practice that encourages social awareness, debate and active participation in civic life.

Characterizations of Youth Agency

Although the ability of young people to engage in political or social action has been recognized by historians for generations—think of the garment industry strikes led by teenage girls in the 18th century in Lynn, Massachusetts (Zinn, 1980), or the courageous SNCC (Student Non-Violent Organizing Committee) organizers who dared to register voters or stage sit-ins at lunch counters in the face of overwhelming racial violence (Carson, 1981)—social scientists have taken a bit longer to recognize the power and potential of youth agency. More often than not, social scientists have characterized young people as passive participants in larger events, as spectators, ground troops, and victims, but rarely as actors with the ability to influence the course of events (Smelser, 1968). Even in the field of education, where young people are ostensibly central players in the learning process, much of the scholarship has characterized their role as secondary to that of the adults who teach, counsel, and administer.

Such portrayals came to a decisive end with Paul Willis's publication of *Learning to Labor* (1981). His vivid analysis and descriptions of the "lads"—those rambunctious and troublesome youngsters who rejected the rewards schools offered in exchange for the hard work of industrial labor—helped a generation of scholars to rethink their assumptions about the nature of youth agency. To Willis, the lads of Hammertown challenged authority, harassed their peers, and openly embraced their destiny as workers in dead-end factory jobs not because they couldn't succeed in the classroom but because they blatantly refused to try. Willis describes their oppositional stances and behavior as a form of resistance, and in so doing he opens up a whole new way of thinking about how young people participate in society and the process of social and cultural reproduction.

However, as important as Willis's insights into the behavior of the lads are, his sweeping characterization of their antics—which are often racist, sexist, and violent—leave readers with the impression that *all forms of oppositional behavior could be regarded as a form of resistance.* Willis does not make a distinction between defiance against an authority and forms of resistance that are consciously linked to social and community change. For educators and youth workers who work closely with young people, such a characterization seems off. If every act of defiance—from cutting class, to challenging adult authority, to committing acts of violence against other youth—constituted a form of resistance, resistance would become little more than an attempt to glorify anti-social and self-destructive behavior. Willis recognizes that the lads' behavior constituted a form of "self-damnation," but he nonetheless regards their self-destructive tendencies as a form of resistance. In so doing, he fails to draw any distinction between oppositional acts and behaviors such as those Henry Giroux has described as conscious forms of critical resistance (Giroux, 1996). Unlike Willis, Giroux argues that youth resistance is distinguished from delinquency and oppositional behavior because it is *behavior that is rooted in a deliberate critique of one's circumstances.* Thus Giroux distinguishes between oppositional resistance (deviant behavior) and strategic resistance (conscious action to achieve a common good).

The youth described in many of the chapters in the present volume not only have the ability to critique the conditions that limit and constrain their lives, but many also illustrate how strategic resistance is incorporated into their daily lives, through reciting poetry (Jocson, chapter 8), organizing (Flores-González, Rodríguez, & Rodríguez-Muñiz, chapter 10) and researching community problems through participatory action research (Duncan-Andrade, chapter 9; Morrell, chapter 7). Strategic resistance among youth is manifest in a variety of ways because it is a form of agency that emerges from what Brazilian educator Paulo Freire conceptualized as "critical consciousness": action + reflection = praxis (Freire, 2002, p. 38). Common throughout all of the demonstrations of critical consciousness illustrated in this volume is the process by which young people reflect and act to transform the communities in which they live.

In order to know whether an act of defiance such as a walkout (Males, chapter 17, this volume), or for that matter even an act of apparent conformity such as forming a study group (Akom, 2003) constitute a form of resistance, one would need to understand the subjective motivation of the actors involved. As obvious as this might seem, this requires that researchers actually solicit the opinions and perspectives of young people and incorporate them into their findings. Why are students dropping out of school, underachieving in math and science, fighting with youth from other ethnic groups, or having babies while they are teenagers? Any serious researcher who seeks to understand the answers to such questions must recognize that young people constantly make decisions and choices; one goal of research must be to learn under what conditions these choices are made. They must also realize that like most human beings there is typically some underlying logic to youth behavior, and that, like adults, young people are also capable of coming up with rationalizations for their mistakes and errors in judgment. Comprehending the nature of their logic and rationalizations are a critical aspect of any research that seeks to effect more just and effective youth policy.

Some forms of delinquency and defiance may be a form of agency but may not be strategic resistance—the forms of conscious resistance to which Giroux refers. In fact, some of the most disruptive behaviors exhibited by young people may be little more than a form of conformity (Pattillo-McCoy, 1999). There are young people who passively embrace societal norms and stereotypes and allow their identities, tastes, desires, and aspirations to be defined by the media and the marketplace. Such youth are more likely to allow their social identities related to race and class define and determine their options and personal goals. This is why acts of defiance by angry, militant, and even violent youth may not necessarily be regarded as a form of resistance. An outsider may attempt to interpret their behaviors as a form of resistance, but if the actors themselves do not regard their behavior as such it would be a mistake to characterize it that way.

Like the lads of Willis's Hammertown, who saw their masculinity as being enacted in the lives they hoped to lead getting drunk in the pubs and toiling on the factory floor, young people who passively accept the idea that they can be nothing more than thugs and hoodlums, or for that matter fast-food workers or college students, may not be resisting anything at all. They may simply be following the "script" (Lopez & Stack, 2001), or a "code" (Anderson, 1999) for individuals from a particular social location. Giroux's point that not all agency can be regarded as a form of resistance is a crucial consideration in the study of youth resistance and is vital to understanding the potential of young people to become conscious political actors (Giroux, 1994).

Why should we care about youth agency and attempt to distinguish among forms of resistance? From an even more cynical standpoint one might ask whether or not it really matters that young people have the capacity to engage in forms of resistance, given the unlikelihood that their activism on either an individual or collective level is going to seriously alter the fundamental alignment of power in the United States or elsewhere. Is our preoccupation with youth agency merely another academic fetish, or is there something "real" and more consequential about this issue?

If one considers the fact that many social movements in the United States and elsewhere have relied heavily upon strategic resistance among young people, the answer to those questions becomes obvious. Particularly in recent times, antiwar movements (Cohen, 1993); immigrant rights movements; challenges to police brutality and the prison industrial complex (Davis, 1996); environmental movements; lesbian, gay, bisexual, transgender and queer/questioning movements; and antiracism movements have all relied heavily on the commitments of youth activists. This has been true in the United States as well as in other countries. Just as the youth of Soweto were able to revive the antiapartheid struggle through their uprising against the racist educational policies of the apartheid regime in 1976, so too may it be young people from marginalized and disenfranchised communities in the United States who step forward to generate a social movement that begins to move the country in a more progressive and humane direction.

The Role of Public Policy in Supporting Youth Activism and Strategic Resistance

Of course, it would be a mistake to just sit back and wait for young people to figure out how to move from oppositional resistance and defiance to strategic resistance and movements for social change. Even if we tone down our expectations, it may also be unlikely that on their own young people will be able to reverse some of the political trends that have contributed to what Valerie Polakow (2000) describes as an "assault on America's youth." During conservative times such as these, youth activism may not be sufficient to advance the rights and interests of disadvantaged youth and the communities they live in. With such a formidable array of obstacles that limit and constrain them—punitive criminal justice policies, narrowly framed accountability measures with no serious effort to improve the quality of schools, dim prospects for employment after graduation, to name just a few—it would be remarkable if young people could find a way to organize for change on their own.

Fortunately, in many communities there are veteran activists who serve as formal and informal mentors, counselors, and supporters of youth organizers. There are also nonprofit organizations, churches, and universities that are providing resources and support to young people so that they in turn are able to play a more active role in influencing policy decisions that affect them and the communities where they live. Organizations such Youth United to Change Los Angeles, Brothers and Sisters United in New York, and Chicano Moratorium in Oakland, California, have been able to facilitate and sustain the involvement of young people in the important policy debates. Yet, as important as their work may be, none of these organizations would be effective were it not for the support of strategic allies.

In addition to allies, youth organizers would also benefit from policies at the local level as well as organizational practices that are designed to foster and support strategic resistance among marginalized youth. The chapters in this volume document the ways that public and private institutions can provide the resources youth need to direct their strategic resistance toward community and social change activities. But too often, rather than encouraging conscious resistance among youth, the mechanisms of policy serve to fortify marginalization and exacerbate disadvantage. Even among policy makers who think of themselves as youth advocates, and who express a willingness to ensure that all youth have access to equal opportunities in education, employment, and access to public services, the ways in which youth are actually treated too often reinforces their position on the bottom rung of the social hierarchy (Fine, Burns, Payne, & Torre, 2004; Valenzuela, 1999).

This is not because we do not know how to improve educational achievement and social equity among all American children. A vast body of research demonstrates the extent to which policy decisions typically do not reflect what we know about increasing social capital, educational opportunity and academic achievement among disenfranchised populations (Valenzuela, 1999).

This is because even those who express support for youth often treat them in a manner that is patronizing and condescending as if those who are older know best and therefore should lead the way. It also occurs because many adults feel threatened by youth resistance either because they cannot control or contain it, or simply because they fear that they may become targets of the anger and energy of misdirected youth. In practice, this results in the punitive and coercive policies this project has sought to address.

Furthermore, efforts to improve academic achievement and civic engagement are too often based upon deficit-based orientations toward youth and their families. That is, policy initiatives begin with the assumption that young people are culturally deprived, morally deficient, and come from families that do not care about them. When this is the starting point for a policy, those who implement it will be more likely to seek to bring about changes in individual behavior and attitudes than in the institutional conditions that perpetuate disadvantage (Briggs, 2002; Rodman, 1977; Valencia, 1997).

Despite such policies, there are a number of lessons about youth activism we can take from the chapters in this volume. Taken seriously, these lessons can stifle the tide of anti-youth consciousness and corresponding coercive youth policy. While several of the chapters herein focus on the ways in which policy practices undermine young people's efforts to engage in the democratic process (see, for example, Flores-González, Rodríguez, & Rodríguez-Muñiz; HoSang, chapter 1; Kwon, chapter 12; Lewis-Charp, Yu, & Soukamneuth, chapter 2) and erode their faith in "the system" we are also left with examples of how to move young people from oppositional resistance and deviance to strategic resistance through which they consciously disrupt systems and institutions that sustain inequality in their lives.

These chapters detail the circumstances under which disenfranchised youth take action to challenge conditions that oppress them and become consciously resistant in the face of overwhelming social, educational, economic, and political disadvantage. All of the cases of youth activism documented in this volume provide insights into how young people struggle in opposition to policies that are not designed around their best interests.

For the remainder of this concluding essay we focus on possibilities for adopting public policies that encourage and promote youth civic engagement. The ideas put forward are based on the notion that it is possible to create *socially just youth policy* that invests in and capitalizes on the capacity and commitment—often emergent and fledgling—of disenfranchised urban youth to participate in improving and changing the society in which they live. We will focus here on the principles that should be reflected in social policy and the ways in which policy makers can articulate a commitment to change that moves well beyond high-minded rhetoric.

The Promise and Potential of Social Justice and Youth Policy: Youth Rights, Responsibility, and Representation

While it is unlikely that public policy alone can cultivate or facilitate youth activism and conscious resistance, some basic principles can be utilized in the formulation of policies intended to support youth civic engagement. In keeping with the focus of the chapters in this volume, these principles are rooted in a commitment to social justice and democratic practice. These principles may seem obvious; yet there is scant evidence of them in institutions across the nation. Any effort to use public policy to promote or protect the interests of young people from low-income and socially isolated communities would need to incorporate a broader focus on the challenges they face—namely, the ways in which they are economically, socially, and politically marginalized and kept subordinate in American society. Without such a comprehensive approach, even well-meaning policy initiatives are unlikely to successfully advance the interests of youth because they ignore the contextual issues that limit their social, educational, economic, and political opportunities.

For this reason, we begin by enunciating certain basic rights we believe must be reflected in policy at the federal, state, and local levels if poor young people in America are to experience a genuine opportunity to grow and develop into healthy, mature, responsible adults who are able to take care of themselves and their families, and contribute to their communities and the society in which they live.

Principle 1: Adopt a Bill of Rights for Young People That Is Consistent with International Standards Pertaining to Health, Well-Being, Safety, and Individual and Social Development

Although the United States is the richest nation in the world, it is also a nation characterized by wide disparities in wealth and considerable unevenness in the distribution of income and the opportunities that generally accompany higher standards of living. Children below the age of 18 are disproportionately affected by these inequities, more so than in any other nation with such a high average quality of life. Nearly one out of every five children in America comes from a household in poverty, and more than 7% survive in families with incomes at less than half the poverty level (Children's Defense Fund, 2005). More than 10% of all children in America are not covered by health insurance (Robert Wood Johnson Foundation, 2005). Furthermore, a disproportionate number of children facing such social and economic hardships are members of ethnic minorities (Children's Defense Fund, 2005). Over one million children in America reside in private or state-managed foster homes and another two million live with someone other than a biological parent. Many of these children are subject to various forms of abuse and neglect. These statistics are particularly appalling in light of U.S. global economic status and relative political stability; it is obvious that it is within our economic power to address these injustices.

Several of the chapters in this volume (Duncan-Andrade, chapter 9; Ginwright & Cammarota, Introduction; HoSang, chapter 1; & Males, chapter 17) document the growing hostility in American society toward youth, particularly those who are poor and nonwhite, with Males explicitly outlining the relationship between this hostility and the social dynamics it leads to. Rather than adding to this list, it is important to point out that with the exception of a relatively small number of national youth advocacy organizations, the neglect of poor young people in America is not an issue that generates much public discussion or debate. America is one of few affluent nations in the world that does not make quality preschool available to all children who need it. It is also one of the only nations that allows young people to be prosecuted as adults for certain crimes, and until recently was one of the only nations that allowed juveniles to be subject to the death penalty for capital crimes.

Most glaringly, the United States is one of only two nations (along with Somalia) that have not ratified the United Nations Convention on the Rights of the Child. The basic assumption underlying the convention is that children—all children—are entitled to special protections and that all nations are responsible for ensuring that each child in its borders has access to the resources widely recognized as necessary for healthy physical, intellectual, emotional and social development (UNICEF, 1989). This basic assumption, and the rights outlined in the convention, should serve as the foundation for all youth policy. While a full discussion of all the ways that American educational, criminal justice, and social service institutions fail to meet this responsibility is not possible here, the following points are those most relevant here. We call on youth advocates and their allies among policy makers to adopt the following policy positions, gleaned from the convention, to draw attention to the plight of America's youth and their vast unmet needs.

> Every child has a right to a standard of living adequate for the child's physical, mental, spiritual, moral, and social development (Article 27.1). This includes equitable health care, child care, education, and protection from institutional practices that contribute to economic and social disenfranchisement.
>
> Every child has the rights to be subjected only to punishment, whether in the criminal justice system or school discipline, that is: (1) administered in a manner consistent with the child's human dignity and individual, mental, and social development (Article 28.2); that (2) takes into account the child's age and the "desirability of promoting the child's reintegration and the child's assuming a constructive role in society" (Article 40.1); and that (3) is cognizant of the degree to which a child's treatment "reinforces the child's respect for the human rights and fundamental freedoms of others" (Article 40.1).

Until American youth policy reflects these most important responsibilities we all bear for America's children, youth will continue to experience the social alienation and disenfranchisement that manifest as social problems.

Principle 2: Young People Should Be Represented in the Formulation and Development of Policy

In the same way that the most successful youth development programs involve youth at all levels of design, decision making, and goals of the program (Watts & Guessous, chapter 4, this volume), so should public policy. This is not merely for the sake of appearing inclusive. It is more likely that adults will succeed in creating effective policy to support youth development and education if they are willing to allow substantive youth input (Checkoway & Richards-Schuster, chapter 18, this volume; Torre & Fine, chapter 15, this volume) Young people often have insights into complex issues such as gang activity, school violence, school reform, that adults are not privy to (Noguera, 2004b). Engaging youth in dialogue about the complex social issues that affect their lives is essential for developing successful policy.

There is, of course, a critical difference between inviting youth to the table and making sure that they have the opportunity to speak, be heard, and influence substantive decisions. All too often, youth attempt to influence policy through uninvited interjections in which they articulate their needs through protest and disruption. Obviously, when they are not invited to participate in problem solving, the most organized youth will resort to protest, and force their way into the policy process through ostensibly antagonistic means (HoSang, chapter 1, this volume) On those rare occasions when youth are able to provided a sanctioned role in the design and implementation of policy, such as recent attempts to involve young people in the development of new schools in New York City, they have proven themselves to be valuable resources in creating solutions that address the needs of all members of a community (Checkoway & Richards-Schuster, chapter 18, this volume; Flores-González, Rodríguez, & Rodríguez-Muñiz, chapter 10, this volume; HoSang, chapter 1, this volume). Of course, allowing youth to offer ideas that are never seriously considered or integrated into policy structures does not constitute youth input.

Again, the reason for involving youth in the policy formation process is twofold: (1) to provide young people with substantive outlets for civic participation; and (2) to increase the likelihood that adopted policies will succeed in ameliorating social problems by drawing upon the knowledge, insights, and experience of young people who are most familiar with the problems being addressed. A broad range of education policy issues including school safety, student conduct and disciplinary procedures, graduation requirements, and other academic standards are all well suited for youth engagement. Additionally, broader social policy issues related to crime (particularly gang activity), public health (drug use, teen pregnancy, sexually transmitted disease), and the provision of youth services are all areas where youth input and insights may prove invaluable.

Principle 3: Invest in the Capacity of Youth Leaders

Involving youth in the processes of policy creation, implementation, and evaluation requires youth to have experience in critical thinking, research, social analysis, and problem solving. Urban youth have demonstrated both the capacity and the inclination for these roles when they are supported by effective educational and youth development strategies (Duncan-Andrade, chapter 9, this volume; HoSang, chapter 1, this volume; Kwon, chapter 12, this volume; Lewis-Charp, Yu, & Soukamneuth, chapter 2, this volume; Strobel, Osberg, & McLaughlin, chapter 11, this volume). But urban youth, especially recent immigrants and linguistic minorities, tend to have fewer opportunities to learn and acquire experience to become active as leaders in their communities (Sherrod, chapter 16, this volume). Without deliberate training and education, youth are likely to lack the skills and thinking required for effective civic participation. Poor urban neighborhoods in particular tend to offer fewer opportunities for adolescents to become involved in community organizations, to exercise leadership in their schools, and to participate in multigenerational organizing efforts.

Effective youth programs build a scaffold for the development of the skills necessary for young people to become activists and leaders in their community. They also impart the skills, both analytical and academic, that young people need to be able to critique conditions and policies that adversely affect their lives (Kirshner, chapter 3, this volume; Morrell, chapter 7, this volume; O'Donoghue, chapter 13, this volume). This scaffolding may include adult or youth leaders modeling certain behaviors, such as how to speak in public, collect signatures for a petition, organize a rally or write a press release. They also provide the young people they work with the opportunity to reflect and process the work and activities they engage in order to insure that they can learn from their experiences. Groups like the Children's Defense Fund and the Center for Third World Organizing also place young people with community-based organizations where they can learn the nuts and bolts of organizing and leadership directly from veterans. Such training activities are crucial if young people are to develop the skills needed to become leaders in their communities.

Principle 4: Devise Strategies to Increase the Accountability of Public Institutions to Disenfranchised Youth and Their Communities

Public policies that aim at advancing social justice must include formalized mechanisms to make public institutions, and the individuals who lead and administer them, accountable to those whom the policies are intended to serve. Research has shown that those with less social capital are less able to demand accountability from institutions purported to serve their needs (Noguera, 2004a). Generally, this means that disenfranchised communities of poor, urban, ethnic, and linguistic minorities tend to exert less influence over schools, social services, police forces, and other public services at local, state, and national levels. In turn, the institutions responsible to the poor most often do not provide the resources that most middle-class people are able to simply take for granted, such as quality education, financial institutions, and health care in their neighborhoods. While lack of accountability to those served is an issue that characterizes the ways in which most public institutions that serve poor people in the United States function (Piven & Cloward, 1979), indifference and unresponsiveness are even more common when those served are young.

Too often, youth demands for accountability fall on deaf ears (Duncan-Andrade, chapter 9, this volume; Lewis-Charp, Yu, & Soukamneuth, chapter 2, this volume; Torre & Fine, chapter 15, this volume), and when repeated efforts to petition public officials are met with bureaucratic indifference, it often results in higher levels of cynicism and apathy. In order to show young people that public institutions in a democratic society can be responsive to their needs and interests, school boards, city councils, social service organizations, and other publicly financed institutions should adopt policies and procedures that insure some degree of responsiveness to the constituencies served.

Public officials should require that youth be represented on elected and appointed boards, even if in an ex officio role. They can also mandate that services provided to young people be evaluated regularly, and that the views of clients and users be incorporated in the evaluation. Finally, public meetings and events can be organized to provide an opportunity for dialogue and feedback between young people and individuals in positions of authority. Policymakers must also hold themselves responsible to all members of their communities, including young people, and they should do this by providing opportunities for feedback on their performance. Until policy makers embrace and act upon the need to be accountable to demands for equity and justice, their part in the social contract that is supposed to serve as the basis for social unity in this country will remain unfulfilled.

Principle 5: Counter the Prevalence—and Impact—of Misconceptions and Distortions About Youth

One aspect of accountability in public policy that is essential for advancing the interests of low-income youth is a willingness to contradict the misrepresentations and distortions that have been used to rationalize targeting youth for punitive measures (HoSang, chapter 1, this volume) With the tendency of the media to sensationalize reporting on crime and other social issues, young people, especially poor youth of color, have often been subject to negative characterizations and debilitating prejudice. There are numerous examples of youth being portrayed as lazy and unmotivated to excel academically, as prone to violence and gang activity, as morally depraved and pathological (Giroux, 1996; Mahiri, 1997). Such images dominate popular media and shape political understandings of how young people should be addressed through policy. As Mike Males (1998; chapter 17, this volume) demonstrates, commonsense knowledge about the rates and severity of youth crimes are woefully inaccurate. Yet such misconceptions serve as the justification for punitive and coercive policies (Ginwright & Cammarota, 2003; HoSang, chapter 1, this volume).

For example, the willingness of several states to adopt high-stakes exams as a basis for determining high school graduation without ensuring that all students have access to quality education (i.e., competent teachers, schools that are adequately funded, etc.) is yet another example of the way in which public policy scapegoat young people. The No Child Left Behind Act (U.S. Department of Education, 2001) has resulted in a system of educational accountability in which the only people who are really accountable for failure are those who lack political power and influence—mainly students (Orfield, 2004), but also their underpaid and deprofessionalized teachers. The fact that there is so little concern expressed over the casualties of these policies—poor students, students who don't speak fluent or academic English, students with learning disabilities, and students who are consigned to the worst schools, all of whom are overrepresented among those who fail—is perhaps the clearest indication that for many policy makers, some students are expendable.

Youth researchers in this volume repeatedly demonstrate how many problems commonly identified as characteristic of individual youth are in fact the result of institutionalized racism, economic disadvantage, and ethnic, linguistic, and class discrimination (HoSang, chapter 1; Lewis-Charp, Yu, & Soukamneuth, chapter 2; Strobel, Osberg, & McLaughlin, chapter 11; Torre & Fine, chapter 15). Their work complements a tremendous body of research on the degree to which hard work ensures academic achievement for only some of our nation's students (see, for example, Anyon, 1994).

This does not mean that young people should not be held responsible for poor decisions when they make them. The other side of recognizing the potential of young people to engage in actions that can change their circumstances is to also acknowledge that they can take responsibility for their own behavior. Anything less would be patronizing and would reflect an unwillingness to see youth as individuals capable of participating in change. On one hand, this means we should not make excuses for young people who prey upon others, who peddle drugs in their communities, who behave irresponsibly and hurt others or themselves. On the other hand, it means that we cannot be content to accept commonsense knowledge, but are responsible for our understanding of the context of economic, educational, and cultural disenfranchisement many youth face. It is also important that we not engage in broad, sweeping generalizations about the nature of these problems such that we that end up disparaging all minority or low-income youth, and create unjust and counterproductive policies. By accepting pathological characterizations of youth, especially nonwhite youth, that is precisely what we have done. Policy makers must take the first step of demanding and disseminating accurate representations of all of America's youth.

The Complexity Inherent in Combining Social Justice in Youth Policy

Policy cannot compensate for public misconceptions and denigration of youth. But more just policies can serve as a lever for creating conditions that promote the academic and social well-being of all young people—especially those who have historically been denied basic opportunities in American society. This is admittedly a complex undertaking. The National Research Council and National Institutes of Health's Committee on Community-Level Programs for Youth's study on youth development programs point to 27 factors that foster positive youth development. These range from physical and psychological safety and security to participation in governance and rule making; from opportunities to experience supportive adult relationships to opportunities to make a contribution to one's community and to develop a sense of mattering and of personal efficacy (Eccles, Gootman, et al., 2002). These studies remind us of the magnitude of the task with which we are charged.

Clearly, knowing the right thing and doing it are not the same. We know a multitude of strategies for increasing academic and economic opportunity and civic engagement among youth. Policy makers are limited by bureaucratic structures and influenced by those with more social power and less interest in equity for youth. Yet when we consider all the things that policy makers could do to foster healthy development and civic engagement among disadvantaged youth, we must remember that policy is a product of the prevailing ideology. The injustices perpetrated against youth in America are not accidental, nor are they caused by a lack of resources. Rather, they are the cumulative effect of an ideology of blame and culture of complacency among decision makers at all levels, who permit the punitive and discriminatory orientation of so many policies. In spite of volumes of research pointing to clear strategies for more equitable urban education and youth development, policy makers continue to rely on punitive and coercive approaches to addressing the crises faced by our nation's youth. Those who delude themselves into believing that hard work and a positive attitude are enough to enable young people to escape a life of poverty simply refuse to see the many ways in which opportunities to grow and develop are consistently denied to the most vulnerable members of American society.

Rethinking assumptions about the nature of poverty in America requires one to recognize the structural roots of disenfranchisement, as well as to challenge the stereotypes about crime and delinquency so that concerns about *morality* are balanced with concerns about *opportunity* and *social resources*; this could move us closer to seeing the plight of disadvantaged youth in terms of human rights. Males's discussion of the ways that our society has disinvested itself of association with and responsibility to a generation of youth reminds us why such a focus is necessary. Our institutions have effectively disowned their children. Recognizing young people's humanity and affirming the rights associated with it could go a long way in developing a commitment in American society toward youth from all backgrounds. Such a commitment is essential not only for the youth who need recognition and affirmation the most, but also for the future of American society itself.

References

Akom, A. A. (2003). Reexamining resistance as oppositional behavior: The Nation of Islam and the creation of a black achievement ideology. *Sociology of Education*, 76(4), 305–325.

Anderson, E. (1999). *Code of the street: Decency, violence, and the moral life of the inner city*. New York: W. W. Norton.

Anyon, J. (1993). Social Class and the Hidden Curriculum of Work. In J. Kretovics & E. J. Nussel (Eds.), *Transforming urban education* (pp. 253–276). Boston: Allyn & Bacon.

Briggs, L. (2002). La Vida, Moynihan, and other libels: Migration, social science, and the making of the Puerto Rican welfare queen. *Centro Journal*, 14(1), 74–101.

Carson, C. (1981). *In struggle: SNCC and the black awakening of the 1960s*. Cambridge, MA: Harvard University Press.

Children's Defense Fund. (2005). Children's Defense Fund. Retrieved July 21, 2005, from www.childrensdefense.org.

Cohen, R. (1993). *When the Old Left was young: Student radicals and America's first mass student movement, 1929–1941*. Oxford: Oxford University Press.

Eccles, J. S., Gootman, J. A., et al. (Eds.). (2002). *Community programs to promote youth development*. Washington, DC: National Academy Press.

U. S. Department of Education. (2001). No Child Left Behind Act of 2001. Retrieved April 26, 2004, from www.ed.gov/policy/elsec/leg/esea02/index.html.

Fine, M., Burns, A., Payne, Y. A., & Torre, M. E. (2004). Civics lessons: The color and class of betrayal. *Teachers College Record*, 106(11), 2193–2223.

Freire, P. (2000). *Pedagogy of the oppressed* (Myra Bergman Ramos, Trans.). New York: Continuum.

Ginwright, S., & Cammarota, J. (2002). New terrain in youth development: The promise of a social justice approach. *Social Justice*, 29(4), 82–95.

Giroux, H. A. (1994). Educational reform and the politics of teacher empowerment. In J. Kretovics & E. J. Nussel (Eds.), *Transforming urban education*. Boston: Allyn & Bacon.

Giroux, H. A. (1996). *Fugitive cultures: Race, violence, and youth*. New York: Routledge.

Lopez, M. L., & Stack, C. B. (2001). Social capital and the culture of power: lessons from the field. In S. Saegert, J. P. Thompson, & M. R. Warren (Eds.), *Social capital and poor communities*. New York: Russell Sage Foundation.

Mahiri, J. (1997). Street scripts: African American youth writing about crime and violence. *Social Justice*, 24(4), 56–76.

Males, M. (1998). *Framing youth: Ten myths about the next generation*. Monroe, ME: Common Courage.

Noguera, P. A. (2004a). Racial isolation, poverty, and the limits of local control in Oakland. *Teachers College Record*, 106(11), 2146.

Noguera, P. A. (2004b). Transforming high schools. *Educational Leadership*, 61(8), 26.

Orfield, G. (2004). *Introduction: Inspiring vision, disappointing results: Four studies on implementing the No Child Left Behind Act.* Cambridge, MA: The Civil Rights Project, Harvard University.

Pattillo-McCoy, M. (1999). *Black picket fences: Privilege and peril among the black middle class.* Chicago: University of Chicago Press.

Piven, F., & Cloward, R. (1979). *Poor people's movements: Why they succeed, how they fail.* New York: Vintage.

Polakow, V. (2000). Introduction: Savage policies: Systemic violence and the lives of children. In Polakow, V. (Ed.), *The public assault on America's Children: Poverty, violence, and juvenile injustice.* New York: Teachers College Press.

Robert Wood Johnson Foundation. (2005). *Going without: America's uninsured children.* Washington, DC: Covering Kids and Families.

Rodman, H. (1977). Culture of poverty: The rise and fall of a concept. *Sociological Review, 25*(4), 867–877.

Smelser, N. J. (1968). *Essays in sociological explanation.* Englewood Cliffs, N.J.: Prentice-Hall.

UNICEF (1989). Convention on the Rights of the Child. Retrieved July 18, 2005, from www.unicef.org/crc/crc.htm.

Valencia, R. R. (1997). *The evolution of deficit thinking: Educational thought and practice.* London: Falmer.

Valenzuela, A. (1999). *Subtractive schooling: U.S.-Mexican youth and the politics of caring.* Albany: State University of New York Press.

Willis, P. (1981). *Learning to labor.* New York: Columbia University Press.

Zinn, H. (1980). *A people's history of the United States: 1492–present.* New York: Harper-Collins.

Contributors

Karin Aguilar-San Juan is an assistant professor of American studies at Macalester College in St. Paul, Minnesota. Her courses focus on race and racism, systems of white privilege, Asian Americans, and urban sociology, and is the author of *Staying Vietnamese: Community and Place in Orange County and Boston* (Temple University Press, forthcoming). She earned a B.A. in economics from Swarthmore College and an M.A. and a Ph.D. in sociology from Brown University. Her chapter is part of an ongoing project comparing youth organizing for racial justice in St. Paul/Minneapolis, Detroit, and Albuquerque.

A. A. Akom is an assistant professor of urban sociology and Africana studies and codirector of Educational Equity Initiative at the Cesar Chavez Institute at San Francisco State University. He received his Ph.D. in sociology from the University of Pennsylvania. His research interests include: urban sociology, urban ethnography, racial identity formation, youth culture, poverty, liberation education, colonial and postcolonial theory, and the African diaspora. He is winner of the 2002 AERA Minority Dissertation Award and has served as a state-sponsored consultant examining educational inequality in high-poverty, low-achieving schools. In 2001 Dr. Akom, along with a group of concerned parents and community-based organizations, cofounded Academic Pathways, an innovative youth development and educational intervention program aimed at getting students from underresourced communities successfully through high school and into college.

Julio Cammarota is an assistant professor in the Bureau of Applied Research in Anthropology and the Mexican-American Studies and Research Center at the University of Arizona. His research focuses on participatory action research with Latino youth, institutional factors in academic achievement, and liberatory pedagogy. He has published papers on family, work, and education among Latinos and on the relationship between culture and academic achievement. Dr. Cammarota has coauthored a seminal article on applying a

social justice approach to youth development practices. Currently, he is the
director of the Social Justice Education Project in Tucson, Arizona.

Chiara M. Cannella is a doctoral student in the Department of Language,
Reading, and Culture at the University of Arizona and is the editor of the *Arizona
Education Review.* Her research interests include youth development, civic
literacy and civic identity among disenfranchised youth, and community
involvement in education. Her current project studies an after-school documentary arts program for low-income youth, with an emphasis on graduates'
evaluations of the program's impact on their lives and civic literacy.

Hanh Cao Yu is a senior social scientist and vice president of Social Policy
Research Associates (SPR), where she oversees much of the company's
research work in youth and education. She received her Ph.D. in education
from Stanford University. Dr. Yu has expertise in integrating qualitative and
quantitative research in the areas of civic competence among diverse youth,
youth development, organizational effectiveness, school reform, multicultural
education, intergroup relations, school to work, and high-risk minority populations. She has also worked extensively with foundations to assess funding
priorities, institutional change, program performance, and effective outcome
measures for a variety of education and community-based programs.

Barry Checkoway is professor of social work and urban planning and founding director of the Ginsberg Center for Community Service and Learning at
the University of Michigan. His research and teaching focus on community
organization, social planning, and neighborhood development, often in collaboration with grassroots groups, community-based organizations, and civic
agencies. He and Katie Richards-Schuster collaborate in research and training
to strengthen youth participation in organizational development and community change in economically disinvested and racially segregated areas.

Jeffrey Duncan-Andrade is assistant professor of raza studies, education
administration, and interdisciplinary studies, and codirector of the Educational Equity Initiative at the Cesar Chavez Institute at San Francisco State
University. He is also a former postdoctoral research fellow and director of
urban teacher development at the University of California–Los Angeles's Institute for Democracy, Education and Access. Prior to his current appointment
at SFSU, he served on the teaching faculty for UCLA's teacher education program and for TeachLA.

Michelle Fine is a distinguished professor of social psychology, women's studies, and urban education at the Graduate Center of the City University of New
York. Her research focuses on theoretical and practical questions of social justice in schools and prisons. Contemporary work focuses on participatory

research methods, policy work on educational and prison reform, and youth activism. Her recent publications include *Echoes: Youth Documenting and Performing the Legacy of Brown v. Board of Education* (coauthored with Rosemarie Roberts, María Elena Torre, Janice Bloom, April Burns, Lori Chajet, Monique Guishard, and Yasser Payne; Teachers College Press, 2004); *Working Method: Social Injustice and Social Research* (coauthored with Lois Weis; Routledge, 2004); *Off-White: Essays on Race, Power and Resistance* (coauthored with Lois Weis, Linda Powell-Pruitt, and April Burns; Routledge, 2004).

Nilda Flores-González earned her Ph.D. in sociology at the University of Chicago, and is an associate professor with a joint appointment in sociology and Latin American and Latino studies at the University of Illinois–Chicago. She studies race and ethnicity, identity, youth, education and U.S. Latinos. Her current research focuses on media discourses on inner-city schools, particularly on how the media criminalize inner-city schools, school activists and students, and how these images shape public opinion and policy. Her book, *School Kids, Street Kids: Identity Development in Latino Students* (Teachers College Press, 2002), focuses on how youth construct identities in relation to school, how the school and its practices shape these identities, and how these identities influence educational outcomes.

Shawn Ginwright is an associate professor of education in the Africana Studies Department at San Francisco State University. He received his Ph.D. from the University of California–Berkeley. His research examines the ways in which youth in urban communities navigate through the constraints of poverty and struggle to create equality and justice in their schools. He is the author of *Black in School: Afrocentric Reform, Urban Youth and the Promise of Hip Hop Culture* (Teachers College Press, 2004). In 1989, Dr. Ginwright co-founded Leadership Excellence, Inc., an innovative youth development agency located in Oakland, California, that trains African American youth to address pressing social and community problems.

Omar Guessous is a doctoral student in the Department of Psychology at Georgia State University. He conducts research to investigate the educational disparities and inequalities that exist in Fulton County, Georgia. Mr. Guessous teaches courses in adolescent psychology, and has published articles on factors contributing to internalizing and externalizing symptoms in low-income, African-American children.

Daniel HoSang is a doctoral student at the University of Southern California's program in American studies and ethnicity, where he studies race, social movements, and political culture in California and the West. He has published several reports on youth organizing for the New York–based Funders' Collaborative on Youth Organizing, as well as articles on a variety of racial justice issues for *ColorLines* magazine. Dr. HoSang worked as a union and community organizer and trainer for ten years in the San Francisco Bay Area before entering graduate school.

Korina M. Jocson is an AERA/IES Postdoctoral Research Fellow at Stanford University. Her research examines the intersections of in-school/out-of-school literacy, multicultural pedagogies, and youth production. She completed her Ph.D. in education at the University of California–Berkeley. Her research is or has been supported by the National Council of Teachers of English (NCTE), the Spencer Foundation, and University of California All Campus Consortium on Research for Diversity (UC ACCORD).

Ben Kirshner is an assistant professor at the School of Education, University of Colorado–Boulder, where he is a specialist in youth development and learning in community settings. His current work is focused on youth activism and youth-adult research partnerships. In addition to his Scholarship, he was an educator in San Francisco's Mission District from 1993–1997.

Soo Ah Kwon is an assistant professor of Asian American studies and human and community development at the University of Illinois at Urbana-Champaign. She is currently a postdoctoral fellow at Teachers College at Columbia University. Her work explores second-generation youth organizing social change practices at the intersection of youth cultural development and community development.

Heather Lewis-Charp is a social scientist at Social Policy Research Associates (SPR). She specializes in qualitative and ethnographic research methods, and has content-area expertise in racial and cultural identity development (particularly white racial identity and racial attitudes), intergroup relations, youth development and civic engagement.

Mike Males is a senior researcher at the Center on Juvenile and Criminal Justice and a lecturer at the University of California–Santa Cruz. He previously worked with children and youth in community and wilderness programs for fifteen years, and has published four books *"Kids and Guns": How Politicians, Experts, and the Press Fabricate Fear of Youth* (Common Courage, 2001); *Framing Youth: Ten Myths About the Next Generation* (Common Courage, 1998); *The Scapegoat Generation: America's War on Adolescents* (Common Courage, 1996); and *Smoked: Why Joe Camel Is Still Smiling* (Common Courage, 1999).

Milbrey McLaughlin is David Jacks Professor of Education and Public Policy at Stanford University, and codirector of the Center for Research on the Context of Teaching, an interdisciplinary research center engaged in analyses of how teaching and learning are shaped by teachers' organizational, institutional, and sociocultural contexts. Dr. McLaughlin is also executive director of the John W. Gardner Center for Youth and Their Communities, a partnership between Stanford University and San Francisco Bay Area communities to build new practices, knowledge, and capacity for youth development and learning. She is the author or coauthor of books, articles, and chapters on education policy issues, contexts for teaching and learning, productive environments for youth, and community-based organizations.

Ernest Morrell is an assistant professor in the urban schooling division of the Graduate School of Education and Information Studies at the University of California–Los Angeles. His work examines the intersections between indigenous urban adolescent literacies and the "sanctioned" literacies of dominant institutions such as schools. He teaches courses on literacy theory and research, critical pedagogy, cultural studies, urban education, and ethnic studies. Dr. Morrell is the author of two books, *Linking Literacy and Popular Culture: Finding Connections for Lifelong Learning* (Christopher-Gordon, 2004) and *Becoming Critical Researchers: Literacy and Empowerment for Urban Youth* (Peter Lang, 2004). Morrell is also the author of two books in press, *Critical Literacy and Urban Youth* (Lawrence Earlbaum) and *Critical Pedagogy in Urban Contexts: Toward a Grounded Theory of Praxis* (Peter Lang).

Pedro Noguera is a professor in the Steinhardt School of Education at New York University and the director of the Metro Center for Research on Urban Schools and Globalization. An urban sociologist, Dr. Noguera's scholarship and research focus on the ways in which schools are influenced by social and economic conditions in the urban environment. Dr. Noguera has served as an advisor and engaged in collaborative research with several large urban school districts throughout the United States. He has also done research on issues related to education and economic and social development in the Caribbean, Latin America, and several other countries throughout the world. Dr. Noguera is the author of *City Schools and the American Dream* (Teachers College Press, 2003) and *The Imperatives of Power: Political Change and the Social Basis of Regime Support in Grenada* (Peter Lang, 1997). Dr. Noguera has served as a member of the U.S. Public Health Service Centers for Disease Control Taskforce on Youth Violence, as the chair of the Committee on Ethics in Research and Human Rights for the American Educational Research Association, and on numerous advisory boards to local and national education and youth organizations.

Jennifer L. O'Donoghue is a doctoral candidate at Stanford University's School of Education. Her research interests include community-based education and public engagement of traditionally marginalized groups (immigrants and refugees, low-income communities, urban youth), youth participation and development, and citizenship and democracy. She is currently studying the characteristics of community-based youth organizations that mediate urban youth's engagement in social or community change efforts. Ms. O'Donaghue has written and presented on democratic education, youth and adult civic engagement, young people's experiences in after-school community centers, and youth-adult research partnerships.

Jerusha Osberg is a doctoral student in education policy analysis at Stanford University's School of Education, and a research assistant at the John W. Gardner Center for Youth and Their Communities. Her research interests include youth voice in school reform, youth civic engagement, and youth engagement in self-directed research projects. Prior to attending Stanford she worked as a teacher in Florida and as a college admissions officer in New Jersey.

Katie Richards-Schuster is a 2005 graduate of the joint doctoral program in social work and sociology at the University of Michigan, where she is currently a research fellow in the School of Social Work. Her work focuses on youth participation, community organization, civic engagement, and community-based participatory research and evaluation.

Matthew Rodríguez is a graduate student in the College of Education at the University of Illinois–Chicago. He is a math teacher at the Pedro Albizu Campos Puerto Rican High School and a member of the Batey Urbano, both projects of the Juan Antonio Corretjer Puerto Rican Cultural Center.

Michael Rodríguez-Muñiz is a graduate student in the Department of Sociology at the University of Illinois–Chicago. He was the editor *Que Ondee Sola*, a student publication at Northeastern Illinois University, and is currently editor of *La Voz del Paseo Boricua*, a community newsletter. Mr. Rodríguez-Muñiz is the coordinator of the Humboldt Park Participatory Democracy Project and is a founding member of the Batey Urbano.

Lonnie R. Sherrod is professor of psychology at Fordham University, director of Fordham's applied developmental psychology program, and codirector of the Center for Action, Responsibility, and Evaluation Studies. His interests also include social policy and program evaluation. Dr. Sherrod's most current area of research is Youth Political Development, and he has coedited special issues of the *Journal of Research on Social Issues* (1998) and *Applied Developmental Science* (2002) on the topic. He is coeditor, with Constance A. Flanagan and Ron Kassimir, of *Youth Activism: An International Encyclopedia* (Greenwood, in press). Prior to joining Fordham's faculty in 2000, Dr. Sherrod was executive vice president of the William T. Grant Foundation, a private independent foundation that funds research on child and youth development. He has been assistant dean of the graduate faculty of the New School University (formerly New School for Social Research), and has served on the staff of the

Social Science Research Council, which builds areas of new interdisciplinary research. He has taught at Yale University, New York University, and the New School University. Dr. Sherrod edits *Social Policy Reports,* a journal of the Society for Research in Child Development, which publishes research of timely relevance to pending policy decisions.

Sengsouvanh Soukamneuth is a social scientist at Social Policy Research Associates (SPR), where she specializes in qualitative methods, technical assistance, and training. She earned her master's degree in education policy at the University of California–Los Angeles. During the past eight years she has conducted numerous studies on youth development, youth labor programs, and education policy. At SPR, Ms. Soukamneuth has served as a co–principal investigator on a number of studies, including evaluation of the *Youth Leadership Development Initiative,* funded by the Ford Foundation, and the study *Challenges in Recruiting and Retaining Out-of-School Youth in Workforce Programs;* she is currently a project manager for the *Ethnographic Study of the Evaluation of the Youth Opportunities Initiative* for the U.S. Department of Labor. In addition to these research projects, Ms. Soukamneuth is the project director for the National Job Corps Capacity Building Project, in which she is responsible for the project design, analysis, training, and technical assistance activities.

David Stovall is an assistant professor in policy studies at the University of Illinois–Chicago College of Education. He received his Ph.D. from the University of Illinois at Urbana-Champaign in 2001. His scholarship investigates the intersection of race, class, and gender in education. Although his work originates from a sociological perspective, his approach is multidisciplinary in that it involves historical, legal, anthropological, and philosophical data to inform his qualitative methodological approach. His current course list includes the History and Philosophy of Education and Critical Race Theory: Race and Racism in Education. Dr. Stovall is involved with youth-centered community organizations in Chicago, New York, and the San Francisco Bay Area. He is currently involved with high school teachers in developing a social studies curriculum at a high school scheduled to open in the fall of 2005.

Karen Strobel is a research associate at the John W. Gardner Center for Youth and Their Communities at Stanford University. Her current research focuses on adolescent development and achievement motivation in school and after-school settings. She has a Ph.D. in adolescent development and education from Stanford University.

Maria Torre is the director of education studies at New School University's Eugene Lang College/New School for Liberal Arts, and a doctoral candidate in social personality psychology at the Graduate Center of the City University of New York. Her research focuses on youth activism, liberatory education, and youth and community engagement in participatory action research. Her most recent book is *Echoes of Brown: Youth Documenting and Performing the Legacy of Brown v. Board of Education* (Michelle Find, Rosemarie Roberts, Janice Bloom, April Burns, Lori Chajet, Monique Guishard, and Yasser Payne; Teachers College Press, 2004). She has also served as a consultant for New York city and state governments, community groups, and colleges interested in establishing college-in-prison programs in facilities such as San Quentin and Sing-Sing.

Roderick J. Watts received his Ph.D. in psychology from the University of Maryland–College Park and is a community psychologist and a licensed clinical psychologist. He is a fellow in the American Psychological Association and its Division of Community Psychology and has served as a program development and evaluation consultant to governmental organizations, schools, foundations, research and public-policy organizations, universities, and other nonprofit organizations on a variety of projects. His research interests include sociopolitical development and activism, manhood development, human diversity, and qualitative research methodology. Dr. Watts has held positions at DePaul University, the Consultation Center of the School of Medicine at Yale University, and the Institute for Urban Affairs and Research at Howard University.

Index

CPSIA information can be obtained at www.ICGtesting.com
Printed in the USA
BVOW05s0040140314

347600BV00008B/216/P